# THE WORLD, THE FLESH
# AND MYSELF

# MICHAEL DAVIDSON

# THE WORLD, THE FLESH
## AND MYSELF

Original edition first published in 1962 by Arthur Barker.
This illustrated and annotated edition first published
in November 1985 by GMP Publishers Ltd
PO Box 247, London N15 6RW, England.

**British Library Cataloguing in Publication Data**

Davidson, Michael
    The world, the flesh and myself.—(Gay modern classics)
    1. Davidson, Michael    2. Journalists—Great Britain—Biography
    I. Title    II. Series
    070'.92'4        PN5123.D1

    ISBN 0–907040–64–0
    ISBN 0–907040–63–2 Pbk

Printed and bound by Billing & Sons Ltd, Worcester, England.

*To Nancy, my sister*

# Introduction

I first met Michael Davidson just before he began writing this book. Our friendship was immediate; it was passionately close and full of laughter. To be in his company was to be more energetically alive in every way—the observations were more pertinent, the wit sharper, the fantasies wilder, while the criticisms could be devastating in their mordant, savage fun. Michael, was in fact, a kind of gourmet of life. Not in the exterior way at all; he had no time for appearances, he looked like a tramp, lived off a pittance and would boil some potatoes and open a tin of stewed steak with a bottle of plonk for lunch. But he had a fastidious taste in the qualities of the mind and spirit, he read widely and loved going to the Reading Room of the British Museum. He spoke German, French and Italian and picked up a smattering of many other languages, which always helped in the endless and persistent search for the boy companion. That was the most urgent quest of all. In old age his camel-like head would be fixed in a grimace of such anguish and gloom if there was no current boy to mother and fuss over. But those times were rare. It always astonished me how Micheal would land on some obscure, small island and within hours a dusky beauty with an ivory smile would be proudly walking at his side.

That precise taste for the finer sensibilities of life in matters of spiritual integrity imbue this book. I believe it to be a heroic document, its intent summed up on the first page: that the more information we have the greater chance of becoming civilised. Of what society terms civilised he had little time for. "But I'd keep one big prison going for a class of criminal for whom society, because itself a principal offender, has defined no crime: the intellectually dishonest and the morally dishonourable—the people whose financial and social rectitude is impeccable but whose mind is a liar and moral facade a fraud: the hypocrites and jockeyers of public ignorance, the purveyors of commercial and political sham and the

falsifiers, for factional gain or private aggrandizement, of the truth."
What a blazing feeling for real human justice lies at the core of this
passage.

But the book is also a revealing story of a man learning to listen
closely to his own confusing truths, learning to make his sense of
them for himself, and slowly learning to respect what others fear and
despise. Here he is after his prison sentence still not learning
caution. "I did openly what it was reckless to do at all, because what
I did seemed the natural, and therefore the innocent, thing to do."
Thus, he pinpoints the factor in all natural rebels, that the acts
which tend to shock society generally spring out of innocence.

His wit is often of the throwaway kind. When Robin Maugham's
yacht was lying in Villefranche harbour, he says: "Robin's Uncle
Willie, Somerset Maugham, came to the quay but refused to come
on board, being averse to small craft." (Of more of what he really
felt about Somerset Maugham see his comment in a letter below.)

Some of this book he wrote at Pigotts, which he described in a
letter as "odd relic of Eric Gill's arty-crafty Papist community." The
first third was hawked around London publishers while Michael
declined in gloom and suffered with mounting irritation the ardours
of an English winter. He was longing to return to Italy. Even a few
years later when in Geneva he wrote, "I want to go back to the
South; there's something there, a sort of immortality, for all those
gods and syrens and satyrs are clearly to be seen in good weather."
Then in the summer of 1961 Arthur Barker, the publishers, bought
the book and within a day Michael was packed and on his way to
southern Italy.

There in a tiny Albergo in Taranto he wrote the rest of the book,
referring in his letters to the boys as 'salami casalingo'. The hotel
was 'fourth class (very)'; he had a small room overlooking the
fishing quay and he ate at a trattoria and wineshop. He lived off
pasta, a little soup and those tiny Mediterranean fish that look like
large sprats; in the evening he would drink a litre bottle of local
wine. The meal then cost the equivalent of twenty pence. By the end
of the year he was saying that his Christmas present to himself was
finishing the book, but after sending it off to the agent and publisher,
who both wrote long enthusiastic letters back to him, he was feeling
in despair again. "The book still seems a dead weight which though
no longer round my neck seems bound to sink like a stone to the
bottom of oblivion."

In April, anger and resentment had overtaken the depression.

"That horrible old gargoyle Willie Maugham, aged 90, is publishing a frank autobiography this coming June." It must have seemed as if everyone was at it. In May he wrote, "Robin Maugham wrote to me about his Maugham book. Who on earth will read it? The dullest family, I'd say: petit-bourgeois solicitors and schoolmasters." His letters were an art form in themselves, sometimes frothing with virulent anger and irradiated with scandalous wit, yet always crammed with anecdotes and acute observations.

In October the book was published and at first Michael was plunged back into gloom because there were no reviews. Then John Davenport wrote a piece in high praise for *The Observer*. But what gave Michael even more pleasure was that Arthur Koestler named it as one of his three best books of the year, also for *The Observer*. Michael was also much delighted with a correspondence in *Books and Bookmen* which said that the "odour of corruption is on every page."

That reader would be much more horrified with this edition for several reasons. Michael found it difficult to leave a book alone. After it was published he made comments in the margins, adding new information, or putting back information which had been censored by the publishers. This edition includes everything that was cut from other editions, in which some names were excised and some thoughts for reasons of prudence. These are now replaced with all of Michael's annotations. But perhaps most interesting of all, this is the first illustrated edition of the autobiography to be published. Before his death Michael had spent some weeks happily going through old files and suitcases bulging with photographs and newspaper cuttings; when these were relevant to the text he pasted them into a copy of the book. From this source book this edition derives.

I am proud for Michael that there is no chance his autobiography will sink to the bottom of oblivion. Truth does not vanish or fade; throughout time it becomes stronger, and new generations will understand and enjoy this story of a man who was a lover of boys. It spawned a few other confessions, but none had the honesty, both mischievous and grave, none was filled with as much socialist passion and libidinous delight, none was written with such perfect syntax and style, and perhaps none was about somebody as complex, fascinating and intelligent as the author of this book.

Colin Spencer

*Asterisks in the text refer to the Notes on page 355.*

THIS IS THE life-history of a lover of boys. It's a first-hand report, therefore, on that heresy which, in England especially, is reprobated above all others.

I suppose it was Arthur James Balfour who wearily remarked somewhere: 'Nothing matters much; very few things matter at all.' Well, to me—now well beyond sixty and no longer giving a damn for other people's opinions—*nothing* matters at all; there's no advantage to be lost by candour, none to gain from deceit. If 'confession' can add even a little to our knowledge of the vagaries of human personality, one might as well confess.

From boyhood I've been a paederast, in the literal Greek meaning of that word, and have been to prison for being one—never though (and the credit is nature's, not mine) a paederast in the peculiarly one-way sense to which even the Oxford Dictionary restricts it. Perhaps 'paidophile' would be a nicer term.

In these chapters I've tried to put down, as frankly as I know how, the sequence of my development from a child little different from any other into what I have remained—an 'eternal adolescent', as a German writer has put it. I can't say *why* I turned out as I did; but I can describe *how* the growth proceeded, and let the story itself throw up the symptoms that seem to have foreshadowed it, what emotional and moral quirks of character accompanied it, and how conduct right through life has been governed by it. Myself, a very ordinary person—I'm of no interest; but the heresy, which after all is that of millions of men up and down humanity (and may be that of thousands more being born today), probably is. And besides, my life has taken me into some bizarre corners of experience and a quaintly varied acquaintance, from prime ministers to bootblacks. These are the excuses for this book.

Trollope, writing his own life, begged nobody to suppose that he intended 'in this so-called autobiography to give a record of my inner life. No man ever did so truly—and no man ever will'. And

Sir Harold Nicolson has recently written, of autobiographies in general: '... the author inevitably seeks to leave to posterity a flattering portrait of himself. The most deceptive of all are those in which (as in Rousseau's "Confessions") the writer, in confessing to pardonable sins, seeks to divert attention from those of his sins that are unpardonable....'

I've done my best to allow my 'inner life', such as it is, to show itself on the surface of my narrative as truly as scum on a pond; and certainly I don't think that the portrait here, if one emerges, is going to be flattering—even the failings which I myself think unpardonable speak up in this confessional. It will be said by some that such unblushing candour is 'exhibitionist'; by others that it's 'courageous'—which is equally silly. The simple fact is that truth, pared down, becomes untrue.

And it's *truth* I've aimed at; without that the thing would have no value. I haven't consciously, within the bounds of memory, evaded, suppressed, shied off or embroidered; and I don't try to justify, condemn, plead, complain or apologize. I've just tried to tell the truth.

One can't write the tale of a pretty abundant life without mentioning an awful lot of names. But mine has been a *double* life, a visible and a secret; I shouldn't like to feel that mention of a name here even remotely implicates its owner in the secret. Only a few, still living, who appear so much as guessed that I had a secret. Nobody, therefore, need be embarrassed (though some, I'm quite sure, will be incensed) if his name crops up in these pages; nobody, who isn't explicitly, is included in my 'confession'.

\* \* \*

I can see in my mind no more than four pictures of my father; in one only is he in his right mind. I can see and smell, after nearly sixty years, the tweedy breadth of his shoulders and the soft fawn curve of his beard as I looked down from my perch astride his back—he lumbering about the dining-room floor on all fours making growling noises like those (I supposed) of a bear. For he called the game 'playing bears', though for me, really, it was my first taste of riding—I was too small then, I think, to have been yet led about on our old grey pony Winky. I know it was the dining-room floor, because this picture contains the fat moulded Victorian legs of the big table and the slippery pigskin seats of the Chippendale chairs and the leonine claws on which the sideboard stood;

and I can't remember my father's ever coming into the nursery. That is my only remembrance of him sane and sober, and like other people's fathers; and my earliest image of him.

Then I can see him being helped by a cabman out of the one-horse victoria that had brought him back from St Peter Port; see him staggering into the house with his face grey and striving above the fair beard, supporting himself against the pillars of the porch, first on one side and then on the other, hand-over-hand through the front-door; while I, puzzled and I suppose frightened, watched from among the tall buttercups which shone in clouds over the paddock beside the tennis court where Winky grazed, and where a couple of Guernsey cows were pegged out on short chains because, I had been told, too much of the over-rich grass could 'blow them out'. My next picture is less visual than a memory still living in the ear. I am standing at the bottom of the stairs—the stairs I was learning to slide down on a tea-tray—and looking up to a kind of mezzanine landing on to which my parents' bedrooms opened, and from where the staircase turned back on itself to reach up to the real first floor. Their door was half open; suddenly there was a shout, a terrible scolding shout: 'Go to hell! Go to hell!' That was all; but my mother came out of the room and down the stairs with her face, usually so laughing and gentle, looking white and hurt. And I can hear myself saying (like a smug child in a melodrama, it sounds to me now): 'Please don't go to hell, Mummy, promise you won't go to hell.'

These three pictures belong to our house in Guernsey where we lived for about ten years. We went there when I was one year old, after my father's public behaviour in London had become so impossible and his adventurous investments (in such insecurities as gold-mine bubbles and illusive South American railways) so impoverishing, that my mother carted us all off to the Channel Islands—where, if drink was doubtless cheaper, so were other things; and where my father was out of reach of the family's dulcet disparagement. We left Guernsey in 1908, when my great-aunt Annie's death made us better off, and I was eleven.

The last picture of my father comes from Hampshire, which became our home after Guernsey. It is of being taken by my mother to his room, to be shown to him as he lay in bed paralysed, unable to frame words with his useless mouth; fondling with his thin, uncertain hands, like pressed leaves, the Toy Yorkshire terrier, Taffy, my mother had bought for his amusement. His face,

I remember, looked grey and sunken and unsmiling, sagging on one side; the fine brown beard, shaped like the Czar's, had turned ashen. Thus he lay altogether for eight years, being fed and washed like a baby by Coeshall, his male nurse who had come to us in Guernsey, having all those horrible necessary sanitary things done to him by Coeshall's faultless, gentle hands. He was little more than fifty when at last he died; I was thirteen.

My father's paralysis though, wasn't the consequence of drink; its origin was a fall on his head in the Rocky Mountains.

I must have been about five, I think, when my father vanished from the Guernsey world of us children; and became a vague, secreted being, mysterious and a little frightening beyond his bedroom door. Mainly my sister Nancy and I forgot all about him; but we hurried on tiptoe past that door, as we hurried by the creviced boulders near the tadpole pond or certain parts of the woods which we supposed to be inhabited by uncanny creatures. But at the same time there came into our lives a new and lovely figure: a tall bald man with a shopman's moustache and a funny half-limp caused by one foot which splayed out sideways like a sea-lion's flipper. This was Coeshall; throughout the next eight years he was a beloved friend of us all—and my most beloved friend other than my sister—and indeed remained so for very many years after my father's death in 1910; when he had to leave, he found himself a job in a Southampton nursing-home in order to be near us. At my first meeting with him I said, without waiting for introductions: 'Can you mend broken horses' legs?' He, who must have been harassed by this sudden translation into a strange household and a new and exigent job, didn't hesitate; he followed me into the box-room, where our more cumbersome toys, with the croquet things, my big brother Eardley's carpentry bench, and so on were kept, and brilliantly repaired one of my favourite toys—a finely modelled horse with a coat of real hair called Cubby, sent to me by my Aunt Annie. From that instant I knew that I had a wonderful friend; much later I was to realize that knowing Coeshall, and his selfless devotion to us all, had given me my first knowledge of disinterested human goodness.

Soon we couldn't imagine life without Coeshall; he was a rock of male wisdom and strength on which we all leaned. If there were any problem like mending a steam-engine or catching butterflies or playing cricket, it was 'Ask Coeshall'; he was never too tired in his scanty spare time to play with us or work for us; and for my mother too, coping alone with the conundrums of three growing children and financial stress, he was a fount of advice and support. Of course we laughed at him behind his back—Nancy and I were horribly giggly children: at his polished bald head, his careful striving to utter aitches where aitches belonged, his funny lopsided gait. But he was a stickler for 'knowing his place', and constituted a kind of middle-class of his own between us and the servants; he had his own little sitting-room where he had his meals alone, and on Sundays, going to church (where inevitably he was a sidesman), he made a point of setting out a little ahead of us or following shortly behind—never familiarly abreast of us. I can see him now, dear Coeshall, in his angular Sunday suit and bowler hat, reverentially holding a large prayer-book with a purple marker and striding along in that comical Charlie Chaplin walk. We, however, insisted on his being one of the family—an elevation which enraged our disagreeable butler in Hampshire, Roffey; whom I hated, and whom I once accused to my mother (probably quite unjustly, but with a pleasurably exhibitionist quiver of fascination) of peeping at me through the bedroom keyhole while I was sitting in my round tin bath.

In Guernsey old Dr Aikman used to call once or twice a week to see my father: a wonderful Dickensian personage in a frock-coat and billowing Prince Albert whiskers; he would come spanking down the drive in a shiny one-horse brougham and alight ceremoniously with a little black Gladstone bag. He belonged, of course, to the syrup-of-figs school of physic. In Hampshire it was brisk young Dr John Fraser who doctored us, modern enough to drive out from Southampton in a jolly little De Dion Bouton. Now and then, in the holidays, Dr Fraser—he had a handsome military face and a man-to-man breeziness which somehow enhanced my shyness—used to take me for a drive on his rounds; and one unforgotten day he asked bluffly, out of the blue, if I 'played with myself'. This overwhelming question—as any personal prying always has, and still does—made me squirm with embarrassment; not because of the subject, which I guessed at, but because I was ashamed of not knowing exactly what he was talking about: somehow I felt that at my age, about twelve, I should have understood what he meant and should already have been performing this secret act, whatever it was, that he seemed to expect me to perform. Mortified to the point of sweating, I whispered 'No'; and he, thank heaven, left it at that. But the question had quite spoilt the fun of the motor-car; I no longer watched the whirling countryside, or Dr Fraser's changing of gears and squeezing of the horn's big rubber bulb, but shrank into a trembling reverie about 'playing with one-self'. Obviously, I thought, it belonged to what we in the lowest of the Lower School at Lancing had been taught officially to call 'smut'; a matter which had scarcely interested me until then. I can remember in my first term being one of a gathering of small boys in the crypt of Lancing chapel: a charmingly eerie underground chamber of squat pillars and spreading vault, used before the splendid likeness of St Ouen which soars like a stranded Ark on the Sussex Downs was 'opened'; listening to the limp voice of a cleric whose identity I've forgotten. 'Smut is *dirt*', he kept repeating: 'smut is *dirt*—with the flat insistence of somebody declining mensa, mensa, mensam; an insistence that didn't impress me one way or the other.

No doubt poor Dr Fraser's inquisitiveness sprang from the highest motive; perhaps he felt that, as medical man to a boy with an ineffectual father, he could take it upon himself to stand *in statu parentis*; I'm certain that my mother, so wise and courageous in most spheres yet so diffident about 'unpleasant' matters, wouldn't have dreamed of giving him such an impertinent mission. Anyhow, his interest in my moral metabolism, however well-meant, had just the opposite effect: he put into my head speculations and mental turbulences which hardly had stirred there before, and started a train of thought which, like a running flame, was soon seeking any morsel of fresh fuel. Of course, I had vaguely heard boys at school 'talking smut'; but I wasn't yet ready to be interested—while aware that I should be interested before long. But coming *unnaturally* from an 'official' adult like the doctor, under a pose of man-to-mannishness that was egregiously false, it acted first like the shock of an unfair accusation and second like a match that set off a creeping fuse. I can't help feeling that the healthiest way a child can acquire sexual knowledge remains the old-fashioned one of 'picking it up'—because that is the most *natural* way; whether it comes from adult or contemporary doesn't seem to matter—the essential is that it should come *naturally*, through relations of mutual trust and the security of equality; and utterly free of embarrassment, shock and the malignancy of 'sin'. Perhaps there are schoolmasters who can meet these conditions; but school-masterishness must patently be unnatural.

I don't suppose that Dr Fraser's gaucherie did me the slightest harm; I do know that the incident is still today, after 50 years, engraved in my mind. In fact, because in bodily development I lagged well behind my age, I didn't reach the delights of pubescence until three or four years later.

I know nothing of my father's character; except that, my mother so often said, he was charming and 'clever' and always gentle and kind—until drink defeated him. I don't know what I inherited from him, besides a taste for alcohol; and in those remembrances of the Guernsey house which, when I conjure them back to life, at once bring him to mind and throw some light on his clouded and unexplored nature, I can see no clue to the intelligence and sensitivity that he surely must have possessed. Yet certainly they display an adventurousness and curiosity about other lands and peoples—and that, at least, I have always had myself. There were the big hairy rug with its brown dog's muzzle that was the skin of a grizzly he'd shot in the Rockies; the suit of Samurai armour with its monstrous visor which he'd brought from Japan; his collections of coins, drawer on drawer of them, in a special tall cabinet; another of quartzes and ores gathered while prospecting in Florida and California and I don't know where else; the snow-shoes, like lacrosse rackets, he had had in Alaska; the wonderful dancing puppet, as big as I was, with its multitude of strings—not a Sicilian puppet, for its face and clothes, exquisite and gorgeous, were oriental; looking back now, I think it must have been from Java; the black astrakhan cap, like a fez, got, I suppose in Russia (I can remember a photograph in that cap, which stood in the Guernsey drawing-room: the dreamy, bearded face, a wide-winged collar, and the shiny silk lapels of a frockcoat—like a portrait of a melancholy Abdul the Damned). There are other memories too, evocative and sad like dead flowers, which seem to point to duller interests: the old scarlet golfing jacket—stained from what weather-beating or spilled drinks?—which I transformed into a military tunic; the double-barrelled gun, with its oyster-blue oiliness, unlifted from its rack, I think, in my lifetime; the gold-topped malacca walking-stick, with which I played drum-major; the mellow loveliness of the velvet smoking-jacket that hung like a corpse in a little-opened cupboard; the antique top hat in the hall, with the pile rubbed the wrong way, which we children used for dressing up; and, of course, the soft luxuriant smell of cigar-smoke. But none of these things tangs of the 'intellectual'; and I can recall no books in Guernsey beyond some tomes about mineralogy or numismatics and a huge leather-bound Cruden's Concordance, apart from our own books and my mother's library novels; 'changing the books' was a weekly ritual, meaning for me a drive to St Peter Port in the governess-cart, behind plodding old Winky.

Yet each of us three children had some small talent, and a fair imaginative reach; we all very early evinced unfashionable appetites for writers beyond the usual run of children's books; sooner or later we each developed an instinct to procreate something or other from our own intelligences, and my sister Nancy became a talented writer. This sort of 'intellectuality' was unheard of among our relations; for them, braininess was suspect and the word 'aesthetic' indecent: 'art' meant the opening day at the Royal Academy and our Auntie Maudie's drawing-room warbling of 'Clementine' or 'Come into the Garden, Maud'. True, this particular aunt owned, as people did in those days, a box at the Albert Hall; but I think its occupance was a submission more to social requirement than to a yearning for the works of Handel. Without a doubt we three were 'different' from our cousins, who bored us to death when we met them; what puzzles me is whence this difference came. Not from the dull Davidsons, my father's paternal relations; nor from our mother, whose wonderful qualities comprised an unbounded fund of love and understanding, a practical wisdom and a simple unphilosophical religiousness spiced with a bubbling sense of humour—a gentle commonsensical intelligence without any pretence to intellectuality. Perhaps, though, that enlivening strain of Jewishness which entered into her family towards the end of the 18th century, and thereafter erupted in one or two Childers descendants with some unwonted flush of brilliance or unorthodoxy, had something to do with it; and I believe too that the Freelings, my father's maternal forebears, may have bequeathed, with their exuberant taste for alcohol, that little bit of extra mental and emotional energy which so often is laced with neurotic instability.

And there was Ma'moiselle, a personage in my earliest years whose memory is blended infrangibly with my father's because, I suppose, of the piquancy of her departure. Ma'moiselle—she had no other name to us—was a French-Swiss governess whom my sister Nancy and I detested but who, bless her heart, gave us the foundation of our tolerable Gallic accent: under her tutelage, we learned to play our games and say our prayers in French. But one sudden day Ma'moiselle disappeared—whisked out of our lives like an 'unsuitable' book, and without so much as saying goodbye. A sort of hush swathed the house for a day or two; and if my mother had been capable of pursing her lips, which she wasn't, she would have gone about with pursed lips. Ma'moiselle was no longer mentioned. Years later—I don't remember how: perhaps by way of the servants, perhaps from some prattling aunt—we learned, my sister and I, that Ma'moiselle had been caught out in some juicy intrigue with my father—whether as tempted or temptress I never learned. Or perhaps it wasn't the virtue at all of that stern and—to to us children—unfeeling spinster that had been arraigned; perhaps her crime had been to smuggle booze to my father's bedside after physical collapse had deprived him of the daily drive round the bars of St Peter Port. Anyhow, we were jolly glad to be rid of her.

This is all I ever knew of my father; except, too, that he was at school at Wellington—I suppose because his father had been a soldier. One other recollection, though, comes to me very vaguely: a dim yet delightful impression of his reading aloud to us 'Uncle Remus', and singing the jaunty-sad Plantation Songs of the American South. I wish I had a clearer, more *physical*, memory of that.

Sometimes, in later schoolboy years, I would overhear in drawing-rooms the hushed voices of my aunts: 'So sad, you know —such a *clever* man'; or, 'Such a tragedy—he had immense charm before he took to. . . . The Freeling blood of course—'

The Freeling blood it was. My grandfather, General Edward Davidson (both my grandfathers were Victorian major-generals, neither, so far as I know, ever hearing a shot fired in anger), married Eleanor Freeling—one of a large brood of brothers and sisters most of whom drank like fishes. My great-aunt Annie was one of them. One of the brothers just managed to succeed to the family baronetcy before quickly dying of drink; a couple more drank themselves into the grave before their turn in the title came. Aunt Annie (who confusingly had married a brother of my Davidson grandfather) also was a steady tippler—though as children we knew nothing of this when we went to stay with her at Brockham Court in Surrey. But I can clearly remember, hugged to her immense bosom, being kissed by her great loose fleshy lips which, after luncheon, used to be stained plum-colour with claret; and, so we learned years afterwards, on the evening her dead husband lay screwed up in his coffin ready for next day's funeral, she got so tipsy that she toppled, with her great weight, against the death-chamber catafalque and knocked my great-uncle Frederick flying. Uncle Fred had been a Master in Chancery, whatever that may be. Aunt Annie, who was rich and whom we venerated with a great deal of cupboard-love mingled with awe because she was so huge and grand, must have weighed twenty stone; my principal memory of those visits to Brockham, before she died in 1908, is of driving about the sweet green lanes of Surrey behind a pair of whacking fat greys, charmingly named Silverthread and Iceberg: she billowing in jet and bugles at the back of the open landau, a mountain of a woman in a black topknot of a bonnet like Queen Victoria's, with my little mother in grey chiffon and a sunshade squeezed in beside her; while I sat perched on the box beside Dewdney the coachman, in silver buttons and rather shabby trousers—only for a round of afternoon calls, or on other formal occasions, did Dewdney sport a cockade, white breeches and topboots; then, I was not allowed on the box, but Albert, the knife-boy, was dolled up into a tophatted 'tiger' and set beside Dewdney with his arms punctiliously folded.

Another life-size image of Aunt Annie comes to mind. During one of her annual visits to us in Guernsey, I burst for some unauthorized reason into her room one morning and found her in a strange condition of bulging undress. 'Jest a minute, child', she said blandly, 'I'm jest washing me neck.' She always spoke like that, rhyming 'just' with 'jest' and saying 'me' for 'my', which seemed very odd to me; and I remember wondering why she didn't wash her neck in her bath, like other people—and then I thought that, since Aunt Annie couldn't possibly fit her huge folds into one of the round tin baths we used in those days, she presumable never had a bath.

Aunt Annie adored us all, and spoilt us with wonderful expensive toys—partly, doubtless, because my father was her only nephew (she and Uncle Fred had had no children), but mainly because she dearly loved my mother for her own sake—as everybody did who knew her. But she adored my brother Eardley most: he got the best presents, and a pony was especially hired for the time of his stay when he went to Brockham—while I had to ride one of the old carriage horses, held on a leading-rein by Dewdney mounted on the other, my feet stuck in the stirrup-leathers above the irons.

After the successive deaths of my great-uncles, the baronetcy

moved farther and farther afield, through a receding line of
cousins; the last that I can recall was the sixth, Cousin Harry, who
lived in Elm Park Gardens. A notion of the high Freeling mortality-
rate can be given statistically: Aunt Annie's grandfather, Sir
Francis, was the first baronet, created in 1828; the last, who died
in Australia just over a century later—and with him the entire
family—was the eighth. All that remains today of the name is
Freeling Street*: a grey shabby slum off the Caledonian Road in
north London; I hope they drink there too.

This Sir Francis, my great-great-grandfather, was the creator
of the Post Office; it was from him, in 1834, that the young
Anthony Trollope got his first job—'the old man showed me signs
of almost affectionate kindness, writing to me with his own hand
more than once from his death-bed', says Trollope's Autobiography.

---

* This is no longer true: my sister's youngest son, Nicolas Freeling, who in
1962 had a novel coming out with Gollancz, assumed the name after Nancy
had published some books under her baptized names of Anne Freeling.

THE FIRST YEAR of my life, 1897, was spent in Inverness Terrace, in a small furnished house taken for my long-clothes season; my parents had been travelling about so much that they had no fixed abode. Inverness Terrace was chosen, I suppose, because that part of Bayswater ('barbaric Bayswater', Frederick Rolfe, that self-crucifying genius, called it) was a humdrum hive of Davidson relations—not one of them distinguished from the rest by any divergent vice, or impregnated with some quickening virus like the Freeling taint. Every terrace running north from Kensington Gardens—Gloucester, Westbourne, Porchester, Inverness—seemed to harbour a Davidson of Tulloch: each as dull and plain and tubby as the other, each living in a dull and ugly house, each belonging to a dull and undeviating club. Only my Uncle Alan Davidson, a cousin of my father's whose wife, Aunt Maud, was one of my mother's sisters, did something quite un-Davidsonlike at the very end of his life: he jumped in front of a tube train on the Piccadilly Line—because, it was presumed, he could stand no longer from the other side of the dining-table the prattle of my poor Auntie Maudie. But even this single departure by a Davidson from the Bayswater code was denigrated, rather than mourned, by the family. 'It's the Thompson blood coming out,' they said, Thompson being the maiden name of Uncle Alan's mother.

His desperate act was performed from the platform of Down Street—a tube station demolished decades ago; where an illuminated sign frequently announced that the next train was 'Passing Down Street'. I was in Zululand at the time, about 1920; but later, after Aunt Maud had been a widow for a few years, I was rattling one day through this station in her company when she suddenly leaned towards me, placing a gloved hand harrowingly upon my knee. 'You know, darling Micky,' she said, 'I never pass Down Street without thinking of my dearest Lanny.'

Somewhere among the northern mists of Ross-shire there dwelt a remote Cousin Duncan, known to his tribesmen romantically as The Tulloch. All past owners of Tulloch Castle seem to have been called Duncan, and were highland bigwigs; in the 18th century one or two of them were Lords Lieutenant of Co. Ross and M.P.s for Cromarty; they served politely in the Guards and married the daughters of other Scottish bigwigs.

There was nothing romantic about the Davidsons of Tulloch who lived in Bayswater at the turn of this century. To me, looking back, they seem like a podgy, and much less pigmented, variety of the Forsyte species: Harrow School and Porchester Terrace—that's how I see them; the few males who bothered to work tended to be affluent stockbrokers or lawyers—like my Uncle Alan and his lanky son Dick, both Old Harrovians, whose office was in Spring Gardens, under the Admiralty Arch, and later in Bolton Street, Piccadilly (handily next door to Down Street). One of them, Cousin Arthur—known to us children as The Little Tub because of his humpty-dumpty shape—was my godfather; he was pretty rich, an unemployed bachelor, and eked out his unlively days parsimoniously between his club and the Bayswater house where he lived with a spinster sister. But on a birthday near the summit of my first decade he suddenly sent me a marvellous steam railway-engine—my knowledge of the Bassett-Lowke catalogue told me it had cost over five pounds, a good sum for a toy in those days. This bit of lavishness gave me faith in Cousin Arthur's godfatherly intentions, and confidence in my rights as a godson. Yet when he died, he left me a brusque hundred pounds: a blow I still resent today. I suppose he had heard about The Little Tub: the Bayswater Davidsons of Tulloch always took themselves seriously.

The wreck of the *Stella* in 1899 on the Casquets, off Guernsey, is the first thing I remember. Or rather, since I don't believe one can remember anything that happened at the age of two, it must be that disaster's sequel about a year later which gives me my earliest recollection.

Because of tidal treacheries in the St Malo gulf, the Casquets were then, and had always been, a snare for seamen. The legendary White Ship ran on to them in the 12th century; a *Victory* of the Royal Navy was wrecked there in the 18th. In my childhood Guernseymen spoke of these rocks reverently; I don't think any Light marked them until after the *Stella*'s loss.

The *Stella* was one of the regular packets from England, which ran in those days two or three nights a week. She went down at the Casquets in fog; and with her sank a present for my sister Nancy from Aunt Annie. It was a very special Japanese doll, with real hair and kimono and every feature and furbelow authentic. Months after the wreck, it was delivered at our house by the postman—the postman, wearing the double-ended 'shako' of those days, who was our childhood friend and whose crooked neck held his bird's face permanently canted over on to one shoulder, so that he seemed always to be peeking at us like a genial sparrow. After all this time divers had rescued Nancy's doll with what was left of the mailbags. I can see now, for some reason, the long squashy parcel: the shiny yellow oil-cloth it was wrapped in—as if Aunt Annie had foreseen some watery adventure—and Nancy's name and address painted in black; I can smell it still. But when we opened the parcel, I saw death for the first time. The doll lay limp and drowned; its face seemed to have melted away; the lank coils of raven hair had fallen from its head; the silken garments were sodden and rotted. It was a horror I've never forgotten; not since, have I seen death so dreadfully stark and sad—not even in a dozen wars of varying dimensions; and always, through life, when I have heard or read the word 'drowned', or thought of the fact of dying, or encountered a corpse, I have smelt again the dank corruption of that dead doll and remembered the wreck of the *Stella* in 1899.

Mafeking, I suppose, is my next memory: a fringe of little union jacks flickering round the top of our porch—or perhaps they belong to a clearer picture, from a couple of years later, of Edward VII's coronation: staying up late for the fireworks, spellbound by the Governor's review of the garrison at Castle Cornet: the soldiers in scarlet, the officers with clinking sword-scabbards like my tin one, the sailors harnessed to field-guns by white ropes—just as my own lead sailors were.

I can remember, still with a pang, my first personal tragedy, my first agonizing amputation from a beloved—it must have been when I was about four: the departure of my nurse, Essa. I have never known her real name, what she looked like I haven't now a notion; but I can remember her grey nurse's bonnet and long cloak and the sweetness of her hugging arms, the sound of her crying, and of my own, as we waited in the porch for the carriage that was taking her away from me—down to the White Rock to catch the English boat. Essa, until then, had been my all, my tender husk—almost a womb that still contained me: everything comfortable, and safe, and warm, and loving. Her cruel and sudden going seemed like the end of life—if infants can conceive of life's ending. But not for long: very soon she was replaced by my mother, who increasingly and enduringly became the centre of my being; and by Coeshall, who came splendidly into my life like a paladin, and did carpentry for me, and played soldiers with me, and mended the toys I broke, and stood up for me when I was beastly. In all the years I loved him, I can remember Coeshall's being angry with me only once. It was at Bitterne, in Hampshire, years later, during a summer holiday from Lancing; we were playing tennis at which, as in all games, I was very bad. He returned me a smasher, and with it won game and set. 'Oh, Coeshall, you *are* a sod!' I shouted; and it took him hours to forgive me for using what he called dirty language. It was no good my telling him that it was a word we all used among ourselves at school and didn't mean anything really: Coeshall was very religious, and very proper; he was, he told me, grieved. 'What would your dear mother say?' he said sorrowfully. But he promised not to tell her; in fact, Coeshall, like my mother, always spoilt me dreadfully.

I quickly forgot Essa; and when, with horror in her eyes, my mother told some five or six years later that she had read in the paper that Essa had been murdered in America by a black man, I didn't really feel sorry at all. I simply felt proud that I had *known* somebody who had actually been *murdered*—and what's more, by a black man.

But more than anything, from those infant days, I remember Molly. Molly was a wooden doll; I adored her more even, I think, than I loved Essa, or my mother, or Nancy, or Coeshall. I carried her about wherever I went; I took her to bed with me; the day I lost her for a few hours was a day of fearful sorrow—until the infallible Coeshall found her in the box-room. To tell the truth, Molly wasn't a doll at all. She was naked; she had no arms or legs: she was a stocky pillar of wood, like a short rolling-pin, with a plump kind of knob at one end for a head. She was, to be sure, a phallus; though I don't imagine I can have realised that at the time —I can't remember being aware until much later that I had one of my own. I haven't a notion why I loved this thing so much; but I've wondered since whether it be possible that my infant worship of Molly may have portended that Priapean worship which was to dominate my mind right through life.

Through that Guernsey decade, I wasn't conscious, I think, of any sexual curiosity. Like many of my kind, I arrived in this tantalizing domain very late; and until well into my 'teens, didn't wake up to these bodily capacities. But I do remember plainly two little incidents around my ninth year that helped, I suppose, to encourage the growth of that prurience which later became absorbing, and to give me a hazy inkling that the tiny tag between my legs could be put to uses other than the watering one. I think they made the smallest impression at the time—but it was an impression that endured.

Behind the house, there was a farm tenanted by a couple pleasantly named Chick: we could get into the farmyard through a door in the high brick wall that separated it from our drive. One evening I wandered through just at milking time and stood in the cowshed watching one of Chick's farmboys massaging the teats with his expert hands. With the boy squatted on the low stool, our heads were about on a level; the fair down on his jaw, I remember, curled in interesting whorls. He must have been about sixteen. He looked at me suddenly with his frank, snub face and said, grinning: 'You can milk yourself, you know; why don't you try?' I ran out of the shed a little frightened; and guessed that he was referring to some process more complicated, more secret, than 'making myself comfy', as my mother used to put it.

The second unforgotten encounter with indecency happened after I had begun to go to school.

My beloved Essa had been succeeded in the tutorial chain by our first governess, Miss Walsh: a cross woman with a moustache and a primness as constricting to the affections as the stays she bonily wore were to her bosom—a primness which compelled her to pronounce words like 'spoon' and 'prune' with the umlaut-ü of 'gemütlich'. This, for us, was Miss Walsh's only saving grace; whenever she uttered a word of the soon-tune school, she gave Nancy and me the signal to collapse in a fit of delicious giggles, well worth the probable rap with Miss Walsh's ruler—giggling was a favourite nursery pastime. Then came Ma'moiselle; and after her, a rather agreeable spell of daily convent, where gentle French nuns, smelling of clean flannel and wearing white habits embroidered with red Sacred Hearts, were fussily kind and taught us nothing.

Then, for my last year in Guernsey, I went to school as a day-boy. I suppose there was no good 'private school' on the island; I was sent to the preparatory department of Elizabeth College, in St Peter Port—a Channel Islands version of a public school—and had to wear a hateful blue cap with white spokes radiating out to its rim: already I was resenting an imposed uniformity. I can recall nothing of the slightest interest or value about Elizabeth College; except this absurdly memorable encounter with the American boy. That's all he ever was to me—'the American boy'; but he was much bigger than I was, perhaps as old as 12, and I felt flattered that day by his walking with me. He was a bit of a swaggerer, and prided himself hugely on his range of swear-words; suddenly he let out a brief, snappy word with a sound and feel I liked very much. It had a satisfying smack to it, like hitting one's fist deep into a pillow; and it rhymed with 'muck', a word I loved because it belonged to the pats of steaming cowdung which the men in Chick's yard threw up into a cart with forks like big tridents—hot, lively muck with the oozy smell of farmyards. I asked the American boy what this lovely word meant; and he said: 'You better ask your mother.'

So when I got home I asked her: 'Mummy, what does fuck mean?' I can see this scene clearly: she was arranging flowers in the drawing-room, and wore one of her long, drooping dresses with a high frilly neck and billowy sleeves. She wasn't angry, and didn't even ask where I had heard it. She took me on her knee and gently told me it was a *very*, *very* nasty word which people like me must never dream of using; only common rough men said that word, and I was to *promise* her that I would never even *think* of it again. Of course I promised. Then, when His Rev. came to tea that afternoon ('His Rev.' was our name for the new curate, a muscular Christian who had become almost a member of the household; he nursed, in fact, a passion for my mother, of a virtuous, clerical sort), he took me down the garden to play croquet, and quite spoilt the game by giving me a sermon. God, he said between hoops, was listening to me the whole time; and if ever I used a wicked word whispered to me by the Devil He would make a note of it. I remember wondering how God, so good as well as so busy, could know about tiny little whispered wicked words. So I couldn't ask His Rev. what this special one meant.

After this I privately rejoiced in my new word. Wandering about by myself in the remoter parts of the garden or down in the fields, I would say it sharply, ffooffing the 'f' and kicking the 'k' as hard as I could; and be thrilled by the audacity of daring God and playing Tom Tiddler with the unspeakably forbidden—a better guiltiness than stealing strawberries from under the nets when old Butt, the gardener, wasn't looking. But also I *knew* that this wasn't just a swear-word; but something vast and portentous and thrilling and secret.

\*    \*    \*

It's difficult to write about my mother; to dare to, would be like trying to draw the profile of infinite goodness. I cannot remember her ever, *ever*—right up to the time of her death in 1940 at the age of 75, when I was in a Spanish prison in Morocco, held as a spy—doing an unkind thing, or an unjust one, or a niggardly or a foolish. I cannot remember her ever complaining—about the unhappiness my father's drunkeness must have meant, about the problems her wise, tidy mind had to cope with in restoring to viability the muddle of our affairs which my father's fantasies had accomplished, about the incontinences and shabbinesses in after life of her children—but especially mine, and the shabbiness was mine; though Nancy's amorous vagaries of course distressed terribly my mother's Anglican rectitude, and even my brother Eardley, six years older than I and a pillar of upright conduct, strained to some extent with his marital mutations the unbreakable fabric of her maternal tolerance. The truth is, I suppose, that like most mothers she couldn't believe that *her* children were capable of *real* turpitude; they might give the illusion of transgressing the simple code of her upbringing, of going off the rails a bit—but it could be only illusion: at heart they were blameless. And, of course, she knew nothing of the new-fangled psychological theories that were then raising their improper heads behind, so to speak, the back of the Church of England: there was good and bad, and no neurotic nonsense in between.

I, to my shame—her youngest, and therefore the child she spoiled most—constantly gave her pain, and fear, almost from the moment of leaving Lancing; constantly saddened her with my fecklessness and ambivalence; constantly was a sponge in her slender banking account, as it became after the 1914 war ('the widow's cruse', she ruefully called it); constantly allowed her to torment herself with the horror of my possibly going the drunken way of my father (there was that dreadful day when I arrived the tiniest bit tipsy at one of my aunts' tea-parties: I can *feel* my mother's sorrow still); and constantly, I know, infused her other anxieties with a tremulous and unformulated surmise that my adventures in love, if there were any, were dangerous and un-mentionable. Yet the sternest reproof she ever permitted herself, once I was grown-up (and in my childhood I never saw her angry), was to say, almost apologetically, with her sweet, pensive smile: 'You know, Micky darling, I lie awake at night *worrying* about you.' She only knew me, after the first war, through my years of failure; she was dead before I became a lopsided journalistic success. How happy it would have made her, if she could have seen my name displayed in the newspapers as a 'distinguished' foreign correspondent—the adored but disappointing son of whom she so terribly wanted to be proud: 'I want to be *proud* of you, Micky dearest,' she used to say so often. How thankful I am that, four years before she died, a carefully constructed falsehood spared her the crushing knowledge that this son had been sent to prison for what was then the most shameful of offences.

The one topic which made my mother almost stern, and sad-faced, and a little frightening, was that of drink. She was for ever telling me what a terrible thing it was, how it had ruined my father's life, how it would ruin mine if I ever touched it—it was 'in the blood', that Freeling blood; alternately she commanded me or implored me never so much as to touch it. I wasn't allowed, as a child, to see any alcoholic decanter or bottle; when my Uncle Eard-ley Childers came to stay, he drank his evening whisky-and-soda out of sight, and even Aunt Annie's claret at meals appeared, in my mythology, as medicine. I don't know why my mother didn't make us children sign the pledge; perhaps she wrote off the Band of Hope as Low Church, or a little common. Coeshall and His Rev. added their oratory about drink to her pleas; they promised me, if I even sniffed the stuff, mental collapse in this world and damna-tion in the next.

Whether as a consequence of this propaganda or not I don't know—but at a very early age I became fascinated by the notion of drink. Clearly I can remember, when my mother gave a picnic-party and we drove out in a wagonette full of children to L'Ancresse Bay, gazing at the door marked 'public bar', through which the coachman hurried after hitching up his horses, with a sort of gloating awe; the same whetted awe that I saw once in Rome, on the face of a small boy who stood spellbound outside a bordello off the via dei Greci, hotly watching the files of men going in and out.

And I remember the pleasurable feeling of guilt as I deliberately inhaled the forbidden smell of beer that hung in the air outside. Later, when I was 14 or 15 and living in Hampshire, I evolved a special solitary fantasy, in which I assumed the decayed graces of a drunk who had known better days, now reduced to beachcombing on some Pacific waterfront. Sometimes I was the younger son of a duke (this was after reading, I think, 'Dorian Gray') whom alcohol on the heels of some nameless scandal had dragged to the depths; sometimes a great cricketer, the hero of my school, in the same condition. I would reel about behind the house, out of sight of my mother in the drawing-room, and stagger among the currant-bushes, paying repeated visits to a secluded pantry-window where, using a tap just inside I would knock back *burrah pegs* of neat water. I was unshaven, and dressed in dirty white drill; and stumbling about in my drunken fashion I could hear the murmurs of the passing swells who had known me in my splendid past: ' So sad; such a tragedy. . . .' This was one of my favourite secret games: I can't imagine why.

Yet I didn't turn into a drunk—not a real one. Since I was 17 I have drunk an awful lot; and I hope to go on drinking for as long as I can swallow—preferably the gloriously inferior wines of southern Italy. I adore drink: either sozzled contemplatively in a delicious melancholy of solitude, or swilled in company as a fecund base for talk. The good fortune (and no merit of mine) which saved me from becoming an alcoholic, a compulsive drinker who wants brandy for breakfast, was mainly, I think the physiological fortune that midday drinking makes me ill: I like to start at six in the evening and drink steadily on until I'm ready for bed. Midday drinking, I'm certain, spells many a drinker's doom; while an evening's soak never did anybody harm. But I've found, too, that drink distracts: it lowers the intensity of appreciations other than of itself. Conversely, other appreciations distract from the cerebra-tion of drink. I cannot drink and work well, drink and make love absorbedly, drink and listen to music mentally, drink and read a book sensibly, drink and *see* squarely the things which looked at intelligently give me a pleasure of the mind. And I cannot do any of these things and at the same time drink well. When I drink, I do so for drink's sake; the other, more exacting, employments of one's time mustn't be allowed to spoil it.

●     ●     ●

My mother was a Childers of Cantley: a family as rum, in their abstemious way, as were the Freelings in their rakish; and as deceptively dull, in an extrinsic way, as the Davidsons were positively so. I've never known a Childers go off the social rails, or commit any interesting extravagance (unless Erskine Childers' self-dedication to Irish liberty, which brought him a firing party's bullets, was an 'extravagance'); yet beneath their immaculate conformity was a bubbling and comic gaiety and they produced one or two men of brilliance.

I say 'of Cantley', because that was how the reigning squires were known while Cantley Hall, in Yorkshire, was still their home; but the house and, I regret, the money, went out of the family before I was born. Forty-five years ago, while on a first-war 'young officers' course' in Doncaster, I went to see Cantley: a big, brown, gentle house dating, I dare say, from the Stuarts; it was empty and sad, and I couldn't get inside. Probably today it is flats, or pulled down for a 'building estate'. I prowled round the little church in Cantley village, where Childers younger sons had been vicar; it was full of Childers memorial brasses, Childers tombs, and ghostly repining monuments like the Childers family pew. Even then, nearly half a century ago, one had the feeling of a bit of England dead; today, for all I know, they've mixed the Childers dust into the cement of their nuclear piles—as the Turks, at Famagusta in Cyprus, once used the stones of the splendid Frankish fabrics for their seaboard military building.

The Childers were always punctiliously conformist—my own kind of conduct would have been, to them, as unthinkable as the ultimate crime of cheating at cards; conformist, too, as sportsman, in an era when 'sport' was a gentlemanly word unstretched as yet to include the pools and mechanised nine-pins. A forebear, Leonard Childers of Cantley, bred around 1700 the 'fleetest horse that ever run at Newmarket', called Flying Childers—a contemporary engraving of him winning the Leger at Doncaster used to hang in our hall, all four galloping legs almost horizontal with his belly; my great-great-great-uncle, Col. Michael Childers, one of Wellington's trusties at Waterloo, devised the 'Childers Fly', still used, it's said, on the Tweed—it was he who sold command of the 11th Light Dragoons, later 11th Hussars, to the 7th Earl of Cardigan, of Balaclava infame; Cousin Hugh, a Gladstonian cabinet minister many times over, played at Lord's in Government v. Opposition matches (but cricket then, and properly, was a 'game', not a 'sport'); my Uncle Eardley, a half-pay major, hunted regularly with the Quorn (luckily for him Aunty May had money); and Cousin Charles Childers was a famous polo player in India. I mention these museum paraphernalia because they seem to indigitate a very unlikely stock from which to breed an omnilateral unconformist like me; though I did inherit a certain aptitude for horsemanship.

They must, 700 years ago, have come out of a home for waifs and strays. Thirteenth century records contain such expository names as Henericus de Childerhus, William atte Childerhous and Philip del Childirhus; there was an Isabel Childhers under Henry III. The family is dubbed 'respectable' in the reign of Edward III; and one of them was in attendance on Henrietta Maria—for some reason, Cromwell gave the family a special pardon for sticking to the Stuarts. But the Childers first recorded by Burke is Hugh, Mayor of Doncaster in 1604; half a century later his grandson acquired by marriage the Cantley estate; and Cantley, at the end of the 18th century, received a chatelaine who surely must have endowed her descendants with that tincture of eccentricity and occasional brilliance which henceforth lifted them now and then from the rut of landed-gentry dullness. She was half Jewish.

My mother, most English of Englishwomen, used often to joke—with something of a boast, too—about her 32nd-part Hebrewness. And I'm pretty sure—whatever may be the origins, outside my own chemistry, of my many obliquities—that my little 64th part, combined with the Freeling taint (which included a discriminative intelligence), must be the source of any inventiveness I may be capable of.

John Walbanke Childers of Cantley, colonel (before his brother Michael) of the 11th Light Dragoons and A.D.C. to the Duke of York, married in 1797 (just 100 years before I was born) Selena, third daughter of Lord Eardley. That's where our Jewishness came from; for this Lord Eardley, my great-great-great-grandfather, was the son of Sampson Gideon, the Rothschild-Sassoon of the 18th century, whose father Rowland Gideon was an Abudiente Jew from Portugal. Sampson Gideon, who died in 1762, was financial adviser to Pelham; he personally financed the Government's resistance to Bonnie Prince Charlie in '45, and every loan raised for the Seven Years' War was his. George II offered him any honour he liked to name. His response seems whimsical: he chose a baronetcy—not for himself but for his 15-year-old son, still at Eton. Both the boy and his sister, who married the 2nd Viscount Gage, were baptized in the Anglican faith: 'he breeds his children Christian', wrote Horace Walpole in 1753.

Anglicization continued: Sir Sampson, in 1766, married the daughter of Sir John Eardley-Wilmot and in 1787 assumed the name of Gideon-Eardley; two years later he got a peerage. His two sons died while he yet lived, but he left three daughters. Selena brought the Gideon blood to Cantley; another married the 12th Lord Saye and Sele; and the third espoused a baronet called Culling Smith.

The Gideon girls thus married 'well'; and so did their husbands —there was plenty of Eardley money. The disappearance of the Childers share of it has always been a mystery to me: no Childers that I know of was a spendthrift—none would have dreamed of wagering, like the 3rd Sir Robert Peel (so Bobbie Peel, Beatrice Lillie's husband, once told me), a quarter of a million pounds about the lengths of two legs of the same chair. My grandfather's uncle, for example, the younger John Walbanke Childers of Cantley, son of Selena Gideon-Eardley, must have been a pretty solid character; he was M.P. for Cambridgeshire and married Anne, daughter of Sir Francis Wood Bt and sister of the 1st Viscount Halifax. Their daughter Lucy, espoused one of the Edens, the 4th Lord Auckland. George Auckland was the 5th baron in my boyhood; his cousin Anthony Eden was three months younger than myself. Thus the exotic seed of Gideon was projected into the Auckland Edens but not into the branch which produced the future Prime Minister.

Yet all this affluence vanished; and by the time I was born, Cantley had gone and most of the family seemed to be living on half-pay or the crumbs that had fallen. Certainly my grandfather, Major-General Eardley Childers, a grandson of the Gideon-Eardley heiress, was.

Sampson Lord Eardley liked his new nobility and, bereft of a male heir, sought to perpetuate himself through his daughters in descending order of grandeur. His Will ordained that his adopted name should become that of Lady Saye and Sele's children; failing them, of the Culling Smith heirs and failing them, of the unbetitled Childers heirs. It's a pity, I've often thought, that those Saye and Seles were childless: Twistleton-Wykeham-Fiennes-Gideon-Eardley would have been a fine surname. So the Culling Smiths stepped in; and the next baronet was called Sir Eardley Gideon-Culling Eardley.

This Semite brilliance, mixed into the Childers monotone, quickly brought results; at the age of 37, Hugh Culling Eardley Childers was sitting on the Government Front Bench with Palmerston. My grandfather's first cousin, he was doubly a Gideon scion, both his parents being grandchildren of Lord Eardley. Almost continuously, from 1864 till he died in 1896, he held one Office or another—pretty nearly everything except the Foreign Office and No. 10. Gladstone gave him the Admiralty when he was only 41, and he abolished flogging in the Navy (Victoria wrote: 'The Queen *hates* the system of flogging, but sees no alternative. . . .'). About 1885 (according to 'Conversations with Max', by S. N. Behrman) he became Max Beerbohm's earliest object of caricature; the 12-year-old Beerbohm was so impressed by the sight of the Chancellor of the Exchequer with his billowing Lord Salisbury beard that he drew him over and over again.

But in the family, Cousin Hugh's fame rests on the great accomplishment of putting beards on the faces of the Royal Navy. There exists an amusing correspondence between Hugh Childers and the Queen, in which Victoria gradually comes to a reluctant approval of beards in the Navy: insisting, though, that they be kept 'short and *very clean*'.

There at least is a memorial: the bearded sailors of the Navy. But the excellent portrait by his second daughter Millie which in my childhood hung in the National Portrait Gallery has long been hidden in the cellars. Yet this very obscurity is a sort of monument to an attractively unsnobbish matter-of-factness: I shouldn't think many other men have *thrice* refused the G.C.B.—the Garter in those days wasn't given to commoners; and as well, at the end of 50 years of political eminence, declined a peerage.

Cheam School, a century and a quarter ago, was an evangelical counterpart of Eton. Cousin Hugh's schooling had to be Low Church, because his uncle Sir Culling Eardley, in whose Brook Street house he was born (in 1827) and who was his political, as well as pastoral, mentor, was founder of the Evangelical Alliance. Cousin Hugh, though, disapproved of Cheam; 'sneaking and spying were universal', he wrote later, and deplored the 'mixture of boys above fourteen with Juniors'.

Yet he sent two of his sons to Cheam; but the one I remember, Spencer, went to Eton and another to Harrow. Cousin Spencer, a

Gentleman Usher to King Edward VII after a lifetime of soldiering, had a huge fund of Childers charm and good looks, and we
children loved him; my sister Nancy, to be sure, told me that when,
as a small girl, she was dandled on his knee, he seemed a bit more
affectionate than an elderly cousin is expected to be—but that may
have been an early flowering of her romantic imagination. Cousin
Spencer wrote the official life of his father.

Brilliance again, and unfamiliar heresy, descended to another
descendant of Selena Gideon-Eardley: Erskine Childers.

Erskine's was an astonishing career in any context—more than
ever in that of the Childers family; yet the faithful likeness, surely,
of his hankering, restless, quixotic spirit.

Clerk in the House of Commons; rough-rider in the imperialist
ranks against the Boers; yachtsman and author of 'The Riddle of
the Sands'; passionate propagandist of Irish freedom; writer on
guerilla warfare in *The Times* Boer War history; sailor and airman
in 1914 and winner of the D.S.C.; loving England, England's enemy
after 1918 in Ireland's cause; and finally, in 1922, victim of Ireland
herself—shot against a wall at the age of 52 by the very Irish for
whom he had fought, for whom he had spoken at Westminster in
1921. What a gleaming story of honourable mutability, of immutable courage!

His son, 'young Erskine', though brought up in England, gave
all his later energy to the Irish Republic and held various portfolios
in De Valera administrations. After I had met young Erskine while
he was a schoolboy at Gresham's School in Norfolk, he described
me—so one of his fellows told me—as a 'pervert of the worst type'.
This was a bit unfair: during our brief meeting in a study full of
boys, he really had no chance to collect any evidence. But I think
I did write to him once with over-effusiveness; I was only 26 at
the time.

*       *       *

In 1865 my Childers grandfather (his elder brother had been
killed at Sevastopol) was galloping about with the Royal Horse
Artillery in Burma, where my mother was born in that year. Twice
again Childers descendants were to visit that enchanting country
of exquisite people: in the first case, to meet a dreadful death; in
the second, my own, a wonderful happiness. Somewhere about the
time of the first war, the widow and daughter of Cousin Charles,
son of Col. Spencer Childers, were murdered by dacoits while

travelling through the country—Charles, my boyhood's idea of a cavalryman, had retired from Hodson's Horse and was breeding polo ponies in India when he died. And I, in 1949, was there as a journalist: a few blissful months in the company of the gentlest of boy 'bearers', Maung Té-hung, who taught me to take flowers and candles to the lovely gods of the Shwé-Dagon, while he daintily performed the prettiest devotions. The memory, inerasable, of that small brown sobbing figure in its chequered *lungyi*, waving, wavering, meltingly abandoned on the Rangoon River jetty when I left, still brings back my own flooding tears which so astonished my companions in that beastly seaplane.

I never saw my grandfather. But I remember my grandmother, before her marriage Henrietta Mostyn, whom we called Gan-gan; I can see her in her widow's weeds, thin and stiff in creaking black silk, sitting on a high-backed chair at Sutherland Avenue. A great gold chatelaine, like a cart-horse's brazen insignia, jangled temptingly from her waist. But she seemed too remote to be real; like somebody's picture in the history book. Some years ago I made a pilgrimage to Sutherland Avenue; it had harrowingly come down in the world. But 60 years ago it was a pleasant sort of limbo, and a permissible dwelling-place for retired Generals' widows or the dwindling in-laws of people like those Davidsons of Bayswater. And not far away there was a marvellous great lion, red against the sky and made deliciously sinful by standing on top of a public-house in the Harrow Road; and on Sunday mornings there was the fairyland High Church of St Mary Magdalene's.

One thing which I know enthralled me at Sutherland Avenue was the Childers escutcheon embroidered in colour on a piece of silk. I loved to pore over it in conjunction with Burke's heraldic description, gleaming in my mind like knights in armour: 'Cross-patée gu. between four oval buckles, tongues erect, az.; a fess embattled. . . .'; and above it the crest, 'a cubit arm erect habited in chain armour and holding in the gauntlet proper a buckle. . . .' I remember being captivated by the word 'fess', supposing it to be connected with the French *fesse*, which somehow I had discovered meant backside. Later on, when I was years older, these curious heraldic images began to assume a kind of sexual mystery; the 'tongues erect', the 'fess embattled', the 'cubit arms erect', became pregnant with a stirring, recondite meaning which I found exhilarating; and at home, during meals, I would absorbedly examine the crests on the spoons and forks. Most of them had the

Davidson crest, a hand holding a heart; some, my mother's, the buckle gripped in a gauntleted fist. 'Don't fiddle with the silver, darling', my mother would say; but I, eating prunes and custard, would continue to see them in my mind, and think how marvellous it was that my two families should be betokened by these groping, grasping hands. Could this childish absorption, I wonder, somehow have been a symbol of the 'eternal adolescent' I was in after years to be?

# 3

I MUST HAVE been about nine that Sunday when we walked to St Martin's Church in Guernsey, filled with excitement because we were going to see the new curate (at that time a new curate was of greater interest than a new sputnik is today). 'What will His Reverence be like?' Nancy and I speculated; and from that moment the Rev. Edward Moor was to us 'His Rev', or 'Rev'. 'Oh, you are a rotter, Rev; you've bowled me out first ball', we would say; I never heard any of our family, not even my mother, call him 'Mr Moor' or 'Edward'.

Poor Rev: it must have been a horrid moment that day, processing out of the vestry behind the choir and in front of the rector—a morose old buffer with a beard called Ozanne—while all the parishioners, including us children, gawked at him. 'Why hasn't he got a stole?' I whispered to my mother. 'Because he's still only a deacon,' she said behind her prayer-book. 'Why is his hood mauve?' asked I, who knew only Oxford and Cambridge hoods. 'Don't talk in church,' she said.

Very soon he came to tea; in a white blazer with mauve piping, smelling of pipe tobacco and with a huge Adam's apple oscillating above his round collar. I was impressed when I found that he'd played cricket for his university; but puzzled by the discovery that the mauve stood for Durham—it seemed odd that our curate should have gone to a university that couldn't surely *really* be a university at all.

Then he was dropping in for tea almost every day; he became part of us—as much, almost, as Coeshall. But, like all children I dare say, we always spotted what was comic in the people we were fond of; gobbled it up delightedly and over and over again regurgitated it in our abominable pastime of giggling. In His Rev we found lots: he pronounced 'God' as if it were written 'guard', and made words like 'book' and 'good' rhyme with 'food'. 'And G-a-a-d said in the g-o-o-d b-o-o-k', we would declaim, imitating His Rev in the pulpit, and writhe with laughter. We treasured his mild commonnesses—we were frightful little snobs —and nudged each other deliciously when one of his anticipated habits appeared; such as twisting a corner of his handkerchief into a sort of spill and wiggling it up into his nostrils one after the other. His nostrils were large and white and curved out like twin railway tunnels from his long bony nose.

But one of His Rev's habits, I resented privately and angrily. To my father, lying upstairs paralysed and tortured, he always referred when he thought he was out of our hearing as 'the Man'—as if he were naming 'the Devil', or 'that swine'. This note of malice, doubtless, was a mark of his devotion to my mother: a chivalrous protest against the source of her unhappiness; but I felt it was a presumption: what, I thought, had our curate got to do with my father? He was in love with my mother, though I didn't realise it at the time; so enduringly devoted, that when we left Guernsey he followed, and got himself a curacy in Southampton, so as to be near us; his first vicarage was in Bournemouth, still within reach (what better upholstery than Bournemouth's hydros for that genial, muscular pewside-manner?). My mother encouraged His Rev's chaste fervour largely, I think, because she thought his faithful attendance provided a good manly influence for her children; it continued for years until suddenly he married 'Lovey-Dear'— another source of unending mirth for Nancy and me: that a clergyman should address his hefty spouse, an ex-hospital matron, as Lovey-Dear seemed excruciatingly funny, and rather Trollopian.

His Rev was a large and abiding and much-loved appurtenance to my boyhood. Yet I don't think he subscribed an ounce of influence to my development; at a time when I might have been drawn to religion, he struck no single inspiring spark; when I longed for a guiding hand into the world of books, he offered me 'Eric or Little by Little'; when I was hungry for *knowledge* of any kind, he gave me lectures about bad language. For all his pipe-smoking and cricket-playing and geniality, he was negative.

But he was 'good' through and through; and it seems surely unfair, though comical, that my most vivid memory of him should be sexual. We were picnicking, as we so often did, in one of Guernsey's gorgeous coves; after our bathe, His Rev and I went to dress behind some rocks out of sight of Nancy and my mother. It was the first time I had ever seen a man naked; and I threw him sidelong gloating glances as he flayed himself with his towel, glowing, I expect, with a manly healthy-body-healthy-mind exuberance. I was mesmerized by his hairiness, and the paraphernalia it encompassed; and by the disclosure that my vague notion that a clergyman could have nothing between his legs was ill-founded. And today I remember His Rev's private parts more clearly than I remember his pulpit face.

He ended up—dear man, he was built for preferment—a Canon of Winchester. Passing through there one morning in 1943, I called at his lodgings in the Close; I hadn't seen him for nearly 30 years. 'Hullo, Rev,' I said. Not a gleam, not a hint of the young curate of my childhood, of the Galahad who had loved my mother: he referred neither to her nor to Lovey-Dear, both dead; but talked dimly of diocesan affairs: the bored, endowed, Established ecclesiastic. And then he pronounced his perfect epitaph: he asked me out to a Rotary luncheon. Little did he know what picture I had in my mind.

\*    \*    \*

Chiefly, my Guernsey memories cling to my mother's companionship. All Guernsey seems now to shine like midsummer; but a special ecstasy clothes the image of our times together: shadowing her while she was 'doing the flowers', pruning the roses or devising with old Butt changes in her loved herbaceous borders; skipping beside her, hand in hers, when she went round the village for her weekly 'visiting' of humbler parishioners (an extraordinary piece of patriarchal impertinence, that seems to me now; yet she was happily welcomed always); driving in Winky's trap down to the town to 'change the book'; and, for sheer lovely cosiness, sitting with her while she worked at her endless church embroidery—I like to think that St Martin's may still today be using the intricate and beautiful frontals, altar-cloths, markers for the Gospels and the lectern, which she worked and gave.

While she was at her stitching, I would do my 'embroidery' too, or the crochet-work I loved, or I'd be dressing and undressing Nancy's dolls; for as a small child, my solitary employments were often girlish; though I liked playing cricket with Coeshall, catching tadpoles down in the fields, or playing with my soldiers or trains, I spent a lot of my time at 'unmanly' games. Nowadays, I suppose, the sophisticated would read into this a disposition towards a 'passive' sexuality; a sign that I was going to turn into the 'camp' sort of queer. But they'd be wrong: I can see now that this was the beginning of an inveterate 'motherliness', the broody fussiness with which I've coddled all my boys—plaguing them about warm underclothes or changing their wet socks, and trying to 'feed them up' after they were already full. I suppose every true paederast's emotional foundation is this maternalism; I know that in all my relationships, other than the most casual, I've been driven just as much by a passionate protectiveness as by sexual interest—the second, for all I know, may be an extension of the first, as a mother gets sensual pleasure out of suckling. And even during actual bodily play, *my* pleasure—beyond the mental joy of seeing and touching, which is intense—comes from a consummate privity to *his* pleasure; if that's absent, the whole process seems absurd and pointless. My own orgastic conclusion may happen as a mere afterthought, if it happens at all—that too depends on *his* desires. I'm seeking an analysis of my own emotional lusts because, if I've found it, it's typical I imagine of most 'normal' lovers of boys: the prepulsion is pretty much that of a mare nuzzling and licking her foal.

Another quartering of my mind contains the precious comradeship of Nancy: bowling our first hoops together; comparing together freshly found delights in the books we were reading; sharing together the endless comicalities of our grown-ups; almost mystically happy together in that secret density of the woods we called 'heaven', where we created our games of the mind and told each other stories—projections, I fancy, of the books we had read; but the stories were Nancy's mainly: she had by far the greater power of fantasy, and was the devourer of books and it was she who, after we had gone to bed, fabled us to sleep through the open door that joined our rooms with the vivid inventions of her romantic mind. Hers was always the dominating personality; as later she dominated her worshippers. It's strange to think that from that immaculate childhood unity, that perfect comradeship, there sprang our two aberrant paths in life—and the curious graph of her progress from High Anglicanism to Atheism to Anabaptism to Catholicism, gathering adorers and protégés on the way, becoming a gifted writer and achieving at last through a philosophy of love a warmly human saintliness.

My brother Eardley I remember nothing of in Guernsey; he was away at Lancing most of the time, or staying with Aunt Annie. He was six years older than I, and felt, I suppose, it was his duty—

his sense of duty was always stern—to take the place of my father: then, as ever since, he seeeems a distant and alarming person— never, in his company, have I been without a feeling of embar- rassment and inferiority. All my life I've been frightened of anybody set over me, or in any way having the whip-hand of me: headmasters, commanding officers, employers, editors, bank managers—I knock on their doors with clammy hands and a sense of unspecified guilt—what Aldous Huxley called the 'nausea of the threshold'. And I can't remember ever not shrinking from meeting new people, or encountering scarcely known ones; always, shyness and a feeling of inadequacy have made me refuse invitations and dart round a corner on spotting some-one less than a close friend. Even today, old enough to be most people's father, I want to hide in the background at a party; to be discussed, to be questioned about myself or what I'm working at, fills me with an angry panic —a facility for social euphuism may screen my misery, but under- neath I'm sweating with shame and resentment. I still remember the horror of that weekly dancing-class at St Peter Port—my initiation, I think, in the torture of self-consciousness: the hateful stares of the strange children, the mothers and governesses sitting in patronizing rows round the walls; and the terrible, shrill, ladylike vowels of the dancing-mistress commanding: '*By* yourself, Michael!'—and I, alone in the focus of those unanimous eyes, frozen in the failure of my awkward hopping. I learned there what agony is; and I've never learned to dance.

But mostly, about Guernsey, I remember the lovely things: the ecstatic, endless summer hours on the sand and rocks of those incomparable bays, and the blue warmth of their gentle sea; the soft feel of foxgloves, the cosiness of Ragged Robin—like being at home again after thinking one was lost; the miracle of maidenhair and the curled young fronds of the giant ferns that grew in the rambling gulleys; the eerie evil of Deadly Nightshade with its exquisite greenish peril and name like the City of Dreadful Night; the dear antiqueness of Fuchsia—when, a year or two ago, I found some in my Sicily garden, childhood rushed to my head faster than the wine I was drinking. I remember the long happiness of 'hay- parties', those heavenly Guernsey functions when one could play at pitching with the haymakers and romp in the building stacks; and the parties at Government House, where there stood, in the grounds, a marvellous Japanese 'pagoda'—it leapt back to my eyes, far more vividly than it did in actual Japan, when I saw Michael

Pitt-Rivers' museum of oriental follies in Dorset. I remember the exotic Guernsey things: ormers, the island's private breed of oysters though really more like giant limpets; the tarred smell of the wicker lobster-pots which bobbed beyond the rocks; the 'patois', a Norman-Breton dialect; the island names, like Le Patourel, de Saumarez, Ozanne, Cloety and Sebeer—he kept the sweet-shop handily near the entrance to our drive.

I remember my first authorship—infantile imitations of our Red Fairy Book and Blue Fairy Book; it sticks in my mind because, though my mother then nourished hopes that I would go into the Church, I told her, displaying my bound volumes made of wired writing-paper, that I wanted to be a 'writer'. And become one I did, after years of feeble shilly-shallying; but not an artist, not an intellectual—a journalist; and journalists are mere butterflies that die in a day.

I remember, too, the three little ragged boys from the village I brought to our house to collect fir-cones beneath the great trees in whose monastic heights the rooks lived, to birds'-nest down in the fields or unearth slow-worms in the wilderness below the croquet-lawn; or rather, I remember the swamping sadness I felt when I was told that my father, in a moment of law-giving lucidity, had forbidden me to play with 'village boys'. There wasn't, that I know of, a grain of sexuality in this childish friendship; yet I've wondered since whether the denial of it to me mayn't have helped to engender that predilection for 'lower-class' boys which has guided my searches. Asiatic, Arabian, and African boys are 'class-less' in my erotic manual; but anywhere in Europe a 'public-school voice' or its equivalent acts as a sexual taboo: I've had romantic attachments for boys of my own class, as I had for W. H. Auden when he was 16, yet without wanting to raise a physical little finger.

It was these little boys, I remember, who taught me the enchanting game of tip-cat. 'Tip-cat, tip-cat, that's the game to play', we sang in our tuneless trebles, tipping the little wedge of wood into the air and sloshing it with our sticks as it fell. But who plays tip-cat nowadays? I wonder if it's described in Norman Douglas's 'London Street Games'?

But Guernsey came to an end. Aunt Annie's death after Early Church on Easter Day in 1908 transported us to England; it was a move from the nursery into life, from unclouded summer into a henceforth of turmoil. It meant, I suppose, the end of Paradise.

Among our legacies from Aunt Annie was Stevens, whose baptismal—though never uttered—name was inevitably Martha. Stevens had started in life some 50 years before as Aunt Annie's kitchen-maid; and she had climbed steadily upwards until, long before we came on her scene, she was Aunt Annie's maid—and, one might say, Aunt Annie's prime minister. At Brockham, Aunt Annie had been a magnificent and elephantine empress who had spoilt us when it was her whim to do so and vanished when it wasn't —presumably to tipple comfortably in her own privacy. It was Stevens who bossed us about, made us wash our hands and told us what we mustn't do. But her sharpness and vigorous omnipotence were sweetened with so huge a lovingness, that we adored her; and were delighted when she came to us at Bitterne in Hampshire.

Stevens' face was exactly like the Red Queen's in 'Alice'; and being totally bald (she had neither eyelashes nor brows), she wore a wiry wig, reddish-tinted and the shape of a cottage loaf, which gave her a spry look and often slid sideways into the askew angle of the Red Queen's crown. Her speech was quaint—and of course with the rest of her gave us endless giggles. She had no trouble at all with her aitches, knowing precisely where they should be and demonstrating this confidence in her *written* spelling as well as in her utterance. For example, if while she was away our Aunt Maud (wife of Alan Davidson) came down for a night, she would write to my mother: 'hi ope mrs halan henjoyed er hevening with you hall. your haunt hannie would ave been appy been there halso. . . .' She simply reversed the customary usage of the aitch, and eschewed capitals altogether; I suppose she was expressing thus a kind of inarticulate pride in her divinely apportioned 'station'. She was a steady letter-writer, all about the family's doings—our family's; for after Aunt Annie's death, her whole being was devoted to Aunt Annie's chosen relations.

It seems apt that Stevens, always sharply idiosyncratic, should in religion have been an Irvingite, daily on the lookout for the Second Coming.

Old age retired her while I was still a boy; she went to live on her Aunt Annie annuity with sisters near Paddington. Once, returned from France where my Roman Catholic aunt had taken me for my first-ever visit abroad, I put up with Stevens for the night on my way home through London. The sitting-room was evacuated by the sisters; the table was laid with the silver and china left her by Aunt Annie; and 'Master Michael' was ceremoniously waited on by dear Stevens in cap and apron, with her flat old Red Queen's features beneath the jaunty auburn wig. Stevens, I think, would not have enjoyed the world which has succeeded her own; hers was a sort of *goodness* that today seems extinct.

Bitterne, 50 years ago, was a country village on the road to the Hamble 'ports' of Bursledon and Botley, and two or three miles from the River Itchen, beyond which spread the slated suburbs of Southampton. Today, those suburbs have joined up with Bitterne village; and our house has been pulled down: industrialism is a great extinguisher.

The houses round had grand names like Bitterne Court, Bitterne Grange, Bitterne House, and down towards the river there was Bitterne Manor, which was a real manor house owned by Sir Something Macnaghten, cousin of our nearest neighbours the Culme-Seymours. There Nancy was later to live during one of the mutations of her married life. Ours was just a cottage, named after the huge yew tree which, with the Portugal laurel higher up in the garden, was one of our twin minarets, and whose beloved frayed smell becomes pungent in my nose whenever I think of the name 'Bitterne'. It stood on the slope of a plunging hill, so that the length of the garden climbed upwards like an escaladed plinth. The bottom gate led on to a levelled track to the stable and coach-house, then the kitchen-garden rose slowly to a plateau holding the house, lawn and rose-garden, from which the rest of the garden, with Portugal laurel, shrubberies, herbaceous borders and the glorious White Heart cherry-tree, rose again to a strip we had levelled ourselves, under Coeshall's generalship, for a rough tennis-court and cricket-pitch. And backing the house there was a steep 'cliff', remnant of the knoll out of which the whole place had been gouged, where the chicken-runs and my rabbitry, with sunken wiring, sprawled among the bushes. Here, and right down half the kitchen-garden, was a sumptuous tangle of currants, gooseberries and raspberries which in season we guzzled from the bushes: I can feel today with a pang of joy the scrape along one's palm as one culled a handful of currants from their thin, knobbled twigs. My mother must have had a genius for finding houses: Les Mériennes, in Guernsey, was a childhood heaven, and the Bitterne cottage a boy's delight. There, too, it seems to have been always summer; I can't remember winter at Bitterne—except for that delicious moment just before tea, when Alice the parlour-maid brought the lamps into the drawing-room. We had had electric light put into the house when we came; but in the drawing-room my mother clung to the lovely, limpid light of oil. (Alice, I remember, brought a younger sister to be housemaid; she was called Gladys, which my mother thought much too flighty for a housemaid. Gladys became Bessie for the rest of time.) Agnes, who had been Aunt Annie's cook, joined us at Bitterne; we were told to call her 'Mrs Roffey' when she married the unpleasant man who became our manservant. Later, there was Emery, the pantry-boy, son of a neighbour's coachman: goldenly pretty in the pale grey 'buttons' he put on in the afternoon to answer the bell; the 1914 war dashed my inchoate schoolboy plans for his seduction. And then there was Sait, the gardener; a taciturn man in a green bowler-hat who, three times married, had had 24 children.

From Guernsey we had of course brought Tommy, our adored black-and-tan dachshund, who was older than I; and Billy, the sea-gull with a broken wing which we had salved from the rocks when still almost a nestling. I don't know whose inspiration brought into being our Bitterne menagerie; I've never been sentimental about animals, except horses. Anyway, before we'd long been there, ten or more feet of the yew-tree's great voluted trunk and lower branches were wire-netted round for a pair of squirrels, Ricky and Ticky; Jenny, the mongoose, ran about the house like a cat; parts of a verandah were wired in to make aviaries for flocks of exotic birds; a red parrot walked solemnly about with Billy the sea-gull; Nancy had a couple of tortoises; I'd got a stud of ginger rabbits; and to old Tommy and my father's Taffy were added Eardley's wire-haired terrier and my mongrel-retriever. What happened to all these creatures I haven't now a notion; and I think the load of their looking after fell mainly on our doting, long-suffering mother—certainly when we were away at school.

My mother never was a social person; duty rites like 'calls' and garden-parties bored her. Her contentment was complete within her home, her garden, her church and above all her family; almost the only social exchanges I can recall at Bitterne were with gentle, faded Mrs Culme-Seymour, whose daughter Violet was a friend of Nancy's, the delightfully jolly spinster sisters, gaily irreverent pillars of the church, called Fanny and Amy Bramwell who lived at Bitterne Court, and perhaps once a year remoter acquaintances like old Lady Swaythling over at Swaythling. My mother lived first for her children; and then for her own sisters and brother and the complicated network of trans-Childers relations.

Her eldest sister Edie, my Roman Catholic aunt, lived at Sutherland Avenue while her husband Louis Jackson was still alive, which wasn't for long in my time. I can dimly remember Uncle Louis, a retired Royal Navy commander who looked exactly like George V, in whose term in the old *Britannia* he had been. Better than Uncle Louis himself, I remember his sword and cocked hat and the pictures round the Sutherland Avenue dining-room of warships half-sail and half-steam. But Aunt Edie is as vivid today as if she sat here with me; she was indeed a vehement force in my life—though I believe the only lasting effect of her influence was to arouse an anger against the narrowness of English upper-class Catholicism at that time (much more recently, some beloved Catholic friends have given me a different view). She was very short and roundly tubby; yet with a briskness and vigour of mind that seemed to contradict her figure. Her shrill, dogmatic voice was embarrassing in public places. Like most 'verts (as my mother called her, in a fond amused way), Aunt Edie was an unflagging propagandist; she didn't, of course, proselytize head-on—that would have been vulgar, like the Salvation Army; she simply made it clear in every word she uttered that Roman Catholics, led by herself and the Pope, were superior and privileged beings; and that, having adopted the Pope's Faith, she shared his infallibility. Aunt Edie had the answer to everything, and *knew* she was right no matter what the topic might be. ('Darling Edie—she *is* a dear old silly,' my mother would fondly murmur after a dose of this positiveness.) Her Catholic world was definitely a class one; and for Catholics of another social sphere she used the adjective 'little', which in her mouth contained a wealth of affectionate patronage: 'Such a nice little priest came to tea', she would say, meaning that he was rather common; 'those dear little nuns' was a declaration that they were as certain as she of Paradise but would occupy a part of it beyond, so to speak, the green baize door. Aunt Edie was my mother's favourite—or anyhow most trenchant—sister, and we saw more of her than the other aunts, whom she long outlived. Fortunately, I found her awfully funny; besides, she was tremendously kind and her maddening complacency had not killed her Childers sense of humour.

After Uncle Louis and Gan-gan had died, she settled in James Street, an odd slum-turning off Oxford Street: probably because it was handy both for Spanish Place and Farm Street (then the scene of Father Bernard Vaughan's fashionable fulminations). Her bosom Farm Street friends were Lady Margaret Orr-Ewing, a Buccleugh daughter, and a Mrs Gunnis—the mother, I've guessed since, of Rupert Gunnis, compiler of the only scholarly catalogue of the Byzantine antiquities of Cyprus, where he was A.D.C. to Sir Ronald Storrs and where I, through the terrorist years, fought my battle with Field-Marshal Harding. Lady Margaret's name still makes me sweat with horror: it was her brooch, a legacy to my aunt, which I stole. But that bit of *louche* folly belongs to a later period.

The next sister was Beatrice, our Aunt Bee. I always thought her lovely, mainly because of her wonderful hair which in her early 'twenties had turned a brilliant white. Like my Aunt Maud, she was completely brainless; but while Aunt Maud's inanity was made up for by a bubbling and laughable frivolity, Aunt Bee's was forgotten in an ineffable and gossamer sweetness; she was like a lily so fragile and fragrant that one wants to pray to it: drooping and tenuous like a pre-Raphaelite pang. But she too was blessedly funny: it was her absorbing custom to illustrate her tranquil remarks with her hands, making ideographs in the air to denote even abstractions like colours. 'Green', she would say in her mellifluous, languid, voice, describing some material she had seen at Harrods or the Army and Navy—and her pale fingers would draw out like elastic an invisible thread of verdure, as if displaying the exact shade she had in mind. 'A box', she would remark, peremptorily paralleling her two palms in front of her. We children adored watching her conversation, vying with each other in guessing the next aerial depiction.

Aunt Bee had married her cousin, Forbes Woodhouse; whose mother like Gan-gan had been a Mostyn and whose father, of Norley Hall, Cheshire, was a county swell, Deputy Lieutentant and High Sheriff and the rest. The Woodhouse money came from Marsala vineyards in Sicily; still today you can see the name labelled on bottles in *alimentari* winnows on that island.*

It's always been a puzzle to me just where, and why, the 'trade' line was socially drawn in those Victorian-Edwardian days; even as late as my boyhood it was unthinkable for a haberdasher or a flour-miller to find his way into any family that flattered itself it

---

* 'L'industrie vinicole fut introduite à Marsala par John Woodhouse en 1773', says the *Guide Bleu*.

was 'upper class'. Some social historians may draw the distinction between retail and wholesale—the former being 'in trade', the latter not; but this would be incorrect: even after brewers and distillers had become 'gentlemen', people like boot-and-shoe manufacturers or wholesale chemists (the odd ennoblement notwithstanding) were still looked down on—while estate-agents, auctioneers and suchlike, were on a par with bank-clerks and dissenting ministers. E. F. Benson (whose 'Dodo' was then the rage in every drawing-room while the stealthy 'eternal adolescents' of the day purred over his 'David Blaise') wrote a hilariously cruel best-seller about a newly coroneted 'tradesman', full of *nouveau riche* solecisms like calling the drive the 'carriage-sweep', which made him the Nancy Mitford of the 1910s; in either mood, Society or homosexual, he was an enchanting novelist. Today, dead nearly as the dodo, that 'in trade' snobbery's been succeeded by perhaps a worse; the new patricians seem to be those profuse enough in vulgarity and self-advertisement, flashy enough in their modes of getting and spending money, to augment the daily excrement of the gossip-writers. It's the humdrum, the unostentatious, the mug who doesn't know how to fiddle his income-tax, who nowadays is *déclassé*; the city slicker gets the best seats.

In Uncle Forbes's time, anyhow, to be a wine-grower, and hence a wine-seller, was socially immaculate—in Italy, after all, half the booze is branded Marchese This or Conte That. He was rich enough when he married Aunt Bee, though one of many younger sons, to take a big house in Hertfordshire, have a home-farm as a hobby, keep a stable of a dozen or so horses, and hunt his own pack of beagles—all paid for, apparently, by people who drank marsala. Nancy and I, when we were shipped off to Micklefield, were cold with terror from the moment we were met at Sarrat station by the dog-cart till we thankfully caught the train to go away again. I was speechless with shyness throughout the stay: terrified by the endless passages and doors I couldn't recognize, terrified of losing my way; terrified of the lordly butler and the two supercilious footmen; terrified of doing the wrong thing at those ghastly family prayers before breakfast, when the entire household was whipped in by the butler to kneel round the walls of the dreary dining-room and listen to Uncle Forbes's mumbling of whatever he mumbled; terrified of saying the wrong thing, or anything at all, during the huge, solemn meals; terrified of my cousin Ralph, a lanky, superior youth at Eton, and of his sister

Mary, an inarticulate mannish girl who (this was before my real horsey days) thought of little but hunting; and terrified finally by my uncle and aunt: the kindest couple in the world, really—and yet they seemed unapproachably distant and august. I think they must have been constrained, poor dears, by the clockwork rota of the Micklefield formalities, and had no time to be human to small nephews and nieces. Anyway, all the lovely things there were spoilt for me: the horses, the hounds, the pretty toy-like farm, the wonders of the harness-room. I think my natural child's shyness was congealed for all time, set into permanency, by my feeling of defencelessness at Micklefield, by the knowledge that I had no loving lap to run to when I was afraid of 'doing the wrong thing'. Probably, it was because of some crisis in my father's illness or behaviour that we were sent there on our own; I never told my mother what agony these visits brought—knowing by instinct that everything she did was meant to make me happy, I didn't want to hurt her feelings.

After 1914 it became known that all wasn't well with Uncle Forbes and Aunt Bee: there was a family rumour even that they were *living on capital*—a thing so indecent that it couldn't really be said aloud. While I was away at the front, they moved into a slightly smaller house; still conducted, though, on a pretty lavish scale. And then, in 1917, the full portent of the war became apparent: a whisper went round—I heard it myself during an invasion of aunts into my hospital room in Vincent Square after I was wounded at Paschendæle. 'Do you *know*,' it said, 'that *poor* dear Forbes actually travelled by '*bus*?' Poor Forbes! Poor dear Aunt Betty—after the war they went quite broke; and lived in a tiny cottage on postal orders sent them weekly by various relations, with Uncle Forbes doing the washing up. Yet they were happier, my mother told me, in their Darby and Joan penury than they had been in grandeur: a simple country couple who adored each other. I don't know how Uncle Forbes lost his share of the wine-takings; but there are still, I believe, Woodhouses at Norley Hall.

And then, Aunt Maud—Auntie Maudie she was, when we were specially fond of her, and she of us; severely Aunt Maud, when in her frowning mood, perhaps after ructions with Uncle Alan over the size of her bill from Harrods. They were living, by the time we came to England, in Cranley Gardens; always fearful of being behind the mode, she had whisked Uncle Alan across the Park when the proper moment came; perhaps this incontinent wrench from Bayswater carried him also a tiny way towards that psychical storm which exploded in Down Street tube-station. Aunt Maud always seemed gripped in a hot fever of fashionable endeavour: always rushing out for bridge or a tea-fight, dressing for a luncheon or dinner-party. Never, though, in the intoxication of her social whirl, would she overstep fashion, do anything that so much as verged on the *outré*; never would she have dreamed of making up her face—just beginning then, I suppose, among *fast* females; a hint of rouge in the evening, and powder for the nose, was as far as any *lady* could go. But her clothes seemed as frilly as her mind, her hats and hair as shrill as that loud Childers voice in which, with her endless empty-headed chatter, she drove Uncle Alan nuts. She had tremendous gusto, and kept us in fits of giggles, giggling with us; we adored her, laughed at her, were maddened by her in turn. Darling, feather-brained Auntie Maudie; she went slightly out of her mind, and had to be looked after, before she died somewhere in the '30s.

They had an only child, a tall dull boy called Dick, whom I remember while he was at Harrow. He remained dull; but did one thing which I've always admired: while up at Magdalen he set to to learn Modern Greek, and spent the vacations in Greece—I think he meant to go in for the Diplomatic. But after soldiering in the war, he died very young of consumption, as it was then called. Theirs was a drawing-room trialogue of tragedy, those Alan Davidsons: grumbled through the connubial decades to the tune of Aunt Maud's frantic gaiety.

The aunts and my mother answered each other's letters by return of post, so that the spokes of family chatter were perpetually revolving; penning their variants of the swift, slanting, punctilious hand of the day, and breathlessly criss-crossing all four faces of the folded sheet. This feminine habit, a corollary doubtless of the penny-post, must have maddened the letter-writing classes right through the 19th century: 'all that chequer-work', Jane Austen says in 'Emma', and Trollope's females, naturally 'crossed' their letters indefatigably.

Younger than the four sisters was my Uncle Eardley Childers, who came to stay once in a blue moon; and he gave me, as a boy, a meal or two at The Rag, in St James's Square—surely the dullest of military clubs: compared with it, the In-and-Out in Piccadilly seemed almost jolly, even with its reminiscences of Spion Kop and the Ashanti. I esteemed him hugely: because he was wonderful to look at, with his easy military languour and slim, assured figure,

his good looks and casually exquisite clothes; because he hunted
with the Quorn, which seemed to me the most splendid thing
anybody could do; because he was a hero—at least, the villagers in
Leicestershire where he lived gave him a hero's welcome, with
flags and a brass band, when, a Green Jacket captain, he returned
undamaged from the South African War; and because he was
richly gifted with the Childers charm. He hadn't a penny of his
own above a retired major's pension; but he'd married a well-to-
do woman whose magnificent aunt, Mrs Perry-Herrick, gave him a
cottage on the Beaumanor Park estate. She was aunt, too, of the
Curzon-Howes; and 'the lovely Mary Curzon', so famed for her
beauty, so frequently portrayed in the Society weeklies, was a sort
of family pin-up—though she was no more of a relation really than
Uncle Eardley's cousin-by-marriage. His wife, our Aunt May, a
sharp, thin woman in a permanent spotted veil, spent most of the
year at Bordighera; and Uncle Eardley was able to live agreeably
at Beaumanor and keep two or three hunters.

For me, Uncle Eardley's memory is graven for ever in Southampton docks. I got a passion, which I've never lost, at about 12
or 13 for looking at ships; and often used to bicycle in and prowl
for hours round the quays; without venturing, though, up any
gangway. One day, staying with us, Uncle Eardley took Nancy and
me to the docks; and almost before we knew it, we were boarding,
behind his debonair, confident grace, a Union Castle liner. The
quartermaster on deck stopped us firmly: 'Sorry, sir, not without
a Company permit.' Uncle Eardley turned on the man his quizzical,
Olympian smile; languidly gave him a visiting-card which announced nothing more impressive than 'Major Eardley Childers,
Army and Navy Club'; and said, in his slow, exquisite voice, 'Do
you know *who* I *am*?' Even we children were awed: so patrician, so
commanding, so *charming*, was this obscure retired soldier, that
the quartermaster was disarmed; we were, instantly, so to say,
piped aboard and had the run of the ship. That's the perfect
portrait of my uncle; that, indeed, is the Childers flair in a nutshell.

So much for my mother's family: all of them amusing, sweet,
charming, and a bit crackers; but none, I must say, supplying a
clue to whence came the aberrations in their youngest nephew's
character.

How far, far closer we were, in my Edwardian childhood, to the
past than to what was then our present—fraught, unknown to us,

with silent change. We spoke and thought still in the idiom of Trollope and Thackeray; an old soldier, about 1905, rolled up his trousers to show me his Crimea musket scars, and talked of Inkermann as if it were yesterday's battle: the 'Franco-German war' seemed only the other day—and Napoleon III's widow was a lively figure among us; we were terrified of 'mad dogs', believing that, once bitten by one, we should start biting each other; little cut-glass bottles of smelling-salts stood about in drawing-rooms; white dust from the raw roads lay like frost on the summer hedges; our evening 'pumps' wore silk bows straight from an earlier century—how I was shot back half-a-century when a few years ago I found Lord Kinross wearing just such pumps! Our aunts looked down their noses at a name like Lady de Bathe (Lily Langtry), or raised their eyes skywards over Mrs Humphrey Ward's; my luckless Uncle Eardley, married in 1888, missed by a short head absolute possession of Auntie May's considerable 'fortune'. We looked backwards, never dreaming that the future could stray far from the familiar; nor that within a handful of decades that morsel of mental autonomy we kidded ourselves was 'free will' would have been wolfed by a technological diabolism to which we're powerless to say 'boo' and which sends solecisms and sophistries tumbling off our parrot tongues before we can taste how horrible they are.

# 4

THE CHRISTMAS TERM of 1908 was my first at Lancing; a few months before I reached 12. Looking back now, I see those four or five years—I left when I was 16—as one sees sometimes a stained glass window from inside a 19th-century English church: the lifeless, sullied glass between the stucco of its mock-gothic mullion and jambs, turbid and dingy, dust-encrusted—yet pierced in a few chinks of faulty leading by dazzling, joyous beams of spangled sunshine, single and irrelated: filaments of stark happiness. That's how Lancing seems: dull and purposeless and silly (those lunatic icy baths on winter mornings!)—yet the precious source of some ecstatic bouts of emotional ebullience; for it was there I began to live emotionally, and to discover that the *mind* was capable of vast pleasures.

I suppose dozens of my contemporaries were killed in the 1914 war: those godlike athletes I feared, the angel-faced choirboys I was before long entranced by, the long-nosed bookworms I liked, those golden boys at the bathing place in whom I was soon seeing a new, mystical beauty—extinguished, still almost in their pubescence, in defence of things like the free marketing of marsala. I remember few; and fewer still, to my knowledge, reached any eminence. Lancing, 50 years ago, taught one to be mediocre; which, I suppose, accorded with the wishes of its founders: it was meant for the progeny of parsons, and aimed doubtless at a yearly output of archdeacons with an occasional episcopal highlight. I can see clearly R. H. Twining, a long, gangly, good-natured boy: now a life-peer and colonial pro-consul; and a stocky lad called Ritchie —was he sandy-faced and small?—now General Sir Neil Ritchie. E. C. B. Jones, a kindly intellectual in the 'Seconds'—did he become a distinguished music critic? And a scholarly swell called Arundell Esdaile, far above my station, who became a grandee in the British Museum; another named Driberg—older brother of Tom, later a good political and journalistic friend of mine. There were the three Imeritinskys, all princes—George's name I've seen now and then since in the social columns. And there was a boy in Head's House named Douglas—we never met at school—known to be the only lord there at that time; I got to know him in London in 1917, and his father, Percy Queensberry, who as Lord Douglas of Hawick had gained eternal honour by going bail with Stewart Headlam for Oscar Wilde. Very vividly I remember a charming, monkey-faced boy, G——: gay, bright-minded, humane, one certain, I'd have thought, of 'success'. He was gallant in the war, I heard; for years after, poor chap, his name kept cropping up in papers like the *News of the World*: 'Public Schoolboy's Cheque Frauds', 'Ex-Officer on False Pretences Charge', and his prison sentences got longer and longer. Poor G——, he was so nice: as a criminal myself, I hate to think of his sparkling spirit dulled and calloused in the sorry nick; and wonder what quirk in his sound nature took him into that rut.

I can think of only three or four old boys I've known in after years. Evelyn Waugh I've never known; but he was there with Tom Driberg, a decade or less after my time, and Tom has told me a story of the two of them at the high altar in that great surging chapel. Both were holy boys, as both today are pious in their eminence—though Tom's harp will be a High Anglican one, and Waugh's a Papist. They were serving together at one Sunday's Eucharist, and setting out beforehand the altar furniture, pretty as *putti* I expect in purple cassock and little lace cotta. They disagreed over the placing of some article—a canonical dispute settled by Waugh's planting the thing where he wanted it and saying: 'What's good enough for me is good enough for God!' (In fairness to Waugh, Tom's text may have read: 'What's good enough for God is good enough for me'—but I prefer the first version.) Then there's a colonial servant I've met somewhere in the Far East, name forgotten; and dear Henry Audley, whose distinctions, besides a gentle charm, combine a fine talent for designing hand-painted glass with being the 23rd baron. And there's that dashing Brighton figure, the Count Willie de Belleroche, son of A. Belleroche, and himself a painter, writer on Brangwyn and Sargent, and shrewd acquirer of pictures. When, in Brighton not long ago, I mentioned our school above Shoreham, Willie tossed his patrician head and exclaimed: 'Of course, I was put down for Eton—I went to Lancing because it was nearer!'

I didn't go to Lancing for Willie's reason; but because the fees were what my mother could afford, and the religious 'tone' was what she wanted—High Church, and plenty of it. So much of it, that I believe there was, for boys, a surfeit of statutory holiness: full-dress matins and evensong each week-day; early Communion, sung Eucharist with sermon, and evening service every Sunday; and last thing each night those lugubriously intoned 'house prayers', always ending with 'prowling about like a lion, seeking whom he can devour'—an uncomfortable thought, I felt, to go to bed with. Even then we weren't finished: there was the obligatory kneeling in pyjamas by one's bed—though nobody counted the number of seconds one stayed there. Chapel, in fact, I loved: adoring the slender soaring of the fluted pillars; inspired, tipsy, with the heady splendour of the plain-song—and it was in that chapel that I first *heard* music; watching, with a queer mystical happiness, the faces of certain of the boys; enjoying, in the same way I enjoyed, say, 'The Ancient Mariner', the more moving liturgical moments. But this joy in chapel wasn't religious; it was emotional, 'aesthetic'; perhaps, too, sexual.

I was bored by and despised the platitudinous burbling in the pulpit—except when the great Adam Fox was preaching: there was in him an exciting intelligence which even a boy could sense and, holy as I'm sure he was and is (in his canon's stall at Westminster), a spark of Swiftian satire. Yet I don't believe Lancing's religiosity defeated my mother's purpose and turned me unreligious: I rather think I was born without the capacity for religion: without the mystical gift which, surely, is the *reality* in religious experience. Or else I believe—and I say it in all sincerity and without blasphemous obliquity—that mysticism, for me, is a kind of distillation of sexuality; that religion, in me, seems an atavistic recrudescence of a worship of the ancients (which, however, lives to a degree in all of us, even in bishops); that the deity, for me, is the principle, the mysterious 'Let there Be', of generation; and that, for me, its symbol is the phallus. I don't mean that I've consciously got a pet religion of my own; I'm merely trying a rough rationalization of my governing *instinct*. And I don't mean that what I'm seeking to describe has anything to do, beyond an unquestionable origin in it, with physical sexual sensation, with what's called lust, with carnal gratification; that's important too, heaven knows: but in another compartment. I'm talking about a fierce and transcending joy of the *mind*; a kind of spiritual gloating over a unique aspect of beauty; an experience of apprehension that I can only describe as *mystical.* The moralists will execrate, the pundits doubtless pooh-pooh me. But here I'm stating, as far as I'm able, the truth about myself: my highest, most intense, pleasure or happiness is of the *mind*; and comes from seeing, being with, touching, looking into the mind of, a boy who, emotionally, mentally, rather than bodily, is *simpatico*; and from visually absorbing the multiple delights of his nakedness. Any sexual *acts* which may, and generally do, accompany, follow or precede this mental joy are adjuncts—prologue or epilogue to the essential monograph of the mind. It was at Lancing that I first had this experience, which I call love.

The 'Great' Bernard Tower was still there for my first term: head masters seem to gain that endorsement as easily as emperors. His successor was the Rev H. T. Bowlby, from a House at Eton: tall, with an embittered look. Fortunately for the boys, he had a limp; which easily christened him Dot-and-carry, and took some of the awe out of him. I don't think I ever spoke to him; but if I saw him lurching through the cloisters I would bolt round the nearest corner: my eternal guilt couldn't face, even anonymously, such august authority. I've often thought that, shorn of his tasselled square and silk M.A.'s gown (like a Greek Archimandrite's, his clothes always seemed cleaner than his underlings'), he may have looked quite an ordinary person; especially after I read in the paper, many years later, that he'd got into some trouble, poor man, about a small girl in a railway carriage.

I hadn't then invented my book-and-candle for exorcizing the spoof out of Olympus. But it should have worked: to a small boy, a Head Master surely belongs to super-humanity. I've simply to concoct in my eye the image of, say, royalty or the episcopate sitting on the lavatory for the mystique which makes their ascendancy to dissolve: how can an archbishop, in such a posture for such a purpose, remain hallowed? It couldn't have worked, of course, against the divinity of the Roman Emperors (and probably the earlier Popes); or for the Neapolitan Bourbons who, with their courtiers, cheerfully defecated among the Farnese marbles—for Italy's a country where the private functions aren't privy ones. But in England it's infallible, when one wants to knock the sham out of some of our institutions; I can think of nobody but Lord Beaverbrook (to his staff, a pretty august potentate) who can retain his lustre while giving audience to senior employees from the throne of the W.C.

There were an awful lot of parsons: Tommy Cook, Breathy Bond,

Little Lukey, dear W. H. Ferguson who became Head of St Edward's School in Oxford; Westlake, whose sublime liturgical voice took him to Westminster Abbey as a minor canon; the great Adam Fox, walking slowly along the cloisters like a careful cat, stooping slightly and led by his huge supercilious nose. He was a scholar—about the only one there—and the perquisite of the Sixth: but I admired him hugely, and always think of him as a mixture of Deans Inge and Swift. I can remember Adam Fox as a just-ordained deacon; now he's a Canon of Westminster and biographer of Inge.

The other masters, full of good intentions, I suppose—are scarcely worth cataloguing. There was a quaint chap called Glasspool, immortal because of the wonderful class-room oath that enlivened his peppery dreariness: 'Phut and bunker', he'd shout, spitting slightly, 'it's all phut and bunker!' Of course we were convulsed; I've often wondered, knowing the hearts of men, whether this attractive euphemism weren't designed to excite as well as intimidate us. There was J. F. Roxburgh, just down from Cambridge, a bright-star-in-the-east of academic innovation and later, first Head of Stowe; and dear, dusty, disillusioned 'Uncle George' Smyth, my house master; and a sprinkling of hearty young Blues. And I remember a bland youth from Cambridge, reputed widely to have 'cases'—liaisons with 'tarts', or pretty boys, to whom he gave cream-buns in his rooms.

Piety and playing-field prowess were the things that mattered; learning, it seems to me, was a mere chore which parents paid for. They crammed people through exams for Sandhurst, or the 'higher certificate'; but not a single master, that I can remember, *taught* one anything, inspired one with an excitement to learn. The subjects I liked—English, history, geography, Greek—stayed dead for me in the mouths of these dull men; my French, after four years of 'learning' it, was poorer when I left Lancing than the legacy from Ma'moiselle that I started with. Even 'divinity', the sublimities of the Bible, was a joke under the pale management of Little Lukey—the Rev Harold Lucas, who also 'prepared' me for Confirmation. 'Please, sir, what's a whore?' 'Please, sir, what does "lay with" mean?'—these were the questions 'divinity' meant: not for prurience' sake, but because Little Lukey seemed to be sitting under that blackboard simply to be teased.

Another agreeable opportunity for teasing came with the imposition upon us of the 'new pronunciation' of Latin. We in the Third Form would try to work Uncle George Smyth round to the declension of *causa*—hitherto pronounced 'cawza' —in order to say, with resounding emphasis, when we reached the plural, 'cow's arse'.

Nobody told me *how* to read, *where* to find the secret of literature: Shakespeare was a bore to be learned by rote, Milton a frightful slab of construing. Nobody showed me, though I felt it was there, the splendid vitality and warmth of Greek: it was all accents and breathings, just as Latin was vocative and ablative and 'by, with or from'. I learned to make efficient Latin verses—as interesting as making mail-bags in Wormwood Scrubs. Never a word was offered about music or painting, philosophy and the imaginative mind; never an interpretative notion mixed into the stagnancy of history or geography. It's the negation of the Lancing teaching of those days, as well as my own choice of going to war in 1914 instead of going up to Cambridge, that I blame mainly for the ignorance and intellectual waffling that I've carried through life (I blame of course, also, but less, certain debilities, like fecklessness of character).

I learned almost nothing there in the academic line. But I learned three things about myself; or rather, three enduring facets of my nature began to shape themselves, which hadn't been manifest before. I woke up to *emotion*; and I saw quite clearly where the most compelling part of it pointed. '(Sexual', then, wasn't really a definition within my knowledge; and the word sex, of course, except for denoting male or female, hadn't yet been invented. I don't think there was any consciousness of 'sex' in that early flow of torrential emotion: it was a chaste worship, a starry amaze.) The other two developments must have come unrecognized; but there began at that time two trends of character that have decided almost every wilful happening in my life: a vacillation and irresolution, like a recurrent moon-madness; an obstinate restlessness that stops my persisting in anything once started and drives me to change to something new; and a comfortable independence and don't-give-a-damn for other people's opinion, with a knack of getting my own way.

One of those shining shafts of Lancing memory comes from the cloisters round the Lower Quad: a beloved highway of imitation gothic, stonily echoing; with wide embrasures, spacious and continent, looking on to the green soft sward of the Lower Quad. The determined gothic of the older buildings wasn't too sickly; it had a veracious restraint; but what I deeply loved were the splendid Sussex flints, faced and embedded and primevally true, of which the older walls of the school were built. (One of the things I liked to think about while I was at Lancing, was that two masons, the same two, had for 50 years been tinkering away at raising the huge chapel; and their fathers, perhaps, for 50 years before that. I'd like to believe that their grandsons, today, are at the same work.)

In those cloisters—hence the memory—a wonderful ritual took place on fine evenings after chapel, after tea, and for 40 minutes or so before herding into the different 'house-rooms' for Evening School—the equivalent of 'prep': a kind of ogling strolling in Vauxhall Gardens, a flirtatious promenade along the Sunny Side of Piccadilly. 'Coming round?' one asked one's chosen friend—but strictly, on pain of the most frightful sanctions, one of one's own age and status; and arm-in-arm, always arm-in-arm, one went round and round the cloisters, meeting one's acquaintances, discreetly descrying the bloods, and above all making eyes at the tarts, the 'tweetles', the pretty boys. I wonder if this exhilarating rite is still performed? It was genuinely beautiful: the antique graciousness of the cloisters, the O.T.C. band practising on the quad (the obbligato, one fancied, to a garden party: I hated the brassiness of the bugles and their silly boy-scout tunes, but loved the side-drums, which seemed to go straight back through Waterloo and the Peninsula to Blenheim and Malplaquet), the awareness of friendship implicit in our linked arms and in the entwined twos and threes parading by, and that delectable, romantical surmise—one had but the foggiest notion of its meaning—as one caught and held the fluttering eye of a passing 'tweetle'.* Then one made the round again, yearning ahead for a second go at those sidelong eyes.

In fact, there seemed to be precious little practised sexuality in my time: I remember seeing only two performances in all four years: little exhibited masturbations, one in the dormitory one 'bath night' when I and the exhibiter were alone for our weekly hot tub (but bath nights could be a trap for the sexy: Uncle George Smyth often slinked through in silent shoes on the watch for just that); the other in the 'Groves'—that barbarous and bad-smelling enclosure of the 1910s for the school's communal excretions. There was a modicum of talk about 'rubbing up', as the phrase there went, which indicated that people did it; had I at that

* a 'tweetle', strictly, was an older boy's 'favourite': c.f. 'winger' in the Royal Navy; or 'batty' in the 1916 trenches—see David Jones's *In Parenthesis*.

time had more appetite, I should probably have discovered more evidence than I saw without looking for it. But of emotional, sentimental sexuality there was plenty: dozens of people had 'cases', an attachment for some Underschool urchin; dozens of smaller boys were 'tarts'—willing to make voluptuous eyes or accept furtive gifts of chocolate—or were some grandee's 'tweetle'. Nowhere, nor since, I think, have I seen exchanged so many meaning glances (of which the glancers barely knew the meaning) as 'round the cloisters' during those enchanted evening ambulations of 50 years ago. It was the fashion; and I was alone, as far as I know, in seeing with absolute clarity, before even my first explosion of love had blown me sky-high, that it wasn't just fashion for me: that here was the unchanging direction I was to follow. It seemed, for me, the normal direction; and quite natural that I should follow it.

It was 'round the cloisters' that I first saw Manson. I used to 'go round' perhaps with old Mellersh, a brainy myope I liked a lot, or a nice snub boy called Bosanquet, one of the cricketing family; but nearly always, whoever else might come, with gentle, untortuous Tom Webster—with whom a 'Sunday walk' over the Downs, in a unison of comprehension without words, meant a brimming of simple friendship; and whom I loved in a taken-for-granted, complacent way until one dreadful sun-drenched morning in the summer holidays of 1912.

Two or three days earlier I had watched from the Southampton quayside the exultant sailing of the *Titanic*, and still was moved by that prodigious scene. Now, sitting on the redolent lawn between the roses and the yew tree, luxuriating in the grandeur of a Turkish cigarette—my first day, I remember so well, of legitimatized smoking—I goggled in the *Morning Post* at the story of the ship's impossible loss—and caught sight suddenly of a swimming inch of print at the bottom of the page: Tom Webster, aged 15, had died horribly in a railway accident.

The detonating pang of that paragraph is still with me. Only four times since, I think, have I felt that same concussion of incredible death: the telephoned horror in 1927 of Christopher Millard's sudden dying ('Stuart Mason', friend of Robbie Ross, Wilde's literary executor); Nina Hamnett's telling me over a gin, in her breathless gossipy way, at the Fitzroy in Charlotte Street in 1941, that Phyl de Chroustchoff had killed herself in the gas-oven; the Reuter flash, that midnight in Tokyo, when Ian Morrison of

*The Times* was blown up in Korea; and the B.B.C. announcement, casually heard with cocktails on board Robin Maugham's yacht in Valetta harbour, of Sir Henry Gurney's murder in Malaya. It's the violence of such impacts, I suppose that shocks one so lastingly: the news that Felicia Browne, the girl I'd been engaged to marry, had been killed fighting for the Spanish republicans, and that of my mother's death in 1941, brought me in a Moroccan prison, had the gentler pain of the expected. (The sorrow of death, anyway, is a milder one than the sorrow of separation from the still living—the cruellest of all compulsions, perhaps, in this determinist life; and one which people of my sort, peripatetic both in geography and in love, must perennially expect.)

Manson,* my boyhood love, had been given, unjustly I expect, by the cloister connoisseurs the label of 'tart'; it was inevitable, with those great languishing eyes beneath their sable lashes, and the lovely Gainsborough face. No doubt the way he dreadfully greased his hair and smarmed it backwards into a clinging scalp enhanced the tartish look; I longed for it to be rumpled, unoiled, like a satyr's—yet adored the entrancing occiput its flat glossiness revealed. I suppose he was 13, I was nearing 15. It began in the cloisters; but it was in chapel that the sudden tidal wave of worship hit me and knocked me head-over-heels. I haven't the slightest idea why: I suppose it was some angle at which I caught his face, some light and shade upon it, some tilt of his head—all I know is that my spirit soared with those fluted pillars into the gothic height, and I walked out of chapel feeling as I didn't know human beings could feel. He had become my 'tweetle'; and for eighteen months or so he obsessed me: the thought that he was in the same world, the incessant awareness of his propinquity, somewhere, doing something; the image of his face and head and eyes and smile; the craving to touch him, to be with him; and later, after seeing him in the swimming bath, the sight of his nakedness. But I don't think, in all the length of this passion, I spoke to him more than twice.

We were in different houses, he in the News, I in the Olds; in different grades of school society (bureaucracy hadn't then thought up the term 'age-group'); and the Lancing law against the slightest consorting—even by glance—between people of disparate ages was as rigorous as any Hindu caste barrier. So this tremendous passion, this typhonic devotion, had to be conducted by signal: the signal, of course, of the eyes; a furtive wave across the breadth of a football-field during, say, a house-match; my ecstatic whistling of the first antiphon of our private catch tune when at last, after patient watching from the mullioned window of my 'pit' (instead of doing my reading), he came across the Upper Quad, and dutifully responded with the second bar ('pit' being the Lancing name for study). I can't think how much time I lost over lurking, waiting, prowling, in the hope of a glimpse of Manson; what an economy it would have been if I could have met him openly and licitly—and, then, how quickly probably the infatuation would have been over!

Sometimes, I managed to send him a note, saying perhaps: 'Groves, tonight, 21 minutes past 7.' Nowhere less romantical than the Groves could be imagined, with that permanent urinary-carbolic stink; but no other common ground, fairly secluded, could be legally reached by both of us. (The Groves were the central depository for ordure of anybody, of any House and any age: the stand-up part was both sides of a zinc-faced wall, open to sky; the sit-down, two rows of door-less cubicles with buckets full-up by evening. It was icy-cold there in winter, and high as old horse in summer; I never crapped again in so humiliating a place until, in the Korean War, I had to use the American Army's.)

Then, in Evening School, after quakingly watching the clock, I'd put my hand up at 7.20 sharp: 'Please sir, may I go to the Groves?' I'd write on a special board my name and destination and the time; when I got back I'd have to put the hour of return. I think three minutes was allowed for the Groves—so there wasn't much time. Then I'd rush off with the beating heart of a lover—but without the slightest notion of what I wanted to do, if I found Manson there. I never did find him; perhaps our house-clocks were different; perhaps he didn't bother.

But I did meet him one Sunday afternoon, when we had to go for 'walks' within delimited bounds, carrying under our arms those ridiculous straw-hats, which it was bad form to put on one's head, and weren't used at all on week-days. How I made the arrangements I can't remember: the tryst was at The Ring, a charming roundel of trees a mile or so over the Downs, between the '16-acre' above the college and Chanctonbury; I took Webster to keep cave, and my weekly 'tizzy's' worth of chocolates from the Grubber in a paper-bag. He came: I suppose for the sake of the chocolate; and while Tom watched from the clump's verge, Manson and I sat tongue-tied and stupid. Perhaps we talked for a minute or two about cricket; and then trudged separately back. We met once again, on the Lower Field when nobody was about; the dead tree-trunk may still be lying there with engraved on it ECMCD—the cryptogram of our espoused initials.

In the holidays, and even after I'd left, I sent him letters: in which, I hoped, the burning fires of my love glowed through formal words intended for parents' eyes. Day after day I watched for the postman, and felt the frightful anguish of disappointment; not more than twice in eighteen months he wrote—something like: 'Dear Davidson, hope you're having jolly hols. I went to the military tournament, yours ever E. C. Manson.' These letters, precious and sacred as the Host, I'd kiss in the locked lavatory, and put under my pillow at night. No names, surely, could be thought of more heavy-handed than Ernest Claude: to me they were pure poetry, and my new motor-bicycle was christened Ernest while my retriever mongrel, publicly called Curly, became secretly Claude.

This, of course, was 'calf-love', a 'childish infatuation': the thing for which grown-ups tease, and perhaps permanently wound, their burning offspring. But I can't see that, in intensity and volume, this schoolboy love, this pubescent emotion, was any less of a thing than others succeeding it in the later, mature years (or rather, the years of the 'eternal adolescent'); just as I can't see that these last were different, in strength and truth—though I admit I'm in no position to judge; but then, nor is anybody else—from 'normal' people's loves. Love is love; and a daffodil's a daffodil, in a suburban backyard or a Sussex coomb. But adult mockery of calf-love (at any rate in my day) wasn't so obtuse: I believe it springs from a jealousy, a selfish misgiving lest, if certain lofty secrecies aren't tantalizingly hidden from the young and emancipating pleasures denied them, some power over them will be lost; just as the ruling coteries of nations, especially dubious dictatorships, hasten to restrict sexual liberty knowing that it fosters an appetite for other liberty (remember the duchess who asked her lover: 'Is it really true that the lower classes do this *too*?'; and the judicial concern, in the 'Lady Chatterley' trial at the Old Bailey, lest ordinary working people should spend 3s 6d on the Penguin edition).

It was, I suspect, the moment that I first saw Manson naked in the swimming bath that I first perceived the fierce joy, the mental exaltation, that surged up from *looking* at naked boys: a fascination I've never ceased to feel and have always sought to experience. In those days it was boys a year or two younger than I; since, myself halted for good, so to speak, in emotional adolescence, it's been adolescents.

The deplorable ambivalence which has dogged my career, or negation of a career, since emergence from childhood showed itself at Lancing in a perverse switching from one purpose to another. Destined to go up to Cambridge, where my brother by now was at Jesus, I'd gone on the Classical Side. After a year or two, I asked my mother to let me change to the Modern whence, finding that I loathed the thing called Science and was stone blind to that called Maths, I went back to the Classical; and then, nearing my 16th birthday, announced that I wanted to leave school and become a designer of railway locomotives. I was allowed to; and entered the London & South-Western works at Eastleigh as a 'pupil', at considerable cost to my mother; but after a few months, towards the beginning of 1914, abandoned that and again tempted by the university started swotting Greek in order to sit for Little-Go. No sooner had I scraped through the first Part of Little-Go than the war came; and I threw up Cambridge to plunge into the sterile military life to which nobody was less suited than I. I excused, to myself and my mother, these lunatic mutations by saying that at Lancing I was learning nothing, that vocationally my road was the railway, that after all it wasn't, that King and Country called me; but in fact, the mould of my lasting instability had set. My poor darling mother, who always spoiled me, always gave way to my wishes, let me do these things; I've wished since that she'd tried to be sterner than she was capable of, and as sensible as she really was.

Lancing, however, also revealed that precious faculty of getting my own way. I wasn't a rebel there; I didn't flout the absurd conventions—that would have made life uncomfortable. Rebellion in plenty began almost at once after leaving.

But, without consciously planning to do so, I gently eased my way into a niche of my own. In form, I was clever enough to be top, or somewhere near it, in the subjects I liked without doing very much work; in those I disliked, I cheerfully let myself be bottom, and somehow appeased the masters by displaying an independent intelligence and turning on, doubtless, a bit of Childers charm. Detesting football, I got myself an unprecedented dispensation on condition that I 'ran' instead; this meant jogging contentedly for a spell over the Downs and then lying, for the rest of 'games', in a hot bath in the changing-room. Somehow, early on, I acquired 'library privileges', which meant I could go in, when others couldn't, and read what I wanted to (I remember being exhilarated, and feeling a bit devilish, over the first appearance in the *English Review* of the 'Everlasting Mercy'). Then I got 'my Privileges'—just what this brought I can't remember, beyond the right to put a 'soft-arse' (Lancing word for cushion) between me and the hard form on certain occasions like 'lectures'. Unusually young, I was given a 'pit', and at long last had privacy. Only one thing was needed for social complacency: House Colours. With a certain amount of effort, I wedged my way into the house team for the Five Mile—the annual cross-country over the Downs; and tottered in last man of the Olds foursome. But Olds won the cup, and thereafter I could wear round my neck the silk scarf, silver-grey and white, of aristocracy. I've never had an ounce of public ambition; and had none then. I was content with social comfort and an unworried saunter through the boredom of most of it.

But it wasn't all boredom; there were things I adored. I loved chapel, and of course swimming naked among the naked—both brought an immense emotional joy of the same sort of quality; I loved Sunday walks with Webster, and watching cricket with him —those glorious House or School matches when one didn't have to play oneself but could lie on rugs round the edge of the field gorging chocolate. And I loved too—proof that a good deal of happiness was there—the sweet, nostalgic sentiment of our singing, at the last chapel of term, 'Lord, dismiss us with thy blessing . . .' But there were things that were torment: the barbarous compulsion of the winter-morning cold baths; the pervading chill of the place, and the warnings that sitting on the snapping hot-pipes would give us piles, the odiousness of the Groves (not that I've any objection in themselves to ordure and public defecation), the deadening ennui of most form-work, and the humiliation of 'beating'—not the pain of the cane on the bum, but the pompous ceremonies of it: as inhumane in miniature as the calculated degradation of an English criminal court.

Into sexual knowledge we had—properly, I believe—to delve ourselves: I can think of few things more damaging than 'instruction' from such a clot as poor Little Lukey. This cleric, 'preparing' me for Confirmation, did have a go: rather like Dr Fraser years before, he suddenly popped the question, did I 'abuse myself'? Truthfully, and squirming with shame, I said No. Did I know about it? Yes, I answered; and then he trapped me into the only offence of sneaking I committed there. Who'd shown me? he snapped, in that cold, tight-lipped way; and before I could think, I'd said S——. For long after I quailed under the burden of my beastliness, and was terrified lest S—— should get into a row: he was so nice, and impressively salacious. Another three or four years, and he was dead in France.

Two more memories of the Lancing time: of 1910 and 1911. I was sent for in form by Uncle George Smyth: by the table where he dished out the weekly 'tizzies' of pocket-money, he told me, with that undertaker's professional regret used by schoolmasters and the B.B.C. when announcing death, that my father had died and I was to go home. I was unmoved, I remember, except by the delight of going home. Various Davidsons came down gravely, thinking of their trains back, for the funeral; of which I recall little but the cold fricassee of chicken. That—and the great sadness of our beloved Coeshall's departure. The other is of George V's coronation. We got two or three days' holiday, and Nancy and I stayed at Aunt Edie's funny little Oxford Street flat, to which little priests paid excited, whispering visits. We didn't see the crown-and-robes procession; but had seats, for the Royal Progress next day, in the Spring Gardens stand looking on to the Admiralty Arch. What sticks in my mind isn't the procession but the gorgeous get ups of the people in the stands; with us was my Uncle Eardley in his full-dress scarlet, and somebody else who wonderfully jangled and dangled with the accoutrements and Ruritanian sabretache of a hussar. I suppose this must have been the very last public ceremonial when the onlookers too, not merely the actors, turned out in their moth-balled splendours.

One other tiny and absurd incident of my schooldays I will record, because—for reasons which I cannot, but psychologists perhaps may, discern—it has stayed in my mind like a framed photograph for 50 years. Going back to Lancing for the summer term one blazing May morning, I sat by the open window of my third-class branch-line carriage and looked out on the sunlit strawberry fields we were rattling by, towards the Hamble river. Suddenly a fine rain came blowing in at the window, softly and warmly spraying my face while I gazed unbelieving at the cloudless blue sky. It *can't* be raining, I thought; and poked my head out to see better. From the carriage ahead of mine a huge penis obtruded; at

Fratton station its owner, a hefty naval rating in bell-bottoms, got out. The sight was so outrageously unexpected, my English bump of propriety so blushingly flabbergasted, that it took me a little time to see how beautifully funny that shower of rain was; and its image, at once ludicrous and awesome, became indelibly branded on my imagination—so that ever since it has remained my emblem of the Royal Navy, side by side with the White Ensign. That is a sacreligious admission, of course; but one cannot teach good manners to one's imagination.

Tea under the Portugal laurel was the seal at home of high summer: those flaming Junes which now seem of a piece with long-ago happinesses. High in its branches we'd built, with Coeshall as architect, a fine plank roost; below was the hammock I sometimes slept in on hot nights. The tree's shadow meeting that of the cherry made a dark cavern of coolness to dive into after whacking croquet balls about in the full sun had made one's tingling heat unbearable; tea and strawberries and my mother's welcoming serenity seemed paradise. One such afternoon, my brother, down from Cambridge for the summer vac, was urging in his indulgently didactic way that municipal socialism was England's need, or something of the sort: the latest Shaw, the last Wells, the Webbs on local government, Fabian tracts, lay about on the ground. Eardley was then at the height of his 'progressive' years—and he'd just got engaged to a 'progressive' Scots girl, his first wife, whom he'd met on the Rome Express. He was full of 'fads', as our aunts called them—and as I became: vegetarian, syndicalist, free-thinker—but he annoyed me when he declared pompously that 'riding was degrading to horseman and horse'. He had an able brain, though unadventurous; and with it an abiding sense of civic duty, deciding that the best way to serve the community profitably was to read for the Bar and then become a Town Clerk—he switched, after fighting through the war as one of the Royal Flying Corps' earliest pilots, to medicine, and became a flourishing G.P.: the Childers charm proved a bedside aid to a great professional ability.

Shaw and the Webbs weren't in my line then: the 'Soul of Man under Socialism' was a good enough revolutionary gospel for me, and at 15 I'd made up my mind that 'art' meant the intoxicating sensual 'wickedness' of Wilde and Beardsley (plus Anna Lea Merritt's 'Love Locked Out' and the annual Academy bathing-boys of H. S. Tuke). But Eardley's predications acted like a developer in my latent insurgence; and after I'd met the Farquharson family, I became pretty well anti-everything. If Dr and Mrs Farquharson were here today they'd be Aldermaston marchers and Peace Pledge canvassers; in 1912 they were I.L.P.-ers, suffragists, vegetarians, anti-vivisectionists, atheists—and of course their three boys went to Bedales. The middle son, my age, became my prescriptive companion; but it was the youngest, Maurice, whose subtler friendship I craved. I was still too unversed, though, to make a move—not that their 'isms' included the puritan one. Yet I think it was the doctor and his wife who really inspired me: they were so beautiful, in a white-haired, Renaissance way; and the first people I'd ever met who were truly *idealist*. Every second, it seemed, away from his Southampton practice, away from her household, was given passionately to some selfless cause: I, as the boys already were, was swept into all this; evening after evening, when I was at home, I was carrying the purple-and-green (were those the colours?) banner of a Votes-for-Women march, or distributing I.L.P. leaflets, or being 'usher' in some proselytizing gathering. I became 'minutes secretary' of the local I.L.P. branch, under Fred Perriman, a socialist saint with a sergeant-major's moustache; I went to political meetings, understanding little of politics: I heard the young Winston Churchill's Gibbonian grandiloquence in the Liberal cause, and the sanctimonious charm of Ramsay MacDonald; I remember Fenner Brockway, very young I suppose, splendidly animating a small soap-box crowd by Southampton's Clock Tower. Socialism, and its accessory infatuations, in those days were a Faith, an idealism, a spiritual intoxicant, an inspired protest: not the professionalism of jealousy and jobbery it seems to be today. I believe the Farquharson influence was tremendously good for me; it supplied a spiritual and mental impetus which my mother's Anglican church couldn't and the sterility of Lancing teaching didn't; and it fertilized the seed of that hatred of social cruelty and injustice which has been one of the few good and constructive ingredients of my later-life character.

My mother agreed that the Farquharsons were 'nice'; but gently sighed because their goodness was godless. And she began to be socially, and perhaps morally too, perturbed because before long I was bringing working-class boys, younger than I, home to tea: she was never a snob; but she couldn't understand why I chose this sort of companion—and in those days, of course, differences of clothes, manners and so on, were tremendously sharper than they are today—rather than the 'nice' boys existing in the neighbourhood. Nor, really, could I; in the manner of the proverbial picture-goer, I only knew what I *liked*. There was a charming telegraph-boy I met in the Southampton swimming-baths; he very nearly took Manson's place in my heart, and would have if the spurious romanticism of the war hadn't abruptly removed me from him.

I think I was a beastly little prig in those I.L.P. days. I remember one evening after dinner, when Aunt Maud and Uncle Alan were staying, behaving as if that unhappy little man were a public meeting, telling him that his dividends were filched from the workers' labour; I must have been shamefully rude and impertinent. But Uncle Alan never liked me in any case; nor I him; but he was always kind. Once, when I was staying in Cranley Gardens, he took me alone with him to the Coliseum, then the most 'family' of the old music-halls, I in my very first dinner-jacket. We sat in one of those little boxes there were at the time, and he didn't speak a word the whole evening; we came back by tube (passing Down Street) in a mood of sorry gloom.

Meanwhile, experience of—but still more, reveries about—erotic pleasure were galloping ahead. I was about 16 when I first discovered almost by accident the tempestuous bliss of the orgasm; and increasingly I was yearning not only to share this bliss, but especially to *perceive* its enjoyment, so to speak, in another boy. About now, too, I was introduced to another mode of pleasure that's endured—I didn't *acquire* it, because it had always been there, in the underneath; I simply learned to relish it consciously, as one learns the flavour of garlic. An older boy, son of another doctor who lived in a doctors' row overlooking Southampton's main public park, taught me a number of tricks: one of them, to watch from his upstairs room the town children in the park, boys and girls, through a pair of field-glasses. We used to see some exciting sights; it was my practical initiation into the *voyeur*'s pleasure: the acute joy of watching, unknown to the watched, some ecstatic privacy.

Aunt Annie had left me, besides some money and treasures to be mine at 21, £50 in cash for spending as I liked. My mother let me buy a motor-bicycle; and I began, nearly every hot day when I had pocket-money, to ride it into Southampton and the public swimming baths. Mixed bathing hadn't then come in, and nobody worried much about nakedness; I went there to *see* as well as to bathe: to a constitutional worship of sun and water, there was added an obsessive awareness of phallic worship. One day—I can see him still: nice-looking and youngish—a 'horrible man' got talking to me, edging his conversation towards sexual things: Makes you feel like something, don't it, this 'ot weather? Like to come to my room? I bolted with embarrassment (and anyhow, with a physical horror of older people); it was a long time before I realized that this chap was already what I was later to become—as the judges put it, a 'menace to society'.

Soon after leaving Lancing, I was motor-bicycling daily over to the L. & S.W.R. engine-works at Eastleigh. First I was in the drawing-office, making tracings; later, wearing overalls, on a lathe; both these tasks I was bad at, being bored by them. I don't know what I had expected: perhaps, having at the age of about 10 lectured the assembled household, maids included, on the working of locomotives, with wonderful lantern-slides made by myself, I thought I should be at once giving advice to Dugald Drummond, then Locomotive Superintendent, an august Jupiter with a Glasgow accent; or at least driving engines myself. Anyway, within a few months I was insidiously hinting to my mother that I wanted, after all, to go up to Cambridge.

We half-dozen pupils, being 'superior' to apprentices and skilled workmen, had a room of our own for eating our sandwiches in. The rest, except one, were older than I and of a different kind: I liked, in small doses, the brash filthiness of their talk, but was bored by its unchanging subject: the shop-girls they'd 'felt'. But Bubbles Parker was discriminate and delightful, and we were great friends; he used to come over to tea with us or I'd go to Fareham House where he lived with nice old Lady Parker and his elder brother Billy, whose grandfather had been a renowned China Seas admiral when Raffles was creating Singapore and Rajah Brooke appropriating Sarawak. A year or so later, Billy and I were to soldier together through the opening weeks of the war, until its fortuities swept us poles apart.

Already a double life was contriving its impinging parallels. I'd discovered, on the borders of the Docks or backing on to the River Itchen, certain secluded voids, waterside *terrains vagues*, which the ragged boys, aged from seven to 17, used as bathing places. Fifty years ago, England's decent negligence about 'indecency' stood about where south Italy's remains today; and here the boys, free of by-laws and the interdictory itch of legislative spoil-sports, swam and played unselfconsciously starkers. And driving off towards Eastleigh on a hot summer morning of 1913, I'd be tormented by the magnet of this knowledge; till I turned the machine's head round and made for the water: to watch for hours these bathers. This happened so often that Drummond wrote to my mother—saddened enough already by my various short-comings. I've forgotten how I explained the truancy; probably I said I couldn't resist going for a bathe. This was a period when the magnet was irresistible: perhaps because awareness of this pleasure was so novel and violent. It accounted, too, for the first show of my innate laxity about money; for some reason one day, perhaps the hope of meeting some special boy, I was determined to go to the swimming baths; but had no pocket-money and, having been badgering my mother recently, didn't dare ask her for more. I went upstairs and smuggled out one of my suits, which I sold to an old-clothes'-man in Southampton for three or four shillings. This has stuck in my mind as one of the shabbiest things I've ever done; I suppose because I was cheating my mother.

Nancy, by now, had left Pelham House, the girls' school in Seaford where she'd been while I was at Lancing; during May Week, she'd tumbled into love with a friend of Eardley's at Jesus (she tumbled into love as easily as I did; her first passion outside Pelham House had been for a holy and unresponsive shop-assistant called Arthur, who served at Holy Communion at the church we went to at Bitterne—but this had been quickly nipped in the bud). To Christopher Southward, however, she got engaged; and indeed married him early in 1913, with a marquee on the lawn and family hosts in feather boas—and me in my only, ever, tail-coat. Chris was a charming and intelligent youth with a rubbery face and an almost total absorption in music—Nancy, and his marriage to her, were, I think, little more to him than a kind of *cadenza* between movements. He was a first-rate violinist and also studied the viola with Lionel Tertis; chamber music was his passion, and he was in, among others, André Mangeot's string quartet. Chris's father was an elderly cleric with a Low Church beard; a Cambridge don, later Master of St Catherine's, who had taken to wife, as his second, his housekeeper. The second Mrs Southward, whose flamboyant bosom and out-and-out commonness gave our aunts and cousins plenty to talk about at the wedding, had necessarily had a lot to do with Chris's upbringing. Aunt Maud, anyhow shaking her head over Nancy's marrying a potential music-master, asked Chris to luncheon while we were all in London; and afterwards came rushing round to my mother. '*Dearest* Clare,' she exclaimed, 'how can you *dream* of allowing *darling* Nance to *think* of marrying a man who holds his knife like a *pen*?' But my mother did, of course; and before the war had come, Chris and Nancy went up to Holt in Norfolk where he had become one of the music-masters at Gresham's School.

My clearest memory of Nancy's wedding is the touching figure of my cousin Tom Field in his Osborne or Dartmouth uniform—touching it seems now, because three years later he was killed at Jutland, aged 16. His father, Cousin Mostyn, was a breezy, bearded admiral who then had just 'got his K', as the saying goes; he was Hydrographer to the Navy; only the other day, at the Royal Geographical Society, I saw his name on some Admiralty charts.

I remember, those summer nights when I slept out in the hammock, a special and guilty enjoyment which, I suppose, was the beginning of my lasting cult of nudity. When the house, and the village beyond the crest of the hill, were silent and asleep, I used to run about the dark and spectral garden stark naked, and even push through the laurels and climb to the top of the tall fence by the road—daring, with an odd excitement, the outer world to see me. I got from this a wonderful feeling of wildness, and an exhilarating guilt; though the guilt, probably, came from the knowledge that my mother would be angry—for nakedness seemed even then a splendid and inspiring thing.

When I had got my way about going up to Cambridge, I went to stay with Eardley who, married now to Cathie, had a house there; and started cramming Greek with old Mr Southward. I was entered for Cat's which, besides being cheaper than Jesus, had also the advantage of having my sister's father-in-law as Master-to-be. I think nice old Southward must have cheated a bit over my cramming; for he set me to learn 'The Frogs' almost by heart—and when I came to sit for Little-Go, it *was* 'The Frogs'. After that—the first and only real examination I ever went in for—we waited at home for the telegram, trembling; especially my long-suffering mother. I think in those days there were 'classes' in Little-Go, or grades of proficiency. When the telegram came, it just said 'pass'. I didn't care: I'd got through—that was all that mattered. I was going to Cambridge, that very October.

Instead, I went to war in August.

## 5

VERY YOUNG I'D begun to have toothache; but I kept it secret, and every time my mother said, 'Micky darling, isn't it time you saw the dentist, just in *case*—', I made excuses and contrived that she should forget. I was so cowardly about pain, sudden, imposed, unknown pain, that the idea of the dentist appalled me; I preferred the ache I was familiar with. By the time I was 17, I knew I had some pretty rotten teeth at the back, but with a vague faith that they'd come out by themselves and all would be well. I've always kidded myself that reality, when it's horrible, must be an illusion: that disagreeable things will quickly be transmuted into agreeable ones.

But when, on August 3rd, 1914, I motor-bicycled down to take the King's shilling, I was terrified by the thought of these teeth; I was afraid that either, because of them, the Army would reject me; or, taking me, would force me to a dentist. I was also slightly worried about my age, less than 17½, and about having no parental authority. They signed me up at once; asked no questions and gave me no kind of medical examination at all. That was the first thing I learned about the Territorial Army of 1914.

Then they said, 'You've got a motor-bike?' Yes, I said. 'Here's £25,' they said. 'Now it's ours. But you can keep it and ride it; when we want it we'll tell you.' I went home a soldier: richer by £25 and still the tenant of my own machine. I was like the owner of a Stately Home who is paid by the Nation to live in it. That was the second thing I learned.

A short time before, a nice youngish man called Sebag-Montifiore who lived between us and Fareham had asked me to become a Territorial officer in a new regiment being formed—Billy Parker, he told me, was a captain in it. Always too shy, or too cowardly, to say 'No' or 'Yes' on the dot, I answered that I'd see. But to myself I said the thing was absurd: how could I, a socialist and a devout anti-militarist, join these capitalistic Territorials?

And then, almost before the same summer's hay-making, I went and joined them. I suppose it was largely the fevered romanticism of that July's tail-end that made me once more turn the future upside-down; but I think chiefly it was that structural inconstancy, or impotence to reject a chance of change. Ever since—since, that is, I began to think—I've believed that Cambridge, while it couldn't of course have lifted the basic spell that's governed me, would have carried me a little nearer to emotional maturity (and given me some of the intellectual training I've always lacked); but the war, the sterile military life, nailed me for good to ungrowing boyhood: it was just a game. Had I possessed my brother's moral solidity, I would, propelled by patriotism into the war, have common-sensically gone up to Cambridge after it—as he, with realist deliberation, returned from it to walk the hospitals. But common sense has never pointed my personal way; impulse and expediency have done that. However that may be, I shed my socialism over-night; and 'England' became my shining oriflamme.

The regiment, obviously, to enlist in was Billy Parker's, the one in which Sebag-Montefiore had offered me a Terrier's unconvincing swagger: the 9th Bn The Hampshire Regt. It was a very odd affair; and showed, surely, how greatly the War Office planners were misjudging the nature of the coming war. It was mounted on bicycles; and offered a remarkable sight when on the march, with its majors and captains and warrant-officers, fat and thin, pedalling away at the head of their troops strung out along the road like a sand-coloured cycling club (the C.O., Col. Johnson, was allowed a sand-coloured motor-car). I didn't pedal; I had the motor-bicycle the War Office had bought from me, and after finding out what the destination was, just went there in my own time. It was that sort of regiment—in which the private soldiers were designated 'Cyclists'.

Our first (and only, while I was with the battalion) destination was Chichester. I can't remember going on parade there, or doing anything of a military nature beyond one or two guards; but I remember snobbishly having a suit of private's uniform made by a local tailor, sleeping in a local pub, and going home on the Government's motor-bicycle more or less when I wanted to. Bubbles Parker had gone off to the Navy; but Cyclist Davidson, M., and Capt. Sir William Parker met now and then 'off duty'—Billy was my company commander: much older than I was, but always delightful and kind.

My mother came over, unfussily loving; and with her unerring eye for *rightness* accosted a tall, jolly spinster of about 40 whom though wholly a stranger, she *knew* to be perfection the moment she saw her in The Close. My mother explained that her lamb was astray among the rough soldiery; and Miss Glover, and her mother, sweet and precious as antique lace, made their lovely little house my Chichester home. The old lady, who was like a portrait of St Anne, was the widow of Canon Glover and sister of Robert Bridges, the Poet Laureate; Miss Glover combined the sweet goodness of a nun with the unpatronizing jollity of the best sort of aunt. If there are degrees of angels, these two sit high in Heaven. Their house was too tiny to sleep me; but any afternoon cans of piping water and towels straight from the hot-cupboard and bath-salts were ready for me, and downstairs there were lashings of hot scones and buttered toast and cucumber sandwiches and chocolate cake. The house was called The Treasury, welded by age and goodness into the fabric of the Cathedral; inside it was a treasury of beautiful things, and books, and a·spiritual and intellectual richness. Nothing almost, in all my life, ever planted in me such an enduring and happy sentiment of *gratitude* as those afternoons at The Treasury, in the company of those two angelic creatures.

A near neighbour in The Close was old Canon Codrington, who came in sometimes to tea; his brother, a general, was, I think, one of the earliest V.C.s; and it was the Canon, I learned years after, who paid for the boyhood training that set Eric Gill on the way to the first rank of English sculptors. There was some connection there too, I forget what, with General Sir Bindon Blood, Queen Alexandra's equerry; this especially pleased me, because 'Sir Bindon Blood' has always seemed one of the most magnificent comic-heroic names in history, like somebody out of Congreve.

Quite recently, the late Mary Gill, Eric Gill's widow, told me that both the Glovers (whom she'd known in her youth) were dead; and that The Treasury was now lived in by Chichester's Town Clerk. I hope he's a worthy Town Clerk.

About seven years later, after the war, I stayed with the Glovers again on my way down from Norwich to visit 80-year-old Edward Carpenter, on the Hog's Back—where, as one's great-aunts used to recall being patted on the head by the Duke of Wellington, I can say I was pinched on the bum by England's Walt Whitman.

In 1914, because I'd never been *shown* it, poetry meant almost nothing, and Mrs Glover's sisterhood with Robert Bridges seemed only an interesting label. But in about 1922, when I was drunk with poetry and exchanging almost daily letters about it with the schoolboy Wystan Auden, the connection became hugely important; and I planned passionately to show Auden's verses to the Poet Laureate. But I never managed to meet him; and that plan, with no harm done to Wystan, came to nothing. All this, however, and Edward Carpenter, belong to another period.

One other Chichester happening has remained notable: my first seduction, if that's the word—my first physical experiment with a younger boy. He was Steve, the boot-boy at the pub, about 14: ugly, unenthusiastic, and not very clean. Yet that spectacle, that tactile privity, that exalting intimacy, left me inwardly inspirited for days and weeks after; and for a long time I dwelt with an intense mental joy on the details of the experience (it was ages before one occurred again).

In the meantime, my family were pulling strings. Uncle Eardley, by now 'dug-out', as was said then, and a Full Colonel in command of a remount depot, went to Lord Roberts, a friend of the family since our cousin Hugh Childers was Secretary for War; and 'Bobs', in splendid retirement, mentioned the matter to Lord Kitchener. This of course seems utterly ridiculous—that the country's most eminent soldier and its War Minister should bother about an obscure 17-year-old; yet this is what happened—the England of 1914 was like that—and within a short time the *London Gazette* recorded my temporary commission in the 43rd and 52nd Light Infantry, the Oxford & Bucks. I had wanted to be a cavalryman; but my mother said she couldn't afford that, and in any case the Oxfordshire L.I. was Uncle Eardley's regiment and in a way a family one—a Twistleton-Wykeham-Fiennes cousin had been his contemporary in it. It was, of course, a 'good' regiment, traditionally brigaded with the Rifle Brigade and the 60th Rifles (the three are now combined in the Green Jackets). And it had pleasant distinctions: a 'gorget' of cord and button on the tunic's lapel instead of the common-or-garden badge, and a sword-belt of a unique design, square-buckled, and worn with both shoulder-straps. Altogether, if I had to be on foot, it was as good as anything short of the Brigade of Guards. But I didn't want to be on foot; and before very long I found a way of getting myself horsed.

The Army, when it didn't know what to do with or wasn't ready for you, had the agreeable habit of sending you on leave. As soon as my commission was gazetted I went home; and stayed there several weeks as exempt as a private person, except for the excitement of going to London to have uniforms made and the vanity of appearing in them when they arrived. I forgot about the bicycling Hampshires, who before long went off to India; and I don't think I gave a thought to the grotesque paradox of my position: 17 years old, uneducated, experienced in nothing, untrained (except in some parade-ground facilities acquired unwillingly in the O.T.C.), a juvenile complexity of negatives; yet authorized to know better than multitudes of grown men, and paid 7s 6d a day by the Government to do nothing.

After the usual day or two of looking for 'other ranks' in order to draw the flattery of their salutes, I returned with a rush to my childhood fondness of riding—I hadn't done any, hardly, since Aunt Annie's coachman Dewdney taught me the feel of a bridle and something of a seat. In those few weeks of leave it became a mania. Nearly every day I went into the New Forest for a ride: cub-hunting had started, and I subscribed to the New Forest Foxhounds (I remember my thrill of pride when I saw later my name printed in the list of subscribers). Generally I hired the same mount; a big, raw-boned black called Emperor, who pulled uncomfortably, but, unlike most hirelings, had liveliness, sense and a nice action over ditches (about the only sort of fence the country had; Uncle Eardley, used to the Shires, would have despised it). I don't think I ever saw a fox killed; I didn't want to. I hunted for the exhilaration of the unknown—for every run is an unknown; for the thrill of finding, and the tensity of watching hounds working; for the electric joy of hounds' giving tongue, of riding for a purpose and within a pattern; for the physical pleasures of the sight and sound and motion of a hunt; and, most of all, for the delirious thrill of being one with one's mount in the split-second moods of horsemanship which hunting supremely enjoins. And, too, for the long, tired jog home, ruminating the day's cud, with a stop or two for a pint on the way.

In the evenings I devoured all of Surtees, knowing Facey Romford and Pigg and the earl and Leech's drawings by heart; and read every book about horsemanship and horsemastership I could find, and magazines like *The Field* and *Bailey's*. I was a natural rider, and could have been really good, I think: I had the seat without looking for it, the hands, and the understanding, the 'feel', of a horse; and a horse knew me. Riding became a passion which, like most boyish enthusiasms, swamped all others—even the growing, secret, urge towards boys. In a way, it was a predestination: it was riding that was my emotional salvation through the futile wastage of the war; and riding again, my chief happiness in the two infertile years in South Africa which followed it.

There's no loneliness, no boredom, when you feel a good horse quicken into eagerness under your legs' pressure, and see his neck and ears liven at your touch of the bridle.

Then orders came: Fort Brockhurst, one of the antique keeps which encircle Gosport; in this crenellated citadel, with its vast gravel quadrangle (which helped pleasantly to raise, if one didn't look too hard, a collegiate or monastic mirage), the Regiment had set up a 'New Army' branch of its Cowley Barracks Depot near Oxford. Here I learned the rigid solemnities of regimental life (like starting school all over again), and here I learned bit by bit to drink. I suppose there was an interest, and novelty, in pretending to be grown up and a real soldier through this winter of 1914; and the Gosport monotony was broken now and then by brief leaves at home or in London and by 'courses' away: at Hayling Island; in a deserted Oxford College; at Doncaster, whence I made my pilgrimage to Cantley. I can't remember learning much from these courses, though I was trying to take my soldiering seriously and generally came out pretty high in the 'tests'; but they left a trail of fervent though transient friendships—there remain today the faces of Robin d'Erlanger and Eric Gunning, both of the Rifle Brigade, of a charming red-headed boy called Andrews whom I'd known at Lancing, of a grave Goldilocks remarkably named Julius Caesar, and a few spontaneous physical ebullitions.

I can recall only two of my fellow-officers at Fort Brockhurst—both three times my age and both, in intellect and outlook, delightfully unsoldierly. Neither, obviously, need have joined the Army at all, each could have found some cushy, opulent 'warwork'. Yet, old as grandfathers, they chose to be junior combatant officers: it's hard to think of a higher chivalry.

George Calderon, an important dramatist and member of that Hispano-English family renowned in art and letters, was nearly 50 and a subaltern in my regiment: a gay, whimsical, slightly ironical person, bubbling with wit and good humour and ever ready with kindness and the sensible solution of some tiresome military problem. His slim, Iberian good looks were made martial by a little black moustache. In less than a year's time he was dead at Gallipoli.

My other friend was much older—I thought he must be 60: a white-haired ensign in the Grenadier Guards, for some reason attached to us. His name was Heneage: tall and rather bowed, with long legs that gave at the knees, and the face of a sweet old eagle—a gentle Tiberius: his uniforms always seemed loose and wrongly buttoned. When we were in London together he'd give me a meal at his club, the Marlborough, and often we'd go to a play. He was kind and amusing and civilized; I never thought of him as so much older, or that our friendship was incongruous. Later, of course, I wondered; but he never said an equivocal thing, nor hinted which way his inclinations were; he seemed, in his courtly way, to ignore as completely as I did the difference in our ages. Alas, after I left Gosport I lost touch with him, and never ran into him again. All my life, like a child at a pantomime, I've been so agape at a new episode that I've forgotten the one before—another trait of adolescence, I suppose; and many fine friendships have withered away through my fault—my fondness hasn't diminished, but I've been too selfishly absorbed to look back, to take the trouble to write or telephone; and then as time goes on that awful sense of guilt shuts finally the door.

One day at Fort Brockhurst I was casually looking at a War Office circular: . . . Machine Gun Corps . . . young officers invited to volunteer . . . officers will be mounted . . . MOUNTED!—the word shone like sunshine, like a sign from Heaven specially for me; I rushed off to the adjutant and put my name down. Before long I was at Bovington Camp in Dorset: later the Tank Corps depot, and then a vast cantonment of wooden huts on the galloping Wessex wold, with Lulworth Cove for bathing, Weymouth for a civilized dinner, and Blandford for a drinking-stop on a good afternoon's ride. In command of the whole place was a marvellous old boy of about 80, a full colonel with a white tuft on his chin like Lord Roberts's and the comic stiff-collared khaki he'd worn in the Boer War. He probably thought of a machine-gun as a sort of improved arquebus; as we did, indeed, ourselves—those unwieldy iron-age Vickers-Maxims with their brass fittings and water-tanks for cooling, and the cumbersome great tripods, that weighed a ton and seemed to make dents in the bones of your shoulders. Though without any mechanical bent, I had a quickness of mind and hand that enabled me to shine in our 'tests' in gun-mounting and so on; and having also a knack of *seeming* alert and generally proficient, I got into the instructors' good books. And there was riding-school:

a dismal lot of horses (anybody who has seen the nags for hire in the Villa Borghese at Rome will know just what they were like), and very elementary instruction. Round and round the ring: 'Walk-march, trrrot—keep those elbows in'—the N.C.O.'s in charge seemed satisfied if they could get the young officers, few of whom had ever been on a horse, to bump round at a slow trot without coming off. But one could pick a pony in the evening and go off for a hack over the down.

It was astraddle my 18th birthday that my first 'adult' sexual encounters occurred: that I discovered that grown-ups could behave just as I felt like behaving. I knew by now exactly what I wanted; and though the young men I lived among, in spite of their endless talk about women, now and then paired off in bed for bodily larks, I knew that this was mainly a boyish hangover and quite different from my own yearning. And I still vaguely believed that I and Oscar Wilde—and, I suppose, that unlucky man at the Southampton swimming pool—were the only people since the age of Alkibiades to be *born* with this yearning. Now I learned from experience that there must be quite a lot of men, and even women, who wanted boys; and I was only too conscious of looking contemptibly a boy, with my undersized shoulders and cheek as smooth as eggshell—two years earlier I hadn't even reached puberty.

While at Gosport, I'd been an honorary member, like all Army officers stationed locally, of the Naval Club in Portsmouth—the Royal Navy run neck-and-neck with the French Army for munificence, as I found again in 1951 when I lived afloat with them in the Suez Canal and the Red Sea; and some evenings I'd go there to sip the weakest gin I could find: it made me feel grown-up. Very quickly I became aware of a podgy, twinkling Rear-Admiral with a furry beard like Cousin Mostyn's: a 'dug-out' in some Dockyard job. He was always there, and began beaming at me over the top of his newspaper or whisky; then he began smiling, and in a day or two asked me to have a drink. Before I knew where I was, I was asked to dine at his house; I felt terribly shy and puzzled, but didn't dare refuse so grand a person as an Admiral. I was puzzled again when at his neat little house full of nautical relics he didn't dump my hat and coat (he opened the door himself) somewhere near the hall, but toddled upstairs with them on his little short legs and hid them in some room. I was introduced to a meek, silent sister; and given a lot of whisky. We had a solemn little dinner, and the admiral made me as tight as a lord; I remember popping in a dutiful 'sir' whenever I could. It was time to depart: the little man bade me come upstairs to get my things—he'd put them in his bedroom. Once inside, he pushed me down on the bed and 'attempted to commit a certain offence'. As politely as I could, deferentially calling him 'sir', I said I was sorry; and managed to skip unsteadily out of the house. But I thought next day I'd behaved awfully badly, by failing to repay in the way he wanted his kindly hospitality; I felt I'd been so ungracious that I couldn't show my face in the Naval Club again.

It wasn't prudery that caused this breach of manners; it was simply that I've always flinched from merely *thinking* erotically about people older than myself. I even feel a certain private embarrassment when my adult friends discuss their sexual doings.

Then, while I was at Bovington, there was the nice, valetudinary aesthete who lived in the Weymouth sea-front hotel where I used to have dinner. He picked me up in the 'palm court', among the wicker chairs: some kind of semi-invalid, though quite young; a wan, hushed person in a brown velvet dinner jacket, whose sitting-room upstairs was softly dim and lush with sombre hangings and little dark drawings by, I imagined, disciples of Beardsley. There was a baby-grand; and after we'd dined and he'd given me a whopping balloon of brandy, taking for himself some barley-water, he would murmur: 'Now I shall play you some purple music'; and I'd swig the brandy while he improvised a pot-pourri of diaphanous melodies. Then he'd come and sit beside me, putting a hand on my knee. 'Won't you *please* be kind to me?' he'd whisper, so touchingly; but brutally, I'd move his hand away, and thank him for giving me dinner. How often, since, have I played that sad man's same role!

A few years after, when the war was over and I was in Zululand, I saw in an English newspaper that he'd died—and left £30,000 to his chauffeur: a chauffeur, I suppose, more obliging than I was a guest. I felt an awful pang, of course, about that £30,000; yet I couldn't ever have been a whore as so many of one's acquaintances are in effect: I've no more been constitutionally able to go to bed with a male old enough to make whoring worth while than I have with a woman.

My other two adventures of this period—one repulsive, though pathetically comic in retrospect, the second quite enchanting—were both connected with my Cousin Florence de Losada. Cousin Florence must have been at least 80 then: she changed her wigs as other women change their hats—auburn, raven, orange: one never knew what colour her hair might be. Her face was a work of art: as carefully perfect as the late Queen Mary's; I always feared it might break, like china, if by mistake she laughed. She had been a Miss Magee, of New Orleans, U.S.A., and first married my cousin, the last Sir Eardley Eardley (for some romantic reason a chamberlain to the Emperor of Austria). Not satisfied, after his death, with remaining Lady Eardley, she immediately married Cliffie de Losada, and became a duchess. As a boy, I was very proud of Cousin Florence; anybody, I felt, could have a lord or two in the family but not so many had a duchess. It's true she was only a Spanish duchess; but Cousin Cliffie (she'd so long been a member of the family, and such a nice one, that he became an honorary cousin too) was a Grandee First Class, and that, I felt, was quite something. Cousin Clifford was the last Duque de Losada y Lousada, a British subject, and a retired commander in the Royal Navy.

It was at one of Cousin Florence's Lancaster Gate tea-parties that I met Mrs T. (for all I know Mrs T. may still be living—and rising 80). She must have been over 30, and handsome in a Junoesque way; her husband, she told me, was in the Navy and away at sea. Somehow I got pinned down by her, and when I said goodbye to Cousin Florence she was doing so too; of course, when I called a cab, I had to offer to drop her. She was staying at the old Langham Hotel, now part of the B.B.C.; I found myself being asked to tea, and artlessly accepted—it hadn't occurred to me that the matronly consort of a Naval captain could be planning to seduce me.

I did my best, at that surprising tête-à-tête, to be polite, but humiliatingly failed; instead of rising to the occasion, I shrank, so to speak, into myself and recoiled from what was to me an impossible task. I don't think Mrs T.'s experiment had the slightest emotional effect on me; except to confirm in my mind by demonstration what I already knew instinctively: that for me the female—apart from the wholly incomparable estate of mother and sister—was only seemly in an aunt-like shape, or in some totally impersonal role like the vicar's wife's.

But the other encounter to which Cousin Florence provided some sort of a bridge was utterly delightful. He was nicknamed Biffy;* and had a wonderful smoky gold skin and the gentle Malaysian beauty of the South China Sea. He was little more than my own age; but as slight and fine as a child and with the sensuous, roguish face of a boy wine-seller in Pompeiian bronze. I thought I'd never seen anybody so exciting. He was then a crown prince, and remained one for four decades. Today he's a ruling Sultan. I briefly worshipped him, before I went to the Front and after; my last sight of him, in those boyish days, was in the Vincent Square hospital when I first came back wounded. I was wearing my dramatic orange-and-black silk dressing-gown—I still treasure the memory of it—which made me feel like an oriental potentate my-self; Biffy had come to see me as soon as he heard I was there; and we managed a few minutes of charming dalliance before a string of aunts walked in, ushered by my gay and lovely V.A.D. nurse, Hope Havelock-Allan, as sweet as she was competent and beautiful.

More than 30 years later, in 1949, I telephoned to Biffy's palace on neutral ground, whither he escaped now and then, for unofficial diversions, from the courtly rigours of his Jovian father's State. An A.D.C., after consultation, asked me for drinks. Alas, I didn't find the Biffy whose delicate image I'd carried so agreeably in my mind's eye through all the years: not even recognizably the same person. . . .

Near the beginning of 1916, we were all moved—those of us who had 'passed out'—to another wooden camp near Belton Park, Grantham. I was now a full 18, and was so eligible for the Front (it's logical enough, I suppose, while both are approved by a perplexed civilization, that the age at which a boy may officially die for his Country should be that at which he may be hanged). We went to Belton to be formed, equipped and trained as full-fledged battle units: a part, though we didn't know it, of the Somme Offensive preparations. We were to be Brigade troops—one company of 16 guns to each Brigade front. All officers in this new Corps were mounted; I haven't yet puzzled out why. If the War Office dream was that section commanders and gun-limbers should gallop up and down their brigade front plugging weak holes, they must have forgotten that the chaps who worked the guns were on foot—I don't think N.C.O.s and gun-teams could have clung for long on to those limbers, which weren't built for passengers. However, this kind of problem didn't worry me; I'd got what I wanted—a horse. The next thing was to get a good one.

By the time my company, the 53rd, could see its own shape, I got myself made transport officer. This wasn't difficult, although my major was a stand-offish chap, not amenable to charm. He had a

Military Cross, but didn't drink; so while I could flatter him over his 1915 exploits, I couldn't approach him through alcohol. Nobody else though, could talk my horsey language, or run a knowing hand down an animal's hocks. So I got my way; and, in an unforgotten happiness, took charge of about eight horses, nearly 20 mules, saddlery, harness and vehicles. The 'officers' chargers' were of the milk-float sort. The best-looking I gave to my O.C.; he was a rotten rider and wouldn't know that this smartish bay had no ideas outside a pair of shafts. I picked the ugliest for myself: a dun-coloured scraggy mare with a ewe-neck and every bone showing. She had a lazy action, forging badly in her long lope of a trot; but she was the liveliest in my horse-lines and had been nicely broken to the bridle—she knew exactly what reins and her neck were for.

I spent the lovely days with my drivers and grooms: cleaning, watering, feeding, exercising; trying out mules as wheelers or leaders—and jolly good mules they were; working on leather, wood and metal—in those days the stuff was *real*, not plastic; riding out with the whole lot for all the driving drill we could get in.

Most evenings I spent at the hotel in Grantham, I forget its name. My closest friends were Billy Mathews and Guy Loftus, both ensigns in the Grenadiers (two or three Guards machine-gun companies were forming too), and both about my age. As time went on, we three dined less and less in the dreary mess, with its drearier food; we went down to the hotel, and dined extravagantly, drank enormously, and behaved abominably, in a jolly uproarious way. I remember another Grenadier with a tiny neat black moustache who always dined there, soberly, aloofly: about ten years our senior; his name was Victor Sassoon—he must, I suppose, have been the Derby winner of 40 years on. My friendships with Billy and Guy lasted until I left England after the war; I stayed with Billy in the country, went to the Loftus' house in Walton Street; and they came to my mother's flat in South Kensington after she'd moved to London. They were both charming; and I discovered then, as I've found so often since, that one can become the greatest friends with people utterly different from oneself. But, of course, we were all three schoolboys really.

Some time in the Grantham months—each of those ancient spans of experience seems today to be in a separate compartment: I look at them as at tableaux at Madame Tussaud, moving from one window to another—Guy got into a bit of a scrape. By a stroke of luck, I was able to get him out of it; but not before there was the shadow of a row, and the poor old Loftuses—they looked about 60 and were as poor as church mice—came tearing up to Grantham like harassed hens. Guy's grandfather, Lord Augustus Loftus, had been Governor of New South Wales when my Cousin Hugh was in the Cabinet and a power in Australian affairs; this tenuous link, and my usefulness in Guy's bother, decided old Mr Loftus that I should be in his son's regiment; and next time I was at Walton Street he told me that Col. Streatfield, then commanding the Grenadier Guards, had agreed to have me and all was ready for my transfer. I was delighted: I fancied myself in the gold-peaked cap of the Brigade, the 'plus-fours' it wore at the time, and the haughtily discrepant tunic. Common-sense eyesores like battle-dress hadn't then been invented: one went to war, as it were, in one's London clothes; the Guards, in the front-line, merely changed their pretty hat for a plain one. I wrote excitedly to my mother; but of course, always right in practical things, she put her foot down: I was already outrunning the constable, and if I joined the Brigade I'd be in Carey Street. She certainly couldn't afford such nonsense. So I stayed in my own uniform; but I set about making it as tiddly as I could. I was forced to wear the crossed machine-guns on my cap; but I clung to my Oxf. & Bucks gorget and Sam Browne; I had tunics made horsily long-skirted, and some elegant corduroy riding breeches; and in Conduit Street I bought a wonderful pair of high boots for seven guineas—the pride of my life till I lost them going down the line in an ambulance. I filed down the rowels of my stubby spurs and wore them high against my ankles; and, carrying my ash-plant hunting whip, hoped that mere foot-sloggers would take me for a cavalryman.

We went on embarkation leave, about May perhaps; and sailed from Southampton. That was a night of high poetry, whose cadence I can still feel: the last time ever that I exulted in a romance which, when I saw war, I found didn't exist. The blustery darkness of the dockside; the echo of nailed boots on the cold flags; the squealing, biting mules as we shoved them aboard; the thoughtful soldiers hung round like penny-bazaar White Knights and stumbling with gentle blasphemy up the slatted gangway; the consecrated swig of whisky when loading was done—*this* was the glory of war, before ever the war was reached. I'd crossed the Channel, of course, dozens of times in the Guernsey days; two years earlier I'd been taken by my Catholic Aunt Edie to Dieppe and Rouen, where she had assignations with Papal counts and smiling monsignori. But on this night I was sailing with Richard Yea-and-Nay; I was among the crusaders—yet loftier than the crusaders: they sailed chiefly for booty and preferment, we were sailing for the pure sake of England! That's how I felt through that long dark excursion to Le Havre, hearing the happy sound of hooves on iron deck, and the petulant whinnies of animal bewilderment. Yet almost next day the shining glamour of my romanticism vanished like hoar-frost; no sooner was I in the war than I longed to get out of it—for a fresh change of direction. I found I loathed the whole business.

I wonder what kind of a soldier I was? Pretty bad, I think: beneath the dapper illusion of keenness and efficiency that I managed, almost unconsciously, to create, I really was lazy, bent on getting through unpleasantness as comfortably as possible, and even, spiritually, rebellious. Even at that age I hated—as I've hated it since in other branches of society—the moral solecism of arbitrarily setting one man over others (though well content to be among the privileged few); had I been born in classical Rome or Athens, I'd certainly have wanted to be of the slave-owning class—but I'd have hated the principle of slavery. I privately saw through the spuriousness of these stupid colonels and majors and the hypocrisy of the generals; but of course, for an easy life, I 'conformed'—indeed, I was generally the blue-eyed boy of my seniors: I was smart, impeccably clockwork on parade, and quick and thorough in carrying out orders; I was clever and glib; and, most important, I had the right sort of 'voice' and manners. And I wasn't tongue-tied and gauche; although when *sent for* by superiors I become clammy-handed and guilty, I can switch on an easy equivalence when they come to me or I meet them on common ground; this I found useful with self-important seniors.

I was adjudged a 'good officer'; but I wasn't. I used to dread with belly-kneading fear a moment when I might have to make a quick military decision affecting the lives of men. I knew nothing of military theory, and precious little of practice; and was never apt for quick decisions anyway. I wasn't good for the men: I was too sorry for them, and shrank from 'checking' them or 'taking a name' or doing anything to add to their miseries and discomforts. I was 'familiar' with them—a disgracefully unofficer-like lapse in those days; and I made favourites; the pathetic elderly, homesick for their wives; the youngest and prettiest. My idea of fun was when, say, marching my chaps to the weekly 'mobile bath-unit', to ride on ahead to some estaminet and lay on beer all round for them; or to hang around in their billet trying to get across that dreadful Officer-Other Rank gap. They liked me, called me among themselves 'the boy' (I was the only person in the company who didn't shave), but I don't think they 'respected' me.

And then, I didn't hate the Germans; I couldn't believe that the unhappy grey-green huns we were supposed to shoot were any more guilty than we were. I remember my anger when Sir Ivor Maxse, G.O.C. 18th Division (and brother of Leo Maxse, a prominent true-blue journalist), harangued the 53rd Brigade shortly before the Somme was loosed off. He sat there on his horse, his pennant, Lancer-borne, behind him and his patrician chorus of red hats and red tabs around him. 'We're out here to kill Boches! We're out here to kill Boches!'—that was his reiterated theme, and he pronounced the word 'boshez'. I suppose he was right: that was what we were there for. Yet I loathed his sergeant-major's bayonet-practice tone: the flashy, fiery way he was lusting to kindle in us hun-hate and blood-love. The cult of 'hate' in war always seems to me a token of moral dubiety: a substitute for the compelling righteousness of 'our side' which isn't there: a confession that, in our G.H.Q. heart-of-hearts, we know it isn't the 'just' kind of war that could be fought without hate—without stories like one we were told: that the Germans were boiling Belgian babies to make oil.

Yet I enjoyed these 'inspections'. There's a stately pattern in ceremonial, the architectural sweep of a huge and romantic mural that has some sentimental charm; and, in it oneself, one feels that one's giving the tiniest dab with the artist's brush. Besides, it was the only time we ever saw our general. Days beforehand, days of precious training time, would be devoted to brass-burnishing and saddle-soaping; then the Brigade would be drawn up on ground well behind the lines—ground chosen, when possible, for its provision of a suitably impressive entrance for the principals: the G.O.C., followed by his Lancer and his incarnadined shop-window Staff, would come cantering on to the parade and pull up elegantly as the General Salute brayed forth (what a pity the new weapons are abolishing the splendid visual rhythms of the old bayoneted Present Arms). In the glorious finale of the march-past, after I'd acquired Trixie, my lovely little Arab mare, I'd kick her gently on the flank to leeward of the General as we neared the saluting-base, making her prance and cavort deliciously, while I sat rigid, bridle-hand into my waist, and terrifically gave the behind-the-ear Guards salute I'd perfected. I loved that sort of play-acting.

Soon after we'd got settled in behind the lines near Albert (I wonder if the miraculous Madonna still leans over, defying the German shell?), I called at the horse-lines of a neighbouring Brigade company—I wasn't satisfied with my mount. Gosh, I thought, *look* at that grey—and went straight over to Trixie. 'Can't do a thing with it,' said Pocock, the transport officer I was calling on. 'Does nothing but rear the instant you get on her. Nobody can ride it.' She was the loveliest thing I'd seen in the Army: perfect little head, strong, neat legs, good chest and quarters; about 15 hands and seven or eight years old. A hint of an upward curve in the fine neck, but a bit of a ewe sometimes spells intelli-gence. 'I'll take her,' I said. 'Swop you anything you like, bar the major's nag.' Pocock was glad to get rid of her; and Trixie was mine. She *did* get up on her hind legs, straight up, like a circus horse—perhaps she *was* a circus horse; she looked like one and was as clever as one. But if you let her head alone she went down again; I got my saddler to make her a light running martingale and never had a hint of rearing naughtiness again. She was brilliant, and she became loving. She could gallop, jump, change legs like an angel; and, I soon found, had been broken to polo. She was the sweetest of rides, and the sweetest companion. Trixie became my beloved, always first in my thoughts; now all I wanted was the *right* groom-batman. I found Thompson, a rather plain slow-thinking country-boy, a little older than I was. The two of them, in the next 18 months, were my only friends at the Front.

Once, in the becalmed weeks before the battle of the Somme, I found myself within 20 or 30 kilometres of my brother's aerodrome. I rode Trixie over to call, on a shining blue Norman day with static floes of white fleece dressed across the sky. It must still in 1916 have been a fairly happy-go-lucky war, for pilots of the Royal Flying Corps were able to take their visitors for a joy-ride across the German lines. Eardley took me up in a single-engined biplane (was it called a Bristol?), with no guns at all, which moved about 60 miles an hour. Our bare heads, mine aft of his, stuck up into the wind like paddlers' in a canoe; we couldn't talk, and he passed information back to me scribbled on bits of paper—'Jerry's support trenches below us now', and so on. I was just as timid then as I am today: frightened silly both by the emptiness beneath and by any imagined speck in the hostile distance. Yet I remember moments of ecstasy, in that first flight, never caught again: a sense of supermundane, of godlike detachment; of being on a par with the clouds—something, perhaps, of the ecstasy felt 45 years later by the first astronauts, except that they are on a par with the stars. But the distinction is one of physics, not of emotion.

When we went into the Somme trenches some weeks before that famous July the First, I left my transport to my farrier-sergeant and took over a section. I can't remember now whether I was ordered to do this or whether I did it out of pride—the kind of vanity that's often made me quixotically do rash or dangerous things I needn't have done at all. Sometimes the guns were mounted defensively in the front-line; sometimes, from a support position, we did 'indirect fire'—shooting blind over our own chaps' heads at map-reference targets. I hated firing my guns: I was horribly afraid we might kill somebody, boche or no boche—a sentiment I certainly wasn't paid to have. The front then was fairly cushy; but the odious ugliness of trench life sickened me, and the sharp distinction between the men's conditions and our own relative comfort and safety nagged tiresomely at my conscience. I began drinking a lot of whisky—3s a bottle I think we paid.

I wasn't terribly frightened yet; but I'd learned to be cautious. My attitude to the beastly danger of being blown to bits went through three stages from beginning to end. First, a confident curiosity, like a child's at the zoo, when a shell burst—an inquisitive eagerness to look for more; and from the front-line parapet, a brash cockiness about getting a look at the Germans. Secondly, a respect for the things that happened, and a sensible care about ducking and sticking to cover. And thirdly, a constant, inexpungeable fear, rising often like a blister into near-panic and a grab for the whisky. In the first two, one felt: it can't happen to me. In the third, one knew it could.

There was the pleasant jolliness of 'winning' in the first advances of the Somme 'big push'—like an early rush of election gains giving a false rosiness to one's Party's prospects. I saw my first dead men (when somebody had been hit in the trenches, I didn't go to look). But now one walked over them: green, translucent faces, the flesh of plovers' eggs, under the summer sun; later turning black and matt like spoiled photographs. One got used to them: as I suppose nurses get used to bedpans. There was the excitement of the strings of Jerry prisoners: poor bewildered fellows, with their hands aloft. Once I and Thompson went down a deep German dugout and found five of them; I'd got a pistol, Thompson a rifle, and they'd had the sense to dump their arms; but I think I was more scared than they were.

Then after all, we weren't winning; and I had the horror of Delville Wood. The place had been captured by some highlanders, and I had to take my guns up that ghastly hill to 'consolidate'. I remember the Jocks lying dead as we went up the hill; I remember wanting, for courtesy's sake, to stop and pull down over the bare buttocks the kilt that death here and there had jerked up. I got my guns into position; and then waited terrified, praying that somebody would win the beastly battle and stop the pandemonium that was blasting the wood, and us, to bits: the shelling was like a Naples street at New Year. Suddenly a colonel appeared, a battalion commander, and sensibly plumped into a shell-hole. Habit, I suppose, made me jump to attention and give him my terrific salute. He asked me about my guns, and then said: 'I shall recommend you for a mention, young Davidson.' I suppose this was because he was flattered by my salute. Of course, I heard no more; anyway, I wasn't out for medals—I prayed only for a comfortable life.

The Somme cooled down and set in a new mould of deadlocked trenches; we returned to a troglodyte routine. If anybody wants to see that Somme battle in immortal truth: to *know* its feel and smell, horror and humour, courage and waste, he must read David Jones' 'In Parenthesis': certainly one of the great English poems and the best book written about that war.

Thompson had turned into a dumb, devoted friend: as one's Chinese or Malay factotum becomes. He spoke in sniffs and grunts, but his gentle presence was also a comfort; he looked after me with the objective care he gave to Trixie. One of his tasks was to arrange hot water and my canvas bath; and somehow he got into the habit of drying me himself after I'd had it. We both enjoyed this, I think; though neither stepped over the purely ablutionary border (I never had anything 'to do' with my soldiers—I suppose they were too old for me; but I've been told it was often a part of trench life). Anyhow, sexuality at the front was for me generally quiescent, except as a casual self-contained chore; but I remember visiting, driven by the jeers of my comrades, a brothel in some 'back areas' town which had a notice outside the front-door: 'Other Ranks 5 p.m.-8 p.m.; Officers 8 p.m.-10 p.m.' A bulbous woman started to caress me; but horror made me rush out, throwing down a wasted 25 frs, or whatever the fee was.

Leave was the occasional ecstasy. One early morning, covered with the dirt of war, I rushed to the Savoy for a sumptuous bath. A Ganymede of a page-boy took me up and, crazily, I told him to come back in 20 minutes to dry me. To myself I argued that, being accustomed to being dried by Thompson, it was my right to be dried by a Savoy page-boy (but I knew I was pretending). In 20 minutes there was a knock on the door; wrapped in a towel, quivering with excitement, I opened it. A sleek personage in a tail-coat stood there: 'You are aware, sir, that we have our house-detectives in the hotel . . .?' In a panic I pulled a five-pound note out of a pocket and dumbly held it out; he took it and went sleekly. I dashed out of the place, without the divine breakfast I'd been looking forward to. That was my earliest encounter with the danger of the forbidden; the terror of it darkened my leave, and I didn't feel safe till I was on the boat again. But I'd bought a polo-stick for Trixie.

The illusion of my proficiency paid dividends: I was sent to another division as a company's Second-in-Command—I had already a 'second pip'. There was a terrible span of battle at Nieuport, on the Belgian coast between Dunkirk and Ostend, where the Germans tried an attack and my poor company commander was killed. But we were pulled out of that nightmare fairly soon, and I had acting command for some time—how utterly inadequate I was for the charge of a company of men, yet how enormously I enjoyed it! For my memories now of that time are almost wholly of riding and roistering: of course I'd brought Trixie and Thompson with me to the new company; and I became practically part of the brigade staff. The brigadier-general, a nice, rather 'queer' non-Regular, made a pet of me; we drank and dined and rode together every day. There was one fantastic excursion, on some other part of the front where the line was still 'fluid'. The brigadier said: 'You'd better camouflage that pony of yours: we're going on a reconnaissance'. I dappled her over with soot, and next day rode out with the brigadier and brigade-major and our orderlies into open country; there was a wood, about 500 yards away—suddenly we saw Germans, also mounted: both sides turned and galloped like blazes for cover. That was my 'cavalry action'.

It was the summer of 1917. After Nieuport we 'rested' blissfully on the coast east of Dunkirk. Looking back, I can see only the bliss: riding down with the men to bathe from those miles of gentle sand; knocking a polo ball about on the firm beach with the brigadier; entering Trixie in a brigade gymkhana and spoiling it by getting drunk and breaking a stirrup-leather at the water-jump; taking Trixie, and Thompson on another pony, and riding them, both of us naked, into the sea.

My brigadier-general, poor chap, was sacked for some reason; there came a severe fellow named Buchanon-Jardine who turned hate upon me: I suppose I'd become much too cocky. But I remember another period of rollicking fun, in some other 'rest' area. One of the battalion commanders—a Scot in the H.L.I.—and I started a 'hunt'; we collected a bunch of mongrels and, after drinking whisky half the night, we'd be out at 5 a.m. after hares— the colonel huntsman, I whipper-in. We never got a hare, but we had great fun. It was like a skit on Surtees: drinking into the night in a big dug-out that had been German—the Earl and James Pigg, whooping and hallooing, and the colonel blowing on his dented old hunting-horn. 'See what the weather's like,' he'd say; and I'd stagger over to the gas-curtain. 'Dark as 'ell and smells o' cheese,' I'd dutifully answer. But before dawn we'd be in the saddle; and by eight o'clock spruce and fresh on parade.

All my happy memories of the front are memories of Trixie. But the bad weather came, and the winter of Paschendaele. We had by now a new O.C., and my job as 2nd-in-command was to supply the company in the line with rations and ammunition. One night I had left the mules and limbers at the road-head, and was ploughing on foot over the Paschendaele gehenna with an ammunition party, the angular, cumbrous coffins of ·303 gouging and aching into their shoulders. How I thanked God I wasn't a poor bloody Other Rank! Thompson, as always, was with me, close to heel. The shelling was mild, the going hellish: we laboured and floundered over the tacky black churned-up wilderness. Suddenly I was knocked flat: kicked, it seemed, by a mule that couldn't have been there. 'Carry on, corporal,' I heard my voice say; and my poor carriers lumbered on with their job. I lay weightless in the mud; and knew that if my mind was still alive the rest of me wasn't. 'Thompson,' I said, 'I'm dying.'

'Not that, sir, you bleeding ain't," said Thompson in his slow way; and he hoisted me up by the arms like a sack and hauled me to the nearest first-aid post—a good way back. But movement quickly returned and I was able to help him, though my right arm remained lifeless.

Later, I half-woke in an ambulance to hear a R.A.M.C. sergeant say: 'Wouldn't you be more comfortable with them boots off, sir?'—and I felt his fumbling at my boots, taking them off, my lovely seven-guinea boots. I never saw them again.

Later still, under the vague lights of a real building, I heard a woman's voice, a woman in rustling nurse's fig, say crossly: 'Well, *this* is a nice time of night to come in, I *must* say!' I suppose she meant to be jocular; but it was a joke that, just then, made me cry.

Next day, in a haze of aching, I found a red-faced, rotund padre by my bedside. He was asking questions: what was my name? I told him. 'Good Lord!' he said. Christian name? I told him. 'Good God!' he exclaimed. What was my father's name? Walter Burn Murdoch, I told him—and he nearly fell off his chair. 'God bless my soul, I'm y'r uncle!' he hollered. He was my uncle Gerard, my father's brother, whom I'd never seen: a fox-hunting country parson who stumped round his parish in leggings and a red waist-coat below his round collar.

A few more hazy nights and days, with breezy visits from Uncle Gerard; and then I remember being carried on a stretcher aboard a ship, and a voice saying: 'Don't jolt 'im, the doc says it could do for 'im.' A label was pinned to me which said, in effect, 'handle carefully'.

By the time I got to Vincent Square, in London, where my mother was waiting, I could see how comic all this had been (except for my boots). The tragedy was that Trixie and Thompson had gone out of my life.

## 6

SOON AFTER GETTING my refreshing wound, my double life consciously began. I went back to the front early in 1918, but during these glowing months I 'grew up' in two directions: I ceased to be a schoolboy in the social sense and started on an independent course of boozy London enjoyment; and, along a very different parallel, on a quest for sexual pleasure—purposeful, deliberate, surreptitious.

The wound was a perfect 'blighty-one'. A tiny fragment of shell had hit a neck-nerve and paralysed my right arm; the doctors' passing fear that it might burrow against the spine quickly fled, and for all I know that blessed bit of metal is still where it landed 45 years ago. For the time being I could forget that sad and plaintive soldiers' song beginning, 'I wanter go 'ome—' and ending

> I do' wanter go in th' trenches no more,
> Where bullets an' whizzbangs go flying gall-ore—
>> Oh, my!
>> I do' wanter die—
> I WANT-ER GO 'OME!

—surely the most poignant of all that war's yearning songs, when chorused with the soldiers' outside-the-pub nasal mournfulness. And, I'm ashamed to say, I forgot even about Thompson and Trixie; I'd changed direction again, and was wallowing in the satin luxury of the Hospital for Officers in Vincent Square, soon to be exchanged for the Convalescent Hospital for Officers in Roehampton. Everything, then, was 'for Officers', 'for Other Ranks': eager-beaver provo-marshals, nosier than progs, peered into bars to make sure that the two worlds didn't meet under the same roof. All one was allowed to do in one's soldiers' company was to risk death.

I was as well as could be; all I had to do, after the morning's bout of massage, was to learn to sign cheques left-handed and head from

Roehampton for revelry with my arm in a hero's sling. One was supposed to be back before ten but, on the night-sister's right side, one could do anything; and creep in from the garden in the small hours.

That was a very different London. There were still a few horse-cabs about; Coventry Street didn't yet 'belong' to Piccadilly—it was a street nobody went into except to reach some theatre. One didn't eat in Soho, and only eccentrics went into public-houses—the word 'pub' had scarcely appeared; one met, outside clubs, in bars like the Carlton at the bottom of the Haymarket, Prince's in Piccadilly, a 'dive' opposite Brown's Hotel—the Savoy was too far just for a drink. One still had one's hair cut at Truefitt's, who made George IV's wigs; and after a night-before one went to Heppel's in the Haymarket for a 'pick-me-up.' Basil Hallam, so soon to be killed, was singing 'Burlington Bertie'; Teddy Gerard seemed as naughty as *La Vie Parisienne*; and Beatrice Lillie was the rage. I was in the stalls one night with Bobby Peel, then in the Coldstream, while she was singing her famous Bruce Bairnsfather song and throwing little Old Bill dolls into the audience. Bobby caught one; and said, quite solemnly: 'I'm going to marry that girl.' I don't think he even knew her then; but he married her, and their son, the 6th Sir Robert, was killed a generation later.

It was a London where 'Boat Race night' rowdiness was the rule —everybody expected to be killed as soon as his leave was over, and there was no blackout or blitz to send one home. One riotous night with Jasper and Humphrey Plowden, sons of the Chief Metropolitan Magistrate of the day, I was arrested for D-and-D; somehow, during the evening, I had acquired some 'dirty post-cards' which were in my pocket. At that time, in police-stations, they didn't take your belongings away from you; they looked through them, and gave them back to you. All that night members of the Force, sergeants and constables, kept opening my cell's little trap-door: 'Oy—let's 'ave a look at them cards?' At Bow Street next morning I was fined the usual; by Mr Plowden.

I'd rudely ignored Uncle Eardley's efforts to make me a member of the Army and Navy Club—I couldn't face all those colonels. But my cousin Leslie Childers had put me up for the old Isthmian, at 101 Piccadilly; before joining the Scots Guards for the war, he'd been a Clerk in the House of Lords—he was a grandson of Cousin Hugh's. The Isthmian (years ago defunct) was a jolly place devoted, it seems to me now, almost wholly to drinking; at least, that's all I can remember doing there. I remember a dear, calm youth called Brodie in the Black Watch; Humphrey Yorke, like a kind aunt, and his portly elder brother Alfred, later called I think Hardwicke; and a beautiful, heartless boy called Dicky D——, in the Life Guards; he took me to Sandown races and then jumped me into bed in the club-bedroom he was staying in. I never saw him again. And there was Lord Fitz as everybody, page-boys included, called him: the most marvellous character outside Trollope. He was Lord Fitz-Warrene Chichester and must literally have been born in William IV's reign: a tiny old man with dundreary whiskers and inseparable top hat, who stumped about the place muttering 'Egad' and 'damme, sir', and complaining about everything. Yet his grumbling was benign and everybody petted him: and I treasure him as a flesh-and-blood link with a past as remote, almost, as ruffles.

It was Mike Bruce who first took me to the Carlton bar. He was a burly, florid person who had been badly wounded in the head and who drank far too much for his wound; hugely amusing and charming, though sometimes he wanted to fight people he saw in bars, and to flaunt the fact that, descendant of Robert the Bruce, he was the premier baronet of Scotland, ex-cowboy, ex-prospector in Canada, ex-barman, and author of small volumes of rollicking verse with titles like 'Songs from the Saddle'. I think, before he died, he had married four times and become something in the film world. Mike, of course, was born too early: with his gusto and rococo brilliance he was designed for the film-studio—or else too late: he would have enjoyed the Regency.

The Carlton bar was the resort of a coterie of exalted down-and-outs. Poor, tottery old Clan, a family connection of mine through a Childers-le Poer Trench marriage, appeared sharp at 11 a.m. for his breakfast of port-and-brandy; after a couple of those, he was able to turn his mind to the question of pre-lunch drinks. In his youth he'd been the best man across country in County Galway, and had married Belle Bilton, a leading musical comedy star of the 'nineties. But in 1917 poor Clan was a bankrupt and never sober: resentful of the justified asperities of Mary Clancarty, his second countess; furious with the family Trust that administered him like a National Assistance Board; indignant about the new wartime drinking hours; yet he voiced these angers with an unfailingly gentle courtesy—I never saw him impatient or captious, though often somnolent. He looked like a very handsome Nonconformist, with his thick grey hair, the bowler hat and morning coat he always wore together, and high Gladstone collar—a defrocked Non-conformist, perhaps.

Then there was 'Q', elder brother of Lord Alfred Douglas: I seem to remember a strange twist to his Neronian face, giving him a malevolence he didn't really possess; the last time I saw him was after a dinner at Prince's, when he and his son Cecil Douglas, who had been at Lancing with me, set off for Hammersmith where they lived obscurely. Shortly after, Q married a Cardiff fish-monger's rich widow, who presumably wanted to be a marchionesss; a hard-up and down-to-earth countess, still alive today I think, told me at the time that she'd arranged the match and collected a useful commission on the dowry brought by the bride.

And I just remember Kim Manchester's joining our table. A Hogarthian group it must have been: me, aged 20, drinking with an earl, a marquess and a duke—each a battered reprobate old enough to be my father and all three insolvent.

But it's one of my few prides that I knew Percy Queensberry; a high courage was needed, in the London of 1895, to go bail for Oscar Wilde and to punch that odious father's head in Bond Street; as it's one of my enduring pleasures to have been a companion of old Clan's. It was quite a dance sometimes easing Clan into a cab and seeing him home to Cadogan Gardens, after fishing him out of the old underground Oddenino's, where he used to go to sleep, or from Rector's—almost the first, I suppose, of London's night-clubs; or Romano's, or perhaps from Rosa Lewis's Cavendish; but he was immensely lovable and humorous, with a rarely gentle and uncalculating spirit. He must, in the Belle Bilton days, have been one of the last true 'stage door Johnnies'.

Sometimes his eldest son, Killy Kilconnel, came to the Carlton: a quiet young man with spectacles—almost an eccentricity, at that time, in anybody less than grey-headed; often Cecil Douglas, now and then with his elder brother Drumlanrig, husband later of the artist Cathleen Mann. Cecil was an agreeable companion; he'd lost a leg early in the war, while one of those breathtakingly gallant Flying Corps pioneers. We used to go some afternoons to an odd place above a Piccadilly tobacconists called the Carlisle Club; it must have been one of the very earliest non-pub-hour drinking clubs—or else it was illegal: I remember only that we could drink there from the Carlton's midday closing till somewhere else's evening opening.

But my closest friend at this time was Bertie Eaton. He was a

couple of years older than I, and had been badly wounded with
the Grenadiers: a wonderfully calm and steadfast person, no
matter how much roistering we did; his greatest love, besides the
girl he later married, was a lean, scarlet Mercedes racing car. Our
first stop in the morning from Prince's Gate, where he lived,
would be the Hyde Park Hotel; sometimes in the evening we'd go
to some 'do', though neither of us liked parties—perhaps Lady
Clan's little weekly dance at Cadogan Gardens; and I remember
our going, unwisely, to a rather formal affair at the Savoy where I,
tipsy and anyway unable to dance, stamped on the toes of the
Prime Minister's daughter, Megan Lloyd George. Like all my
intimacies in this department of my life, friendship with Bertie was
wholly 'hearty'; he was the most normal of young men, and would
have been horrified if he'd known about my other life.

Sometimes, after I'd left hospital, I'd stay at Prince's Gate at the
end of a 'heavy' night and sleep with Bertie, both of us supine with
whisky—having finished the night, probably, by giving drinks to
the policeman on the local beat. One morning, just waking out of a
drunken stupor, I heard alarming footsteps stumping up the stairs
to Bertie's attic; and scarcely daring to open my eyes saw his father
burst into the room. 'How *horrible*!' roared Lord Cheylesmore,
major-general, Colonel of the Grenadier Guards, A.D.C. to the
King, and I don't know what else—and stumped down the stairs
again. When we went down and helped ourselves to a spot from
the decanter, the old man was still fuming: 'Don't understand you
youngsters, sleeping *disgustingly* like that, and drinking at eleven in
the morning!' So often since, this kind of situation has put comedy
into my evasive life: the most innocent actions given an impossible
misconstruction, the most guilty unrecognized, even encouraged;
but that day I was very upset on Bertie's behalf. I was awfully fond
of him in a perfectly ordinary way.

This was one side of my 'growing up': drinking far too much
with older people, many of them far from reputable. But London
was a disreputable place for a boy with a taste for temptation to be
let loose in; yet if many of my companions, like a few I've mentioned, were disreputable at least they were unvulgar in a way that
people aren't today; there wasn't the ostentation, the flashy
flinging of money about for the sake of displaying it of which the
pretentious 'bar' in every sitting-room nowadays seems to be the
symbol. One drank—and how one drank!—but ungarishly, from a
decanter; not from the semblance of a saloon-bar designed, one feels,

to shout that money's no object. But this curious economic rule hadn't yet been devised: that the more a man productively earns, the more he should be taxed; while the more he unproductively spends, the less he should pay in tax. A film tycoon couldn't then showily entertain his friends, and charge a good part of the cost to the Exchequer.

Yet in fairness to the manners of 1960, one must acknowledge that they're backed by a precedent from Byron's day: ' It is only that they love to throw away, Their cash to show how much they have a-year . . .'

When I left hospital, arm out of its sling, I began deliberately pursuing my secret wants. I didn't look for boys 'on the game'—I hardly knew there were any; remembering the delights of boyhood bathing places, I started to explore London's swimming baths—I'd slip away after lunch, making some suave excuse to Bertie or whomever it might be, and spend the afternoon till the evening's drinking appointment at some borough pool. Because I had to wear uniform, I couldn't go to the '2nd class' baths in the poorer districts which I haunted in later years; but to the 'first class' in Westminster or Victoria where I wouldn't look so out of place.

Because, I suppose, my sexual objective has never been primarily physical gratification, I've never liked 'prostitutes'—people, I mean, for whom the primary objective is payment. Of course, every sexual transaction contains an element of 'prostitution'; a girl expects a present or a seat at the pictures; a bride—even at St Margaret's—wants position or security; a young man, from his patron, male or female, hopes for a new suit; a boy needs cigarette-money or a new inner-tube for his bicycle. 'Love', whatever its form, requires a tit-for-tat—it's a kind of natural law. But for sexual pleasure, for emotional happiness, the 'love' must come first, the honararium second in the scale of preference. No fortuitous 'pick-up' could ever attract me unless genuine sexual interest were his *first* motive—or unless there were a touching need of 'mothering'; the frequent combination of both hankerings in the farouche boys of Berlin was one of that city's enthralling features in 1930-33.

At that stage of my development, in 1917, I was less interested in *doing* than in *seeing*—or perhaps less daring than I became, and so largely contented myself with seeing. I discovered some swimming baths which amply supplied the needs of the *voyeur* I was becoming: generations of 'dirty old men', apparently, had systematically bored peep-holes through the wooden partitions between every dressing-box—observation-posts which, to my knowledge, remained unaltered by the City Council for the next 30 years at least. Mixed bathing, then, was still municipally considered indecorous; most baths were as a matter of course labelled 'men and boys only', and generally there were more boys than men. What a complete reversal in the social conscience has occurred in these 40 years—in the last ten or 20, indeed; and especially since the doctrinal inundation of the Montagu Case: the public awareness of homosexuality has become so general, the fear of a sexual fifth-column so publicized—a sort of English spectre of Alfred Krupp or Prince Eulenberg—that nowadays the bikini type of bisexual exhibitionism is almost desperately encouraged and the old 'men and boys only' has been given the savour of decadence.

I became, as the years went by, an authority on the swimming-baths of London; I could have compiled a guide-book to them. They were as much the habitual playgrounds of youthful voluptuousness as any Roman or Greek *bagni* can have been; and very recently, notwithstanding the restringent vigilance of today's ubiquitous authority, I've seen overt juvenile orgies that would have surprised any of our prevalent fetichists of moral welfare. What might surprise him more, is the argument—not perhaps outrageous when solemnly considered—that such behaviour among the young *is*, in a sense, moral welfare; though doubtless not the etymon from which acquiescent social discipline derives. The exalting freedom of nudity, solitary or in company, releases naturally—*not* perversely—other freedoms, of the mind, the spirit and the body. A smooth, untimid, eruption of these freedoms, as natural as an errand-boy's whistling, surely must lead to moral health (if that's what moral means); their constriction, to deformities of the spirit. Of course, they can lead too by derivation to pretensions to further freedoms, inconvenient to whatever brand of 'law and order' obtains. That's why, no doubt, in disciplinary religion, nudity is often the chief bugbear of prudery; and in some conventual orphanages washing below the belt is put on a par with going to the W.C., while in Israel one sees the ringletted sons of Talmudic Jews wearing long black stockings like old-fashioned nursemaids', with their short knickers: they're not allowed to see their own knees.

Now and then there would be a brief, bewitching encounter in one of the dressing-boxes; but generally the delight was reticent and contemplative; and I'd go back exhilarated and mentally flushed to the evening's drinking appointment. I remember one gathering in the Duke Street *pied-à-terre* that Bertie fleetingly had: one of his young woman friends, intuitively percipient, suddenly said: 'There's something fishy about Michael—I think he's a woman-hater. I believe he likes little boys!' Of course I roared with laughter; my double life had taken shape.

While still at the front, I had suddenly decided to stay in the Army after the war. I wrote to my mother, knowing she would like the proposal. Uncle Eardley was put on the job again; and not long after I was gazetted a Regular Lieutenant in the Oxf. & Bucks L.I. I don't remember now just what brought me to this absurd decision; I knew that I disliked the military life, at least in war; probably I saw myself pig-sticking in India or playing polo at Khartoum, and I believed of course, that, if we won it, this war was going to end wars. I suppose I thought that as I was picking up a trade, I might as well stick to it—a trade, what's more, that included horses among its tools. I knew that in authority's eyes, though not in my own, I was a fairly competent soldier; and that at least I was conscientious—I've always conscientiously, urged by an 'on-your-honour' feeling, done my best in jobs I've undertaken, especially when paid to do them: a kind of high-minded sub-servience, I suppose—like a club hall porter's.

But though a Regular, and as such sensible of a snobbishly agreeable superiority over 'temporaries', I was still seconded to the Machine Gun Corps; and at the end of my leave, towards the summer of 1918, I was posted to the Bucks & Berks Yeomanry. They'd been turned into a Machine Gun regiment, attached to a brigade in Belgium; and, the Lord be praised, out of the line. That short sojourn among the yeomen remains hazy: a few horseback paper-chases which were fun; a quiet, ungregarious subaltern called Alston, a nice farmer's son—we used to go for sauntering rides or walks, and talk about trees, crops, hunting; the flat plough and scrappy woods of the countryside. With the Colonel, 'Freddy' Cripps (oddly incongruous brother of Sir Stafford's), and the Second-in-Command, Crocker Bulteel—both, I think, race-course swells—I never reached how-d'you-do terms. In October came word that we were to go up for an attack; I remember clearly the deadly, cold fear, like a nagging hangover, that this prospect infected me with; I told myself I *couldn't* face it, *couldn't* endure shell-fire again—I'd had enough of it; and the glorious respite at home hadn't cured my cowardice. I even played with the old, old notion of shooting myself in the finger—as one promises oneself now and again, when hope (the true fuel of life) seems petered out, the repose of suicide, knowing one won't do it. And then, incredibly, fear could be laughed at: the move up the line was postponed, cancelled; there came the trembling rumour of armistice.

'Oh, it *has* been signed, has it?' asked someone casually, when the signallers rang through that November 11th; and I won, or lost, a case of champagne—either way, we drank it. That night, in our village near Courtrai, we and the Belgians made bonfires of the doors and shutters, and the people threw out their furniture for burning. That freezing night, five of our soldiers died celebrating sweet Peace—one was found dead in a field next day, beside an empty jar of rum; two, drunk, fell off a duckboard bridge into the icy canal, one had his face blown away by his best friend's triumphing Verey pistol; what irony of the Cease Fire killed the fifth, I can't recall.

The regiment, like Frankish mercenaries before some Parthian fortress, blasphemously settled down to besiege the torpors of Demob. 'Get them out on parade, send them on route-marches, keep them fit'—down came the orders from above. But I, the Regular, went straight off home—once more on leave; in time to see Bertie Eaton marching along the Mall with the Grenadiers in some victory parade.

My mother by now had left Bitterne, dividing two-thirds of her possessions between Nancy and Eardley, both now busy with parenthood, and squeezing the rest into a tiny flat off Queen's Gate. Of course there was a room for me; generally I reached home hours· after she had gone to bed, and breakfast became a torment of dissimulation—the commanding need to disguise from her worried eyes the symptoms of morning-after malaise. By 1919 I was conversant with the processes of 'picking up': as easy as winking at that time when a multitude of yearning faces, young and old, used—in Holbrook Jackson's words about Francis Thompson— to 'haunt the Embankment, the cavernous arches of Charing Cross, and the black and dusty colonnades of Covent Garden ...'; and one shameful night which still, 40 years later, puts me in a cold sweat when I think of it, I smuggled a boy into Queen's Gate while my mother was asleep and smuggled him out with the dawn. The criminality of that folly, of course, lay in the hair's breadth of chance that might have given my mother an odious sorrow and a confirmation, squalidly shocking, of that dread, scarcely comprehended, which I'm sure had been hovering in her mind almost since my boyhood. I recall the questioning heartache, the image of a prayer in her eyes, when one morning I crassly took home a ragged Glasgow boy I had found singing for money in the Brompton Road—I wanted to give him an old pair of shoes, I explained. Yet never did she utter any word of that anxiety; I think it was an adoring faith which forbade her accept such fears about a child of hers. Now and then, through the years, she would say: 'Darling Micky, I *do* wish you'd find some *nice* girl and settle down'; and her contentment was touching when, in Berlin at the end of the '20s, I became engaged to Felicia Browne; the strange, haunted painter whose youth of selfless abnegation and inner suicidal torment was ended in Spain by a bullet from the Franco side. That engagement was short-lived; and my mother never knew that in 1935 I did actually get married—to a refugee communist from Germany. It would have appalled her: a marriage of political expediency arranged by 'the Party'—it happened in the St Pancras registry office and ended an hour later in the nearest public-house.

What extraordinary and churlish paradox of procreation is it, I wonder, which allows a woman of such consummate goodness as my mother to bear offspring harbouring so much badness? And here I don't mean some sexual divergence by itself—that needn't be bad; but those moral improbities and basenesses it so often carries like parasites.

\* \* \*

By the last year of the war, my mother was feeling the pinch; a part of her money had been in Russia and the bolsheviks, naturally, weren't paying dividends to imperialist widows in South Kensington; while some railway in Latin America had also, less reasonably, become infertile. Yet I, just then, seemed to be swimming in money; and was spending it with the compulsive improvidence of a boy at a fun-fair. Already I'd developed that myopia for money which has made me incurably confident that while there's cash in my pocket today, tomorrow won't matter—or, like the proverbial old lady, that funds in the bank last as long as one's cheque-book.

On St Mathias' Day in February 1918 I had become 21; and on that day solemnly called at Uncle Alan's Bolton Street Offices to receive my inheritance and his advice. Overnight, after living and getting into debt on a subaltern's pay—half-a-guinea a day I think it was then—and a tiny allowance from my mother, I became the possessor of a thousand or two, which seemed to me an infinite fortune. A five-pound note in those days would go a long way, even in London's most extravagant square-mile; but in little more than a year's time it had all gone. And more than the money: a couple of good George Morlands left me by Aunt Annie, my share of the family silver, some fine Sheffield Plate, a lavish gold and enamel snuff-box like a coffin that had belonged to a Freeling ancestor, a flawless set of 18th-century Regimental colour-prints—I don't know what else; all these things went up the spout one by one as I ran short of money. I don't know what a Morland rates today; mine must have been worth then many times what I got for them over the counter of an acute dealer. I behaved as ridiculously with my little possessions as one of those adolescent clerks one reads about who runs off with his firm's petty cash; I haven't changed much in the long succeeding years. I've always seen terribly clearly into the hungry minds of those unhappy boy embezzlers; and thought, often, that I'd probably have done the same had I been in such a situation.

My mother, for my 21st birthday, gave me a great pigskin dressing-case full of compartments and pockets and silver-topped bottles and ivory-backed brushes, blazoned all over the place with the Davidson fist. It weighed a ton; poor darling, she doubtless saw its lasting my lifetime: how could she have dreamed, in 1918, that the aeroplane would make such splendidly ponderous pieces of luggage as useless as battleships? She begged me, of course, to cling on to the securities Uncle Alan had handed me: 'Don't break into it, Micky darling; remember those bolshevists have made a big hole in the widow's cruse.' But I argued that a hundred a year was no good to anybody. Perhaps I was right; but what dividends that small amount of money might have paid had I spent it at Cambridge, or lived for four comfortable years in Rome or Paris and acquired some aptitudes and civilizing *knowledge*!

No detail arises today from the cumulus of bars, restaurants, theatres and parties which I suppose spread across the winter of 1918 and the early part of the first year of peace; except one—an odd Christmas Day luncheon which old Clan and I solemnly ate together at the Berkeley. I can't think why; or where my mother can have been, or how the two of us came to be on our own on that Christmas morning of 1918; but I have a clear picture of Clan, looking like a dissolute archdeacon, nudging in the direction of a dowdy old couple on the far side of the room, and saying with an infinitude of chuckling scorn: 'Lord *Weir*—that's *Lord* Weir!' This was an iron-and-steel magnate, I think: one of the first industrialists to be co-opted into a War Cabinet and one of the first of the technocratic peers. I can't remember whether Clan told me what prompted his comical disdain; perhaps, being always—notwithstanding his chronic disreputability—a seigneur in the grand style, he disliked the Lloyd Georgian new nobility; more probably he thought that Lord Weir may've had a hand in the new licensing laws. After a good quantity of wine, and into his second or third brandy, old Clan began muttering about 'her ladyship'; I never heard him name Mary Clancarty as anything but 'her ladyship': a formal courtliness of an earlier age, with an adumbration of the formality of his relations with his second wife. I don't recall seeing Clan much after that curious festivity; he lived on until 1929; and was yet to have, poor fellow, before he died, a bit of police-court trouble about the bankruptcy laws. He was wonderfully handsome still, like a silver-point drawing from the dawning 19th century. I've always kept an affection for him; not only because he was a museum-piece of a period that was ending even before 1914, but also for the innate goodness, the charm and kindly courtesy that survived among the wreckage of his former splendours. Worldly failure is often more attractive than success.

Then, suddenly, after choosing soldiering as a profession and giving Uncle Eardley the trouble of contriving it, I gave it up. I had changed direction again.

But no impulsive option set this new course; I wasn't even aware that it was going to happen. It came, I think, as the climax of an unconscious revolt against a life which, deep down, I was realizing was quite incongruous—a sort of safety valve that blew off before worse explosions occurred. I seem to remember now, during those long weeks of London leave with their growing appetite for esoteric experiment, feeling more than defining a dawning disquiet: a skulking dubiety about my fitness for peace-time soldiering—or rather its fitness for me. Uncle Eardley still seemed a paragon, of a plate-glass window sort—but then, I wasn't an Uncle Eardley.

And above all I think, I was secretly wondering how my stealthy pleasure could be made to tally with the tight-laced curriculum of the regular Army; somehow I felt that the extrovert atmosphere of a regimental Mess wouldn't be the best for the pursuit of boys.

But all this, I know, was but a shadow of uneasiness; and when, my leave up, I reported at Cowley Barracks, near Oxford, I travelled down cock-a-hoop: a bit clammy, as always, with shyness when on the point of meeting new people; but never dreaming I was capable of making of myself such an ass as I did make—that very evening. Cowley was still in a state of semi-war undress: there was no full-fig in the evening—one wore patrol dress or even khaki. I arrived towards what I call drinking-time; changed into 'blues' and made for the ante-room where, alone and probably indecorously early, I primed my sense of elation and armed myself against fresh faces with a series of whiskies-and-soda. Now, I was by then a fairly hardened toper; I knew how to behave, and decorum seldom deserted me till the small hours of the morning—I could, in an earlier phrase, 'hold my liquor'. But not that evening, I couldn't: something went click in my mind, and on far fewer drinks than I was used to I got stinking drunk—I tried to buy whiskies for unknown senior officers, I talked out of turn, I tumbled over chairs; finally I was put to bed. I don't suppose anybody ever has behaved so shamefully on his first evening in a Regular mess. This exhibition was so alien to my own idiom, organic and temperamental (at any rate at that age; as one grows older, I suppose, one's social censorship becomes laxer), that I believe it was the expression of an emotional rebelliousness, an unapprehended urge to escape—and as such I've always been grateful for it.

Next morning, by an austere adjutant, I was sent off on leave again—the Army's way, in those days, of getting over a headache: its own, and mine. The fear that the story of my disgrace should reach Uncle Eardley, and so my mother, was, thank Heaven, unfulfilled. But she disapproved of this renewed leave: 'So bad for you, darling Micky, all this idleness. And I'm afraid that London—' and I knew that the spectre of fast living and the demon drink was haunting her mind. After some weeks of vacillation and lazy wondering what best to do, the interpretation of the Cowley nightmare was shown me in, so to speak, a sudden Annunciation of my own. 'Sir, I have the honour . . .' I wrote impulsively to the Secretary of the War Office, sending in my papers; and so ended my stay of one night with the Regular Army. My mother sighed: 'Well, darling boy, I suppose you know your own mind. But it does seem rather futile, all this chopping and changing—'. Then I saw a fresh light: I must go abroad. I didn't mind where I went, but go I must—into singular, emotive countries, among garish, sensuous people: I wanted colour and warmth, fleshly and climatic; and the romantic tropical symbols (as I saw them), like coral reefs and the Southern Cross, of a natural and candid nakedness.

The trouble was, in 1919, that shipping-space couldn't be found; every berth, in any direction, was booked for the next year or more. But one of my Auntie Maudie's bridge-playing cronies— and here can be seen the importance of being born with the right connections—was a certain Lady Anderson whose husband, Sir Alan, was a shipping magnate of the first water and held, therefore, a corner in cabins. Dear Aunt Maud, over cucumber-sandwiches, secured for me a berth in a ship which happened to be bound for South Africa; so to South Africa I went.

Near the middle of December Bertie Eaton drove us down to the West India Docks: my mother, my Catholic Aunt Edie, and me; and with what little of my money was left inscribed in a Letter of Credit—travellers' cheques then probably hadn't been devised—I boarded the *City of Dunkirk*, of the old Ellerman & Bucknall Line, a 4,000-ton cargo-boat with iron decks, a Lascar crew, and curry-and-rice daily for luncheon. Sailing, as a tramp's sailing always is, was delayed: I spent that evening in Charlie Brown's allegedly *louche* saloon-bar, watching attentively for symptoms of Limehouse's silent iniquities.

We were headed for the Cape direct, 24 days at sea; thence eastward to Simonstown, Port Elizabeth, Durban and Beira, in Portuguese territory. I was booked to Durban, and had some notion of making a way up to East Africa, just becoming the moneyed colonists' Arcadia. I wasn't moneyed; but there had been talk in London of my joining a group of ex-officer hearties, organized by a breezy brigadier-general, who proposed to dispossess a few dozen Bantu kraals by means of brawn and public-school principles. Somehow, I can't remember just why, this beefy proposition is linked in my mind with a gay meal, more than 40 years eaten, at Claridge's; at which I was fascinated by my neighbour: a child, so she seemed to be, as tiny and exquisite as a petal, fragile and delicate and airy like a soap-bubble, dainty as an

ivory doll and yet friable like a puff-ball. This gossamer creature
was a professional dancer who had recently become Viscountess
Uffington; her stage name had been Olivette, so of course I christened her Uffilette. What made her memorable to me was my
sudden sight of her in epicene shape: Gracious! I remember
thinking, what a boy she could have been! It was the first time that
I was consciously aroused by a girl—not because of, but in spite
of her femininity. I don't know whether lovely little Uffilette, as
entrancingly neuter, to me, as a Balinese dancer, ever became a
Countess of Craven.

The *City of Dunkirk* carried one other passenger: a fat and
costive Dutchman conducting four racehorses to Capetown. They
were housed in stalls like packing-cases lashed on the forward well-
deck: my heart bled for them in their 24-day confinement. The
Dutchman too remained confined; he eased himself into the saloon
to eat unsociably his curry-and-rice, and now and then saw to his
horses; but for most of the 24 days stayed evasively in his cabin—
throwing a furtive glance over his fleshy shoulder before slipping
into it and slamming the door.

The Dutchman was sinister—and properly so; for the *City of
Dunkirk* was like a ship in one of those seafaring thrillers, and
everybody in her a stock character of a Maughamish tropical
drama. The Chief Engineer, of course, was a Scotsman, a teetotaller and anti-tobacconist; a suffering, angular man who would
lean over the rail and tell me in mournful Clydeside that the sinful-
ness of the *City of Dunkirk* merited the doom of the Cities of the
Plain—he was referring, though, to his shipmates' consumption of
liquor and not to the juvenile lecheries performed in the tiny
deckhouse on the poop, where lodged the two apprentices. The
Mate was a boozy, concupiscent chap, bluff and cocksure, who
boasted spivvishly of the 'perks' he could derive from the general
cargo before the voyage was over. The Old Man lived a secretive
life in his cabin beneath the wheel-house, appearing in the saloon
to eat curry-and-rice with Jovian ill-humour: he plainly despised
his passengers and disliked his officers. The Old Man disapproved
officially of alcohol—no drinks could be bought in the saloon—yet
over Christmas he locked himself in his room and wasn't seen for
36 hours. Not much of that Christmas for me survived even into
Boxing Day; I can remember climbing dangerously towards midnight up to the bridge, and finding the Mate stretched on the deck
of it, fast asleep. It was said afterwards that the ship had been

adrift for 24 hours, but I think this was an exaggeration: there must have been a fairly sober quartermaster at the wheel.

Although the saloon was apparently 'dry', the steward did a good trade in bottles of whisky, and determined carousing went on in the cabins—the Mate's, mine, the 2nd Engineer's; its volume was swelled when we reached Capetown, as Wagnerian brass swells the sonorities of wood and strings, by the company agents, customs men, stevedoring gangers, harbour hangers-on and others, who trooped thirstily through our doors.

All this was very amusing; and a fragment of mercantile marine experience which I've never seen again. But the enduring fruit of this voyage was the maiden encounter, in my own eyes and being, with some of those fine and adventurous things one had read about in Marryat and Hermann Melville: the measureless languor of the equatorial sea; the far fountain of one's first whale or the grinning belly of a shark; the snowy flight, like blossom, of Mother Carey's chickens, and the silver thrill of a flying fish's sad slither on deck; the awe, the iterated anguish of Coleridge, when for the first time one watched the huge circling silence of an albatross; and I remember the sharp pleasure, looking aft one glittering dawn, of the peak of Teneriffe hanging high up in the hazy sky like a chunk of gold-hot coal—80 miles distant, I was told. Thirty-nine years were to pass before, with Robin Maugham, I landed at the base of that peak and drank Spanish brandy at the Bar Atlantico in Santa Cruz.

In the fore part of the ship was one-half of this ocean fantasy: drinking with the manly mariners, in a mood of Yo-ho-ho. But aft, on the poop, a different world dawdled on the slow tropic swell: there lived the two apprentices, their isolation during a watch below almost inviolate. I was barely half-a-dozen years older; and passed long dallying hours with them: one, a genial, sprawling oaf with tireless powers of obscenity, the other a reticent creature of a touching tenderness, whose amorousness was more fastidious. They were good, happy boys; it's odd to think that today they may be Commodores of a Line—or at the bottom of the sea.

Then, one sunrise, we were anchored before Table Mountain: a picture postcard of itself; and feeling that strange suspension, as if time were pausing, that comes with the stillness of engines.

On Durban quayside, three weeks later, I was crying like a child when the *City of Dunkirk* drew past The Bluff and swung east-

THE WORLD, THE FLESH AND MYSELF    101

ward: she'd been savage, but she was 'home'; and I yearned for
her protectiveness. For the first time in my life I was alone: in a
strange land, knowing no single soul. Instead of being elated by
my independence, I was sobbing, I suppose, for my mother.
But this self-pity soon departed: hand in hand, no doubt, with
the tremors from the night-before's farewell. And there, ahead,
lay Africa.

## 7

SINCE THEN I'VE lived on other continents, seen other parts of Africa; each, in time, has found its own level in my heart; and Africa, Black Africa, all of Africa below the Niger River, stands low in my roll of affection. (The French, in Morocco, used to say that 'Africa begins at Marrakesh'; for me, Timbuctoo marks the frontier.)

It isn't simply that African soil and lushness seem to breathe out, like a dragon, a malignancy harsher than does, say, the Malayan jungle or an Irrawaddy swamp: I've a feeling there's a pursuant spite in the evil humours of Africa, next to which those of Asia are timid and passive, like a nettle's sting—though no soldier who has patrolled in Pahang will believe the jungle leech isn't spiteful! Certainly fevers and suppurations can be more obstinate in Africa than elsewhere; but my subjective sense of an African miasma belongs rather, I think, to a notion of spiritual void; I've a feeling that within the splendour, the rank opulence of the gleaming human swarm, there's an imaginative nullity: that pleasure is *mindless*, like the slow-worms of my Guernsey childhood which, much as I loved them, seemed to be headless at both ends— and enjoyment as callous as Henry's VIIIth's gnawing of mutton-bones.

I've tried to justify this personal warp by telling myself that the Africans of the bush have no literature, no fund of accumulated thought as distinct from belief, no retrospection of imaginative enterprise—none of the things from which intellect is made; and that, for as far as they can see back, they've more or less been the bondsmen of somebody or other—foreigner or tribal tyrant. But then, I remind myself, the Berbers of the North African *bled* also for the most part are illiterate, also exist on the edge of brutishness —and yet have a life of the *mind* as well as of the physical senses; while the Tuareg aristocracy of the Sahara, whose mode of life, though borne on the backs of negro slaves, couldn't delve deeper

into human squalor and indigence than it does, possess, when not
too lazy to exert it, a ranging imagination as high and wide as the
stars. But they are navigators, using instinct and eye, and even
nose, for compass: to whom, from a camel's saddle, the sands and
the savannah seem less circumscribed than does space to a modern
aeronaut. And then, I reflect further, the Berber has a liberty—
climatic, geographic, politic even—far more pliant than the Black
African's; and the Tuareg 'noble' possesses, on his side of the
Desert's rim, personal freedoms unequalled probably anywhere
on earth. But I'm getting into anthropologists' stuff, beyond my
own powers of misjudgement. I'm aware, though, of some lack in
myself that makes me seem to miss, south of the Niger, a brightness
of *spirit* which has rejoiced me elsewhere, from the Atlantic to
Japan.

All this, of course, came years after that first arrival in Durban.
What came immediately, came to the surface like a child's pencilled
rubbing of a penny, was the outline of a constitutional proclivity for
the underdog: an inborn proneness, as to hay-fever. Two things
showed me which way my sentiments faced—and were to face for
the rest of my life. The first was the pack of 'prancing niggers'—but
poles apart from the naif and homely sophistication of Ronald
Firbank's—who between their ricksha-shafts leaped and capered
like grotesque marionettes near the landing-stage, waiting for the
White Man's shillings; not having then the intelligence for thinking
about it, I *felt* that these pathetic mountebanks, with their horned
and feathered head-dresses more extravagant than Prince Mono-
lulu's, were a parody of themselves: that these bizarre garbs were
no symbol of a proud and barbaric 'Africanism' but the badge of
Bantu abasement. The Durban ricksha-pullers were like cheapjacks
with funny noses; but they were no cheapjacks—I was told that
only a few years put an end to their working strength. The second
thing happened on the broad and empty footpath of a wide and
empty street. Towards me came a hefty young African whose
mouth and mind and hands were glued to the soft, secret twanging
of his Jew's Harp—yet a few yards from me, automatically it
seemed, he stepped off the ample pavement and passed me in the
gutter. I remember my feeling of shocked humiliation; and bent
on deferring to the next African I met, I got off the footpath—but
so did he, and we met in the gutter; he looked at me as if I were
mad. Thereafter I made a point of making way for African women
on trams, helping with bundles and so on; and was regarded, by

Black and White alike, as having a screw loose. At that time courtesy to the kaffir (as the people were generally called) wasn't yet a criminal offence; it was merely lunacy. These were my first sights of 'colonialism'.

There are, I suppose, three kinds of rebelliousness: the bread-and-butter sort, kindled when people who see they're getting a raw deal try to bash authority; the philosophic, which brings academics, Karl Marx or Bertrand Russell for example, to an intellectual conclusion; and the romantic or emotional, which impels men like Cunninghame Graham, who can't hope to get anything out of it, to make fiery speeches from Nelson's Column. I was born into the last division; just as I was born with a taste for chewing nasturtium leaves in the garden: I just can't help taking sides against the man with the big stick—against the men who use *power*, and its attendant instruments of enforcement, to order for the sake of their power the lives of people who lack power. My rebelliousness, I suppose, is animated less by compassion for the oppressed than by loathing of oppression; I feel almost strangled by anger when I see, as I've often seen, official violence carefully, deliberately unleashed, 'justice' hypocritically manipulated, liberty and even the necessaries of life vengefully restricted, truth derisively falsified to accord with a propaganda 'line', financial prerogatives capriciously exercised—so that the euphemisms of power-politics may be justified and the immunities of a super-taxed few secured. So I don't claim good marks for benevolence because I find myself, willy-nilly, on the side of the powerless against the powerful; it isn't a generous altruism that puts me on the side of the black and the brown and the chalk-faced, or of any people in any form of vassalage. I just can't help hating the evil that's at the heart of power—any more than I can help suffering the precipitous sensations of vertigo, when, by mistake, I look down from a height.

It may be that I am like that because I'm naturally on the side of the naughty boy against his avenging elders. Sexual crankiness is so often accompanied by other emotional *Krankheiten*; one non-conformity generates other nonconformities (a reason, I suppose, why society approves the rolled-umbrella frame of mind); and the stories of many notable or notorious men show that insurgency against something or other is a frequent one. Byron, Swift, Voltaire, de Sade (a precocious social-democrat), William Beckford, Swinburne, Samuel Butler, Whitman, Wilde, Edward Carpenter,

Corvo, Roger Casement, were all sexual eccentrics; and all congenital rebels of one sort or another; and even the Rev. C. L. Dodgson, that diffident and emotionally aberrant deacon, revolted through Alice and the Snark against the tyranny of logic.

I hadn't much money left by the time I got to Durban. The steward's bill in the *City of Dunkirk* had been large, and a fortnight's hold-up in Capetown, where the stevedores were on strike, had cost a lot—although I had passed the hours of sunshine watching the Cape Coloured boys basking their abandoned, gamboge bodies on the tarry rafters of a disused wharf, the evenings had been spent without pecuniary thought for the morrow. I found myself jobs: first as a 'tallyman' at the docks, trying to count the bags and bales which the dock 'kaffirs', like endless ants, trotted sweatily up the bouncing gangplanks, terrifying as tight-ropes; and then, when I found I couldn't count, as an envelope-addresser in a charitable office. But it wasn't long before I got what I wanted: hired as apprentice-assistant by the leading farmer of Zululand at a wage of £5 a month and, thrown in, the Africa of Seton Merriman and 'Jock of the Bushveldt'.

Zululand 40 years ago was still, though beyond the time of warfare, the romantical, aboriginal land of Chaka and Tsetewayo; it had, garbling Surtees, all the glory of savagery and only one per cent of its danger—and by savagery I mean innocence of the corruptions of civilization. There were still *impis* of warriors, but they danced and hunted instead of fighting; the men still carried a fistful of assegais and an oxhide shield like a kite; they wore still nothing but a sporran of monkeys' tails over their genitals and a backside apron of buckskin; and they still bounded like joyous animals over the rolling game-paths of the veldt, uttering barks of triumph and stabbing the air with their javelins like shadow-boxers. A royal scion of the House of Chaka still sat on some cow-dung throne—Diniswayo was his historic name, and he had 80 wives and 300 children. Huge palpitating iguanas, like dragons, sprawled on the river banks; and as one rode, reins loose on one's horse's neck, by a sudden escarpment, baboons stalked and swore, tails rampant, among the scree above. Bushbuck and duiker vaulted like dolphins through the green surge of the veldt; and northward but a little, the real big game roamed. This, plainly, was paradise for me; and all travelling, north of the 100-mile road from Durban, was on horseback.

Zululand was only then being 'opened up' for the White settler

—which meant, of course, that the natives' commonage of veldt had begun to be whittled down. The pasture was among the richest in the Union: splendid for both butter and beef—the country was to be a cattle-raising Eden. But the tsetse-fly was already quietly nipping those hopes in the bud; within a few months I was helplessly watching my own few head of cattle lie down one after the other to die, killed by a kind of sleepy sickness; and some years later the country was turned over to sugar-cane. But then all was joy: for the farmers, wealth lay ahead; for the Zulus, the farmers meant wages—and wages were the means of getting together the dozen cows wanted for the buying of a wife.

K. N. Young, my farmer, had a handsome russet face like a ripe William pear, and white hair though he wasn't yet 40; his wife, sweetly dumpy and pinafored, smelt of hot bread and pumpkins. They were immensely kind to me—with a hint of presbyterian astringency in their bounty; we ate an enormous amount of homely, wholesome things, and the bedclothes tasted of sweet herbs; but drink was taboo and tobacco frowned on—I came to feel that my cigarettes were a foolish indulgence. There was an austerely prospering simplicity about them: they were like a couple in a covered-wagon happy ending. His father, a Scots immigrant I think, had built up the biggest butchery business in Natal; Mr Young, as I always called him, was the richest and earliest settler in Zululand. He was an inspiring teacher: full of farm-lore and veldt lore, with a jaunty talent for imparting it. In a few weeks I'd learned more from him, on his subject, than I'd ever learned from anybody else; and soon, having an accurate mind, an exemption from laziness when interested and a conscience about doing thoroughly an accepted task, I became useful to him. But some while later, after my own farming adventure had failed, this time of simple and immaculate happiness was cut short by one of my sillier follies: a pack of tawdry indecencies acquired aboard the *City of Dunkirk* was discovered by Mrs Young while I was away on a big-game drive, left lying in a bedroom drawer.

For I was wildly happy: each day was a fresh exhilaration, physical, spiritual and even literary—this was a world of the imagination, made real by living. We were pretty high in the Zulu uplands, ten or 20 miles beyond Eshowe, the nearest township; down the deep gullet of our country the wide shallows of the 'Mshlatusi river swashed over the rocks like a fast tide. I can remember today the uncontaminated joy—the perquisite, surely, of angels—that I felt on those fresh African dawns: running down the stony hill-path to the cattle-kraals below; seeing the milking through—drops translucent as sap on the beautiful black hands of the 'boys'; gauging, as I turned the crank, the pitch of the separator's humming—too fast, and cream was lost with the skim; too slow, milk came in with the cream; and then, splendidly hungry, being towed up the cliff short-cut by Greydawn, Young's utility pony, hanging on to his wiry tail; and eating a huge breakfast beginning with yellow mealie-porridge and lashings of cream. And the tremendous sense of creative fruition in compelling the plough-shares along their course behind a team of 16 oxen, holding true the bite of their gleaming blades and watching with a craftsman's excitement the curling breaker of the furrow: or those days of god-like solitude when, pig-scales hitched to the saddle like a lariat, I'd go off on Greydawn for a 40-mile round, taking in a couple of farms to weigh some porkers for old Young's butchery. Greydawn wasn't a lively ride; but he had a comfortable ambling pace and the surest eye for ground: you could go to sleep on his back, and he'd get you there.

Having, by luck, some feeling for languages, I quickly got myself the use of basic Zulu—a nice basic tongue anyway. It's a 'click' language, though not extravagantly: the Bushmen, I've heard, talk in a regular pizzicato of clicks—Zulu has only three. The simplest is like a governess disapprovingly tut-tutting: tongue against front teeth: the word for 'no', *tsa*, begins with that sound; so does the name of King Tsetewayo. The next click is fiercer, made against the palate rather than the teeth: *in-ntètu*, for instance —the *nt* representing a loud 'n' with a click to it; this word, ordinarily translated 'cock-box' is the name of the half-nutshell which Zulus from puberty on wear over the top of the penis to restrain any public manifestation of amatory interest. The third is the click made by a cabby against his back teeth when speaking to his horse: *in-kleng-kla*, 'pig-trough'—there are two clicks there, the *kl* snapping out twice like a whip-crack. I was proud of my Zulu (and, obviously, still am); and when, leaving the Youngs, I moved ten or more miles northwards to run a virgin farm for a sleeping partner, I could talk to my natives. Here, I was plumb in the veldt: midway between Eshowe and the next township, Empangeni—and they were 50 miles apart. Thornbush, laid in wide circles above the stream, made the cattle-kraals; a couple of wattle-and-daub rondavels housed the natives, another for the separator and churns and one more for me—there was the farm: with 1,000 acres of roughly charted veldt.

The Zulus, then, were still uncivilized enough to let you go away without shutting your door or locking up your money: improbity wasn't yet a convention. If, after pay-day, the young men wanted a lark with a woman, they said: 'Let's go down to the Mission Station'—there was one 20 or 30 miles away. The Mission girls, with their gingham bodices and hymn-books, were said to acquire a more liberal attitude to male performance than the kraal-code allowed—and that was pretty liberal: conceding to adolescent boys and girls almost any sexual trick short of 'penetration' (an offence which exiled the over-zestful youth from his kraal and barred him from every other kraal within his tribe). But Christianity was believed by the pagan to remedy this. Should anything, in a White man's store, be missing from the till, it was the 'educated' clerk from the Mission who was suspected. Discovering this sort of thing, I found myself disapproving of Missions: it seemed to me that conversion took away the immemorial moral usages, solid as the hills, but failed to make valid a new set in their place. In 1947, at Bamako in the French Soudan as it was then (where there are plenty of Pagans; the Muslim, as elsewhere, are as unconvertible as the Pentagon), an American Baptist told me he had 25 converts in his congregation—'but,' he added ruefully, 'they all wear *gri-gri* under their shirts: they come to God because they hope He'll bring them better-paid jobs; but their real faith remains in *gri-gri*.' It's not the fault of Christianity; the fallacy is that of wanting to drink new wine too soon—of imposing a new concept of human life on a mind unready to grasp it. You can't make a mustang pull a milk-float by wetting his forelock. Decades of observation in various 'missionary' countries have persuaded me that the only good mission is a medical mission—with 'conversion' kept 'on request only', like a special book in a library.

I had acquired certain surgical dexterities which, looking back now, fill me with horror and which, had I foreseen them, I wouldn't have believed my squeamishness capable even of watching: I suppose Special Branch policemen, too, sometimes marvel, incredulous, at their willingness to bash up suspects. But then—bravado, I dare say, quelling queasiness—I thought nothing of castrating bull-calves and young boars or performing acts of midwifery on a cow. Gelding was simpler than peeling a prickly pear: with your penknife, while a couple of boys held the victim on its back, you made a slit in the scrotum and popped out a testicle as you would a broad-bean from its pod; and then scraped, but never cut, the anchoring cord until it severed—a good splash of creosote with a paint-brush on the wound, and your patient scampered free looking merely a bit crestfallen. Meanwhile your assistants would be watching with glistening white eyes for the delicacies they'd quickly broil on a skewer (an appetite that at the time sent shivers down my spine; yet decades later, in Morocco, I round that ram's balls done in a *tajin* are delicious). As for obstetrics, I can't say I relished putting my hand deep into the vagina of a newly calved cow and clearing the afterbirth—but I did it. A medical chore that daily dismayed me was jabbing a brushful of red lead into the pathetic eyes of ophthalmic calves—it seemed to hurt them much more than emasculation did.

We were doomed, though. To our cattle and horses, we who lived northward within the orbit of the big game, the tsetse-fly was as inexorable and unanswerable as, 40 years later, fall-out must seem to human beings who live within range of the nuclear menace. The fly brought a murrain called *n'gana*: with the symptoms, and the terrible subsidence into death, of human plague. Game, of course, and native cattle were immune; but livestock brought up from outside the tsetse belt lay down and died: no prophylaxis was then known, and no cure. It seemed as inevitable and as horrible as old age. Some extraneous animals, by breeding or some freak of constitution, became 'salted'; and were worth their weight in gold. This circumstance brought me a personal anguish which revives still today when I think of the little mare I named Nancy, after my sister.

I found her at Empangeni, the dusty hamlet of wooden 'stores' and corrugated iron that was the railhead of the coastal line from Durban. She was a dainty bay, about five years, with charming manners and that responsive liveliness when being saddled that's so entrancing: a fast and untiring ambler—the eccentric camel's gait which, dull and facile though it be, is ideal for long rides over the veldt. And she was salted, her owner warranted: £25 was the price. I'll tell you what, he said—ride her away now and pay me in a month's time: if she isn't as much alive then as she is today, I won't take a penny! It was a fair deal: I rode home exultant, and in love; the next four weeks were a honeymoon. Besides, Nancy was the first horse I'd ever had of my very own: Trixie had belonged to the Army, and I'd hunted on hirelings. One admires or covets somebody else's house, horse, book or pictures; one *loves* a thing when it becomes one's own—buying something in a shop can become a sacrament. The little mare was *mine*: saddling her, making much of her, riding her over to Ken Young's to show her off, were stanzas of a nuptial poem.

The month's grace up, she took me to Empangeni to pay: it was like riding an angel. I handed over the £25, and after a few drinks to Nancy and her proved immunity, set off for home. About half-way, she suddenly went limp; in my thighs and hands I could feel the liveliness go out of her—like the electric light dimming with a fault at the power-station, like a motor engine plumply losing its 'pull'. I can see now, as if I were at this moment on her back, the abrupt droop in her neck, the alertness leave her ears. Like a wheat-field suddenly feeling a storm-cloud's wind, her coat was staring. The last five miles I had to lead her; she scarcely had the will to walk. It took her, I think, two days to die.

The cattle were dying too: each morning two or three more would show the pathetic dropsical swelling of the dewlap, the tell-tale hollow behind the ribs, the creeping debility that brought them, like Belsen's doomed, to the comforting ground. Some farmers propped them up with scaffolding of wattle-poles, believing that while they were on their legs there was hope. But there was no hope: n'gana's poison was relentless, and we had no antidote.

The little mare's death and the shambles of the cattle-kraal broke, temporarily, my heart; and I went back to Ken Young's— in time to set off, with old Greydawn and some of his natives, on a great Game Drive across the White and the Black 'Mfolosi Rivers 50 miles to the north.

The idea was to drive the Big Game, harbourers of the tsetse-fly, northwards into the empty wilderness of hill and bush that rose towards Swaziland; if one couldn't kill off the carrier of n'gana one might, it was hoped, shove it on to somebody else. All the White farmers joined in with squads of their 'boys'; the Chiefs mobilized the *impis*; the veldt thundered with the dancing feet of warrior Zulus, thumping in splendid naked ranks and painted and feathered up to the nines—Seton Merriman come true.

There was savage poetry in those nights of wild encampment beside a trickling nullah; with great fires to keep off the marauding carnivora, the strips of buck-meat hanging from the trees, scarlet in the flames' light, and the burnished black youths squatting over their meat and chanting the old epics of war; and now and then the roar of a tantalized lion. But I hated the slaughter of the daytime—I can see now an open plain dotted with the corpses of zebra, shot down as the harmless striped asses cantered across the muzzles of the white men's guns. My Zulus had a pretty poor opinion of me; I was a rotten shot, and each time they urged me to kill, I prayed that I should miss. I loved near dusk to wander off to a water-hole and sit down-wind like a stone: a warthog sow with her litter might come down to drink, a kudu bull, perhaps, with splendid spiralled points, and some of the lesser buck; and it was fun to come upon a couple of great lumbering White Rhino, which one could drive along like sheep; fun, too, deliciously terrifying, to hear a whispered warning from the 'boys' of a likely bit of bush for a Black Rhino's charge; exciting, and beautiful, to see the deadly flash of a Green Mamba across one's path. There was beauty and horror and plenty of Boys' Own Paper thrills in the ten days of that Game Drive; and when we turned back for home, the Big Game too turned round and reoccupied the country we'd tried to evict them from.

Then came the awful chill of my return: Mrs Young had found my poor little pornography. In a panic of humiliation, I went off to Durban; and there followed my first attempt at a ménage with a boy—my first blundering hope of playing both lover and mother.

\* \* \*

He was 16, and Welsh: I've often thought it was the beautiful name of Mervyn*that gave the conclusive fillip into infatuation. I was still conceited enough to feel it was more aesthetical to fall in love with somebody called Belisarius than with one called Bert.

The sorcery of Zululand's splendid innocence hadn't worn off: I wanted Arcadia, an idyll of unending tenderness; and thought that 'we'—I and a boy, any boy—had merely to live together in sunlit candour for life to flourish and happiness to be infinite. I hadn't yet learned, of course, what every paidophile has to learn—that the lifetime of his loves, if he gets any, endures no longer than his boy's beardlessness; they pay the penalty of a butterfly's freedom and, as a child out of last year's clothes, grow out of themselves. Not rarely, they ease into friendship; but that fierce and mystic delusion which is the sexual lunacy cannot span more than three or four years at most: suddenly, overnight like an overblown flower, it is dead; the unique and magic boy has become an ordinary young man, and one can look at the curve of his cheek without feeling a pang and an ineffable joy. Ideally, if one can use the word in so reprobated a context, the paederast is, as the Greeks knew, a pedagogue: his loves should pass in succession through his life as pupils progress through a master's class; and like the master he should see that each owes him at the end some mental or spiritual growth. But this is an ideal scarcely possible to attain, in this prying world, outside parts of Asia and the Mediterranean.

It wasn't so much Mervyn's prettiness that bowled me over—the First XI prettiness, as I remember it, of any prep. school story—as the sheer contiguity of his boyhood (like a child's begging to be given something for the sake of its being 'mine'); and I didn't stop to discover whether there might be affection there too. Within hours of our meeting he had become my partner in a pig-farm; within days, his family had given their assent; within a week I was sailing to England to try to make pigs and pounds-sterling out of my infatuate dream.

I went steerage in the *Euripides*, of what in those days was called the P. & O. Branch Line (I remember rejoicing in her 'Greekness'); and in Queen's Gate confronted my poor mother with an instant need of £1,000. She sighed sceptically during my glowing description of the fortune to be made by pig-raising in South Africa; but as usual her wise dubiety dissolved under the warmth of my exuberance and her own doting; as usual she was compliant, protesting gently. And, as usual too, she said nothing about the loss to herself of this money's income—the capital of course came out of my ultimate inheritance. 'Darling Mickey—I lie awake worrying about your frittering away your money,' she said; and a week later I sailed again for Durban in the *Kinfauns Castle*, an aged Victorian-looking vessel with two tall and thin funnels.

This time, money lying in my pocket, I compromised with commonsense and went second; I can see now up on the first-class boat-deck the magnificent Lord Lonsdale whose whiskers and Cruikshank nose and yellow barouche and grey frock-coat were as renowned up and down England as any year's Derby winner. Generally, I noticed, he attended the dashing and youthful Countess of Mar and Kellie; while Lord Mar, huddled in rugs, sat in silence beside the angular Countess of Lonsdale. I'm glad I saw just once this genial magnifico: it seemed like peering over the edge of the 18th century.

I remember the swaggering pleasure of sending a marconigram

to Mervyn; and I remember the unbearable excitement—like breaking up for the holidays, like the first dim glimpse of one's Christmas stocking at the bed's foot, like the morning of release from prison—of swinging in early daylight round the Bluff at Durban and searching madly for the sight of Mervyn's face on the quay.

I had learned from Ken Young in Zululand a lot about livestock; I'd learned nothing about farming economics—and besides, the motions of money have always been to me inscrutable. Of course the farm failed; of course, too, my experiment in bucolic love. I hired the first small farm I saw because it looked romantic and the furnished cottage was pretty: plunged into it without observing that the rent was absurdly high and the cost of pig-fencing huge. It was by the coast south of Durban, near Umzinto; a tame country with none of the reach of Zululand; and with neighbours a mile or two away, proud of garden-gates to their homesteads and neat avenues of eucalyptus. But there was a good wild ride to the sea over five miles of scrubby veldt, and bathing and sprawling among the rocks; though sharks and the weight of the Indian Ocean forbade swimming out.

The Major was our nearest neighbour. I never found out what sort of 'major' he was: he talked vaguely over his whisky about past 'campaigning' but was too old to have fought in the recent war; a huge lump of a fellow in his khaki drill, with a grey clipped moustache and a breastplate of white hair reaching to his neck: leg-of-mutton biceps which he'd display braced saying, 'Feel that, young man', and a great belly loosely belted round with a bando-leer. He had a gammy leg, got in some act of violence, and walked with a steel-pointed stick; though he could ride with anybody. 'Women—keep 'em where they belong', he used to shout, glaring at his cowed little wife who scuttled away after bringing out the whisky to the stoep; and he regularly beat the small orphan nephew who lived with them. 'Make a man of him', he'd snap, fondling the stick. I was terrified of him; though flattered by the paradox of deference I could feel in his arrogance: like many 'colonials' early in this century, he found a sort of snobbish kudos in patronizing someone genuinely 'English'. Soon he was almost daily nosing about our place, stumping uninvited into the house, breezily inquisitive. 'How much capital you got? What's your property in the Old Country? Want to get a woman in here—a man ought to have a woman, you know, if she's kept where she belongs. Got any whisky?' And then: 'What's this boy you've got here?

Put him to work, do you? No good, having a boy about the place, I'd say—anyway, see that you make a man of him.' And it was The Major, in the end, who gave our faltering comradeship its *coup de grâce*; and to me another lesson in what I might expect for the rest of my life.

But before that moment came, I could laugh over The Major behind my horror of him; and he was useful. Through him I got a nice little grey cob for Mervyn; and word of the very horse I was dreaming about for myself. The son of the storekeeper along the northern road—a place like part of a film-set: where men drank Cape brandy sitting on sacks of maize,and one ordered a whisky-and-water with one's groceries—was fortunately short of cash and wanted to sell his horse: a splendid black gelding standing more than 16 hands. I'd never seen a handsomer horse; he had a spectacular action and the spirit of a bushbuck. I got Lonestar (he had a white lozenge on his forehead) for £35; when I left I sold him for £45—the only 'commercial' deal in all my life I've made a profit on. The day he was led over to me by one of the store 'kaffirs', I incautiously tried him on a snaffle: he galloped me all the five miles to the sea without a stop, and then back. After that I gave him a double bridle; then, nicely ridden, he had the manners of an angel and the looks of a prince. He could jump too—unusual in South Africa, where there isn't much to jump. Lonestar was a superb, *happy* ride; as happy a ride, in another way, as Trixie had been. I rode him in two or three township horse-shows, and always won the Red ticket; this wasn't my riding's doing: he was simply far the best mount in the district.

All the same, I know I rode him well: Lonestar wasn't anybody's ride, and I wouldn't let Mervyn up. One day, taking Lonestar at a rather showy walk past The Major's place, where he was drinking whisky on his stoep with a visiting Boer, I heard his violent voice say: 'Look at *that* now—that's the *English* seat: *that's* how they sit a horse in the Old Country!' This gave my vanity a wonderful pleasure—and still does.

We had stocked up with sows; and I'd brought down a couple of Ken Young's Friesland cows-in-calf from Zululand, at £25 a head (this was 1920) plus rail. But from the start the money seemed all to be flowing out, with nothing coming upstream: the bacon-pigs swallowed more in cash then they amassed of flesh; the porkers snouted beneath the sunken fencing and ran away their weight; our Hindu gardener's wages were higher than the worth of the greens he so torpidly irrigated. Our only possessions which showed a profit were the horses—and that was huge: but the profit was pleasure. I thought, as I have always, that things would come right in the end; we rode, and bathed among the rocks, and up at the store gossiped and swaggered like cowboys.

But also we quarrelled. It was much more my fault than his: I shouldn't have blamed him for being incapable of giving the affection I'd bargained for; nor, a townee, for being a good deal bored and lazy through these months of pastoral sameness. When one builds a castle in the air, it's childish to complain because the castle doesn't exist; it was I who had dreamed perfection: nobody else could be reproached for an awakening to imperfection. Djuna Barnes, in her agonisingly exquisite 'Nightwood' (written perhaps on the *terrasses* of the old Dôme and Rotonde in Montparnasse), said: 'To love without criticism is to be betrayed.' Yes: but oneself is the betrayer.

We were often in tears; yet there was one interlude nearly daily when we both were happy. After our midday meal we would lie side by side in the bedroom and I would read aloud: the 'Jungle Books', 'Black Beauty', Morris's 'Norse Sagas', 'Richard Yea-or-Nay'—these are some that I remember. The bed stood full under the wide-open window to get the smell of the veldt; Mervyn would snuggle up to me as the young do when their imaginations are engrossed, lost in the story; and we'd scarcely notice if our cook or one of the 'kaffirs' came by.

One day, so absorbed in 'Jock of the Bushveldt' that neither of us had heard a sound, something made me look up at the window: The Major, sitting on his horse with the steel-tipped stick across the pommel like a gun, was glaring in at us. Without so much as yelling, as was his habit, at the front-door, he'd ridden quietly round to our room at the back. I can hear today the snort he uttered; and see his horse's yellow teeth as he jerked its head round. He spent the afternoon, we learned later, riding round to all the neighbours to report the 'disgusting' thing he'd seen.

This was the end. Not because of the neighbours, who quite failed to play up to The Major's indignation; but because poor Mervyn turned on me. It was he who rallied to The Major's side; and accused me of blackening his character and doing the opposite of 'making a man of him'. Of course he was right in a way; although his eyes were wide open well before I met him and there were only half a dozen years of age between us. And yet, looking back now across 40 years, I can't think of a single other friendship with a boy, not one, that ended in recrimination and 'moral' odium.

I sold up, at a big loss of course. Mervyn had his grey cob and a share of the wreckage; and I took a train to Johannesburg with, as my sorrowingly indulgent mother had feared, nearly all the money I had coaxed from her 'frittered away'. I didn't 'fall out' of love with Mervyn quickly; as time took me further from the reality, the dream appeared increasingly real; and I'd pore with sugared misery over the snapshots I had of him. There's always some pleasure in heartache.

When I see the name 'Jo'burg' I think of Mrs Ecks*and of the Wemmer Pan—much less of the horrible, heartless, brassy spivishness of the place. These two memories are related in the way that a child's sweet belongs to the nasty medicine it follows: from the hothouse grotesqueries of Mrs Ecks's non-stop bedroom farce, I would rush out to the clean seclusion of the Wemmer Pan, that splendid gold-mining sump, where nothing ruffled the basking water but the splashing of boys' bodies. The Wemmer Pan was a splendid green-edged sheet of water, locked within a ring of huge, black, pyramidal slag-heaps—the vomit of the Witwatersrand.

I'd supposed that in Johannesburg job-finding would be easy; but it was quickly plain that a diffident incompetent with no aptitude for brokery wasn't in demand. One had the feeling of being in a colossal flea-market—where the diamond-rings were real and the cheap-jacks lived at the Ritz. In between the financial baronetage—the Beits, Baileys, Joels, Schlesingers and their like—and the untouchable Natives, shoved down to abysmal levels of squalor by the crumbs of prosperity they flocked in to sweep up, the town seemed to be peopled by auctioneers, bookmakers, share-hawkers, carpet-baggers and 'agents' of every sort. They punted their money all day on each others' wares, and got it back again all night at each others' poker parties.

A Small Ad. in the *Rand Daily Mail* took me to Mrs Ecks's office; a young man of good appearance &c was sought—to make money, apparently, hand over fist. I'd never had a high notion of my appearance; but I'd learned by now that in South Africa a certain *English* way of speaking, and English manners, could be an asset. I remember walking past the door several times before that sense of deficiency let me screw up my courage; but once inside (as always later, when calling on somebody like Mr Nehru, or facing the awful frigidity of a pawnbroker), the usual intelligent 'charm' took over and hid my clammy cowardice like a false beard.

I had never seen, in real life, anybody like Mrs Ecks. Perhaps the Queen of Sheba was like her; perhaps, if the Israelites had had their Boadicea, she would have been like Mrs Ecks. Not much more than thirty; so tall and broad that the huge tumuli of fat that bellied like spinnakers through the floridly expensive clothes didn't seem ungainly; beautiful ( I suppose) in a flaming Jewish way; and she moved, in spite of that vast bulk, with the serpentine elegance of a Phillips Oppenheim adventuress, while the wide face, luscious as trifle, seemed to flaunt a luring lasciviousness: a Miriam, was Mrs. Ecks, of the Neapolitan School, very well fed. Yet that face held a paradox: hand in hand with the bawdy simper, a hard ruthless intelligence gleamed through the authoritative horn-rimmed spectacles, and one felt that a ferocious personality lay embedded in all that fleshy femininity. She was wonderful, was Mrs. Ecks, and to me quite repulsive in an enthralling way.

She was a brand-new experience; and in any case the first 'business-woman' I had met. She owned, of course, an 'agency'; the job was selling-on-commission. Before I knew where I was, I was sent out to hawk round the flashier shops a new-fangled contrivance connected with window-dressing. Timidly I'd ask for the manager; feeling foolish, I'd display the gadget and explain what it did; blandly I'd say, when he picked holes in it: 'Well, I don't think much of it myself; but you see, if you buy one I shall make a sovereign for myself.' I didn't, of course, sell one. Mrs Ecks, instead of firing me, asked me to dinner; and later put me in her office, paying me a pound a week for doing, as far as I now recall, nothing.

Mrs Ecks lived in Parktown, the 'smart' end of Jo'burg: flowery avenues of ochre-coloured, gabled villas, opulent and 'modern'; where the only visible Natives were white-liveried servants. I was brought, like a new dog, to the Ecks mansion; and made aware of, rather than introduced to, Solly Ecks (an auctioneer of course): a whirlwind of secretive energy, detached and incurious, who dashed in and out of the house like a visiting plumber who's forgotten his tools—he didn't seem to belong; and of Izzy, who also lived there: a small, morose, white-faced man, tongue-tied and pent-up—smouldering, obviously, with some ineffable passion. Izzy 'travelled' in women's underclothes, and made a very good thing out of it; he was also Mrs Ecks's lover—an idiosyncratic sort of lover, I was soon to be told. I became aware, too, of a mercurial movement of people called Reuby, Sammy and Hymie who streamed in and out to eat, drink and play poker. I wasn't allowed to see much of any of these people, being kept in a corner by Mrs Ecks like a kind of pet; yet all the time I knew her, and through all the intimacies of our confidences, I remained to her 'Mr Davidson' and she to me 'Mrs Ecks'.

I hadn't dreamed, up to that time, that any town could *feel* so immoral as Johannesburg did—'immoral' in the fields of manners and ordinary social ethics; now I couldn't believe that anything so utterly *fictional* as the Ecks household could be real. It was like sitting endlessly in a cinema. The furniture, florid and expensive, seemed always to be changing—Solly, presumably, kept moving in fresh bargains from the auction-rooms. There was always masses of rich food about—all cream and aspic; and people kept on pouring out whiskies, as they used to in those jolly William Powell and Myrna Loy films. Solly moved restlessly from guest to guest, saying a few breezy words, mostly about money—speaking his formal lines while his cryptic mind was elsewhere engrossed; Izzy glowered darkly in an alcove, tense and gnashing, suffering, jealous eyes fixed, like claws, in Mrs Ecks's huge flesh; and Mrs Ecks herself, lushly bossy: a horn-rimmed Theodora, trailing eroticism yet ironclad in hard-headedness.

Soon Mrs Ecks was treacherously telling me about poor Izzy's eccentric passion. (I was constantly being whisked up to Parktown: like a dog on a lead.) She would take me into her sitting-room, the one where Izzy was allowed his sessions, and set me in front of her —facing the full moon of her voluptuousness; and she would talk and talk about unutterable privacies. Izzy, her lover, she said—his bald head barely reached up to the great prow of her bosom— wanted only one thing from her: to listen to a string of obscenities uttered in her satiny, caressing voice. 'Filthier, filthier!' he would exclaim (she assured me) in a frenzy of excitement; until he had had for the moment enough. That, if she was to be believed, was Izzy's sex-life. I remember feeling horrified: not by her salacity (I always enjoyed 'dirt'), but by the implications of its issuing from this mass of female fleshiness; and yet fascinated, as schoolboys are fascinated by medical dictionaries—fascinated too by the discovery, quite new to me, that 'grown-ups' could behave in such peculiar ways. And then it dawned on me that Mrs Ecks was getting some occult pleasure out of talking like this to *me*: watching me, eyes behind the horn-rims like microscopes, to see if I was responding with a gratifying excitement. And when she told me that poor little Izzy was in a torment of jealousy on my account, of all people, I realized that she *enjoyed* making him jealous.

'But that's ridiculous,' I remember saying. 'You see, Mrs Ecks, I can never like you in *that* way—I like boys!'

She was furious: not disgusted or scandalized, but downright indignant. 'I shall have that altered at once,' she said with managerial decision, 'I shall have you cured'; and at once telephoned to Johannesburg's most expensive psycho-analyst.

I went to the man only once; and consciously, lying on his sofa, refrained from exposing my unconscious. Deliberately, I edited my answers; for I knew that I didn't *want* to be cured. I don't think, through all the ups and downs of my life, despite all its humiliations and futilities, I have ever wanted my fundamental emotional nature to be different—not even when I went to prison on account of it; because if that nature, the essence of myself, were changed, then the 'I' that I know, the 'I' that is myself, would cease to exist— I'd be somebody else, a notion which is inconceivable. One may despise oneself; one may regret one's incapacities, ugliness, weakness of mind, deformity of character; and know oneself to be a rotter; but one cannot contemplate surely being a *self* that isn't one's own self. I have often, during 40 or 50 years, tried to see myself as a 'normal'; but the attempt has been as ineffective as searching for the end of infinity. 'He is a poor creature who does not believe himself to be better than the whole world else,' Samuel Butler observed. 'No matter how ill we may be, or how low we may have fallen, we would not change identity with any other person.' So I gave that psycho-analyst no help.

I never found out why Mrs Ecks made a bee-line for me from the moment I went into her office. I was ugly then, as I've always been; and looked, I suppose, a hobbledehoy though I must have been 23. Perhaps she was excited by sheer youth; perhaps it was that 'colonial' snobbishness which found pleasure in the authentic English; perhaps there was some lure in a Gentile (Mrs Ecks didn't know about my 64th Part). I could, I expect, have made a good thing out of becoming her gigolo—even a purely verbal one; but I wasn't able to for the same sort of constitutional reasons that a few years earlier had prevented my attempting a homosexual 'trade'.

The Parktown interlude had given me a good deal of amusement, and taught me some strange novelties about human desires; but before long I found it sickening. I went back to England.

The night before I took the train for Capetown, after dark, I was stopped in the street by a boy. It was Mervyn. I've forgotten now why he had come to Johannesburg; I remember only that he was charming and friendly and ready, I think, to start all over again. Of course it was too late; but the extraordinary chance of this meeting reopened for me a wound that had almost healed. I rather enjoyed the gentle pain of it; I have always been sentimental.

## 8

IN LONDON, IN 1922, came a tiny occurrence, silly in itself, which gave another warning of what my heresy must bring; or rather, which made me a stage more sensible of that tumour of furtive 'guilt' that my unconformity with society was ineluctably planting in my soul—guilt, though, that I've never correlated with *ethics*, but with the anathema of one's fellow beings. This incident also, such is the paradox of fortuity, jumped me obliquely into the trade of journalism, to which I was plainly predestined by my limited abilities and in which, so far as I've stayed anywhere, I stayed.

Until supplanted by Lansbury's 'Lido', a strip of the Serpentine in Hyde Park had been insulated by tradition and a surprisingly unprudish Board of Works for the bathing of 'males only'. There was a wonderful lot of juvenile nudity there: screened from strollers behind by a fenced rampart, and from boaters ahead by a delimitation across the water. Baron Corvo of course knew it: 'Through the foliage, exquisitely lush and vivid, he could see the arches of the bridge. . . . Before him was the green grass, the gravel path, the silver water, and the microscopically clear expanse of the other side, verdant, brilliantly bright. . . . Miscellaneous males of all ages from seven to seventy, came hurrying . . . shed dun-colours; and slipped pink into the water. . . .' That's how I saw it; and I was, like Corvo, fond of going there on a summer's day.

On this day, which was to leave a permanent bruise of private shame, I had taken my bathing-drawers and, aware of the notice 'bathers only', was sitting on the grass wondering how chilly the breeze blowing from the Marble Arch might be—besides, I had lent my slip to a boy who was shyer than most about going in with nothing on. All at once the delicious scene was harshly shivered: I was being astonishingly spoken to by a policeman, being ordered to 'go along' with him out of the bathing enclave; I was *in the hands of the Law*. By not instantly undressing and plunging into the water, by dallying on the bank fully clad, I'd broken a Parks Regulation—that was all; yet walking away under police escort, I felt that each of those staring eyes was boring into my secret mind, that every man and boy discerned that I was 'like that', that I was being arrested for *thinking* illegal thoughts. I became parched with shame and humiliation—all my privacies, I thought, were lying bare.

This was rubbish, existing only in my own mind; yet it left me through life with a pursuing anxiety: a furtive, backward-glancing, collar-turned-up sensation of being watched by a special branch of Orwell's Thought Police. Later, *real* involvements with the Law led logically to the physical and worldly disruption of imprisonment, but made no 'spiritual' imprint; they soon became interesting, but not very important, museum memories. Yet that 40-year-old illusion, that sharp, subjective throe of 'guilt', has endured for good. It was my first encounter with the police; and it coincided like a sock on the jaw with reveries which until then I hadn't connected with 'shame'—thoughts that to me were joyous and clean but seemed, with the jarring incursion of the policeman (who was merely saying 'move along please'), to become infected with a kind of social scabies. Of course, it didn't modify my thoughts; it only complicated them.

That day, I felt chased by devils—London seemed impure. I telegraphed to my sister in Norfolk that I was coming down: I knew I should feel safe with her.

Nancy's rambling, ramshackle house, sequestered within girdling beeches and tangled garden, had become a kind of disapproved school for literary young men. When she had lived in Holt, where her husband Christopher taught the fiddle at Gresham's School, she had shocked J. R. Eccles, the Head, and the rest of local respectability by hoisting the Red Flag during the 1921 railway strike and by letting her three small children run naked in the garden, performing their infant improprieties in view of the main road. Swayed, probably, by acquaintanceship with men like Bertrand Russell and Julian Huxley, and especially by the friendship of Lancelot Hogben, she had slid from the High Anglicanism of her upbringing into the emotional void of free-thinking, but hers was too ardent a nature to stay there long, and soon she was seeking spiritual experience under such varied teachers as a Baptist and a Brahmin—until finally her mystical desire found fulfilment in the

Catholic Church. Obviously, Nancy was considered officially to be an unsuitable companion for the poetical boys who flocked to her house; and for the sake of Chris's tutorial security she went to live in the remote country. The boys followed her when they got the chance; and after they'd gone up to Oxford or Cambridge they came in the vacations to stay at The Beeches.

I've never known another person who so magnetically drew, as Nancy did, such a volume of devotion, emotional and intellectual—indeed, adoration; but especially from men with yearning and sensitive minds. She possessed an unbounded store of spell-binding 'personality'; and of a fervent sympathy which she poured like spiced wine into souls thirsty for love. She could shape hearts with her charm as witches would wax—though her spells, if sometimes emotionally prostrating, were made wholly of goodness. I don't know if she was 'beautiful'—she had the wide, plump face of our great-aunt Annie and an untidy bob of straight hair; but she had wonderful eyes, and a huge lot of people fell in love with her. Her lovers, from the middle-aged to the sixth form, worshipped her; and she adored their worship, lavishing on them in return the unrivalled balm of her understanding and sympathy—there must be hundreds of people today who've been happier for knowing Nancy. Yet if this rapturous love of hers was two parts maternal and healing, it was one part Circe's desire for possession: steeped in Malory, she saw herself as the ideal lady-love, and clad her worshippers in shining armour; but it didn't escape her that Guinevere and Galahad were as fleshly as any. The craving to possess, though, remained dominantly emotional: physical love was a fragment of a whole.

The truth is that Nancy was always a mystic: she was always, from childhood, seeking an ideal love, spiritual love; searching for some mystical or philosophical system through which she could become united with perfection. To her, all 'love' was part of perfect love, part of the divine; love of animals and *things*, love of people in general, love of the flesh, love of the beautiful in experience, were all part of the same thing—love of God: if there was *love* there couldn't be evil. Her morality was the corollary of this ardent, mystical humanity: 'right' and 'wrong' in their arbitrary and conventional shapes were as movable as sheep-hurdles when they obstructed the way of deserving emotion or deserved sympathy. She believed, or rather felt, that goodness meant the beautiful—the quality of happiness; evil, synonym of the ugly, meant unhappi-

ness. For her, at that time, love, literature, music and the romanticism of all three, were the channels of grace. Later, perhaps, this
faith seemed deficient and undisciplined; her emotional affairs, I
suppose, were getting out of hand: she came to need the safety and
symmetries of order and, especially, a spiritual, mystical outlet for
her abounding genius for love. She discovered them in the Catholic
Church.

Her favourite reading of those days reflected her romantic
nature: Shakespeare—but Romeo rather than Lear; the lovely
intoxicants of Swinburne; Malory and arthurian Tennyson;
Cervantes, Kipling, and above all Dickens. She would cross
England to see, once again, Martin Harvey play 'The Only Way'
(the 'Tale of Two Cities' was for a long time her best-loved book);
and the first of her books, 'Great Gifts'—whose pacifist hero was
drawn from Lancelot Hogben—bore the nom-de-plume 'Anne
Darnay'.

'Great Gifts', published by Collins about 1922, must have been
the earliest fictional condemnation of the war in which personal
revolt against it, 'conscientious objection', was the heroic act.
Lance Hogben, while up at Cambridge, almost friendless and a
social fish out of water, had suffered for his pacifist faith and
courage—and, too, from poverty and working-class origin. Nancy
poured love and understanding and her unflagging sympathy on
him; and, I believe, brought him from emotional misery to the
tranquility that made his brilliant career possible. He, with his
gifts and spiritual valour, was the hero of that novel; and the first
of Nancy's protégés.

For the next 20 years she was bringing up four children; but
about 1940, living in Ireland (it was with her, in that year, that our
mother died), she began writing again: three religious books,
printed privately and without a name; and, in the 1950s, two
animal books for children published by Hutchinson: 'The Good
Beasts' and 'Ranjit of the Circus Ring'.

By this time she was a Catholic of some ten years' standing; and,
bodily, the almost total invalid she is still today; and at this time,
in the first years of the last war, she did what I imagine no woman
has ever done before: she created and guided a work for and among
priests which spread far beyond the confines of Ireland and
anonymously wrote for them books of human and spiritual counsel
whose authorship, for the thousands of priests who possessed them,
remained unknown. This work was recognized by the highest

Church authorities and one of the books received the special blessing of Pope Pius XII. Her two children's books, by 'Anne Freeling' (her baptismal names), contain some of the most exquisite animal portraiture in English; and, in a charmingly entertaining way, gently remove, in the mind of any child-reader, the barriers of class, colour and religious prejudice through a common love of animals. 'The Good Beasts' was intelligently chosen for a prize in London schools by the L.C.C.

Without Nancy's companionship, mine wouldn't have been the perfect childhood it was; without her flooding love and example during those years at The Beeches, I wouldn't ever have gained some small qualities of mind that I perhaps have. We were out of touch for some three decades after the 1920s—I abroad and she in Ireland; but now, in old age, that precious companionship has been restored to me, even if only by post.

My sister, by my definition, is one of history's 'great' women; she is also as good a saint as any in the calendar. She is already beatified in the hearts of all who have known her; she should certainly be canonised—she's worked miracles enough in the healing of sick souls and the mending of broken hearts. Priests and others with some illness of the spirit or problem of the mind are still sent to her bedside to be cured by her wisdom and charity. And, her youngest son Nicolas wrote to me recently, she's still 'the best of company'; for Nancy's goodness isn't of the starched sort—nobody can laugh so happily at the funny side of things as she.

I poured out to her my agony on the banks of the Serpentine; and the unarguable fact of my bondage to boys with its rider of sexual allergy to women. I don't suppose I knew, then, the word 'homosexual'. Nancy took this avowal with that perfection of tolerance and understanding which perhaps is synonymous with saintliness and certainly was with her nature. Her chief advice— after conjuring me to make any relationships *positive* with love and some sort of mental contribution, rather than leave them mere sensual negations—was: 'Well, Mike old boy, do be *careful*.'

Although The Beeches was a house to which people were constantly bringing their emotional bruises to be bathed in Nancy's wisdom, it was also an exciting, happy house where literature was for ever being talked, poetry being read, music being played. At week-ends, when Chris appeared, his practising violin would faintly, from a distant room, wail and sing and reiterate some stubborn phrase; he would abstractedly join, vaguely ironical (his was a world of technique, and fingering, and a private love) in the talk at meals, and quickly vanish, to practise more. Visitors brought loads of new gramophone records—the Brandenburgs, Jelly d'Aranji's Beethoven violin concerto, Mozart quartets; or Nancy, curled on her calves in a shabby armchair, would enthral us with the magic of her literary romanticism and the wise harmonies of her boundless heart.

All this to me was intoxicating. I was in a novel world of the mind, and discovering fresh realms of experience like poetry which seemed as exciting as the emergence of a new sense; and, though I don't suppose I put it like that, I was at last getting some *education*. An important inspiriter of this mental development was Walter Greatorex, senior music master at Gresham's School and a principal worshipper at The Beeches. One day when I was staying in Holt with Chris, Walter—familiar with my freshly impassioned interest in poetry—said to me: 'There's a boy you'd like to meet—writes very good verse I think. His name's Auden.' So in Walter's rooms I, twenty-six years old, was introduced to Wystan Auden, then 16; and there began a poetical relationship which for two years or so absorbed me.

By now, I'd become a junior sub-editor on the *Eastern Daily Press* in Norwich. My sister knew the Cozens-Hardy family who, with other 'whiggish' Norfolk people like the Colmans, the Gurneys, the Copemans, owned the paper. Arthur Cozens-Hardy, the Editor, a complaisant man who amiably deferred to the judgement of his subordinates, gave me the job: for the first time in my life I had real 'work' and was being paid a wage.

A wonderful character on the *E.D.P.* was Mr Cook. He was one of those old-fashioned reporters who wrote their copy in flowing pencilled italic, words linked together like a string of performing elephants and most of them forming obligatory clichés like 'floral tribute'. Mr Cook's special perquisite was the coverage of Sandringham: a right that he prized as aldermen prize a knighthood. He was, of course, an anecdotal chap; his most treasured memory concerned a Sandringham shoot in Edward VII's time. Mr Cook's task was to dodge about behind hedges while the royal party, joined by their ladies, were having their picnic luncheon. On this occasion, he would relate, he suddenly observed his Majesty detach himself from the company and stroll nonchalantly round to stand against the hedge behind which Mr Cook was crouching. 'And—'

(at this point his voice would sink to a reverential hush) '—*I saw the Royal penis!*'

One of my tasks, as 'local page' sub, was fashionable weddings—important news-stories on which Mr Cook lavished his most powerful descriptive writing. Once, dashing with my blue pencil through a sheaf of pencilled flimsy, I was brought up dead by the sentence: 'After the ceremony, the marriage was consummated in the vestry.'

Auden, as I remember him then, was tall and gangling, with fair hair limp across a pale forehead and clumsy limbs apt to go adrift; and an odd, cogitative face that was frighteningly unboyish. He seemed too engrossed in *thought* to be boyish; it was the face of a mind far older than its age and already had that look of puritan sternness which signifies contempt for all intellectual time-wasting. He was very like what he is today—already Stravinsky's 'big blond intellectual bloodhound'—but fairer and less rugged. His face wasn't, of course, yet rutted with those singular corrugations which seem like the seismic result of terrific intellectual commotion; but the tenderness of its boyhood was oddly combined with an extra-ordinary grown-up austerity.

I was bewitched at the first meeting; not by a physical attractive-ness, which I didn't find (beyond the general one of adolescence), but by the blinding discovery, as in a revelation, that here was wonderfully joined that divine freak called genius with the magical age of sixteen. The maturity of even his smallest remarks, a kind of inspired wisdom which, in his company, one couldn't help being aware of, was alarming; and I knew instantly that, though ten years older, I was shamefully his inferior in intellect and learning. But he went to my romantic head like one's second Pernod; I saw that I had found my boy Keats or Chatterton, on whom I would lavish all I could muster of literary maternalism. I was in love; but I think I deliberately chose to be in love.

This passion was conducted mainly by post. A two-way stream of letters, poems and books flowed almost daily between Norwich, where I was working, and Holt, where he was at school. He sent me every new poem he wrote (in his small, adult hand; that looked much more legible than sometimes it was), and I returned long letters of criticism or rather discussion; and through the post we discovered to each other any exciting writers that had come fresh to us—I remember particularly Edward Thomas, Robert Frost,

Jefferies and de la Mare—or copied out passages of special relevance in our reading. I devoured the *London Mercury* and *Times Lit. Sup.*, and ordered for him every new book of poetry and criticism (Wystan told me recently he still has many of the books I sent him in those days).

It must have been a strange, and rather touching, correspondence. Mine were love letters as well as literary ones; though I did my best to filter the love out of them, so afraid was I of offending his detestation of the sentimental. His were calm, mature, rigidly unemotional. I tremble still today when I think what nonsense I must often have written; for my outlook on poetry was a romantical, traditionalist one, and sadly uninstructed. Although I was supposed to be the counsellor, the critic, of ten years' seniority, I learned much more from Auden than I could teach him. Yet my letters, and my association, can't have been valueless; not many years ago, sitting with me over the yellow wine of Epomeo on the island of Ischia, Wystan said: 'Michael—you don't know what you did for me in those days.' Perhaps my encouragement did indeed help him to encourage himself to go on writing poetry—helped to dissuade him from abandoning it for psychology; perhaps I played a part in making poetry his profession.

At that time he had schooled himself in Freud and Jung, and had made up his mind to become a psychologist. When I urged him to be a poet he declared in effect that for poetry to be a modern reality it must, like everything else, become a matter of science and that henceforth the poet must be scientist. He saw the world in technical terms and modern life as a scientific transaction and was determined, whether he wrote poetry or not, to fit out his intellect with the finest technical equipment. It was in science that he found *truth*; and Auden at 16 loathed sham and falsity. That is why he abhorred easy emotionalism and sentimentality as a teetotaller abhors alcohol; why, probably, he loved to load his conversation and work with the specialist terminologies of the sciences, physical, mental and spiritual—their use, I suppose, was an entrenchment against the romanticism of the unscientific. And that was why, when I took him to The Beeches to meet my sister Nancy, he disliked her—or rather 'disapproved' of her—although his closest friend at Gresham's was one of her most devout worshippers. He was unjust in supposing that the lushness of her emotionalism was merely sentimental; but I should have known beforehand that the meeting couldn't be a success.

He knew, of course—better than I, having the entire psychological pentateuch at his finger-tips—the nature of my feelings for him. I think he rather enjoyed them—he could study me, so to speak, clinically; he once told me, as if stating an interesting scentific fact, that I was the first adult homosexual he had met. But his understanding of my devotion was never more than tacit; and once, when I was fool enough to post him some wretched verses I'd written to him, he never referred to their existence. He was kind enough to ignore their poetic dreadfulness and stern enough to keep silent on the sentiment they conveyed (he knew of course that sentiment far better than my feeble and misguided effusion could tell it).

We met when it could be managed; but before long, our friendship had to 'go underground'. The school authorities naturally forbade it; and then I got a letter from Mrs Auden, formally asking me to see no more of her son. But he wouldn't have this: contemptuous of convention, intolerant of authority—though deferring to both when reason justified—he circumvented them when they couldn't be flouted. He came to stay with me in Norwich, where he had my bedroom while I chastely slept downstairs. I would sometimes cross Norfolk by train to meet him, when some scholastic whim sent him, say, to King's Lynn; from these assignations, carefully organized by post, we would go for 'long didactic walks', to use John Pudney's perfectly descriptive phrase. Auden loved then walking over fen or through wood; and he was always didactic, as he is still today; the walk would be accompanied by a discourse on whatever subject might crop up, spoken in a yet adolescent voice, fluent though somewhat staccato: rich in ideas and knowledge and hot with a teacher's zeal. His blond head would toss backwards as if in muscular reaction to thought, and he'd be much too engrossed by his ideas to watch where his unruly legs were taking him. The magic of his mind was irresistible: I imagine that those on Samos who listened to the young Pythagoras must have felt the same kind of uncannily precocious sapience. Certainly Auden, at 16, had an astonishing aura of wisdom.

It was yet more alarming in later years, when one no longer had the alibi of being 'grown-up'. Many evenings, in an Italian summer, I've been one of a few who, emptying flagons of wine, have listened with awe and only a little understanding to Wystan's intellectually spatial orations. There was a highly 'intellectual' American who tried to turn discourse into discussion; but one cannot argue with Auden—really, one can only listen. That intellect is too big for ordinary folk. Then, towards ten o'clock, he would abruptly stand up almost in the middle of a sentence. 'I like people to go to bed early,' he'd say with severity; and set off a little lopsidedly for his house at the top of the village.

He was always didactic. Once, eating together, I ordered some mushy dish like *pasta e fagioli*. He was at once critical. 'A liking for sloshy food', he devastatingly said, 'is a symptom of infantilism. Only the retarded eat mush. I like people to eat solid food.'

While he was still at school—about 1923—I angered him by springing a surprise which I hoped (with the fevered excitement of a lover bearing gifts) would give him pleasure. I had discovered that some firm of publishers was putting out an annual volume called 'Public School Verse'; and, choosing what I thought the best from my stock, I submitted a poem without saying anything to him. Of course it was accepted; and I had the additional joy, when the book appeared, of reviewing it in the *Eastern Daily Press* and devoting the whole review to Auden. But he was furious and I, in consequence, chagrined. Yet I think his anger was justified: his work by then was far too mature to be ranked with that of school-boys.

But it's been a satisfaction to know that I, and none other, first got Auden 'published', and that it was I who gave him his first newspaper review—humbly and obscurely both; but there's a historical fact for future bibliographers.

About 1924 I left Norwich; and a little later Auden went up to the House where I visited him now and then. By that time I possessed a suitcase crammed with his autograph poems and letters; and for ten years they went with me wheresoever I went. In 1928 they went to Berlin; then to Geneva and back again to Berlin. In July 1933, as a not very bold member of the Communist underground 'wanted' by Hitler, I had to get across the Czech border at an hour's notice. Auden's poems stayed with the rest of my belongings in a room in the Zimmerstrasse. For fear of endangering my Berliner friends, there was nothing I could do from England to get them back. Were they, I've often wondered, blown up by allied bombs? Or will they, one day, be discovered and published with a German commentary? I don't suppose, though, apart from the handwriting, that they bear any clue to identity.

It was in this Norwich time that I came across the contemporary literature of homosexuality—people like Havelock Ellis, Norman

Haire and Edward Carpenter; and began to realize that my condition was much more widely and intelligently understood, though scarcely less reviled, than I had imagined. But it was Edward Carpenter whose work came with the bright light of an evangel; who, in my romantic mood, seemed to say what I wanted said; who gave 'friendship' a mystical, an ideal, meaning—mingling the nobility of the Greek *agapé* with the soft-sweet tenderness of the German *Freundschaft*. This, at the time, was right up my street—look after the spiritual side, I thought, and the carnal will look after itself; and besides, wasn't Carpenter a poet and apostle of human liberty, author of 'England Arise' and 'Towards Democracy'? The latter, I secretly confessed, bored me a bit; as did Walt Whitman except in small doses; but Edward Carpenter was plainly the Master, who had written the homosexual's true gospel (though I didn't like being dubbed 'the intermediate sex').

I wrote him a disciple's letter, and proposed a pilgrimage to the Hog's Back. I can't now remember what Auden had to say to this; probably he was disdainful. An affectionate invitation came back, beginning 'Dear Friend' and written in an old man's hand, shaky but still beautiful. Edward Carpenter was then, I think, over 80.

The house was a perfect Sage's retreat, down to the revolving summer-house in wooded solitude where great thoughts could be penned and the sun's circuit followed. But I was a little disappointed in the Sage. Handsome he was, so far as old men can be, with a white beard, soft and sacerdotal; but instead of the splendid Socratic mind I'd envisaged, inspiring and vivid, I found a feeble old man, beyond conversation, who coquettishly pinched my behind. He wasn't surrounded (after all, this was Sussex), as I had romantically hoped, by a throng of golden youths; but lived with an unromantic railway porter named Fred, middle-aged and portly, with a little black moustache. It showed, I suppose, that it is unwise, having set a person on a pedestal, to climb up and have a close look —one will find that he is very like oneself.

And then, in 1924, I crassly changed direction again; and threw to the winds the nice steady life of comfortable security, with a pension at the end of it, which a newspaper desk then promised me.

## 9

I'VE NEVER REGRETTED that imbecility. It's one's follies that lead one generally to the unexpected, the odd, the excitingly worth-while, not one's cautious, sensible decisions; and had I been wise and stayed at the Norwich desk, that wisdom would have cost me most of the enchanting experiences and friendships which have made my life richer than money could have done. Often I've cast a brief repining glance over my shoulder at the allurements of a secure income and freedom from the travails of penury; and then quickly thanked the fecklessness of my character that prevented my yielding to the temptation: for wherein lies the merit of affluence when its enjoyment is the victim of the monotone duty of obtaining it? I've long been convinced that life should be a matter of pleasure not of duty; and I'd rather suffer for pleasure's sake than sacrifice pleasure for duty's.

So I left Norwich for London.

Ella King-Hall ran a literary agency in Panton Street; and her husband, H. W. Westbrook, an unsuccessful novelist but an able journalist, had founded a short-lived weekly called *By the Way & Interviews*. It had standing rubrics like 'Penny Plain, Tuppence Coloured' and was full of literary chatter; each issue carried an interview with some Grub Street notability. How old-fashioned that paper would look today! I, though, became its sub-editor, and helped in Miss King-Hall's agency. I was paid £3 a week—ten shillings less than my wage in Norwich.

She was a little, bustling woman with a leathery face and hair like a grizzled golliwog, as capable as she was charming. Her brothers were both retired admirals, and a cousin was Stephen King-Hall. The agency lived mainly on P. G. Wodehouse. Every month a new story came in from P.G. and was sold to the *Strand Magazine* for £750—an enormous sum in those days; simultaneously it appeared in the *Saturday Evening Post* in America for about double the money.

Ella King-Hall accomplished something more difficult than collecting commission on P.G.'s output: she sold a story of mine. *The Sketch*, then a dignified weekly in the *Sphere* and *Illustrated London News* class, paid eight guineas for it—a handsome fee, then, for a 2,000-word story. It was about a London docks ship's watchman who, never having been to sea in his life, swaggered in fantasy as a seafaring hero and became to everybody but himself a laughingstock. This brought from Christopher Sclater Millard—immortal as 'Stuart Mason' for his classic bibliography of Wilde, and immortal as a person in the memories of all who knew him—a jocular letter addressed to me care of the *Sketch*. We were already friends; and the kindly letter is a characteristic mixture of Millardian thoughtfulness, irony and downrightness:

'My dear Sir,' he wrote from the famous Bungalow in Abercorn Place, 'Please allow me to congratulate you on your very remarkable short story which appears in this week's *Sketch*. ... You are evidently a writer of experience but your name seems quite unfamiliar to me. ... I would compare you to Joseph Conrad, only I could never stomach that much overrated writer's halting sentences and slipshod English. I am, dear Sir, yours very truly, Stuart Mason.'

Millard was, I think, the most *important* person I've ever met; and he remains so today, 35 years after his death.

There can't be many survivors left from the old Café Royal; I was lucky to be in time to see it before the vandals destroyed it. I remember one evening shyly drinking a beer with Jacob Epstein; and being introduced to an agreeable and brisk young man named Allen Lane—of interest to me as the nephew of the 'great' John Lane of the Bodley Head, yet perhaps even then dreaming of revolution in the book trade. I just missed Ronald Firbank there; I think I should have adored him, pansy preciosity and all.

I came into what today would be called a 'queer set': people like Charles Kains-Jackson, silver-haired and ruddy, who had been a contributor, with Oscar Wilde, Alfred Douglas, Max Beerbohm and others, to that issue of *The Chameleon* made famous at the Wilde trial by its inclusion of the story *The Priest and the Acholyte*, and who had been a friend, until the inevitable quarrel, of Corvo's; and Leonard Green, a nephew of the historian J. H. Green, a writer of graceful idylls about romantic encounters in Dalmatia which he privately printed for his friends. The word 'queer', then, hadn't been invented; the cryptic designation was 'so', corresponding to *comme ça* in Montparnasse. 'Oh, is he *so*?' one would ask, giving a slight italic tone to the syllable. Another verbal cipher in use was the initials *t.b.h.* 'My dear', somebody might say standing outside Wellington Barracks, 'the one third from the right in the front rank—I know *he's* t.b.h.!'—meaning 'to be had'; as the modern queer will say 'he's trade'.

Another friend was Charles Dalmon, a small, white-locked, elfin poet, forgotten today. His verses had been printed in 'The Yellow Book', and he had achieved his 'collected poems'. He had been a friend since the '90's of Franklin Dyall, who appeared in the first production of *The Importance of Being Ernest*; and of Dyall's wife Mary Merrall. Dal, a fragile, feminine creature, lived in Ebury Street, in what might be called guardsmen's country: 'My *dear*', he once said to me, 'my ambition is to be *crushed* to death between the thighs of a guardsman!'

These amusing people were *fin de siècle*; and their emotional shape was as different from mine as mine from a womanizing stockbroker's. They were feminine, aesthetical, fussily elegant; my only womanish traits, I suppose, were the invisible femininity implicit in phallic worship and a pronounced talent for maternalism.

When I came to London I found a room at the top of Gower Street. It cost £1 a week, one-third of my income, but the house had one great advantage—the primary one sought, but so uneasily found, by every homosexual: it was what the Germans call *sturmfrei*—it was free of snoopers. It was the first abode of my *own* in the bottomless well of wickedness which I expected London to be; and the prolonged chastity of the Auden period, with the change from the Quaker innocence of Norwich to London's ineffable promise, had their quick reaction. The high-flying 'spiritual' emotionalism of the last year or two was replaced almost overnight by an insatiable hunger for downright carnal experience—a craving to *know* the physical secrets of as many boys as possible (this was the important delight, as it always has been: my own sensual enjoyment being of much smaller moment).

In that decade after the war 'picking up' was easy: the Embankment and the furtive arches of Charing Cross were peopled with wanderers of every age, and under the colonnades of Covent Garden rows of homeless boys slept. In my restless search—the eternal search, I suppose, for Corvo's 'divine friend, much desired'

—I even discovered a kind of hutment, put together with corrugated sheets in an alley by Savoy Hill, where the boys sheltered at night; and sometimes I'd creep in there, to spend fevered, flea-bitten hours. Once, for the excitement, I paid a shilling for a bed in a common lodging-house across the river in the Borough.

Across the landing in Gower Street lived Felicia Browne. This strange, strained girl, whose compulsive craving for immolation at last was gratified on the battlefield of Spain, had been at the Slade; she now lived in a lumber of paint and canvas, working in a tense way and sacrificing to those she chose to love what energy and money she had. Mental suffering with her was a habit; but the suffering of others, individual or on a social scale, was an injustice that drove her to fury; one felt she wanted to shoulder it all, and somehow atone for it. Our across-the-landing relations developed into affection; and a few years later, in Berlin, we became engaged to be married—though neither of us contemplated going to bed together. Twice I found her with her throat gashed with a razor, once in Gower Street, once in Berlin.

Auden came to see us in Gower Street; and a delightful young Slade student called Bill Coldstream, with whom some 15 years later I did an engaging pub-crawl round the alleys of St James's. Really nice people are sometimes given knighthoods.

At the Oxford and Cambridge Musical Club in Bedford Square I'd made friends with F. C. W. Hiley, a Keeper of Printed Books at the Museum. One evening I asked him where books with a 'decadent', 'ninetyish flavour, treating preferably of the 'love that dare not speak its name', might be found. After telephoning he said that C. S. Millard would be at home to us at 8 o'clock. I was excited over the possible discovery of interesting books, but felt no interest in the obscure bookseller I'd never heard of; and if I expected a furtive purveyor of semi-pornography, I was in for a shock.

The quality of 'greatness', I suppose, comes from the fusion of incorruptibility with *uniqueness*: a personality of such vivid singularity and a mind of such unbending integrity that anybody within their reach finds himself under a spell—feels himself in the presence of the unaccountable and the incomparable. It's got nothing to do with brain-power, or the creative force, or the manipulation of nations, or doing something better than anyone else; it's the power of a unique, immutable personality. Socrates was great; but he won no wars; his greatness was the privilege of those who met him.

Luckily for us, he was recorded. Winston Churchill would yet have been great, within the circle of his acquaintance, had he never entered public life or picked up a pen. Norman Douglas's greatness rose far above his writing. Samuel Butler was great, without reference to 'The Way of All Flesh'. Even dear Nina Hamnett remained incorruptibly unique, and in that sense 'great', long after alcohol had taken the paint out of her brushes.

But the denominator common to these people, besides a unique personality, is intellectual *honesty*, a courage of the mind that's uncompromising. There can be no spuriousness in greatness, no self-deception. That's why men like Corvo, and his dexterous biographer A. J. A. Symons—though the one had genius and the other the brilliance of neon-lighting—could never have been 'great': both were self-deceivers, each in his way was dishonest— the first because he was mad, the second because dishonesty flattered his vanity and paid some of his bills.

If these paragraphs are true, then Millard was great indeed. Mr Julian Symons, who never saw Millard, has chosen in his biography of his brother A.J.A. to call him 'disreputable'— presumably because he had been in prison twice for homosexual offences. Yet A.J.A., who knew Millard well and drew largely upon his vast literary and bibliographical knowledge, and who was lucky to pick his feline way safely over the impediments of the anti-fraud laws, himself writes of Millard in 'The Quest for Corvo' only with affectionate approbation. If anybody's reputation was unreputable it was Mr Julian Symons' brother's; whose 'phoneyness' was a byword in Bloomsbury in the 1920s. Even the assumption, after the launching of the Wine and Food Society, of an omniscient epicurism was factitious; A.J.A. was quick to learn from Mr André Simon, but sometimes he forgot himself: the pose of the connoisseur had become so habitual that once, in the Plough Inn in Little Russell Street, he was seen ceremoniously inhaling the bouquet of a glass of pub gin. On another day he horrified Millard by offering him for luncheon pheasant out of season. But A.J.A. atoned for his elaborate shams and dubious business principles by recognizing Millard's unique quality and by writing the excellent Corvo book.

On that evening I knew I had never before met a man so exciting. It was like climbing up Olympus and having drinks with one of the nicer gods. Lots of ordinary people are equipped with charm, an exactly fastidious mind, a grave and gently sardonic humour, an integrity so forthright that often it was crushingly plain-spoken—

but in Millard these values weren't ordinary; they were the magic of a personality bigger than full-size. He towered over ordinariness, and made little touchy, quarrelsome men like, say, D. H. Lawrence, look dwarfs.

He must have been flush that day, for he gave us whisky, not his favourite Val de Peñas which he bought in Manchester Square at 2s 2d a bottle; and as glass succeeded glass I plainly felt fascination turning to devotion—I was falling in love with a tall, gaunt, grey-headed man well over 50. I bought a couple of books, one of them Corvo's 'Stories Toto Told Me'; and when he saw us from his garden into Abercorn Place he tickled the palm of my hand and told me to come again.

The Bungalow at 8, Abercorn Place—which, like Millard's genius for finding the unique, must have been unique in London—is excellently described in the first chapter of 'The Quest for Corvo', as is C.S.M. himself. Nothing could have been invented to suit more perfectly his quaint, eremitical way of living; in this tiny un-urban oasis of solitude, out of sight and out of sound, his privacy, shared with the squirrel and tits he daily fed, was insulated against intrusion: yet when he felt like drinking, as he often did, some Bass-from-the-wood, or wanted to meet the few he admitted to his friendship, there were buses round the corner: the Bungalow was a country cottage in the middle of London.

He was the son of an Anglican vicar of Basingstoke; but became a Catholic while an undergraduate at Oxford, where he derived some wayward enjoyment from flaunting publicly his friendship with telegraph-boys. I imagine the attraction of Rome was largely emotional and aesthetic; as his later red-tie socialism was more an emotional protest against social injustice than adherence to the dogma of nationalization. His obedience to the Church wasn't very strict; I think he was too honest with himself to obey her formal commands without going the whole hog and renouncing the flesh and the devil, and he had no intention of doing that. He might have made a splendid monk; as he wasn't, he couldn't be a 'good' Catholic. But he died in the Church's arms: in the hospital of St John and St Elizabeth to which, I believe, he left the few hundred pounds the sale of his books realized.

Christopher seldom mentioned his imprisonments, but never tried to hide the fact of them; he regarded them as accidents which, having happened, no honest man would want to conceal. 'My first row', he would declaim in his deep, resonant, trenchant voice, regardless of the curious bowler-hatted looks from strangers at the bar—looks anyway drawn by his startling appearance: his great height increased by the grace and delicacy of his slim figure; a splendid head of thick greying curls, and long, mobile Augustan face; blue shirt and blood-red neckerchief, the inevitable haversack slung over one shoulder and shabby flannel trousers rolled up above his ankles.

He must have been the first person I knew who had been to prison; certainly for the offence which I was then repeatedly committing with rhapsodical fervour. The glamour of his imprisonment of course fortified the fascination he anyhow had for me; while his friendship and collaboration with Robert Ross, Oscar Wilde's closest friend, and the vast erudition in Wildeana that grew out of that intimacy, made him in my eyes O.W.'s earthly vicar. (Once he sent me some pyjamas that had belonged to Robbie Ross; I still recall the feeling of awe with which I put them on—as if they were an heirloom.) He was more than that: he seemed to link me personally with some of the fabulous figures of 19th century literature; it was at Abercorn Place that I met Henry Festing Jones, devoted companion of Samuel Butler and one of the 'three' in that mighty threnody, terrible with anguish, 'Out out into the night ...'; a clerkly little fellow to look at, I remember.

In a day or two I was at the Bungalow again; and stayed the night. Christopher showed me his classic bibliographies of Wilde and Claude Lovat Fraser; his 'Three Times Tried', on which the Peter Finch film 'The Trials of Oscar Wilde' was founded; the famous Corvo letters from Venice, dazzling exercises in literary depravity written in that exquisitely startling coloured script; his collection of O.W. letters and manuscripts; and talked wonderfully about the fun of literary and bibliographical detection. Next day was Saturday. 'I always lunch with Phyl and Boris on Saturday', he said in his soniferous positive voice; and went to the telephone. I heard those same mordant tones: 'I want to show you my new young man—he can even talk about *POEtry*!' He took me to the Plough in Little Russell Street, and I entered yet another new world: the mad, neurasthenic Bloomsbury of the 1920s.

Christopher was probably fonder of Boris and Phyl de Chroust-choff than of his other friends because they, in their odd ways, were as unique as he was in his. Boris's impregnable individualism and egoist probity put him—or rather, happily, *puts* him; for he and I are almost the only survivors of that bizarre, and mainly doomed, coterie—into my category of insulated 'greatness'; his genius lies in a sublime capacity for withdrawal from every facet of life that bores him, in an ability to do perfectly a number of, in the utilitarian sense, completely useless things, and in the intellectual storage of a vast amount of minutiae of knowledge which have no relation at all to the exigencies of a pecuniary world.

He wouldn't cross the road to 'make money'; but will bicycle for hours to discover in the Buckinghamshire woods a fungoid rarity or, on the Berkshire downs, a curious fossil or sherd. Nobody, probably, in England knows as much about the fungi of the world; about the coinages of antiquity; the raising of delicate Japanese seeds; the nature of herbs and spices; the intricacies of Chinese and Moorish cooking; the identification of incunabula; the geography and procedures of mountaineering; the exactitudes of language, classical and modern, academical or dialect; the anthropology and aesthetics of African carvings; the constituents of vodka and the characters of the French vintages; the flora and fauna of the Welsh mountains; the less frequented byways of literature, European and Russian; the regional gastronomies of France and Switzerland; the domestic habits of toads and the psychology of Siamese cats—of all these things, and others, Boris is a savant whose authority is honoured in their different spheres. Yet he has never written a line about any of them.

Cecil Gray, a music critic of the day and biographer of Philip Heseltine ('Peter Warlock'), wrote in his autobiography that Boris was the laziest man he had known 'except Norman Douglas'. This was unfair to both; unless he meant that neither would consent to 'work'. In fact, Boris is the busiest of people, ceaselessly employing his cognitive mind on these inutile interests; or his vigorous muscles in the growing of unusual plants. He was, and remains, a delightful and consummately civilized example of perfected egoism—the quiddity of uncompetitive singularity. So singular, indeed, that I've known him, after expending hours cooking a superb dinner for expected guests, throw the whole meal out of the window because the guests had lingered overlong at the pub. He is, of course, a personage straight out of the Russia of 'War and Peace'; and this, with his extraordinary mind and decorative personality, is why novelists were constantly using him as a character: D. H. Lawrence put him in 'Women in Love', Geoffrey Dennis, a contemporary at Oxford and a Hawthornden Prize-winner, portrayed him in an early novel called 'Harvest in Poland';

and Aldous Huxley too, I think, introduced him into some story.

Boris today, had there been no 1917 revolution, would have owned a huge estate in the Ukraine; and perhaps some of Nikita Kruschev's relations would have been among his dependants: for the Soviet Premier's homeland was also Little Russia and until 1860 serfs would often take the name of their lord. It's amusing to think that Mr K.'s grandfather may have been the henchman of Boris de Chroustchoff's. Boris, though, left Russia when he was ten to go to school in Switzerland, and then on to Harrow and Oxford; yet 60 years in England and western Europe haven't made him less of a Russian.

His first wife, sweet, drunken, doomed Phyl, was the eldest of the three astonishing Crocker sisters, children of an astonishing mother; but the incomparable Phyl—the 'Cornish pixie' Philip Heseltine, who wanted her to love him, called her in some verses— possessed, in addition to her dazzling elfin looks, some magical quality of spirit that seemed unearthly, something of the goblin world. Nobody who knew her escaped adoring her, and forgiving her folly; yet this supremely *lovable* creature, who ought to have been as immortal as a dryad, was doomed—like her own mother and one of her sisters, like so many of that circle of her adorers— to kill herself. Alcohol and some lunatic virus destroyed that unique family. '*I'll* give him a birthday present', Phyl telephoned a friend, of a man she later loved; and on the morning of his birthday he found her dead in the gas-filled kitchen. Her mother, Al Crocker, whose marble-white Giaconda beauty, great black sombrero and black cloak, gave her the eerie look of a witch, also went the way of the gas-oven; and Phyl's sister Joan hanged herself in the lavatory of a mental home. Laura Knight painted them all, I think.

Al Crocker's second husband, much younger than she, was Irving Davis, who ran the Museum Street branch of the book-shop Davis & Orioli, while Pino Orioli, first publisher of 'Lady Chatterley's Lover' and most of Norman Douglas's work, ran the Florentine branch. At that time Boris, rare books being among his pleasures, was working with Irving in Museum Street, and lived with Phyl round the corner in Bury Street where Douglas Garman, brother-in-law of Roy Campbell, also lived. Phyl's youngest sister Beth was A. J. A. Symons' amanuensis in the odd converted tabernacle in Little Russell Street where he double-entered the subscriptions to the First Edition Club, and later the Wine and

Food Society, and shaped his crafty projects; and thus this acre of Bloomsbury was something of a family domain.

For years our *sede sociale* was The Plough, where 'Roman' the potman, a decayed relict of the Romano family, kept our special table free of the bowler-hatted fraternity and where Phyl, through most of the hours of 'opening', held court; though there would be visits to Kleinfeld's, in Charlotte Street (nobody ever called it the Fitzroy in the days of old Mr Kleinfeld, with his Academie Française beard and German-Jewish kindliness); and sometimes to the Cadogan in Chelsea to see Augustus John.

That period, and our Plough group, were remarkable for the number of brilliant, and doomed, composers they contained: Philip Heseltine ('Peter Warlock'), who, one night in 1930, put his head in the gas-oven after carefully putting out the cat; Constant Lambert, then boyish and gay and still fresh from his successes with the Diaghelev Ballet, and Cecil Gray, long-faced and morose beneath his great black sombrero—both drank themselves to death; Jack Moeran, never sober but always pungent and good-humoured, who, drunk, fell into the sea near Dublin and was drowned; Bernard Van Dieren and John Goss—these two perhaps survived the stresses of those days.

We all drank too much; though not many of us were drunks. I suppose we did so because it was the fashion; as blue shirts and wide-brimmed hats were at that time fashionable bohemianisms; and perhaps it had something to do with what's called 'post-war'. But mostly we drank beer in pubs and wine in houses; only the rich, like Cecil Gray, burnt up their livers with whisky. I've seen Cecil, late at night, unable to stand—unable, even to sit; yet able, flat on the floor, to write his piece of musical criticism ('I remember', recounted Pope, 'Dr King would write verses in a tavern three hours after he could not speak').

Nina Hamnett was another, in her peculiarly wonderful way, unique person. She could, I suppose, have been a successful painter as well as a fine one; and her illustrations for Osbert Sitwell's extravaganza about the statues of London show how wittily she could draw. But she couldn't be bothered; she was too fully occupied by drinking and by the succession of young pugilists whom she took to her bosom and bed. 'Oh my dear,' she would exclaim, 'haven't you seen my new boxer? M' dear, he really has *dimensions.*' Walking together one day up the Tottenham Court Road, she stopped at the corner of Howland Street and pointed to a second-floor window. 'In that room,' she said, in her loud upper-class voice, 'Verlaine and Rimbaud lived together; and in that room, m' dear, I lost my virginity.' People had turned to look anyway; for she was an arresting sight, with her lank height, and long, scornful nose, her frayed crumpled clothes and spindly legs in wrinkled stockings; though she walked like a duchess, she looked like a tramp. Nina was easy enough to caricature, as Ethel Mannin unveraciously did in a novel called 'Ragged Banners'; it's less easy to portray the kindness and generosity and humanity that existed within that curious scarecrow frame.

In the 1940s, not long before her violent death, she was spending her afternoons in the Soho drinking 'clubs' which had started springing up; and one evening about nine o'clock I came upon her sitting forlornly and patiently on a wall at the bottom of Wardour Street. 'Nina, what *are* you doing here?' I asked. 'I'm waiting for them to *open*, m' dear', she answered with that glassily bland archness she acquired towards the end of the day; and as I led her to the nearest pub, she learned with surprise that 'they' had been open for more than three hours. She was killed when she fell from her upper window on the banks of the Regents Canal near the Harrow Road; some said it was suicide—but Nina would never commit suicide; as long as the pubs opened on time she was perfectly happy and a determined optimist, with the cheerful courage of her faith in life.

It was a period of elegant pornography; when elaborately exquisite editions, numbered and signed, of beautifully composed erotica were being put out, highly priced, by 'private presses' like John Rodker's Casanova Society or the Fanfrolico Press of Jack Lindsay, novelist and son of Norman Lindsay. Rodker, a sweet, sad poet—husband of novelist Mary Butts—whom a delicately resolute talent had raised from the slough of east-end Jewry, produced lordly volumes of oriental salacity done into the neat and witty English of Powys Mathers, a fat and galvanic man.

Eric Gill, who found no discordance between Catholicism and a comfortable bawdiness, referring in one of his letters to a book by Mathers for which he had done some engravings, wrote '. . . a fat man who lives in Lincoln's Inn Fields . . . "Red Wise" is very good and very naughty—I think it probable that Powys Mathers is the same . . .'

Mathers did live in Lincoln's Inn Fields, with his gifted wife Rosamund, and he was naughty; but he was also good, as writer and companion, and possessed a vast eclectic knowledge and mental ingenuity which made him the original 'Torquemada' of *The Observer*: he was the inventor of the 'intellectual' cross-word puzzle. He was a bellying, rubicund, bearded, guffawing farrago of conversational fireworks, and a mighty drinker of beer; who worked for preference lying in bed surrounded by beer-bottles. Now and then he would fall asleep with a burning cigarette in his mouth and wake to find the sheets smouldering. His output was tremendous, his writing always perfected—I suppose his great 'Thousand-and One Nights' is unequalled in wit and spirit and texture. I don't know how close he remained to his originals, which ranged from Chinese to Arabic; for his translation was all done from the French; but the result was *literature*.

Frieda Lawrence sometimes came to the Plough—D. H. Lawrence had been a friend, not a much-liked friend, of Irving and Boris. There were Frank Dobson, the sculptor; Dora Russell, one of Bertrand Russell's wives; John Somerfield, a left-wing novelist; Bill Empson, that very intellectual poet, who remained a friend for some years and, more than 20 years later, turned up in Tokyo one hectic day when I was there for the war in Korea; Edgell Rickword, also a poet and a co-founder of *Left Review*; Amyas Ross, collaborator in intellectual socialism with G. D. H. Cole, and briefly, before dying of an overdose of pills, a Labour Party politician and husband of Phyl's sister Joan Crocker; Roy Campbell, declamatory and quarrelsome; yet another poet, Harold Monro, a charming drunk and bookseller near the Museum, whose verses about a cat have remained in most anthologies; and Charles Ashleigh, one of my closest and kindest of friends—as a boy of 17 he had somehow become a hobo in America, a convict in Leavenworth for I.W.W. sedition, had published a novel, and was a delightful singer of hobo songs. Like me, Charles was a natural rebel; after 1933, when I came back from Berlin, he and I were associates in the anti-fascist cause.

It was into this fervid and poignant world that I came that Saturday when Millard took me down to the Plough to meet Phyl and Boris. Soon I was discovering, hardly credulous, that nearly all these people were wholly indifferent to one's foibles or vices; nobody seemed to be shocked or disgusted by anybody's unorthodox appetites; one was required only to be amusing, or at least not a bore, and morally and mentally *honest*. The social offences were dullness and sham.

Millard's hatred of the spurious or tawdry was aggressively proclaimed; he didn't believe in euphemism. He detested badly kept beer, imported meat, 'shop' eggs, airless bars, unopened windows, women who showed their armpits or made up their complexions in public; he liked good wine but despised the unctuous affectations of self-appointed arbiters like A. J. A. Symons—as he despised, too, Symons' concern to be thought a Gentile; he loathed pretentiousness and posturing and the slipshod. What he disapproved of, he proclaimed. Once, in a restaurant, when a woman at a neighbouring table produced the implements out of her vanity bag and began to re-embalm her face, Millard called loudly, in his booming, eloquent voice: 'Waiter, bring me a tooth-mug and a basin—I want to clean my teeth!' Entering a stuffy room, he would make a great fuss of gasping and fanning himself: 'Why can't they open the WINDOWS?' he would boom severely at his host or hostess. Yet no sweeter, kinder nature existed; and the spell of his smile was binding. How he would have loathed the falsities of this age of plastics and television and pressurized beer. . . .

With him I used sometimes to meet Symons, then pursuing the quest for Corvo. Christopher wasn't taken in by the young man's suave effronteries, and described him bluntly as a charlatan. But I've wondered whether he wasn't taken in sometimes by Symons' wiliness in finance. Millard himself was so stubbornly honest, preferring to do without a profit rather than make an unfair one, that he assumed honesty in others—even though he operated in that keenest of markets, the rare book trade. Symons, in 'The Quest for Corvo', says he sold the V ice letters to Maundy Gregory for £150—'exactly six times what I had paid poor Millard for them.' But did he ever pay poor Millard that £25? Christopher more than once in 1926 and 1927 said that he was uneasy about these commercially precious letters, which he had lent to Symons for the purposes of the book he was working on; but also because, he told me, Symons had said he thought he could find a buyer for them. But up to his death in November 1927, Millard never told me that Symons had himself bought and paid for them; and by the time Symons' account of this transaction was published, Millard had been dead seven years.

In those middle years of the 1920s I was pursuing a course of blatant wildness: the unceasing search for the 'divine friend, much desired', which, as every paederast must know, imposes a hunger for fresh experiences that's sated only when the 'right' person has been found. This brought me precarious moments. I'd made friends with two page-boys at the old Monico, and provoked the jealousy of a third (there's no jealousy so bitter as a 15-year-old boy's). I used often to go into the Monico for a drink and a word with Dick or Taffy; and one evening found Cecil Gray sitting there in his wide black hat, sombrely nodding over a large whisky-and-soda. Scarcely had I joined him with a drink, when the uniformed doorman came menacingly up: I was to leave the bar and not show myself in it again—the page-boy I'd offended had 'narked'. Gray was charmingly unabashed. 'Well, my dear man,' he said in his queer high-pitched croon, 'if you go in for this eccentricity, you must accept its inconveniences.' The shock of this occurrence was painful and frightening; but I'd come a long way in experience since that moment of panic on the Serpentine shore a few years before. I was getting used to the perils of my temperament.

Dick and Taffy, I vividly remember, were the companions of a specially saturnalian evening when a certain friend and I took them to a Bloomsbury basement room and poured red wine over their white, bare bodies. . . .

And then Millard died; which meant that a vital component of my life had dropped out and couldn't be replaced.

BUT BEFORE HE died, I had one golden interlude with him on the Upper River, the 'stripling Thames': towing up from Oxford until, towards Cricklade, the water barely covered its stony bed; and sailing down with the stream; camping for the night at enchanted places like Lechlade, Kelmscott, Cumnor, the Old Rose Revived at Newbridge.... The last time he had cruised this magically leisured course, along which he knew every lock, reach and tavern, his companion had been Charles Scott Moncrieff, translator of Proust. But this was a third of a century ago and more: today, as I painfully found when revisiting some of the spots on which the image of Millard is graven, the egregious petrol-engine and caravan is everywhere; the tiny, bemused, stone inns where we replenished our beer-jar have been dolled up with 'car parks' and 'cocktail stools', and fleshy females and their flaunting city swains loll under striped umbrellas where we pitched our secret tent.

That was in 1927; through the summer before and over the Christmas of 1926 I had two sojourns in France and a number of happy walking excursions with Phyl and Boris and sometimes Millard—excursions, for instance, to John Fothergill's Spread Eagle at Thame.

During the General Strike of 1926, I combined my evening's drinking with 'work' for the strikers' cause; Millard, carrying his red flag, and I and Amyas Ross, then parliamentary candidate for St Marylebone (where C.S.M. was secretary to the local Labour Party), set out each evening about opening time carrying bundles of the *British Worker*, the strikers' answer to Winston Churchill's *British Gazette*, which we hawked in the bars, clubs and restaurants around Soho and Piccadilly Circus—smart places like Scotts, and 'fast' ones like the Hambone. We had drunk enough beer to drown the insults and rebuffs we got in such strongholds of law and order; but I recall one nasty quarter-of-an-hour in the old Hambone Club, in Ham Yard: a haunt of well-dressed drunks and, just then, of those volunteer strike-breakers, wearing the armlet of Authority, who, I don't doubt, later became Mosley's storm-troops. In the Hambone, at the top of a steep and winding stone stairway, we were set on by a group of these: I can clearly see three of them trying to crack Amyas's leg across a chair. I'm useless in a fight, being numbed by violence, and Millard was getting on for 60; but Ross, who was young and strong, managed with our small help to extricate himself, and we were tumbled down the steps. I've often narrated this story when assured, later, that deliberate cruelty of the Fascist-Nazi sort was un-English and couldn't happen in this country; or when, as in Cyprus indignant denials of British police brutality are issued.

For some weeks on both sides of that Christmas I was walking through Provence or living in the scented hills above Toulon, where the flesh of the thrushes and wild rabbits is flavoured with the perfume of the mountain herbs they live among. Long before this I'd left *By the Way*; and don't know how I'd scratched a living in the meanwhile—I remember being given jobs of 'research' and copying in the Museum Library. Now, on the pretext of 'writing' within sight of the Mediterranean, I'd persuaded my long-suffering mother to let me have some money, a pound a week, on which I lived agreeably on wine and small birds.

Millard wrote: '. . . I have spent most of my time transcribing from Corvo's amazing manuscript his unpublished novel "The Desire and Pursuit of the Whole". . . . I sent you a copy of my Methuen v. Millard pamphlet, so I hope your brother will send it on, if you are still on writing terms with him. Shall look out for you on the feast of purification of our Blessed Lady . . . by which time flowers ought to appear in the earth and the voice of the turtle to be heard in our land.'

The 'Methuen v. Millard pamphlet' referred to the libel action brought against Christopher after he had described in his catalogue a forgery called 'For Love of the King' and included by Methuen's among the collected works of Oscar Wilde as having been 'foisted on the public' as a Wilde play. The case was heard by Mr Justice McCardie in November 1926 and Millard of course lost and had to pay £100 damages; but he gained his point—he proved that the play *was* a forgery, though to do so he had deliberately to libel the publishers. Since the death of Robbie Ross, he had been the guardian of Wilde's literary reputation, and his integrity wouldn't allow him to rest until he had publicly shown that Wilde didn't write this inferior play. In 1925 he had done his utmost to goad the culprit, an adventuress called Mrs. Chan Toon or Mrs Wodehouse Pearse, to bring an action against him for accusing her, in the Press and elsewhere, of forging a number of 'Wilde' letters and verses which she was selling where she could; he had written libellously to Walter Hutchinson, who had first printed 'For Love of the King in *Hutchinson's Magazine*. Finally, he forced the Methuen action by the calculated use of the word 'foisted.'

It was the last of the Oscar Wilde trials and libel cases—distinguished though, by the absence of Lord Alfred Douglas. I never met him; he moved in different fields when, as a boy, I'd known his brother Queensberry and nephew Cecil; and now he and C.S.M. were in opposing camps: Robbie Ross and Alfred Douglas had loathed each other, and Christopher was Ross's devoted friend.

In 1927, after Millard's death, I got myself a job at the Clarendon Press where the Printer to the University, John Johnson, asked me to edit the house magazine and teach English to the apprentices in between 'reading' Goethe's letters and the prose of Paul Valéry.

My principal memories of Oxford are summer ones: of Long Bridges, sylvan and sunlit, the 'town' bathing place along the tow-path from Folly Bridge, where bare wet bodies dived and darted and Robert Dundas of Christ Church, that massive and renowned don, lay on the grass like a contemplative walrus and appraised the scampering urchins around him.

Dundas was one of those Oxford 'characters' famous for foibles and idiosyncracies; and famous for his curt, downright remarks uttered in the jerky, high-pitched contralto that was made to be mimicked. One day, when Wystan Auden was up at the House, Dundas sent for him. 'Oh, Auden—' the great man snapped. 'I wanted to tell you—I can't be your tutor any longer. You see, I'm in love with you—. *Good* morning!' Once, when I was with him at Long Bridges, lying beside parallel bars that had just been installed, he roused himself from his Olympian lethargy to say: 'I presented this gymnastic apparatus to the municipality'; and added curtly, gazing up from ground level at the naked acrobatics going on above: 'Very good investment, don't you think?'

For as long as civic memory went back, men and boys at the 'town' bathing places, like members of the University at Parson's Pleasure, had worn nothing at all; it was an Oxford tradition—a tradition which old Dundas (he must then have been in his late 50s) was mightily concerned to preserve. At Long Bridges he was down like a ton of bricks on the slightest little playful masturbatory frolic among the boys; and when, on the green sward of that lovely tree-encircled backwater, I appeared with my camera and told him I had discovered a 'new vice'--taking photographs with the camera apparently pointing in one direction, while in fact the lense was eyeing another—he went back to his rooms and wrote me a four-sheet letter of close, small handwriting beginning, 'I'm very worried about your "new vice" ': full of grave concern lest the smallest ammunition should be supplied to the reformist assailants of this tradition in the City Council—who, it seemed, were led by the principal drapers and haberdashers of the town. There can have been no other town in England where it was practically impossible to sell a bathing-slip or 'costume'; and to remedy the absence of this market, the aldermanic gents' outfitters were raising the cry of 'decency'. They won, and Dundas lost; and by the time I revisited Oxford in 1941, summoned there by the branch of the War Office that was planning an assault on the coast of Morocco, the verdant candour of Long Bridges had been defiled by rows of bathing-boxes and the place given over to the sexual swagger and simpering prurience of mixed bathing. Presumably 'swim-wear', male and female, sold briskly.

I'd been at the Clarendon Press a few months when I threw the job up and went to Berlin. Felicia Browne, whose devotion to me was deeper and more constant than mine for her, wrote from there begging me to join her; and I, fired less by the pleasure of being with her than by fantasies of prodigious adventure in Central Europe, jumped at the proposal although financially it was lunatic. We were, though, my selfishness notwithstanding, genuinely bound to each other by a wonderful sympathy and, too, by that terrible night when I had gone into her studio in Gower Street and found her slumped on the floor with her throat cut. I remember how she looked up at me with dim, sad, apologetic eyes through her round owlish spectacles; and how I thought, with so much ghastly blood, she must be dying. I rushed out to University College Hospital, fortunately in the same street. My urgent task, when they told me the wound looked worse than it was, was to stop the thing reaching the police. The doctors and the almoner were endearingly understanding; I don't know what claim the Law has to the secrets of a hospital, but no police ever did appear upon our scene.

Somehow I got together £25 and crossed to the Hook of Holland.

## 11

A HUNDRED YEARS ago Thackeray wrote: 'We arrive at places now, but we travel no more.' Yet 30 years ago a train journey across Europe was still an adventure. Ordinary people didn't travel to Berlin, which remained a remote, rather frightening and scandalous city, lying far towards the unknown wastes of Russia; ordinary people didn't travel at all—'going abroad' was the privilege of the well-to-do and leisured, the 'official classes', and un-ordinary paupers like myself and the layabouts of Montparnasse.

As almost always in a new country, especially one whose language I don't know, I loathed Berlin for the first week; and then suddenly, like one of those tiresome screw-tops on bottles that refuse to engage, I found the thread. Suddenly I saw that it was the most exciting town one could conceive of: Babylon, Gomorrah, Rome in decay; and yet galvanic with an intellectual liveliness as bright as the grandiose flood-lighting of *Berlin im Licht*, then just inaugurated. On the one hand, all the *boue* that one nostalgic for it could desire—squalor, drunkenness, penury, an ubiquitous underworld, dramatic violence and despair, the turbulence of gangster politics, the whole spectrum of sexual lust, with some unimagined hues added, displayed like fruits in an open Mediterranean market-place; on the other, a novel flowering—as if rain had fallen after a long drought—of architecture, the theatre, music, satire—a new liberty of ideas, a wonderful release of the individual. Of course, within five years all this exploring spirit was crushed—less, perhaps, by Hitler than by its own libertarian blindness which allowed Hitler to pinion it from behind. Except for Tokyo, Berlin must have been the world's ugliest town, though the new architecture was decorating its periphery with gay, thought-out dwellings which for the first time recognized that light and air were constituents of living. Yet one forgot the hideousness of the streets in their unfailingly provocative excitement: one *knew* that adventure—intellectual, political, sensual—lay round every corner; and there was beauty in the ugliness—the sort of beauty that Georg Grosz drew in his bitter, harrowing satires.

Felicia and I, in the evenings, haunted the Staatsoper or the Kroll, or concert-rooms where new writers like Hindermith and Schönberg were being played: we went to the Volksbühne in the Bülowplatz which was putting on, in superb and novel productions, serious plays of a sexual audacity that would have shocked London for the next 25 years. In the daytime Felicia painted with stubborn absorption; while I surged through the thrilling streets, gloating over the notorious Münzstrasse off the 'Alex', and fascinated by the discovery of a turning from it where a man who wanted a pregnant woman could at any time find just that (I hadn't known until then that there *was* a demand for pregnant women); or I would spend hours at Magnus Hirschfeld's *Institut der Sexual-wissenschaft*, whose unique library was the first victim of Hitler's *auto-da-fé*. I found that the homosexual traffic of the streets began about 9 a.m., the *Strichjungen* hanging about outside (or inside) the best-known men's lavatories, or idling through the famous Passage, the arcade that ran diagonally into Unter den Linden from the Friedrichstrasse; and that almost any street in Central Berlin had its sprinkling of *Stundenhotels* or *Absteige*—small discreet hotels or private flats where a room could be used for an hour or less. An astonishing number of seemingly respectable spinsters and widows, and of dignified elderly men who before inflation may have been living on dividends, let their spare rooms for this purpose, charging M.2.50 for a brief stay and having a working arrangement with a small string of boys who thus knew where to take their transient clients.

I discovered, too, the amazing tolerance of Berlin; the people generally accepted as a human fact, even though many deplored, conduct which in England would have raised cries of horror or menace. Once a policeman appeared when I was having difficulty with an offensive youth whom I couldn't shake off. 'You know,' said the policeman kindly, 'you should be very careful about what boys you pick up—there are some bad ones about.' I had a Swiss friend whom I'll call B——:*a senior functionary in one of the international organizations in Geneva. He kept going a *pied-à-terre* in Berlin; and there one morning, he told me later, he found on his doorstep when he answered the whirr of his bell a well-dressed man in a Homburg hat and carrying the inevitable briefcase. '*Herr B——?*' said the stranger: '*Jawohl*', answered B—— inquiringly.

'I believe you're a friend of a boy named——?' the man went on.
B—— was taken aback; but the visitor hastened to put him at his
ease. 'Oh, it's all right,' he said. 'I just came to call—I always like
to know what sort of man my son is going with.' That was Berlin
in the years that I knew it, between 1928 and 1933.

There must be people who believe that Hitlerism was a stern
reaction to this 'German decadence', or alternatively regard the
Nazi Party itself as a foul edifice of degeneracy—in either case
blaming Germany's blatant homosexuality for the Hitler tyranny.
But both assumptions are false.

Hitler didn't, morally, care tuppence about homosexuality; in
the early years of his power he tried, so to speak, to cover it over
with a clean cloth just as he tried to deny poverty by pushing its
more public signs, like beggars and street musicians, out of public
sight. But politically he used homosexuality, like anything else,
wherever it fitted expediency. Ernst Röhm wasn't shot because the
Nazy Party felt outraged by the abrupt discovery that he was
'having' his Storm Troopers—that had been known for ages; but
because his sway over the S.A. had become a menace to Hitler.
In the Hitler Youth the 'dear love of comrades' was evilly turned
to a political end.

And if the Nazi hierarchy was well larded with homosexuals so
was Wilhelm II's court and so was the Weimar Republic. The
'German decadence' wasn't a national trauma left like a scar by
1918; and it wasn't, I suppose, the invention of Frederick the
Great and Voltaire. If it's a decadence, it's been decaying for a
very long time.


And then I met Werner.[*] I had, of course, surveyed the city's
swimming-baths; and most afternoons was going to those in the
Bärwaldstrasse, somewhere in the wilderness beyond Hallesches
Tor. And there one day, naked beneath the showers, I found the
most startlingly beautiful person I'd ever seen: a living, and lively,
Beardsley decoration for 'Salome'—he might have been the original
Beardsley prototype, except that he was an improvement on the
artist's invention. He had all the Beardsley sin, but none of the
corruption; all the grace and *uniqueness*, but without the epicene
languour. His was the face Beardsley would have drawn, had he not
been dying of consumption. Ivory-white skin, parchment-pale, with
a fervent scarlet mouth and huge sable eyes, full of black fire; a mass
of romping black hair, thick and lively as a bear's, and the figure of

a Gemito fisherboy. To Beardsley he added something of the della Robbia choristers in Florence and a great deal of the famous 'Tripod' satyrs in the Naples Museum. It didn't surprise me to find that this face had been chosen from all over Germany to go on the cover of the magazine published by the Socialist Labour Youth —whose blue blouse and red scarf he wore.

But, I quickly found, it wasn't only his face that was intoxicating; it was a glittering personality and the incomparable *friendship* that he gave—in his magic company differences of age, culture, language, vanished: he made me his equal and partner. *Was ist mein ist Dein*, he pronounced early on; and that remained his rule for the next few years—what was his was mine: he would share, when I was broke, his last cigarettes; and gave to the last drop his love and loyalty. I had found at last the 'divine friend much desired'; if one of us was faithless it was I—never he.

Before I knew what was happening, that first day, I'd been swept on to the back of his bicycle and was whirling down the Friedrich-strasse—to a *schwules Lokal*, one of those 'queer' bars whose discreetly blacked-out façades and sombrely curtained doorways proclaimed out loud their nature, where we drank cognac. He was not quite 15. Then, from the homosexual bar, he bicycled me back to his home in the Zimmerstrasse and introduced me to his mother.

We must have been an astonishing sight, Werner and I: roistering round Berlin with our arms round each other's necks; both with long bare legs and open necks; singing *Wanderlieder* or socialist songs, drinking a great deal, embracing and spooning in public places and generally behaving outrageously—I skinnily ugly and 30 years old; he dazzling in looks, with that astonishing head and face in which the angelic and the demonic were tantalisingly blended.

We camped one summer on the edge of the Uedersee, beyond Eberswalde, where Social-Democrat families in the nude bathed and basked at one end of the lake, and Communists at the other; we walked one snowing winter in the Kalkberge, staying in village inns and leaving the peasants gaping at Werner's vivid narration of invented adventures; when we had no money we went on the tramp, getting food and cigarettes where we could and sleeping in barns or under forest. In Berlin we swam and sang, and drank beer in Socialist or Communist *Kneipen*; and later—this must have been in 1931-32 when Berlin's political conflict was at its fiercest—we together joined 'Fichte', the Communist sports organization, and on Friday evenings bathed in the splendid Gartenstrasse swimming pool which 'Fichte' hired weekly so that its members, young men and women, boys and girls of all ages, could be healthily naked together. The cult of *Nacktbaden* was one of the first expressions of the libertarian bent to be suppressed by Hitler.

And in Berlin we together went the rounds of the 'queer' bars— more, as London's 'camp' young men would say, 'for a giggle' than for a pick-up. There were dozens of places like the *Nüremberger Diele* and *Kantdiele* where middle-aged stockbrokers danced with elegant pansies. But we enjoyed the more specialized resorts like the *Schnurbart Diele*, as it was nicknamed—the 'moustache café'— where men with magnificent moustaches went to meet other men with moustaches. 'I've got a bigger one than yours', one would say to a new acquaintance—meaning, at any rate in the first place, his moustache. There was the 'Mikado' in the Krausenstrasse, a transvestin joint where the men in female 'drag' punctiliously used the lavatory labelled *Damen*, and the masculine women in suits that marked *Herren*; and a place devoted to plump, elderly men who came in little short knickers and sailor suits; and the 'Monte-Casino' at Hallesches Tor, owned by a kind-hearted quean who had built up a team of obliging boys in their 'teens. But the place I liked best—because, I suppose, it was so touching, and tore at my mother's heart—was the 'Adonis-Diele', where farouche yearning boys slumped for hours at the tables, long, yellow hair falling into their eyes and their most urgent desire a pull at a cigarette. Each time the curtains at the door were pushed apart, all eyes would turn to the new customer, each face hungry to be chosen—to be given a cigarette, some beer and *Bockwurst* and, later, a bed to sleep in. These weren't professionally 'on the game' —they would have been elsewhere had they been that; they were just unhappy, homeless boys. I confess that when Werner was much older, and that early frenzy for him had inevitably sobered to serene friendship, I visited the Adonis-Diele pretty often.

But all this covered several years—to July 1933—and two or three returns to Berlin. I can't remember now, in that winter of 1928, how I scraped together a living; of the English lessons I gave, I recall chiefly the failure of some pupils to pay and Werner's anxiety until assured that I was teaching not schoolboys but men old enough to be my own father. I expect I harried my poor mother for subsidies; and I ate frequently with Felicia when she had her own studio, and sometimes stayed there. She had been ill, mentally ill, through those months—the nearest to downright 'mad' I had known her; and once again I'd found her lying in her own blood. It was mainly because of this illness, I think, that we became engaged to marry—though neither of us intended our marriage to be consummated: we believed that this sort of formalized relationship might provide her with something to hang on to emotionally, like a strap in a tube-train. But the formality, of course, wasn't enough; and when I in my selfish way left her alone to go rampaging round with Werner her inner torments increased—she had always known, obviously, and accepted with perfect understanding, my love for boys; yet the presence of Werner made her grin with mute pain. I was to blame: when Felicia needed an emotional strap to catch hold of, I gave her the illusion of one; but to have renounced Werner I would have needed a character a hundred times nobler and stronger than mine. I wasn't noble; and I loved Werner.

Meanwhile my blunderings were sowing more distress for my continually martyred mother. When I wrote to her about the engagement her relief and happiness were unbounded; and she sent me one of her diamond rings to be given to Felicia—a ring, I'm ashamed to say, which came in very usefully, indeed providentially, when we found ourselves stony broke and compelled to make for London. So, when the engagement fell apart almost as quickly as it was made, my mother could only worry about me more than ever; and regret, too, the loss of a diamond ring.

In the new year of 1929 I was back at the Clarendon Press; but by March was away again—to Geneva, where I had found a job in the International Labour Office, a job most men would have coveted, with good pay, little work, diplomatic privileges and that halo of superior smugness which the international functionaries of Geneva at that time liked to wear: the job of my lifetime, promising a fine pension after 30 years of gentle tedium. But I didn't look at it like that; to me it was a step on the way back to Berlin and Werner.

I stayed 18 months in Geneva; and during them rushed to Berlin whenever a week's or month's holiday allowed. And in 1930, soon after I'd been 'confirmed' in my appointment by Albert Thomas, I resigned from the Bureau; collected a month's pay and the money I'd put into a pension fund, and left for the Zimmerstrasse.

By now my German was good. I'd been studying it since 1928, and in Geneva, I'd taken lessons; and it was a language, I found, which like learning to ride a bicycle suddenly came to me with a rush. So, to earn money, I looked round for a book to translate; and persuaded Allen & Unwin to publish a book called *Youth in Soviet Russia*. This was the first of six books which I did into English from German and had published in the early 1930s: all left wing or anti-Nazi.

In the summer of 1932 I was camping on the Uedersee; Werner, then an errand-boy in Berlin, joined me for week-ends. The terrifying Nazi tide had almost reached high-water mark; but here, in the benign peace of that silent lake and its pine-clad dunes, the nightly battles of the streets, the outrageous strut of high boots, the unrelenting rant of Nazi propaganda were far, far away—too far: for here their horrors were diluted by distance; and the bland, negative quiescence of the basking Social Democrats I was living amongst seemed frighteningly ominous: I got the idea that Hitler, already blessed tacitly by the propertied classes, could safely count on the lassitude of the rest.

The ordinary people I knew—wage-earners, unemployed, little artisans, door-to-door hawkers, people employed in 'vice'—loathed Hitler and the Nazis; but the antagonism of most went no further than their private conversation and half of these quickly changed sides after January 1933. (I remember particularly a mettlesome fantasist aged 17 who, habitually vaunting the insignia of a communist Red-Front Fighter, appeared overnight in the full fig of a Nazi Storm Trooper. But that pathetic youth was scarcely a political factor; it was the turncoat timidity of the liberal multitude that let Hitler in.)

The Communists of Malaya, when they started their terrorist rebellion in 1948, were powerful in numbers and rich in sympathy because the Overseas Chinese in South East Asia had seen that the sole group which *did* anything during the Japanese occupation against the hated Japanese was the Communist group. That's why I joined the Communist Party of Germany in 1932; and why so many emotional anti-fascists in England, though they weren't really Communists at all, were drawn to the British Party between 1933 and '39. I'd read the first volume of *Das Kapital* in German, but it was written for less woolly intellects than mine—the *Manifesto* I'd found noble and inspiriting. I was 'emotionally' a pinkish socialist with a sentimental affection for camp-fires, *Volkslieder*, libertarian nudity and fine phrases like 'workers of the world unite' (though I detested organized unity as much as organized games, and didn't much like workers). I was spiritually dismayed by Communist 'discipline' and frightened by the ruthlessness I already discerned in 'the Party'; but my hatred of the Nazis, the disgust I felt for their obscene physical *power*—a bodily, bilious disgust like that aroused by the eating of raw fish in Japan—sent me to it because nowhere else was anything being *done* against the horror that was disgusting me.

My first step towards 'the Party' was taken on Uedersee; I moved down the lake and pitched my tent beside the lean and tempered Communists (as I chose to see them), leaving the Social Democrats to their often obese complacency.

Then, that summer, came the von Papen *Putsch*: and the road was open to Hitler's Brown dupes and their pistols. Even on the Uedersee we seemed to hear the march of the arrogant boots; the shining blue sky suddenly became ugly with threat; rumour reached us that the Nazis planned an attack on the lake's encampments.

It hadn't cost me much thought to perceive, by now, that Hitler wasn't just Germany's venom: that when, as he must now, he secured *power* the world beyond Germany would have to swallow him too. From the Uedersee I posted to the *New Statesman* an article describing what National-Socialism, seen close up, looked like. The *New Statesman* didn't print it; and I concluded that England, even left-wing England, wasn't much interested then in what eight years later was nearly to destroy her.

I was proud of my 'Party card'; it gave one a pleasantly esoteric feeling, as if one belonged to an élite entrusted with great secrets. It made me feel that I'd become part of a mighty force that could save the ordinary people from their own political futility. Yet I can't recall that our Zimmerstrasse 'cell', which met in the back room of a beerhouse, did much. Mostly we discussed; and learned our duties for the day, inevitably soon, when the Party would submerge into 'illegality'. My task was to be the sly performance of liaison between our scattered members and some secret centre—I was to meet people at street corners and deliver messages out of the corner of my mouth.

There weren't more than six of us—I remember a gaunt, sombre young Jew of the clerkly class, coldly charming but so solemnly intent on his own communist soul that it was impossible to get a smile out of him—he was like someone permanently in church; and a tiny, wizened, ascetic Parisian who chanced to play a vital part in this small segment of my life.

This Frenchman, whose mind was as nimble as a squirrel, was our theorist and dialectician; he endlessly lectured and explained, fascinated by his own didactic flow, reverently effusive over the dogmas of Marxism and its sacraments—the mystique of 'the Party' and the sacrifice of a Purge; almost visibly he seemed to make the sign of the hammer-and-sickle at the name of Lenin and to turn towards Highgate at that of Marx. He expounded the Early Fathers—the German philosophers and the French reformists—as theologians expound St Paul; and implored us to use Engels for bedside meditations. With the fire of faith in his hollow eyes and a lifeless skin drawn tightly over the sharp bones of his face, he ought, I felt, to be wearing a hair-shirt. But I couldn't see how all this helped to halt the Nazis; I felt we ought somehow to be goading the ordinary people into an avalanche of massive resistance.

But this odd Marxist mystic was agreeable and kind when out of the pulpit. He worked as a translator in the great publishing firm of Scherl, whose head was Hugenberg, leader of the German-National Party and its private militia, the 'Steel Helmets'; because Hitler, before absorbing these people, needed their alliance, Hugenberg was made briefly a Minister in the first Hitler cabinet. This fact proved valuable to me; the Frenchman got me into Scherl and when, after January 1933, I was arrested by Storm Troopers, the name of Hugenberg magically set me free.

Our work at Scherl was the production of English and French versions of a monthly magazine about industrial machinery. I remember my interview with the dapper, fat-fingered director in charge of this department. He was suspicious of me: in the first place, my German, though fluent, was 'Berliner'—I spoke the 'cockney' of my friends and slum associates, saying 'Icke' for 'Ich' and 'jehen' instead of gehen; in the second, he didn't like my name. 'Na also, Herr DavidSOHN,' he said pointedly, 'Sie sind ja der jüdischen Konfession, nich' wahr?' I told him that Davidson was Scottish and un-Hebrew, but he wasn't happy: every German name ending in sohn was Jewish—surely it must be the same in England? However, he hired me with some distaste; and Scherl then possessed two alien Communists hidden in its pay-roll.

I suppose, after that hideous January's end in 1933, we who loved Germany and loathed Hitler must have felt some of the nightmare anguish of the French in 1940. For us it was the Fall of

Berlin; the city was occupied by an enemy as hateful as any alien invader.

Overnight the streets seemed to have turned Nazi; overnight the air, which before had been soft and warm and human, had become harsh and malignant. Strutting police officers wearing swords flaunted their *Hakenkreuz* armbands—the thing had incredibly been transformed into the badge of Germany. The streets were brown with clumping S.A. free now to bully and chivvy and show their *power*—soon they were picketing the doorways of Jewish shops like Wertheim.

Soon young men one knew, or the sons of one's weeping neighbours, were being manhandled out of their homes—some never to be seen again; others crawling back in two or three weeks with their faces beaten out of recognition. Other people, one knew, little shopkeepers perhaps, began gingerly hanging out small modest Nazi flags, as an insurance. 'Ach, Mensch,' they'd say apologetically, 'wat denn soll man tun. So is' det Leben, nich'?' Life was like that, they said—what was a fellow to do?

The streets were scarlet with Nazi flags—odd, I thought, how *emotional* colour can be: the red flags of the Left had been friendly, enlivening, red like wine or cherries; now this Nazi red seemed the blood of one's friends. The S.A. marched and marched and the martial drums beat on one's mind like sticks. Ceaselessly, maddeningly, like a Chinese torture, the loudspeakers blared at every street corner—the interminable *Die Strasse frei* . . . of the 'Horst Wessel Lied', sickeningly beautiful as a deadly snake. Each day one awoke to the same terrible chorus of brutality, cynicism and hypocrisy: designed to bring under the Nazi power by bludgeoning or romantic blandishment the young men and boys and groom them for death —as fighting cocks in Bali are groomed for the pit. Fortunately for one's sanity the unending clamour became meaningless with time; but the effect dug deep; and the full nausea of those weeks came back to me recently in Sicily when I saw, still unexpunged, the big black stencilled letters of one of Mussolini's ubiquitous maxims across a house-front in Messina: DYING IS NOT DEATH, WHEN IT IS FOR ITALY THAT ONE DIES. I hope, for his sake, that the Duce remembered that comforting adage when he was hanged upside down by the mob: certainly it was for Italy that he *died*.

A monotony of *fear* hung like a pall of smoke over the loveliness of that spring and early summer—at the sound of tramping boots one braced oneself for a blow; the sudden whirr of the door-bell stopped one's heart. Yet in spite of the hideous things that were happening, I was still enjoying life—which was why I didn't take the obvious course of leaving Germany while I could. There was Werner: he was almost grown-up by now, and the intoxication of our earlier years had sobered into a friendship of a quite different, but still wonderful, kind. I had a comfortable job which, though in the service of the heavy industrialists who had carefully fanned Hitler's sulphurous flame, had nothing to do with Nazism. And I still loved Berlin; where, in the early months of 1933, adventure was still abundant.

Because I didn't want to implicate Werner's family in the Communist conspiracy which might at any moment land me in trouble, I'd left the Zimmerstrasse and was sharing a flat near the Bülowplatz with a scholarly fellow-traveller. There was a *Kneipe* near where, in the evenings, a group of us met to drink beer, eat *Bockwurst*, and lament our situation—the Party's leaders had been swept away, the organization had collapsed of itself, and such cautious gatherings as ours were all that was left of communist cohesion. The pub was well-known as a 'Red local'; and the landlord, a courageous man with an engaging charm, was on our side—it was this charm, and the name of Hugenberg, that one March evening saved, perhaps, my life.

The tables along each side of the narrow bar were full. I was sitting with Walli, a sensible woman I liked and the aunt (though she didn't then know it) of my new little love, Kurt. It was Saturday, I think, and the *Stimmung* of the place was almost light-hearted.

Suddenly the curtains from the street were pushed aside and half-a-dozen Brownshirts marched in, pistols in their hands and boots thumping on the bare floor. At once there was a thunderous silence; we watched, and held our breath. They ranged themselves down the central aisle and covered us with their guns. 'Stand up', ordered the head Nazi, and we stood. Then, each of us in turn, he turned out our pockets, looking through our 'papers' and feeling us over for weapons (naturally, none of us had his 'Party card'). *Du bist doch Engländer?* he said to me, using derogatively the familiar second person. 'What's an Englishman doing here? *Heraus!*'—and then I was being marched out between two armed Nazis. All I remember of that brief walk down the street is that I was very frightened.

We'd marched perhaps a hundred yards when the brave little
*Wirt* of the pub came running up behind us. 'Excuse me', he
puffed politely to the Nazis, using to the full the charm of his
smile, 'perhaps you ought to know—this Herr is employed by
Scherl, by Minister Hugenberg—'. Many of the young Nazis, in
those early weeks, were still apprentices in the exertion of official
'terror' and, apparently, afraid of offending their bosses, whose
co-operation at the ministerial top was still precarious. Anyhow,
for some reason and to my surprise, the little landlord's words and
manner did the trick. They let me go; and I badly needed another
drink.

I had reason to be frightened. I'd begun posting articles for the
*Daily Worker* to a 'cover' address in London arranged by Felicia
Browne; had one of these been stopped it would have been simple to
trace it to me.

By early summer Kurt was coming to my flat after school for a
midday meal—lentils stewed with bacon and potatoes and dash of
vinegar was a dish I was good at (I have, in various parts of the
world, often been a competent cook for schoolboys); now and then
he stayed for a week-end, and we would go out into the country,
bathing in the lakes or walking. I gave him a second-hand bicycle,
which he left discreetly with me when he went home.

The Grosse Hamburgerstrasse, into which my courtyard de-
bouched, had been a fairly 'Red' street; now from its doorways boys
in Hitler Youth uniform, when they weren't on parade, watched
and whispered and noted the passers-by. Sometimes, Kurt told
me, they shouted after him—he wouldn't have anything to do with
the Hitler Youth; and they used to eye me and point as I walked
by. For them, the bicycle was the last straw; I've had a lot of
experience of boyish jealousy—it can be venomous: how much
more, when it's sharpened by political malice! One early July
Sunday, Kurt went out for a bicycle ride. After an hour, I knew
some disaster had happened; and at dusk, when Kurt's stepfather
arrived brandishing threats, I knew what it was. This stepfather,
Kurt had told me, had embraced Nazism the moment he was sure
that Hitler had won; now he stormed as much against the 'un-
German' nature of my political soul as against my very German
morals; and declared that he was going to the police.

I filled a suitcase with papers that I wanted to preserve, like
Wystan Auden's poems and letters, or that might embroil the young

man whose home the flat also was, and went to a friend's where I stayed the night. Next day, I got word that police and S.A. were posted at the gateways of my courtyard. It was a midsummer day; I was wearing only an open shirt and plus-fours—fortunately in a trousers pocket were my passport and a hundred-mark note. I walked down to the Potsdamerbahnhof and took the first train to Prague; and then, with nothing but the clothes I was wearing, travelled to London round the edge of the Third Reich, by way of Vienna, Zurich and Basle.

## 12

IN LONDON I called on 'Springy' Springhall, boss of the London District of 'the Party': a big, tough, shorn-headed pugilist of a fellow; agreeable but cold as marble. I think that later—like Wilfred Macartney, author of that great prison book 'Walls have Ears'—Springy spent a long time in prison for alleged espionage in the Soviet interest, and then, after the Red domination of China in November 1949, went to Pekin where he may still be. He was one of those vocational Communists whose faith burns with a painful heat; in his ruthless presence, I felt that, if he made love at all, he did so holding a volume of Lenin in one hand.

To my relief he didn't assign me to the tedium of 'cell' work; I was given jobs nearer the centre in King Street, Covent Garden, and especially at the focal-point of anti-fascist propaganda in a little crooked street off the Charing Cross Road: we worked and talked with fevered enthusiasm behind a charming first-floor bow-window, still standing today, which looked into St Martin's Lane. Here came all sorts of delightful people, united in their hatred of Hitler: Ellen Wilkinson, a Labour M.P., like a pert, bustling, red-headed bird, whose overdraft on her energy killed her; Ernie and Isobel Brown, monarchs of the Friends of the Soviet Union—she a fat, motherly washer-woman to look at, yet one of the knitters of the revolution; jolly old Willie Gallagher, Harry Pollitt's *khalifa*—a fanatical teetotaller who got rollickingly drunk on endless cups of stewed tea and sang irreverent songs like 'Boys of the *you know what*, All British *you know what* . . . But you can't beat the boys of the *you know what*, Who made Old England YOU KNOW WHAT!' Harry Pollitt himself, abstractedly smiling, rather august in an amiable way; various furtive Germans, some of them 'illegal'; Jewish refugees like the writer Alfred Kantorowicz.

Pollitt, off the platform, didn't strike me as the possesser of a 'leader's' gifts. He took me once, with one or two others, to a pub; and I had a chance to watch him off duty, so to speak—though

Communists, like policemen, are never off duty. He ordered a 'small port'—and looked just the humdrum little man who would drink one small port. I remember nothing exciting or vivid in his conversation—no flame of greatness spurted from his mind. He was, I should think, good at working from the book—and the Communist book, like Islam, in those days had for the orthodox the prescription to meet any situation. I don't think he had much understanding of the human personality and its strange modulations. Once, a friend of mine, important in the intellectual quarter of the Party and a writer of talent, went to Harry after a bout of self-criticism and said: 'Harry, I think it's my duty to tell you: I'm a homosexual.' Pollitt snapped sharply in his brisk on-duty way: 'Cut it out, 'Erbie, cut it out!' And that was the end of it: the Party directive was: Cut it Out—as if changing one's nature were an act of will like giving up smoking.

Bill Gallagher, as *good* a man as any I've known, was, I thought, a bigger person than Harry; he had a wider vision and saw life through more human eyes—he was enriched, too, by a buoyant Scottish humour.

Mostly I worked on translations. My first was 'Hitler over Europe', published by Dent's, the remarkable work of a remarkable conspirator known as Ernst Henri, whose real name was Simon Rostovsky. This book, with its successor 'Hitler over Russia', caused a sensation—though not, unfortunately, in the hesitant spheres of government where nobody could make up his mind whether Hitler were a counter-communist godsend for capitalism or a peril for humanity. I got £20 for each of these—I'd been paid £50 for the Allen & Unwin book. I translated, besides, an anti-Hitler novel called 'Shot whilst Escaping' (a Nazi cliché of the day), a charming book of *reportage* on China by Egon Erwin Kisch, and a couple of boring Party theses published by Lawrence & Wishart.

The reviewers called me a good translator. The reason so many translations are bad is that their perpetrators suppose that knowledge of the two languages is enough; the rest is a straight exercise in literal construing. Translators, of course, must re-create the author's thought and feeling, not transcribe his text; departure from the meaning of his *words* often is essential to reflect the meaning of his *mind*. The translator, like an actor, must *live* himself into a new role with every fresh author he tackles.

Soon we had our own Reichstag Fire 'Trial', with Mr D. N.

Pritt on the Bench; my job was to interpret for the German-speaking witnesses.

Dorothy Woodman, who with Kingsley Martin was living then in Kentish Town, asked me to look after during his stay the 15-year-old son of Fritz Torgler, a senior German Communist also accused in Germany with Dimitroff of burning the Reichstag—the boy had been brought to London, smuggled out of Germany, to give evidence. He was charming, and we had fun together—chaste fun.

Interpreting for hours before a big 'committed' audience determined to get the evidence it wants is morally exhausting, as well as mentally. At one point my nerve gave. Young Torgler had been in the box for a long time; I'd been interpreting back and forth—his words into English, the Court's into German—and my mind was frayed, frayed especially by interruptions from some members of the 'public'.

The boy had said that, visiting his father in Moabit prison, he had found him *deprimiert*. I translated this 'demoralised'. 'No, no!' shouted the knowledgeable among the audience, 'not *demoralised*—depressed!' The word can mean either, and no doubt it would have been more tactful to have chosen 'depressed'. It was then that I walked out of the hall in tears, with angry eyes glaring at me as if I'd been a Nazi agent. I recall this silly incident because it seemed to show that political 'stunts', no matter how well intentioned they may be, are bound to contain some taint of corruption—as anything political does. I agree that it was impossible for the honest to be *impartial* about Nazism; but it is corrupt to be dishonest in one's partiality. People at that 'trial' came, of course, with their verdict already given, but to sustain it they wanted to write the evidence themselves.

About this time I became a lowly partner in a group bent on attracting to the anti-fascist cause people in the world of letters and art, and on forming an active association with left-wing writers and artists abroad. The others were: Edgell Rickword, poet and publisher, who had lost an eye and won the M.C. in the 1914 war: an odd, sourly gentle person, already an old friend; John Strachey, whom nearly 20 years later I was to see again in Malaya as Secretary for War; selfless Ralph Fox, one of the saints of Communism, killed in Spain; Tom Wintringham, the strategist and guerilla master of the International Brigade. The first thing we did, I playing a humble part, was to found the *Left Review*, with Edgell as first editor; from which was developed the idea of a Writers' and Artists' International ranging the intellects of Europe against fascism and helping the German writers who were its victims. One of my tasks was to seek the moral support of well-known writers and/or their money, to be sent to the aid of anti-Nazi writers in Germany. I wrote, among others, to Evelyn Waugh; who asked, in reply, whether I would *guarantee* that his guinea, if he sent one, would go solely to *Catholic* writers suffering under the Nazis, and to no other kind. Obviously, in the circumstances of illegality in which our funds were distributed in Germany, this guarantee couldn't be given; and we got no guinea from Evelyn Waugh.

By 1935 I was combining a dissolute life with the earning of a desultory income from translation for the heavy Party journals: long, leaden columns of theory to be printed in the *Communist Review* or *Labour Monthly*, the kind of stuff enjoyed by Palme Dutt —a beautiful mask of a man, but whether saintly or satanic I couldn't decide.

A rare friend of those days, unconnected with Communism, was Tommy Earp. T. W. Earp was known to a narrow public as *Daily Telegraph* art critic and author of a few books on painting. His personality is impossible to describe: with his death a whole inimitable species, of which he was the sole specimen, seemed to become extinct. Like all 'great' character, Tommy's hadn't an ounce of affectation in it—the mannerisms were as natural as the wit was spontaneous; it found physical expression in a roguish, purple face, that bright gimlet eye which pinned one with undodgeable steadiness. to the matter in hand, the unvaryingly close-shorn head— Tommy Earp must have invented the 'crew-cut' long before the Americans; and that extraordinary falsetto, drawling yet musical, in which like a leisured Gregorian chant his exquisite conversation was conducted. He hadn't many close friends, because he *chose* them; being Tommy's friend was like belonging to a very exclusive club.

He had been President of the Oxford Union and probably could have bestrode any sphere of success he chose. But, instead, he preferred the quiet and unobtrusive corners of life that amused and seemed worth-while to his own fastidious and idiosyncratic mind. Drinking was one of these; though I never saw him drunk, even after long hours of unwavering consumption. It was with Augustus John, I think, one of his closest friends, that he worked out, and then proved 'on the ground', a time-table and itinerary

*The Author, shortly before his death*

*At home in Sicily 1971*

*With George Greaves in Tangier 1974*

*With Maung Té-hung at the Shwé-Dagon pagoda, Rangoon 1949*

*With Nicos Sampson and Randolph Churchill at the Leda Palace.*

*Nicos Sampson as a boy*

*With Joseph Anthony, Cyprus 1955–57*

*Eikivhi Suzuki ("Keibo"), Tokyo 1951*

*On the beach of Enoshima, August 1958*

*Mura on a Timbuctoo rooftop 1958*

*With Robin Maugham on Ischia 1953*

*With Field-Marshal Harding, Government House Cyprus 1956*

*With Randolph Churchill*

*At work in Cyprus 1955*

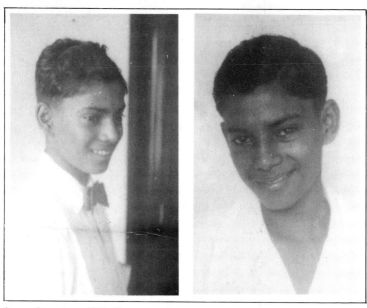

*Somo, Singapore 1950–51*

*In Sicily 1971*

for drinking *legally* in London right round the 24 hours; making use of the special 'opening hours' enjoyed by Covent Garden, Billingsgate and Smithfield, and other legal anomalies like clubs and 'extensions'. Another time, he organized (and won) a point-to-point over a course composed of every public-house on both sides of the road between Ludgate Circus and Charing Cross. The rule was half-a-pint of beer in each. I think Tommy was with Philip Heseltine and John on that famous walk in Norfolk, so wonderfully described in Augustus' autobiography, when a blinding flash of lightning, timed as nimbly as a Jovian thunderbolt, fell upon them precisely on the point of celebrating the Black Mass in a parish church.

I saw Tommy Earp last, two or three years before he died, at the Authors' Club in Whitehall Court—I think he liked it there because it was notoriously empty of 'authors': like everybody who is wholly himself, Tommy couldn't stand posturing. We drank beer till three o'clock, forgetting all about lunch; and made splendid plans which we both knew were fantasy. Then I went to Italy, and Tommy, soon, was dead. He was a happy person who largely was unhappy; the constrictions of his marriage tormented him, yet he was too loyal to free himself.

My behaviour, in these years, was disastrous, and leading me—obviously, had I paused to look—straight to my 'first row'. I was drinking more than usual; and with more than usual frenzy was chasing 'romance': Millard would have disapproved. I had no beloved, though many delusions of love—'in each of them I saw the sign of the one I was waiting for', wrote Carlo Coccioli in his extraordinary novel of Florence and Paris, 'The Eye and the Heart'. That is the impulsion, the motive power, of the prowling paederast —the unending search for the 'divine friend, much desired'. One tried to look, always, beyond the brevity of pleasure.

The 'row' came towards the end of 1936; but a year earlier I took part in a rite which to my adolescent mind seemed as trivial as joining an afternoon 'club'. I got married.

I can't remember my wife's name; but I can still see her fresh Prussian prettiness and soft yellow hair: such sweet girlishness couldn't, one would have said, be the countenance of a militant Party Member escaped from Hitler Germany.

It happened in this way: a friend of mine concerned with some of the Party's secrets, who knew that I wasn't by nature a 'marrying man', asked me if I would do the anti-Nazi cause a good turn by conferring a British passport on a German girl whose legality in England would be valuable. I answered: 'Of course, Henry, if that's what the Party wants'—partly because of a spineless reluctance to refuse anything I'm asked; and partly, though the flame of my zeal for the C.P. (never having been a 'real' Communist) had by now waned to a flicker, because my hatred of the Nazis hadn't waned at all.

So I married her in St Pancras town hall whence we moved to a neighbouring pub for a brief party, and said goodbye. This foolish, and perhaps in the 'patriotic' sense immoral, act has never brought any consequences to me, beyond, I suppose, an extra black mark in my 'file'; but I'm afraid for her it must have been bothersome. I believe that late in the 1940s, while perhaps at the other end of the world, I was divorced for desertion. I hope so, for her sake.

In the middle of 1936 I was living in a mean room off the Camden Road. Here I was 'mothering' a boy called Ray, a truant from home or perhaps reformatory: a touching psychopathic creature who lied and stole and wetted the bed in which he lay until it was time to go to the 'pictures'; but whose nature was so loaded with pathos and need for affection that one was filled with fondness and compassion. Plenty of food cured the bed-wetting; but no amount of coddling could cure anything else; and one day he walked out, taking what little I had—luckily it was a day I'd taken my typewriter out.

Then I had a pleasant Islington friend who came to see me now and then, improbably named Bill Jones; but an insatiable curiosity and the unsatisfied search drove me on beyond the bounds of caution and I became 'known' in the *louche* environs of the old Collins' Musical Hall; had I had the sense to interpret one or two signs, I might have realized that. Bill liked practising on my typewriter; and meeting me one Saturday evening in Upper Street, proposed that we go to my room. This meant taking two buses, and then a short walk; and it wasn't until, as I was unlocking the front-door and a voice said tersely 'Just a minute', that I had a notion we had been followed. Bill was asked his name. 'Bill Jones', he said. 'Now, don't try and come that on me', retorted the detective knowingly, 'I wasn't born yesterday. Come on, what's your name?' Here I put in: 'But it *is* Bill Jones—I assure you it's Bill Jones!' And thus the conversation continued for some minutes: the one part of that sickening evening that I can remember clearly, and still makes me laugh. But after that, 'accompanying' him to a police station, and later, I was too shocked to notice much: the unspeakable, the unthinkable, had happened—I had been *arrested*. I remember being searched, and their taking my keys: the long wait in some lavatory-tiled police-station while they took a 'statement' from poor Bill; I remember being finger-printed and charged—to this day I don't know the wording of the charge. I remember the blessed moment when they said I could have bail —whom would I like them to ring up? And then Charles Ashleigh came, taking it in his stride; and went bail for me and took me to his flat for a drink. Charles's friendship stood that test as few others' would.

There was a week's remand; I had a week to think in. My principal task, plainly, was to save my mother the unbearable sadness of learning what had happened; I had to invent a falsehood plausible enough to convince her. My mother knew of my communist doings and connections with Germany: I wrote to my brother asking him, should I go to prison, to tell her I'd been sent on a mission abroad so secret that no word of it could be breathed and that would keep me *perdu* for as many weeks or months as I 'got'. Again, I discovered how *good* people can be: where one awaits odium, or at least incomprehension, one finds so often kindness. Like Charles, my brother Eardley was generous and understanding; he didn't upbraid me, but said he would pay my lawyers' bill; and agreed with my fiction for our mother. When I came out of prison, he was again kindness itself, helping financially and in other precious ways; I was still shy of him, he was still the big brother; but I saw that he was a much nicer person than I had believed as a small boy, and a far better one than I could ever be.

My solicitor advised me to plead guilty; poor Bill's 'statement', he said, was conclusive; it was a 'first offence', and if I made things easy by refraining from denying what plainly was true, I would almost certainly get probation. He had briefed a nice young man called Mallalieu—the same, I suppose, who later became a Member of Parliament; he would say all that could be thought up in favour of leniency. Of course I agreed to plead guilty: in any case, as I knew that whatever Bill had said in his statement would be no more than the truth, I knew too that nothing would induce me to surrender the boy to the degradation of sustaining it in the box. So, the next Monday morning I put a toothbrush and razor and a Left Book Club copy of John Strachey's 'Theory and Practice of

Socialism' into a satchel and caught a bus for North London Police Court.

It's difficult to unravel one's emotions in a situation so utterly revolutionary as that of being the centre-piece of the Dock—revolutionary because it turns topsy-turvy everything in life one has always taken for granted. Humiliation, of course: centuries of procedural refinement have made the dock in a British criminal court the perfect fount of mortification; while you're in it, innocent or guilty, you're a contemptible worm and you know it—no matter how kindly the Judge or 'helpful' the police; bitterness with myself, I felt, for being so stupid—for *allowing* this to happen; dread, I suppose, of the unknown degradations and discomforts that perhaps lay ahead; but certainly a lively and enjoyable interest in what was going on and what was yet to come. I've always welcomed fresh experience, even unpleasant: human, emotional experience, that is, not technical, like flying to the moon. And I knew that if I were gaoled nothing would ever be the same again—the whole future would be coloured, or stained, by that.

I've always considered that most of the sexual actions one's nature drives one unreasonably to perform are too silly for words. Why, I ask, does one *want* to do such pointless things? Yet at the moment, nothing in life seems so important. When these things are publicly described in the nerveless tones of a dusty solicitor from the office of the Director of Public Prosecutions, and publicly ascribed to oneself, sitting in the dock under the public's goggling eye, they make one feel not only an imbecile but also a monster; in his mouth things which seemed to one perfectly natural become horribly deformed. And that, evidently, is what's intended.

A detective testified to the shabbiness of my room and my apparent poverty; Mallalieu excellently did his best to make bricks without straw; and the magistrate gave me four months with hard labour. He added, in the tones of a headmaster announcing some special benefaction, that in prison I should receive 'psychological treatment'. My lawyer told me, after I 'came out', that he believed it was the squalid description of my lodging that decided the beak to send me to prison; had I seemed respectably prosperous I would probably, for the first offence, have been put on probation. Perhaps that could have been true in 1936; perhaps it can still be true today.

I don't remember the stipendiary's delivering one of those speeches that one sees reported in the *News of the World*; in which the occupant of the Bench improves upon the law by filling it out with his personal indignation and his own moral views.

A year or so ago I saw in a newspaper this paragraph:

> Passing sentence on ——, Mr Justice Stable commented: 'The man who kills does no more than shorten a human life. But a man who corrupts a young lad or girl destroys one—and that is worse.'

Assuming that this means anything at all, and leaving out of account the Judge's apparent desire to reverse the acts of parliament which makes 'shortening a human life' the worse crime of the two, this pronouncement seems to jump straight back to the heresy-hatred of the Inquisition. It is almost a paraphrase of this passage from Bernard Wall's 'Report on the Vatican':

> ... This was the well-known apologia of the Spanish Inquisitors who argued that a murderer only murdered people's bodies whereas a heretic murdered their souls.

It seems likely that remarks like this are prompted more by hatred and fear of heresy than by a heart sorrowing for the countless innocent souls waiting to be corrupted. Sexual heresy must seem to the unswervingly loyal member of the sexual Establishment like an affront to his most recondite and 'sacred' sentiments; and at the present time particularly, when the public has suddenly become aware for the first time how widespread and various these heresies are, he must *feel* that they constitute a positive danger to the *rightness* of his sexual simplicity. This is why, I suppose, a greater sanctity than ever seems to be given nowadays to the word 'innocence'—both by those whose blood boils when they hear of its being corrupted, and by the others who confuse childhood with the first snowdrops of spring.

'As innocent as a new-laid egg', said Samuel Butler somewhere; and that's nearer the mark than the usual comparison—the new-born babe's innocence lasts as long as its elders can artificially and unnaturally keep it swaddled, and often not nearly so long as the elders suppose: the young creature's own bodily senses and instincts will sooner rather than later 'corrupt' it.

Sexual 'innocence', as ordinarily understood, is manifestly *unnatural*—true innocence, I suppose, is the natural progression of knowledge and experience with the creature's growth and under-standing. But 'purity' artificially maintained by prohibition and insulation against knowledge is really a disciplinary device invented by adults: and can, I'm fairly convinced from observation of its opposite, be a contributor to England's psychological chaos.

In Southern Italy 'purity' doesn't exist and isn't expected; a child by the time it can walk is 'corrupt'. The boys unfailingly begin to masturbate in public from the age of six, and continue to do so, with only token attempts at concealment, until they are old enough to be admitted to the brothel or have found a girl whose maidenhead hasn't been as uncompromisingly preserved as her sisters'. Masturbation for the boys (I can't speak for the girls, whose virginity, though not 'innocence', is jealously kept intact by tradi-tion for marriage) is regarded as a normal and sensible accompani-ment to the boyish phase of their development—a matter of course, not calling for comment. In England, of course, it's almost as prevalent; but furtive and shameful and guilt-loaded.

And there is the point. This youthful 'corruption' perhaps has interesting social consequences. In south Italy one rarely hears of the sexual murder of children, of brutal attacks on women by adolescent boys, of young girls being raped, of the explosive lusts of the psychotic or the psychopath. Of course there are murders; but they are 'healthy' Mediterranean murders, acts of vengeance or jealousy; and almost to a man these 'corrupt' boys grow into excel-lent husbands and devoted fathers of seven or eight children. Divorce is practically impossible for the Catholic poor; but there doesn't seem much desire for divorce. There is some homosexuality in the cities, but compared with northern Europe it's insignificant; and though almost any youth is ready for a homosexual frolic or even friendship, that bent doesn't go beneath the surface of his nature—below he is firmly orthodox. I'd say that the Italians are the most 'normal' and sexually healthy of any people—for all the versatility of their concupiscence in youth.

Isn't it likely that this is because from childhood their sexual behaviour is allowed to develop *naturally*, in time with their own growth, as a puppy's does?

Locked in a cell like a hard-class *couchette*, I found they'd taken away my matches; I couldn't smoke till they brought a mug of tea and gave me a light. Then, to keep smoking, I remember lighting one fresh cigarette after another from the stub of the last—smoking seemed the final contact with the familiar, with the real: like the feel of one's mother's dress when going away to school for the first time. It was mid-afternoon before I was unlocked and taken out to the Black Maria.

People who haven't ridden in a Black Maria may think it's as good a way of getting about as any other; I think it's the most terrible that man's invented for the humiliation of men. It contains along each side a row of tiny steel cellules each constructed to receive and hold the human form in a sitting position. Into this canister one is locked; the tantalizing ventilation holes at eye-level are just too small to let one distinguish anything outside when one tries to peer through. The thing jolts and jerks, comes to a stop, moves on: you don't know where you are, where you're going, how long you'll be immured. The claustral pressure of this steel confinement becomes like pillows smothering your mind—you want to scream: but what will screaming do? And suddenly you know that very soon you'll unbearably want to pee. . . . A prison cell is a bower of bliss after two hours in the Black Maria—there you can walk about, fling out your arms, dance if you want to: your will has still *some* room to range in; in the wheeled safe-deposit it has none. This frightful vehicle, this mobile filing cabinet for samples of human degradation, is obviously unnecessary and quite uneconomic; prisoners, meek and unnerved most of them, could just as well be carted about London in a van, like human beings—and there were always handcuffs; there is no need to start their prison life by burying them alive.

After an hour or so, it stopped and we were unlocked; but we hadn't got there yet. This was a kind of prisoners' clearing-house, or 'lay-by' (what words and signs our English roads are being defiled by!); a herd of us was locked into a big cell with a steel-barred gate and left for an hour or so. Then, those of us bound for 'the Scrubs' were inserted into another Black Maria; it was late evening when at last we arrived. I was drained of all spirit by then, and can remember little of 'Reception'. One had a bath; and was marched naked in to the doctor. 'Have you had syphilis?' asked this cold, cursory young man. And then my blessed cell, my home for the next 90-odd days and refuge from the vast grey clanging ugliness outside it.

As I had 'hard labour' I slept in my blankets on bare boards; after two weeks of that I got a mattress. This fortnight of sleeping hard was the symbolic residue of Hard Labour—in practice this old-fashioned penance had vanished, like the treadmill, from the prison rule.

This was the end of October 1936; I would be 'out' by the beginning of February. If one avoided trouble and thus 'earned' full remission, one quarter of one's sentence was pinched off, like the head of a prawn. So I had three months to do; I'd made up my mind to be carefully submissive to the prison rules and to the whims and foibles of the screws whose single uncorroborated word could spell one's doom. Only the 'burnt-out cases' (Graham Greene's leper term seems to fit so well) walk with their eyes open into trouble in the nick—those men so embittered and hardened by familiarity with its grinding evil that the protest of noisy contumacy has become a need, though it hurts nobody but themselves. But it was sadly easy to make a mistake (like failing to fold the blankets just as the screw wanted); and harrowing to know that some pathetic mental deficient was being 'done' because he couldn't understand, or to foresee the fate of the poor fellow who, his mind cracking one evening in his cell, 'smashes up'.

The impressions that have principally remained with me are the unvarying physical *cold* of the place—I used to think that even in summer it must be cold in the Scrubs; the studiedly inhuman *intention* of it—everything in the routine, everything that met the eye and ear (and nose), had been lovingly devised, I felt, to humiliate and dismay; and the shocking number of near-lunatics who'd been sent there—drooling, dribbling wretches who had fouled the Law because, I suppose, they couldn't cope, or couldn't comprehend; or simply happened to be handy when somebody had to be picked up. One such, I remember, mumbled to me in the Brush Shop that he didn't know at all why he was in the nick. I wonder whether magistrates still send droves of mental deficients to prison?

One's clothes were the first vehicle of humiliation one noticed: these sad grey garments seemed designed to make the biggest fool possible of one's appearance—trouser reaching half-way down the calf or bunching over one's ankles; a little boy's coat that made an ass of one's backside or one so big that it slumped off the shoulders; one had either, one felt, grown out of them or shrunk inside them. As for the bare necessities of the toilet—a second-hand razor-blade, used with cold water, left one permanently stubbled; and, being deprived of one's nail-scissors, the horrid hairs of one's nose grew long and repulsive and one's nails were cut with tailor's shears under the eye of a screw. There was the early morning procession to the fetid 'recess', an open bog used by about 50 people, carrying grotesquely one's jerry containing the stinking excretions of the night—which, multiplied by 50, made a considerable hum; the incessant yelling of the screws—'GET BACK inside', when, parading after 'unlocking' in the doorways of our cells, one of us seemed to overstep his threshold; the peering eye through one's door's spy-hole; the careful marshalling of metallic prison noise—the clanging of steel doors, the jangling of keys, crashing of locks and bolts, grating of warders' boots on the iron 'landing', the wiry lashing of the screws' shouts: it was like living in a boiler-makers' shop; the taunt of being 'taken' wherever the whims of the routine sent one by a bum-bailiff with jangling keys.

I suppose some prison-officers (it's odd there are no 'other ranks'), off duty, are ordinary men with gentle feelings; but I found no sign of human sympathy in the screws I had to do with (except, perhaps, the nodding old 'instructors' in the Brush Shop); the worst were the young—the strutting, yelling fellows with the minds of Storm Troopers. I saw no bodily violence, though I heard the sound of it once or twice coming from some poor chap's cell; but *mental* violence was part of the routine. I suppose the men and women who consent to this ignoble life are to be pitied—they too are victims of the prison system; but I've always thought that one who from preference joins a police or prison service must belong to that lowest human caste, which can include cabinet ministers and school bullies—those who enjoy holding *power* over their fellows.

Meals were thrust through a trap. I enjoyed the breakfast porridge and bread and the cheese at supper—prison bread seemed as good as any I've eaten; and the pint of greasy cocoa brought a special comfort. But the midday .mix-up in a tin can was so nauseating that I didn't learn to eat it in three months. I don't know how much, or little, truth there was in the universally held belief that some sort of chloral substance was mixed into the cocoa to halt the stirrings of venereal desires. I know that in prison I lost almost all sexual interest—even the distant sight of the short-trousered captives from A-Hall, the 'boys' prison', being marched about didn't quicken my heart much; though now and then, in my cell, or day-dreaming in the Brush Shop, I would invoke, as a relaxation (like going to the pictures), a douce salacious reverie. I put this mental emasculation down to the numbing of the body by the cold, and still more to the deadening of every segment of the spirit by the harsh metallic ugliness of everything and·the shared sadness of this huge repository of suffering.

I had one visit of about 30 seconds from a dim Anglican chaplain; he didn't come again; and after a couple of months a Prison Visitor turned up—a nice, colourless man with a clerk's moustache who didn't know what to say. Obviously he must have been impelled into this voluntary work by great kindliness and noble intention, but hadn't the knack of imparting it; he did tell me cautiously about the Abdication, about which I knew nothing. 'I'm not allowed, you know, to tell you what's happening "outside",' he said apologetically. (Prison Visitors, of course, do sometimes achieve great and positive good; as I have seen in the splendid work of a great friend of mine. But he is a humanist, a psychologist and a leading writer on penology.)

After the first month I was allowed books from the library. But I wasn't allowed to choose the books; a random couple was dumped in my cell while I was out awkwardly constructing boot-brushes out of bristles and bits of wire. I read them all, avidly; but can remember only one: a life of the Duke of Wellington: and thinking what an odd place this was to read it in. Then I asked for leave to have in my cell Strachey's book on Socialism, which, then reposing in my 'property', I had brought becuse it was long and was the sort that could be read several times. I had to make an 'application' to be taken before the Governor; then was paraded like a defaulter outside the Governor's office; then was ceremonially marched in and told to stand abjectly at attention; then I made my solemn request. I was rather surprised that it was granted; I'd thought that a book so frankly 'political', and near-communist, would be on the prison index.

I must have done about half my sentence before the promised 'psychological treatment' made its sudden appearance. One evening I was abruptly 'unlocked'—anything out-of-routine happened abruptly and capriciously, like air-raids—and marched silently across the dark prison; as usual I wasn't told where I was going. And then, for the first time, I found myself alone with a human being—a person who treated me as a human being. He was a young psychologist, and charming; I was sorry I had with him so few talks. The upshot of my treatment, really, was that he urged me to raise, so to speak, my 'age of consent'; couldn't I, he asked in effect, persuade myself to be attracted by people much older—

above the age, at least, of 18? The risk then, he pointed out, would be less. This wasn't, I imagine, what the magistrate had in mind.

There were 'classes'—voluntary classes for the illiterates, classes in book-keeping and so on. As a diversion, I enrolled for the geography class; and one or two evenings a week was marched to a room where for an hour we sat on benches while a kindly elementary school teacher showed us maps, which I always like looking at. On Sundays we 'C. of E.s' were marched to the prison chapel for Matins, while the 'R.C.s', Jews, Methodists and so on were marched in grey groups elsewhere. We sat in sorry, grey shambling rows; round us screws were posted to see that there were no breaches of the regulations, while behind us the door was locked—it must have been a very Christian spectacle for the man in the pulpit. Now and then on a Sunday afternoon we would be marched back to the chapel to listen to some well-intentioned person come to play us 'pieces' on the piano or sing us songs like 'Roses of Picardy'. I found these occasions humiliating; I don't know why it is that so often charitable benevolence seems insulting.

Once a week we in the Brush Shop were marched to the bath-house for a hot bath and the issue of 'clean' underclothes. The luxury of the hot wallow generally had to be paid for in pain after-wards: reasonably, one was required to clean the bath; but what looked clean to oneself was rarely clean enough for the inspecting screw—over and over again one was compelled to rub and wipe and scrub, without any sort of detergent, to remove soap marks which he violently insisted were still there.

I've written the word 'clean' in inverted commas, because the underclothes weren't always clean. Once, I discovered that I was possessed of the sort of lice known as 'crabs'—which, having been in the nick for over a month, I couldn't have brought from outside; a 'clean' pair of drawers must have harboured them. I knew that to 'report sick' with a minor ailment was almost a delinquency; to report that one had 'caught crabs', no matter where from, couldn't bring less, I thought, than loss of remission. So I said nothing; and for about a week, squeezed in a corner of my cell out of range of the peep-hole, I sedulously shaved with my blunt razor, scraping myself sore. By a miracle it worked; and the nightmare was out-rooted. That was a thing that could, and did, happen in prison in 1936.

Each morning, between breakfast and 'work', we were hustled down the clanging iron turret stairs for 'exercise'; counted at the door into the yard (we were always being counted) and set in single-file motion round and round the concreted ring that was our daily treadmill. I ought to have looked forward to this morning constitutional, breathing God's air beneath the open sky; but I dreaded it. If it was raining we wore little grey tippets round our shoulders that made us look sillier still; but against the cold we had nothing. Our clothes had no pockets, and to get some warmth into my aching hands I would improvise a muff by tucking each into the other's sleeve; but our guardian screws, snug in their overcoats, instantly yelled: 'GET those hands free!'

In those days there was no talking for prisoners called short-term, no 'association'—by the rules, I was supposed not to utter a word for three months except when addressing a screw; and at exercise we were strung out in single-file, so many paces between each. Sometimes, of course, sidelong remarks were exchanged, gangster-film fashion; but it was a dangerous pleasure, if pleasure it was. I've seen few more melancholy sights than this trailing circle of grotesque grey figures, plodding round and round in mute, meaningless gyration; the grey silence punctured by the screws' scolding; even the few brave winter flowers planted in tidy institutional beds seeming tainted by the great grey sadness.

And yet I found the fantastic pattern of this social sadism fascinating. I've always had a godsent capacity for being interested in, and therefore in a sense enjoying, mental and moral pain; and in the Scrubs I was interested all the time—in my own sensations, in the methods and techniques of punition, and especially in the punished and their punishers. It was an experience I've always been thankful for: a privileged view—like getting a ticket to the 'secret room' of Naples Museum—of social cruelty restricted to far too narrow a segment of society. It made me, I think, a humbler and nicer person, and was therefore morally salutary—though not in the way intended by my betters who sent me there. In Erewhon, no doubt, all the wilfully respectable, the smugly affluent, the safely conformist, would have been given a sharp three months as a matter of course; I believe human nature would be more humane if everybody, as a kind of moral inoculation under the National Health, were sent to prison for a spell—but at a time of life after the callousness of youth has softened and before the ageing arteries of sympathy have hardened.

If the purpose of prison is to make prisoners vow they'll not come back again, it succeeds; but it does nothing to deter people from repeating the acts that sent them there. One goes out merely determined to be more careful in future about being 'caught'.

Society gets the prison-population it deserves, as it gets the politicians it deserves. About one-third, I'd say, of the men I saw in the Scrubs 26 years ago needn't have been there at all—their fault was not one of character but of social circumstances; another third *oughtn't* to have been there—they should have been in hospital; the remainder, perhaps, presented a social problem. To this problem our great-grandfathers had an answer in transportation. I would have a kind of Pitcairn Island for society's undesirables—perhaps some of those remote tracts now being used for blowing off bombs; and pack them off with their wives or sweethearts and an adequate grant of money to find their own salvation there. But I'd keep one big prison going for a class of criminal for whom society, because itself a principal offender, has defined no crime: the intellectually dishonest and the morally dishonorable—the people whose financial and social rectitude is impeccable but whose mind is a liar and moral façade a fraud: the hypocrites and jockeyers of public ignorance, the purveyors of commercial and political sham and the falsifiers, for factional gain or private aggrandizement, of the truth. This is the sin that cries aloud to Heaven for justice; and I'd hire those screws I knew in the Scrubs to shout at the sinners.

That third of the population which, I've just said, 'needn't' have been there, included an alarming number of young men who, having a 'previous', had been 'done' for 'suspect'. This means that they'd been 'picked up' and charged with the crime of being a 'suspected person' by plain-clothes 'bogeys' who knew they had a previous conviction. I don't know if this wicked charge is still on the statute book; it enabled detectives to swear that a 'known' young fellow, perhaps harmlessly walking in the street, had been, say, trying motor-car doors: the 'previous', reinforcing the evidence of two policemen, was bound to get a conviction.

A 'previous', if you sail close to the Law, follows you about for the rest of your life; mine has cropped up in various ways, once developing into my 'second row'.

## 13

WHEN I 'CAME OUT' early in 1937 I saw that earning a living
was going to be difficult. Much earlier, I'd 'lapsed' from the
Party; now, I felt, my disgrace and their primness had blocked
that source of translation work. From journalism, too, I thought,
I must be barred. But my brother again was kind; one of his friends
was Norman Collins, a best-selling novelist but not yet, obviously,
a television tycoon. Collins was good enough to recommend me as
a reader to a firm of printers; and diligently I read proofs for the
next few months, 'clocking in' at 7 a.m. and being solemnly
admitted to an aristocratic trade union called the Association of
Correctors of the Press. I took a flat in Kilburn, an excitingly
squalid district well removed from Islington; and my poor mother
(who, with sweet discretion, had welcomed me back from my
'secret mission') again gave me furniture.

Often, going home late at night, I took the tube from Piccadilly
Circus, where the station roundabout and lavatory were notorious
haunts of male prostitutes and plain-clothes bogeys. I was terrified
of its dangers, and at that time hurried through it. One evening I
was brusquely stopped by an obvious 'dick'. 'We know you,' he
said; 'we're watching you.' I felt the same panic, the same sense
of being pursued by hostile eyes, that I'd suffered years before at
the Serpentine. Already my 'previous' had raised its head; I
supposed this man must have been in court when I was convicted.
I took this new horror to my brother; and begged him help me
escape from the leering malevolence which suddenly England
seemed to mean. His comprehension was unwavering; he arranged
with my mother that against my inheritance I should have two
pounds a week while, living abroad, I 'wrote' or found work as a
translator.

Germany was out of the question; I'd never found France
*sympathique* but, with good French, it seemed sensible to choose a
country where that language was generally understood; sunshine,

and the sea were other requirements, and a sexual benevolence uncomplicated by taboos. With my romanticism, and an innate English yearning to play-at-Arabs, North Africa stood out golden from the map; besides Barbary was then still adventurous and bizarre; and to me, with my hunger for novelty, seductively *new*. Gide's 'Si le grain ne meurt' pointed to erotic enchantment; and Cunninghame Graham's stirring account of 'The Furthest West' showed Morocco to be still remote and gorgeously barbaric. I chose Morocco; and at the end of 1937 said goodbye to my mother. It was the most poignant parting from her I'd ever known; I don't know why—we neither of us could know that we wouldn't see each other again.

The 'express' train from Algiers to Oujda, which then ran twice a week, crawled round the devious contours of the coastal downs; past Tlemcen we left behind the neat French vineyards and ran down into the eastern Moorish plain, and from the windows I suddenly saw that I was travelling straight into the pages of the Bible. More than any Arab country I've since seen—more than Palestine—Morocco reproduces exactly the Bible's atmosphere and familiar images: the very idiom, visually, in which the Gospels are written. Here, in flesh and blood, are those coloured pictures which decorated the Testament in floppy covers given one for one's confirmation. Every few minutes one sees Christ riding on an ass—perched sideways on its bony rump and with His long skirted legs rhythmically kicking its belly.

I tried Fez, elegant, arrogant, patrician; but deep in the dusty plain it was stuffy, and I wanted the sea; and there was a chill discernible in the outward friendliness of the people—symptom I suppose of the fervid nationalism and francophobia that was already simmering in that royal centre of theocratic politics. But before I moved on to Rabat, I had an interesting and biologically instructive experience in Sidi Abdullah, the brothel-town of old Fez, so named in honour of a holy man whose neighbouring shrine is greatly venerated.

I'd made friends in a mild way with a boy of about 17; he proposed one evening that we should pay a visit to Sidi Abdullah. The *quartiers reservés* of the bigger towns in French Morocco were cities within a city: self-contained villages with their enclosing walls and noble gates, their own streets and shops selling sugar and candles and *kif*, their own *pissoirs* and police-stations. Nearly every house was a 'bar', with painted females of all ages and garish cubicles off stage for the stilling of desire. The turbid skins of *les femmes* ran through every shade of brown and ivory from anthracite to alabaster; the effect of rouge upon some brown and near-black complexions can be odd. Small boys peered inquisitively into the doorways, bigger ones hungrily; wiry little Berber *tirailleurs* in crumpled khaki, sadly distant from their tribal lands, formed a good part of the clientèle. They demurely drank fizzy lemonade, cautiously bargained a price with their chosen woman, and quietly went away after 10 minutes in a cubicle.

To Sidi Abdullah ('My Lord the Slave of God') we went; and Abdessalem ('Slave of the Peacemaker') procured in a house he knew a charmingly personable young woman with skin the faint matt shade of raw wool. We drank, I remember, in her cubicle a number of *anisettes* which cost more than she did.

In a description of Arab copulation in the *Arabian Nights* it is said of the lover that he 'knelt between her thighs, bending Sweet-Friend's legs about his waist'. This is what Abdessalem did with his sweet-friend: kneeling, bending forward upon her, his bare back clasped and drawn down in the grip of her encircling legs. Thus did they perform; and thus, I discovered, Arabs always do. Once, strolling by a babbling stream in the foothills of the Atlas, I came upon a copulating pair in the seclusion of an olive-girdled dell; so intent were they upon their pleasure, they didn't heed me; they too were exactly in the posture of the *Arabian Nights* and of Abdessalem. Then, after a while in the country, I made another discovery: I found from observation that the Moorish phallus, when erect, does not stand up at an acute angle with the belly, but rather outwards at right angles or even slightly dipped, like colours lowered in salute; and inferred that millenia of coition in this kneeling, declivitous position have modified the erectile mechanism. It's an observation which may have some anthropological interest.

In Rabat I met Mustapha. It was one of those magnetic encounters of the eyes, beneath the evening lamps of the Boulevard Galliéni, that lead sometimes to a brief bit of amusing commerce and sometimes—but O, so rarely!—to an ineffable happiness. From that evening on, Mustapha and I were together for nearly three years; until the fall of France cut brutally our lives apart. Once again I'd found that 'divine friend': Werner was reincarnate in Mustapha—without Werner's peerless verve and glitter, but with the same sweet genuine loyalty and, in place of Werner's peremptory passion, a soft and wistful gentleness.

I supposed Mustapha to be about 14. He thought so too; but since Moroccans counted their birthdays from some unrecorded point in history like the summer the drought killed 50 sheep or the year the *afreet* appeared in the guise of a jackal, speaking with the voice of a man; and since they build their years out of lunar months, it's best to assess an age by looking, as it were, at the teeth. He had the true Berber's sweet oval face, snub and artless, with none of the Arab's semite severity; his tribe were the *Sghana*, who grazed sheep over the plain above Marrakesh.

We went to Beni Mellal in the northern green skirts of the Atlas, where seven streams kept the encircling village lands lush with fruit and flower; and lived in a sparkling white palace where, in the evenings, on the chequered tiles of our patio with its colonnade of delicate arches, Mustapha played on his one-stringed lute small plaintive melodies which hovered up and down among the three or four notes which compose the Arab key, while I sipped red wine and watched his brown plucking fingers. The night we moved into our palace we set out saucers of milk and sugar to please the good *djinn* and a saucer of salt to dismay the bad; but next day we had a plague of cockroaches which Mustapha said had been sent by the evil *djinn*. We slew the cockroaches with brooms till our patio was littered with corpses. Next morning the corpses had vanished: I thought of the cats I'd seen lurking on the top of the patio wall; but Mustapha said the benevolent *djinn* had proved the stronger and the hostile ones, defeated, had carried the bodies of their friends away.

In the mornings I worked: making notes of everything that Mustapha had told me and I had seen; while he shopped and cooked our midday *tajin*. Later we bathed in one of the streams; or Mustapha would teach me to 'fish' for scorpions by poking grass stalks down their holes in the earth, so that they grab it as a crab in a rock crevice seizes your finger.

And once a week the postman blew his trumpet outside our house and paid me in Moroccan francs my two pounds; it seemed to me wonderful that at the bidding of a bank in London a Moorish postman in the Atlas mountains should hand me cash over the doorstep.

But we tired of Arcady; and, besides, we'd decided to make a home for Mustapha's mother and any of his sisters who needed

one. We went to Sla: a fairy-tale Moorish town almost without
blemish which, piling like white lumps of sugar up a hog's-back
hill to its apex over the sea, overlooks from the north the estuary of
the Bou Regreg and, across the river, its ancient enemy in Rabat,
the fortress of the Oudaya.

Malika, Mustapha's sweet mother, was sadly beset by evil *djinn*;
they attacked her with persistent malice, and she spent a lot of
time trying to drive them off—fumigating herself by putting
beneath her skirts a small earthen brazier of burning benzoin;
procuring amulets written by holy men on bits of paper which she
hid among her clothes; preparing magic potions of which fragments
of a dried chameleon were important ingredients; putting out
saucers of salt; calling softly to her favourite saints; working with
her beloved wool—carding, spinning, weaving, dyeing—which,
like bread, milk, whiteness, and the person of a shereef, was laden
with the divine essence: the *baraka*, which signifies quite simply
'the blessing'.

Some Friday mornings I would go with her to the Sultan's palace
in Rabat to watch him ride out ceremonially for the Friday Prayer.
It was a fine, barbaric pageant; and it gave Oumi Malika a good
draught of the especial *baraka* distilled by God's viceregent on
earth. The benefit of this outing was doubled for Oumi Malika if
the Sultan was riding a white horse, and not a black; the sight of
him on a white horse put her in brighter health and spirits for the
rest of the day.

A favourite sight at the Friday Prayer was El Mokri, astride a
solid mule and looking like Abraham. Behind him rode the lesser
Viziers, all riding mules. El Mokri, reputed to be then 120 years
old, had become Grand Vizier 60 years earlier and had remained
Grand Vizier ever since, under four or five sovereigns; it fascinated
me to believe that perhaps he'd really been born in the year of
Johnnie Walker.

No wonder Oumi Malika and a horde of other women with her
were conscious of the *baraka* when Sidi Mohammed V came
radiantly through the gates on a dancing stallion beautiful as
Pegasus! I was too: he looked like God himself—or perhaps the
Holy Ghost: exquisitely hieratic in soft, sumptuous white: rapt,
regal face framed tightly in the snowy cowl of his *burnous*, like a
knight's in chain-mail: no wonder the women broke into the
ecstatic ululation—tongues trilling like aspens within their cheeks
—with which they greet and consecrate any auspicious happening:

the birth of a son, the public display of the bloodstained towel
after consummation of a marriage; or with which they used, from
the housetops, to goad on their men riding out to battle. Behind
this shining seraph came on foot the bearer of the caliphal umbrella
(necessary, Mustapha said, because the Sultan, being himself a
sun, couldn't be allowed to be outshone). He rode splendidly to the
mosque; but returned rather quaintly inside the semi-state coach
given his grandfather by Queen Victoria—looking now, alas, much
more like a nursemaid in bonnet and cloak than like the God one
thought he was.

Fatima came to live with us, Mustapha's eldest sister; a little
over 20 I should think—she'd been married twice, perhaps three
times: it's easy to forget such details. The dark lid of one eye was
permanently shut; so that the other, the colour of bronze, in
moonlight, seemed to glow in rather ominous solitude. Fatima was
beautiful in a wry, sultry way; she was a bit of a witch, given to
incantations and the sticking of pins into the wax image of an
enemy; and there was in her soul a tumult of sombre passion. She
smoked hashish, and sometimes drank wine—privileged sins of
the male, which no woman should commit; and now and then she'd
go off for a couple of days, into the sensual obscurity of some affair
of the flesh. Then she'd come back, sulking, full of dark silences;
and sit for hours huddled over the charcoal brazier, dropping into
the embers black pieces of incense. 'C'est putain, celle-la ma soeur
—hadda l-ka'hab', Mustapha would say angrily mixing his queer
French with Arabic; but they loved each other. He, of course, was
worshipped by the women: the only male of the family, he was
their lord and master, they his absolute slaves.

As master of the house, it was Mustapha's duty to perform our
ritual sacrifices: when, on the Muslim feasts or important occasions
of our own like the completion by Malika of a splendid piece of
weaving, we killed a goat or even—ah, that was grandeur!—a
sheep. I hated it; but was compelled by a horrible fascination to
watch spellbound for the bloody moment. He looked beautiful and
uncorrupt, knitted skull-cap of geometrical colour on his thick
black hair, as he held the poor victim between his knees and, facing
vaguely eastward, said 'In the Name of God!' The ghastly blood
spouted; and was carefully caught by Oumi Malika in a large dish:
when it had cooled and settled, she would read the omens written
on its surface.

Mustapha gave me a tiny silver bowl, like a thimble, for my

hashish pipe—the long stem was of sculpted wood; and a delicate pouch of gazelle-skin for the *kif*. *Kif*-smoking in Morocco was rather like drinking in England; when a friend called, one said, instead of 'Have a drink?'—'Have a pipe?' A reasonable number of pipes, I found, like a reasonable number of whiskies, did no harm and, unlike whisky, bequeathed no hangover next day. One or two neighbours would come in for a pipe:—a fat, jolly local tinsmith; and a dear dignified old chap who had been a *kaid l-mia*—literally 'centurion'—in the Sultan's army about 35 years earlier and retained the honorific title of Kaid. On these evenings the brass samovar would be hissing, for a lot of tea would be drunk; and on the low table there'd be bread and olives and a bowl of oil for hashish makes one hungry.

Soon, still reclining on my mat and cushion, I start to rise in a singular act of mental levitation until, perfectly comfortable and quite unsurprised, I'm suspended near the ceiling and looking down on the others as if from a stage-box. This produces a wondrous, yet quite calm, feeling of disembodiment—or rather of release: the moorings of one's tethered balloon have suddenly been cut; one's no longer *of* this world, but a spectator absorbedly watching it through a stereoscope. Everything is enhanced and transformed as if touched by the hand of alchemy, the commonplace becomes rare, the inelegant beautiful; what before seemed futile now is fascinating; all experience has turned to pleasure: even the hot wafts of the tinsmith's breath seem like perfume. I go on talking as if nothing odd had happened; but now the words of this banal conversation have become jewelled; the old Kaid's voice, which used to be like sandpaper, has acquired purity; no music was ever sweeter than Mustapha's twanging of the *gnibri*; Oumi Malika's fingers as she twirls her spindle move with an incomparable loveliness; the flicker of the solitary candle seems like the light of paradise. . . . And time, like gravity, has been prorogued: each moment is eternal —there's no beginning to sensation and no ending. . . . I was told that under the spell of *kif* the sexual orgasm can seem to be marvellously, almost unbearably, prolonged. I've been sorry since that I never tested this; I was always too interested and enchanted in the hashish heights by what was already going on to think of orgasm; and then, after a bit, I wanted simply to go to sleep.

Of all the semi-mystical, semi-demonaic, semi-'rock-'n'-roll', religious sects, more pagan than Islamic—of which the snake-

charming Aissaoui of Meknes are the most famous—I found the
Ouled Sidi Khalifa the chiefly interesting; I was such a regular
attendant at their unholy communion with the fiend that they made
me an 'honorary member' and admitted me to their private
sessions.

The Children of St Caliph, to Anglicize the name of this delightful
community, were a tribal sect, into which their children were born;
as the holy family of the Cherkaoui at Boujad are all saints from the
moment of birth. It's inherited, this very special *baraka* that enables
the Children to summon their votary *djinn* for the performance of
the divination and other wizardries in which they were adept. To
their public rites, performed throughout the great festivals of the
Muslim year, women came who had been robbed of the kerchief
into which they'd knotted their money, had mislaid their favourite
amulet or suspected their husbands of infidelity; and often the
Ouled Sidi Khalifa told them who had stolen the money, where to
find the amulet, and how their husbands spent their evenings.
Often, it was said, these divinations turned out right; generally of
course they were hedged round with reservations in case they
weren't. What interested me was the wonderful ritual of diablerie
which was the body and soul of the soothsaying—this last was
doubtless two-thirds showmanship; but the conjuration of the
demons, and the biblical 'possession' of men, women and children
by them, was much more than showmanship.

Three or four Masters of the Drum, squatting in a turbaned,
bearded row, start the proceedings by beating out the gruff rhythms
of their sepulchral serenade. Soon they are chanting in unison with
the beat: holding the hollow tambours, the shape of a big sieve,
close to their faces and singing urgently into it—it's in the pro-
fundities of the drum that the *djinn* hear the summons. The phrases
of the conjuring chant are borne on the same iterative stave of
plainsong; and the two-tone thumping of the drums plays on one's
mind like a devil's tattoo. Were it not for the drumming, one might
think oneself listening to the singing of the Office by the canons
of Santa Maria Maggiore.

Firewood is stacked ready in the 'ring', and a pile of straw soon
to become flaming brands. By ones and twos the Children of St
Caliph begin to dance, though that's not the word used—'to get
under the influence' is nearer the intention of the Arabic; they
dance alone, absorbed by their own sensations, compelled by the
hyponotic rhythm of the drums and chant which imperceptibly is

increasing in speed and passion. Soon a dozen or 20 people are capering within the circle of onlookers: prancing, hopping, quivering as with ague, performing a stealthy cake-walk across the ring's diameter, gyrating like epileptics, jigging up and down with their cowls pulled over their faces to obliterate all but the sensations of oblivion—any sort of traumatic motion which will induce that kind of emotional catalepsy that modern rock-'n'-rollers call 'the groove'. The wood fire will be burning by now; presently two or three of the prancers seize a tuft of straw and frenziedly set it alight —then dance away gazing adoringly into the flames, burying their faces in the burning flambeaux as if they were roses, lovingly lathering their cheeks with red fire, letting the flames steadily lick their flesh. Suddenly one ecstatically flings himself into the fire itself, embracing the burning logs with his arms and kissing the hot ashes until his friends pull him away before his clothes catch fire; others are doing the oddest thing of the lot—they pick up a smouldering ember, pop it into their mouths, and spit out a perfectly real, edible date; I have seen a seven-year-old boy do exactly that. These dates, transmuted apparently from red-hot ash, are eagerly collected by the spectators, for the *baraka* they obviously contain.

I've seen them do the same thing at their private sessions—done for their own 'spiritual' satisfaction when no money was taken at all. How the red-hot embers are transformed in the mouths, even of children, into real dates I don't know: there must have been trickery once, a thousand years ago. But now, this thing which has been inherited through the generations, which is absorbed by children with their mother's milk and has become the sacrament through which they're united with the spirits of darkness, there's no conscious trickery left. They believe in their *djinn* as firmly as Catholics believe in the flesh-and-blood Presence in the consecrated Host. And after all, what one believes to be true is, to the believer, *true*.

As for the 'dancing', it's interesting to observe that the present-day Londoners who jive themselves into exaltation are returning to a practice of the ancient primitive Arabs.

We had some nice Jewish neighbours who on Saturdays, when the lighting of a fire was forbidden them, came to us for our charcoal burning in the hollowed stone brazier. Later, they'd send a little girl with a plate of their food, as a present; it was like our food, though more unctuous. 'We may eat Jewish food', Mustapha said, 'but not make love with Jewish daughters. We may sleep with Nazarene women, but not eat their food.'

By 1939 I began writing a book: a chain of sketches describing the things Mustapha and I did and saw—a sort of 'Stories Toto Told Me', only it was Mustapha who did the telling. Later, when I'd done about half, the book was accepted by Lindsay Drummond, who gave me a small advance; but the war, dislocating mind as well as circumstances, cut the thread and when, back in England, I tried to join the ends, I couldn't. There has always been this flaw in my mind: an inability to keep going across the frontiers of mood, to carry a task begun in one emotional climate over into another; it's as if the mind changed colour. Then Lindsay Drummond went out of business: I don't know what became of my manuscript, and poor Mr Drummond lost his money. This was the first of my unfinished books—I've written so many.

The war came. At first, after one's agonized cry of disbelief in a thing one knew must happen, it didn't seem to count; our tranquillities recurred day after day as before, and our happiness—nothing changed. It seemed so far away from Morocco; and France was safe behind the Maginot Line. 'La France, il a beaucoup la force', said Mustapha, 'Le'Zallemand il est vîte foutu'—and that's what most people seemed to think. And then one day, in our tiny self-centred world, the war abruptly mattered a great deal: our £2 a week came to a stop. It seemed a bit unfair that the whimsical hand of fate should choose poor Oumi Malika to be one of the victims of Currency Control—it was a situation which the invocation of the nether spirits couldn't rectify.

But almost as soon as the crisis was on us it had gone—I was earning more than our £2 by teaching English. I can't now remember how I came to know dear Mme A.; I had little contact with any French and none at all with the lofty elegance of Résidence society, in whose table of precedence Mme A. stood high. She was the gentlest of women; and comfortingly worldly—I felt she might be expecting Voltaire to call; and we became great friends. I write here Mme A. not to disguise her name but because, in my ingratitude, it's one of the few that I can't recall. Soon I was going thrice weekly to her kindly house with its pergola of bougainvillaea to read and converse and discuss the contrarieties of English stress and idiom; and she paid handsomely—a thing most useful when she procured me other high-society pupils who couldn't, for the sake of social 'face', pay less.

I took a lodging in Rabat in May 1940, on the dusty edge of a *terrain vague* behind the Balima Hotel, so as to be nearer my pupils; and left Mustapha with Oumi Malika and his stormy sister Fatima in our little house near the topmost mosque of Sla. Mme A.'s kindly and genteel propaganda had procured me a handful of customers from among the affluent ladies of Résidence society, and consequently the torment of a time-table.

I had a guilty feeling that I was swindling these charming students; but they didn't seem to perceive, as I could only too well, the absurdly empirical character of the lessons I gave them. Indeed, my fame was spreading, and learning English from an apparently well-brought-up Englishman looked like becoming fashionable. And the news from the métropole as France—and, so it seemed in Morocco, England too—scampered to defeat, even encouraged this sort of modishness; catastrophe followed calamity but here, on the other side of the Mediterranean, one could not believe it was true. The French, still splendid, still indomitable, still without a suspicion of the terrible change that was to occur in their soul, felt in their hearts that France and England together *could not* go down; and the upper-class women sought nourishment for this faith in the polite study of their Allies' language. This reliance upon hope was even strengthened, for a time, by the anguish of the Pétain armistice—I saw colonels and captains publicly sob their hearts out at an evening party when the news came.

But only for a time: the British attack at Mers el-Kebir cut like a sjambok across the back of French faith. From what I heard from my French friends, military and civilian, it seemed that Churchill's decision to send the Royal Navy against France's ships at Oran was psychologically a disaster in French Africa, whatever may have been its tactical merits; without Mers el-Kebir, wobbly old General Nogués at the Résidence-Générale might have led all Morocco—then of course still a 'protectorate'—to de Gaulle. Instead, he declared for Vichy.

That July 3rd morning I walked slowly to Mme A.'s carrying the *Echo du Maroc* and its bitter headlines: the aghast anger of the paper's report, its sudden, savage, Anglophobia, showed which way French feeling was going; and I dreaded meeting her. Mme A. was in tears—and through her tears she went for me as if I personally had given the order to fire at Oran. She had put her trust in

England—yet behind England's mask was *la perfide Albion*; she had believed in Churchill—but all his splendid words had turned to treachery: how could I dare look her in the face? There was nothing I could say: the ruthless reason of cold-steel strategy was powerless against an *ancien-régime* Frenchwoman's anger in Morocco on that July 3rd. Her friendliness was never again as warm as it had been; though later, I heard long afterwards, the A.'s house became a centre of Gaullist endeavour. When I returned to Morocco in 1947 I made straight for it; but by then dear Mme A. and old Col. A. had both died.

So often, when one moves about abroad, one has to take the rap for any actions of Whitehall—or even of history—which displeases one's hosts. I thought of dear Mme A. and Mers el-Kebir when, some nine years later, I went to lunch in New Delhi with Sardar Patel, Nehru's Home Minister who nipped off the maharajas with the methodical assurance of a gardener using his pruning knife. I was shown in to a little room which contained nobody but Miss Patel, a fierce birdlike little woman whose principal boast was that she had spent more years in British prisons than her father had. She said her father had been held up at the House and would be twenty minutes late—and for those twenty minutes I was at her mercy, made defenceless not only by shyness and the rules of courtesy but also by the nature of her attack. Why, she stormed, had I and the other British saddled her country with Government House? What did I mean by encumbering Free India with the incubus, the excrescence, the white elephant, that was Government House? What did I expect the Indians to do with this monstrous edifice that Sir Edwin Lutyens and a shameful viceregal conspiracy had palmed off on them? Would I, and Britain, provide the money to keep it up or pull it down? Fortunately, the flow of Miss Patel's vehemence did not allow time for replies; but I was trembling by the time the Sardar, calm and urbane, rescued me with a drink—I think only orange-squash.

Meanwhile, in that early summer of 1940, the leisurely social rhythms of French Rabat went on only in a lowered voice, like a child's playing in the hushed passages of the house in which its parents are dying. The 'European' stretch of beach below the Oudaia, had its usual carpeting of half-nude basking Frenchwomen, watched as usual from a short distance by silent, staring Arab boys, huddled and hooded in their woollen *djellabas*, their only movements the dry licking of lips and the slew of poignant eyes. The evening elegance of the French colonialist upper-class was hardly interrupted: the jewelled little dinners that were like essays in perfection, the punctilious *vins d'honneur* for visiting hierarchs of the administration or army, the evening ranks of clinking drinkers under the arcades. It was fun, and beautiful, under the golden burden of the Moorish daytime, and in the shining respite of the nights; but all the time the war bulletins of Radio Maroc kept drilling into everybody's minds with the dental noise of a circular saw; and behind the placidity there hung fear and a gnawing fatalism. The war news, like the Protectorate propaganda about *la France amie* and *la France civilisatrice*, ran off most Moroccan understanding like rain from a roof; only the nationalists, then still largely conspiratorial, jubilated cryptically over the tragedy of France. I suppose the young Sultan Sidi Mohammed, whom then I didn't know, was already perceiving in his adroit political mind—ironically enough, chosen and schooled by the French—what a chance a French defeat would bring him: a chance he was brilliantly exploiting by the time I returned to the country in 1947.

But most Moroccans, urban Arab or pastoral Berber, were unmoved by the Nazarene conflict beyond the sea. Yet among the ordinary people with whom I had mostly lived, there was a great volume of rather patronizing affection for France; almost anybody would have echoed 16-year-old Mustapha's casual touching sympathy. '*Pauv' La France*,' Mustapha would say in his pidgen-French, writing off the Protecting Power with a lingering fondness: '*pauv' La France—il était genti', quan' même. . . .*'

On the afternoon of June 9th we were drinking whisky on the British Consul General's lawn. The house, as I remember it, was a brown block of respectability standing on a peripheral eminence of the French town and charmingly overlooking the sparkling buff plain which, brindled like a paratrooper's camouflage suit, rolled away hazily towards Meknes and Fez. The Consul-General was respectable too, in a gloomy way: a tall, morose man with an air of perpetual disillusionment. Although his post was the Shereefian capital and the seat of the French Résidence, any work more exciting than franking passports and registering British-Protected Persons was done at Tangier, where the foreign missions were. Behind the house ranged a glorious lawn, green and English, shelving gently towards some of those profuse flower-beds for which northern Morocco is so apt.

Here we were drinking Mr Hurst's whisky—and plenty of it; glowering down an imperious nose into the gloom of his own thoughts, he didn't stint his guests: Harry Whyte, an ex-Fleet Street Scotsman; myself and a couple of others; and the Italian Consul-General.

The Italian Consul-General that day drank a great deal of whisky. He was a humpty-dumpty comic of a man: the kind of embarrassing droll whose unlively banter so often humiliates watchers of the 1960 television. He turned somersaults, vaulted over chairs, juggled with bottles, and mimicked functionaries of the French administration. He was hectically gay; for him, apparently, war had no worries.

Next day 60 Italian divisions fell upon the wounded flank of France. Perhaps it was the strain of an unbearable secret that impelled the Italian Consul-General to perform these alcoholic antics on an Allied lawn on the eve of the Duce's facile triumph—though it seems unlikely that Mussolini's plans can have been confided to so humble an official. But what at the time seemed odder was that a British Consul-General should have entertained any representative of the Axis in those dark days—let alone, even fortuitously, on that day of all days; and poor Mr Hurst, who perhaps mildly hoped that his Foreign Office whisky might in some occult way have added power to the Allies' diplomatic elbow, and Britain with him, came in for some sour criticism in and around the Résidence.

The Italian Consul-General, that June 10th, was confined to his consulate; Italians all over Morocco were gathered in for internment, protesting, most of them, that they were against Mussolini's war. In a fortnight's time, under the dictate of the Armistice, they were let out again; the Consul-General's principal anxiety, we learned, during his confinement, had been for the safety of an Italian ship bringing him a new suit of official livery, expensive with the braiding of a Fascist consul-general.

Shortly after the Pétain surrender, we Allied 'ressortissants' began to feel its effects: General Nogués, a negatory man anyway, was choosing the *laissez-aller* negation of Vichy; and a rumour that Britons in Morocco who did not get out quick were to be interned seemed, from enquiries among my French friends, to be approaching fact. Harry Whyte had already left for the neutral enclave of Tangier where he had fixed himself up with a 'string' to the *Daily Express*. I wanted to hang on as long as I could: partly because I was still able to make a living by teaching, but mainly because I shrank from leaving Mustapha. I thought of going into hiding with Mustapha, into Arab anonymity—perhaps moving the family down into his tribal pastures; but that, I saw, would be lunatic: by putting me out of reach of funds, it would do Mustapha no good at all.

Soon there were reports that Axis missions were on their way to Morocco; it was time to be off, and I followed Harry Whyte to Tangier. Mustapha had been with me for nearly three years; it was one of those partings, shocking and apparently intolerable, which in a life like mine ineluctably repeat themselves down the years: one gets over them, and fresh friendships succeed the ones they cut short; but their pain, and the happiness that made that pain inevitable, are branded in one's memory for ever. I gave him what money I could, and a letter to Mme A., who, gentle as ever, had promised to find him some domestic job among her friends. When I boarded the train, I told him that I would come back. Today, two decades later, the picture of him standing on Rabat railway platform is as bright as it was then: the jester's hood of his purple *djellaba* clutched beneath his chin, framing the harrowing brown face in the impeccable oval of a miniature. I thanked heaven for Islam; which permits even a 16-year-old to accept with fatalism the crassest quirks of fortune.

I promised myself I would come back; and on the lumbering journey north I tried to devise conspiratorial ways of doing so— vaguely it seemed that entry into the field of espionage might be the thing. As events turned out, it was to be seven years before I saw Mustapha again; and by then he was charmingly married, and dear, whimpering Oumi Malika, whose only defence against the daily encroachments of tribulaton was the concoction of magic and alliance with friendly *djinn*, had died.

Tangier in 1940 was not yet entirely the international elysium for crooks, outlaws, escapists, drunks, aberrant sexual eccentrics and sedulous voluptuaries of both sexes that since the war it has been. But even then almost any curious thirst could be assuaged; boys or pubescent girls of half-a-dozen races were two-a-penny, guilty manipulators of foreign currencies and the procurers of curious pleasures or illegal commodities lurked at every café-table; and the sombrely sinful streets behind the Socco Chico were full of caravanserai with evocative names like Hotel Satan or Pension Delirium.

But Tangier then was especially a mart for 'intelligence': one of those indulgent patches of common-ground which, like Stockholm and Lisbon, Beirut, Hong Kong and Macao, are as necessary to war, hot or cold, as the public-houses of Fleet Street are necessary to its contending newspapers. For one thing, it belonged to nobody, but lived under a quarrelsome condominium of France, Great Britain, Spain and Italy, in which the nominal sovereign, the Sultan, had practically no say; for another, nearly everybody who lived there was ready enough to sell his services, or the promise of them, to anyone who would buy; for a third, none of the multinational organs of the administration bothered much about what happened outside their own personal rivalries, mainly commercial.

Shabby little men with names like Pinto, Gonzales or Benmoussa haunted the foyers of the belligerent consulates and furtively handed each other slips of paper in the Place de France or the Socco Chico; one at least, a Portuguese, would make his way every Friday from the British legation to the German, from the French to the Italian, collecting his wages from each. (Tangier was the seat of foreign diplomacy in Morocco, and the consulates-general had the local status of 'legation'.)

Drinking at our British table at the Hôtel de France which overlooked the port and the *playa*, Harry Whyte and I, and perhaps George Greaves, would often be flanked by Enemies—Germans and Italians with a sprinkling of Spaniards flaunting their musical-comedy uniforms. When one appeared among these parties of roistering foes, their voices would be raised in calculated but impersonal insult, or hushed into the whisper of artificial conspiracy.

Everybody was drinking enormously. One seemed to swirl from one bar to another in an atmosphere of alcohol and hectic, though spurious, adventure; and the supporters of the two sides of the war aired the slogans of their countries like hearty cup-tie enthusiasts, or passed each other in the street with fastidious noses in the air. Patriotism was vocal, and required no sacrifice. One day, in the patio of the Minzah Hotel, I found two tweed-clad English women, hefty and virile, with muscular grey hair. They were vigorously immersed in Scotch and, as I passed, one was saying in that loud English voice: 'What are we *doing* for our country, you ask, Emmie dear? We are *drinking* for our country!'—and she lifted her whisky-tumbler in a splendid toast to old England. I never saw them again; probably they were quickly off to Britain to work magnificently in the W.V.S. or Civil Service—they were that kind.

George Greaves was already one of the great characters of Tangier. His Australian truculence, his power of verbal venom, the Hogarthian vigour of his satire, and his infinite knowledge of the private lives of anybody who mattered, from the British Minister down, made him a personage to be respected. For his friends he possessed an unfailing fund of kindliness; for those whom he chose to make his enemies, his ruthlessness was waspish. George today is one of the two social pontiffs in Tangier whose good books any visitor—if he wants to avoid leaving, disappointed, by the next boat—must make a point of getting into. The other is that gracious and lovable dignitary who, with the *hauteur* of a Versailles duchess, the *cortesia* of a Papal chamberlain, a heart made of honey and, often, a tongue like a scorpion's sting, rules over Dean's Bar. But in 1940 Dean—the cognomen, like Caesar, has acquired the larger attributes of a title—had not yet reached Tangier; and Tangier was the poorer. Since the war, however, the name of Tangier has come to denote merely the environs of Dean's Bar; and a silent blackball from Dean—indicated from behind his well-bred bar by a subtle movement of those haughty brows, perhaps a flutter of the dark, unfathomable eyes—can seem socially far more damaging than being turned down for the Royal Enclosure.

To sit with George Greaves outside the Café de Paris, or on a pavement of the Socco Chico, was to become a privileged peeper into the souls of the passers-by. His great bulk hunched forward in the cane-chair, chins resting on one hand with an erect forefinger ranged along the imperial nose, trilby hat tilted over the pale eyes, he would watch the passing notables derisively. Suddenly he would explode in an expectorant noise of disgust, like the beginning of a full-blown Neapolitan gob. 'See him!' jerking his head in the direction of a trim supernumerary in the British Legation who was also a local commercial magnate. 'Don't touch 'im—don't *touch* 'im. Poison, that's 'im. *And* he murdered 'is first wife—puts flowers on her grave every anniversary of the day he murdered 'er. I *know*, f—— me if I don't.' His destructive eye would fall on a prosperous-looking Arab. 'That one—used to be the kept boy of a former French Minister: *now* look at 'im—wouldn't tell you the time if he 'ad two watches. . . . Hah! There's P.'—mentioning a famous name. 'In the Foreign Office, he was. Foreign Office my arse!

Only diplomacy 'e does now, 'e does on small girls!' So his social commentary would proceed; until, perhaps, his attention was caught by a comely calf twinkling by in the sunlight. 'Nice drop o' leg', he would observe. 'Cor'—that *is* a nice droppa leg!'

A delightful companion: amusing, informative, generally shrewd: mouthing sardonic imprecation in his fruitily uninhibited Australian vowels; and a wonderful friend—as long as you *were* a friend.

George carried about a favourite antipathy for a certain Col. Ellis, the brother of an industrial baronet and M.P. of northern England. Toby Ellis was a powerful little man in 'the Zone': a Tangier tycoon with a controlling hand in all kinds of ventures from insurance to the town's bus service. He was also president of the Chamber of Commerce and, by way of war service, head of the British legation's department of 'information'; from his office issued, for Tangier's variegated public, roneographed explanations of England's war aims, and into his office went the fruits of back-street espionage. Toby Ellis could hardly have been qualified for this post by his colonelcy, which was of the Veterinary Corps; but his long familiarity with the ambiguities of the International Zone and his intimacy with the heart of Tangier's tortuous commercial anatomy gave him special powers and knowledge. Nearly everybody was a ready-made informer; and the colonel, at the centre of commercial prestidigitation, was excellently placed for the reception or pursuit of political rumour.

Harry Whyte was now compiling the Legation's bulletin of war-news and propaganda, and was a part-time functionary under Ellis; a circumstance which seemed to me valuable when I decided to go into espionage myself.

It wasn't espionage for its own sake—or for the sake of my country—that attracted me: I saw in it a means of returning to Mustapha in the French 'zone', now under the thumb of Vichy. Gusts of vague hearsay were blowing through Tangier about what was going on down there—that German troops were in Rabat, that German officers were in control of Vichy forces in Morocco; not even the legations seemed to know more than the drinkers in the Socco Chico. I thought: Why not go and see? Through Harry Whyte I offered to do so. At first Ellis was interested; until he asked, *Does he drink?* 'Drink?' guffawed Harry, a far greater toper than I've ever been, 'does he *drink*? I'll say he drinks——' That, of course, settled it. I didn't blame Toby for recoiling from Harry's spirited report. But I did tersely remark to Harry that if we'd known beforehand his conscience would require him to err so fancifully on the side of truth, we should have been saved the trouble of broaching the matter at all. I wasn't, and never have been, an 'alcoholic', and could, when expedient, 'leave it alone'.

But there's always been a discrepant tincture of obstinacy in my generally fidgety nature; and once a project has waxed in my mind it doesn't easily wane: I nibble away at its fulfilment like a mouse gnawing in the night. Harry Whyte had been a sub-editor on the *Daily Express*, and knew well the Foreign Editor of the day, Charles Foley (whom 15 years later I was to entice into the foundation of the *Times of Cyprus*). We wrote to Foley: and before long Sefton Delmer called on us in Tangier, flying in from some outpost of the war. In an alcove of the Minzah bar the three of us discussed the plan like conspirators; and the Great Man, looking like a bishop drawn by John Leech, flew on to London. In after years, Tom Delmer was often an amiably mordant drinking companion in some journalistic bar between Athens and Angkor; he would hugely lumber in, full of episcopal moment, enceinte with the intimacies of unnumbered prime ministers, and growl: 'My dear chap, you'd better have a quick one on Lord Beaverbrook while you've the chance'; and one wouldn't see him again for six months.

Foley, to my unbounded joy, thought the scheme worth a small newspaper gamble, and cabled £50; and I slipped anonymously into bated preparation.

By then—the autumn, I suppose, of 1940—the Spaniards had 'taken over' the international zone of Tangier: of the other partners in the condominium, France was out, England's hands were too full and too weak, and Italy was Franco's friend; the Sultan, no vassal of Vichy, was biding his clever time. In one way, this absorption of 'the zone' into that ruled by Spain helped me: it loosened control of the frontier between the two; and although for excise and political purposes Spanish police-watch was maintained, passage across was slightly eased. And this was my plan: on foot and *en arabe* across Spanish Morocco to the southern border town of Ksar el-kebir, whence I'd slip through the frontier posts, Spanish and French, and catch a bus down to Rabat and Mustapha. It was a scatter-brained notion: had I got as far as worming myself into the centre of that individious no-man's-land, between Franco's Scylla and Vichy's Charybdis, I'd almost certainly have been shot. But I was stopped before that.

The first weakness of my plan was that I couldn't go alone. I knew enough Arabic to get through the formulae of an Islamic day, and was fluent in the ritual gestures of social intercourse—when for instance to step out of my slippers, when to kiss my own right forefinger, how to eat with my right hand only (the left is condemned to the basest of purposes and is therefore haunted by devils, which is why Mustapha had given me a silver ring to wear on it); but conversation at once gave me away. Besides, I didn't know the way; and a mendicant pilgrim, dumb by God's will and illiterate, couldn't plausibly walk across Morocco reading a French ordnance map. I had to have a companion: the secret had to be shared. To keep the circle of confidence as small as possible I took the first man sent me: a minikin, mumbling, wizened monkey of a rogue called Abderrhaman ('Slave of the Merciful'), who agreed to guide me down to Ksar el-kebir and over the frontier for a sum so small that I should have been suspicious—half to be paid down and half by Harry on his return to Tangier. But I couldn't afford suspicion: the walls of my little intrigue were too flimsy to pick and choose in. I sent this unattractive gnome to the market to buy me second-hand clothes; and withdrew from my usual haunts to grow a beard. It came lushly enough for me to sculpt it in the Moorish mode, as gardeners sculpt a privet hedge. I did an elegant job: too elegant, perhaps, for a beggar. (I had no fears about my drab hair and muddy pale eyes: in the north fair heads and blue eyes were a frequent Phoenician heritage.) Then Abderrhaman shaved my scalp—I remember what an ass I felt; but I was now physically an impeccable Moor: fortunately, as if a guardian angel in my infancy had foreseen this Muslim interlude, I'd been circumcised; and when, in a river, I washed naked with my brethren I could confidantly (but with ritual modesty) display the bodily symbol of my faith.

He brought my clothes—dressed in which, so odd is destiny, I was three months later sauntering through London, with small boys whistling 'Sheik of Araby' behind me. A long white cotton undershirt, like a nightgown (what grimy skin, O Lord, did it last enclose?); a tattered *serual*—those knee-length knickers with braided flanks and a seat so profound that one can carry home a week's shopping in them; an old doublet, the splendour of its braided buttons now frayed and tarnished; a *djellaba* of coarse brown wool, a good deal tattered but still a splendid garment for sleeping out in; a pair of old slippers, brown and stiff with age; and a dozen yards of butter muslin a foot wide, which I learned to wind criss-cross round my head. I possessed already a red leather purse about a foot square which, containing precious objects like one's *kif* pipe, was slung from a shoulder on a sable silk cord; I loved this bag as I loved Mustapha: he had given it to me two years earlier.

I took only a few pesetas of Spanish money; and sewed some £10 of French francs into the lining of the waistcoat. Into the bag went the pesetas, my silver-bowled pipe and the hashish pouch of gazelle-skin, bread and black olives, and a small piece of paper on which a holy man in Sla had written an Arabic text; this, Mustapha had told me, would always be a good safeguard against the forces of evil.

It was early in 1941 that we set out, I and my ominously muttering companion, one bright, brisk dawn. We'd arranged that I should 'act dumb'; uttering, in conversation, no more than the enigmatic animal noises of the tongueless. This was important because, at the shrines and mosques where Abderrhaman planned to sleep, we were bound to meet others. I wanted to spend the nights in the open, away from the haunts of men, but he insisted that we should have the protection of sanctity, being nervous of djinn and jackals—if he couldn't sleep inside a tomb, he'd have his back against its hallowed stones. This matter of shrines was a ticklish one: Morocco was one of the few Muslim countries where a Christian was still debarred from entering a holy place—to do so could bring the direst vengeance; it seemed that my nights were to pass in uneasy thought not only of Spanish or Vichy bullets but also of Islam's cleaving wrath.

But we hadn't been going long before I saw that Abderrhaman himself was far more frightening than these speculative terrors. He was out of his mind; and to be tied to the apron-strings of a raving madman seemed more perilous than the likelihood of being caught in an illegal masquerade by inimical men. He had the face of a bewhiskered mummy; and strange dried-up eyes that looked, but weren't, blind. At the end of each half-hour's slow walk, he'd squat down, brew green tea in an old jam tin, and light his hashish pipe; but, as well, he was swallowing small pills, which later he told me were opium. He spoke scarcely a word to me; but was steadily talking to himself—shouting to himself, raving, arguing, challenging: since, though, even when yelling he mumbled, I couldn't make out his words, if words they were. We must, to our companions of the evening, have appeared an odd pair: he ranting a deranged tirade into his own ears, I emitting the faint yelps of the vocally maimed. Fortunately, Moors pay no heed to eccentric behaviour or physical deformity, regarding both as the blessed fulfilment of a Divine whim. Now and then, as we walked, he would suddenly stop dead, turn on me with gestures of violence, and pour out an alarming flood of mumbled malevolence.

Soon the stiff edges of my old slippers had rubbed my feet raw, and I carried them in my hand, going barefoot; until stony ground forced me to put them on again. In spite, though, of these worries, we were moving in the right direction; Abderrhaman seemed to know what he was doing, and in his smoky mind had plotted a workable route. I began to think, after two or three days, that he was going to keep his word and deliver me on the French side of the border. One evening, the fourth, I think, he spoke to me reasonably as we approached the shrine we were to sleep in. Here, he said, I must be punctiliously cautious; this was one of the holiest of places where a Nazarene's life wouldn't be worth a pinch of tea if he were caught fouling it with his presence.

It was a small mosque, appended to a great saint's tomb; beautiful with dainty pillars and keyhole arches and a circular patio; it had its custodian, himself saintly, and was nightly a caravanserai of pilgrims. I remember one awful moment when, in a certain part of it, I didn't know whether I should take off my slippers or not; and hung, so to speak, in a panic of belief that I'd committed a tell-tale heresy. Abderrhaman, after his sane warning to me, was that night more maniac than ever; raving and crazily declaiming to our solemn fellow-guests, and terrifyingly pointing to me, as I were the subject of his fury. I shrank into my djellaba and obliviously smoked my pipe, pretending an ecstatic unconcern.

But nothing happened; and next day, pursuing the contours of the rolling down that was the western foothold of the steeps and ravines of the Riff, we found ourselves looking from a charming brink down to the green vale of trees and water from which the minarets of Ksar el-kebir rose delicately. Beyond gently sloped the hills on the French side; and behind, the cork forests and the sweet plain unfolding towards Rabat. I was on the threshold of the promised land. It was then that Abderrhaman dropped his bombshell. 'I'm not coming any further', he mumbled—and offhandedly set off along the path we had just come. I sat, limp with wonder, and watched his horrible mean figure slowly diminish into the distance. The joy of seeing the back of him was muted by this new perplexity: trying to cross the frontier with Abderrhaman would have been bad enough; alone, illegal and dumb in this uncharted world much worse. I wondered why Abderrhaman hadn't simply killed me: he could easily have done so, and, searching with his fumbling fingers, torn out my secret money.

We had, on our way, avoided any place where we might attract the prying notice of Spanish agents. I was determined to keep clear of this big market town; and that night curled up in the open under the camouflage of palmetta clumps. I've never felt so lonely, so *deserted*; as old Italian men, in moments of distress, call aloud to the mothers of their childhood, *O mamma mia*, so I, that bewildered night, whispered to mine. Once in the deep dusk voices came approaching, and passed close: while I froze into the safety of my dark djellaba's hood. Next morning I went to the river to drink and bathe; I still had a little bread left. The rest of the day I spent scouting the land ahead, the Spanish outposts and the French hills beyond: I thought I'd roughly traced a course through. I slept out again, determined to try next morning. But of course I had no food; and was compelled to go in to market.

It was cynically said, in the Spanish Morocco of that time, that one-third of the male population was in the Spanish colonial army, one-third in prisons, and one-third in the police. Moreover, the great weekly *souk* to which the tribes came in for marketing were so cannily watched by the police that every face was known; an unfamiliar one was suspect. Mine was unfamiliar.

I wasn't surprised when I was stopped by a clerkly Arab with a careful hidalgo moustache and a townee's *tarboush*—a palpable 'dick'. Bluff, of course, was useless and when I came before the Spanish police, with their sly, lazy eyes and humid smiles, I told the truth—I was English, trying to reach the Vichy zone for my newspaper. They unpicked my clothes for hidden clues and took my French money (later returned to me in pesetas, at a rate of exchange about 50 per cent in their favour); they were fascinated by Mustapha's piece of magical writing, preserving it in a thick envelope. Their artless delight over catching me was charming: from the way they talked and telephoned and rubbed their beautiful sleek hands and peered at that Arabic text, it seemed that this was an important day for the Axis: a real English spy! Then they locked me into a whitewashed cellule like a Moorish saint's tomb.

They'd given me back my pipe and gazelle-skin pouch and my

few pesetas. I squatted on the sand floor and smoked. I remember feeling suddenly very tired (I'd eaten nothing for a long time); but also a delightful curiosity—I was impatient to see what would happen. I've always loved novel situations.

Then the procession of sightseers began. Every few minutes the key would crash into the lock and some personage dressed with the feminine flamboyance of senior Spanish officers would gaze at me, mouth agape with wonder. These visits continued for some time, and were pleasantly comic. After some hours I was driven in a truck full of soldiers to a military fortress where I was lodged in a charming stone turret. I enjoyed my stay here; I could sit in the deep medieval embrasure of my barred window, and look infinitely out over the boundless fair plain of French Morocco and a broad ambulant river glinting in the sun; and talk to the charming little Moorish soldiers who were guarding me. They brought me glasses of mint tea or a plate of *ksuksu*; I was happy in a negative, *far niente* way. But after a few days, with the determinist inconsequence of a prisoner's star, I was abruptly whisked to Tetuan, to the great civil prison that stands over the capital like a Barbary Pentonville.

This was a prison of great interest. It housed then—besides a vast agglomeration of Spanish Republicans and ordinary criminals, guilty or innocent—an odd but moving miscellany of Allied heroes: men trapped in this Spanish lobster-pot while trying to reach Gibraltar after escaping from German or Vichy captivity. Surely they were heroes: the secret courage and dogged resolution of what they'd done can't have been surpassed in any corner of that war; and here they were in the living burial of Tetuan—*éperdus*, written off, slowly famishing. There were a dozen or more; the pattern of their journey was the same. After the escape, they'd made their way to the Mediterranean, somehow crossed to North Africa (one shipped himself as merchandise in a packing-case), and ridden the westward trains clinging, in the manner of the American hobo, to axles or buffers. One, swimming the Moulouya river with his clothes on his head, had lost them; and on the Spanish side had walked stubbornly on stark naked, until a kindly Moor gave him some trousers. Another had escaped from a German camp only to land in a Vichy one; he escaped from that too. It seemed to me magnificently symbolic, this community of spirit which caused these brave men independently to reject defeat: to march on, each one separately, in an unbending desire to join de Gaulle or the

British and fight again. But on the very last lap to Gibraltar, Franco's Moroccan lobster-pot caught them.

I remember a young Rumanian, one of those athletic Jewish blonds, who, at the Sorbonne before the war, had rushed into the Foreign Legion to fight Hitler and, with the fall of France, deserted from it to join de Gaulle; two stolidly unyielding French *sous-officiers*, well into middle-age and already showing signs of six months' starvation; a young French-Canadian passing himself off for tactical reasons as a Belgian; a declamatory Pole who fondled a rosary and cried to his engulfed wife and children; two boyish Belgians; a hairy French *poilu* of the old sort, inclined to steal one's crusts of bread. They were splendid, knightly men; and among them I was unworthily placed.

There was an open courtyard where we could sit agreeably in the warm winter sun and search the seams of our clothes for lice. We weren't locked into cells but shared a large stone chamber like a chapel's crypt, sleeping in rows on its concrete floor; it was cold at night. We got on well together; though the awful mental darkness of this long sepulture, and its physical decrement, was fraying the nerves of some who'd been there a long time. The thing that exacerbated our amity was food—the lack of it. We were ravenously hungry. Once a day we got a tin of dish-water soup with a few loathsome solids in it; giving one's stomach, if one could eat it, a laxative void. But there was blessed bread; lovely, coarse, gritty, maggoty bread. It was this precious stuff that sometimes brought acrimony: one would scamper with one's bread into a corner, like a dog with his bone, and another, creeping up behind, would snatch the piece one was putting into one's mouth.

I managed to send a message to the British consul; his name, I think, was Moneypenny—or was it Pennyfather? He kindly sent me twenty Gold Flake—I can see now the homely yellow of that friendly packet, seeming in my excited hand to shine like a crock of gold. But I heard no more from the British consul. I perfectly sympathized with the British for not bothering about me; as, naturally, I bore no grudge against the Spaniards for arresting me. Both were right. Sir Samuel Hoare, then, was exchanging British petrol for Franco's malevolent neutrality; and Spain was glad to sell oranges to England: the eruption of a British 'spy' was, to both, a nuisance. But I think it's likely that this strategic commerce between London and Madrid had something to do with my being excused the firing squad and with my eventual transportation to

England, in British custody. The shooting of an Englishman, just then, might have caused political irritation.

About once a week I was taken to a grand office for 'interrogation'. There was nothing forbidding about this; the interviews were garlanded with courtesy, and, indeed, with public-school banter—my interrogator, oddly, had been at Dulwich College and spoke an excellent English peppered with tags like 'my dear chap', and 'oh, jolly good'. He was charming, of course, as Spaniards are to a foreigner even when he's their prisoner. He kept harping back to my scrap of talismanic Arabic, holding it up to the light, looking at it with a magnifying-glass. He couldn't believe that it didn't conceal some incriminating message—because he couldn't believe what I told him: that it was a bit of Moorish magic. It was amusing, six years later, if a little embarrassing, to meet this nice man again while paying a courtesy call on the Spanish High Commissioner in Tetuan; it was the sort of situation one passed off with a laugh.

Change of circumstance at Tetuan was announced, with the abruptness beloved of prisons, by a sharp kick before dawn on the soles of one's feet. One knew, when this occurred, that something out of the ordinary was going to happen; but one wasn't told what. One morning, after I'd been there six weeks, my feet were kicked; I was ordered to get up and come; there was no time even to say goodbye to my friends. Down through the great gate we went, into the sloping road above the town; three policemen and I drove away in a car. We stopped at a café, where my guards allowed me to buy them, and myself, some sour-sweet coffee. I longed to ask whether I was going to be executed or released—I felt it must be one of the two. 'Are we going far?' I asked casually. 'You'll see,' they answered. Always disliking to seem inquisitive, I asked no more.

But it was neither. We drove to Tangier, where I was locked up in the Kasbah—this time in a cell. In the big courtyard where we were put for exercise I came upon Harry Whyte, swept in because of his connection with me.

I was taken before a superior policeman, looking professionally solemn like an undertaker. With a bow, he handed me two letters, open and well perused. One was from my mother, now 75—a brief sad note, written in a hand so shaky and feeble I barely could recognize it. The other was from my brother to say that she had died. These letters must have been in Spanish hands while I was at Tetuan. The superior policeman made a little courteous speech of commiseration.

Then suddenly, some eight weeks after I'd set out to rejoin Mustapha, a clerk came from the British consulate to tell Harry and me that the Spanish had agreed to release us into our country's hands. I was allowed to wire to my brother for £10 to meet me in Gibraltar; and one windy morning we were driven down to the port and put aboard the old *Rescue*, that aged tugboat which used to ply twice weekly between Tangier and the Rock. That night we slept in the *Scythia*, a P. & O. liner converted for war service; built for 750 passengers, she carried on this voyage 3,000. I possessed now nothing but my Moorish tatters: passport, clothes, luggage, had been 'seized' by the Spanish and not restored. Next morning I stepped briskly to the gangway, bent on fetching my ten pounds from the bank, but was sternly stopped by the Master at Arms. '*You're* not going ashore', he said with meaningful disdain; and it dawned on me that I was still 'in custody'. They feared, I supposed, that I'd try to slip back to Morocco. I asked to see the 'O.C. Troops'—the kind of colonel who gets that kind of job; he arranged for the collection of my money.

Before we sailed I was interviewed by 'Intelligence'. Bespectacled sergeants of the Intelligence Corps would suddenly turn up and question me, sensibly, about what I had seen; I made a point each time of reporting the presence in Tetuan gaol of those splendid Allied orphans who had been my friends. I hope I started the wheels of diplomacy turning to their advantage.

Astern of *Scythia* came another big ship; and spread around was an escort of impressive magnitude: a battleship, a small aircraft carrier, a cruiser, and a whole flurry of frigates. It was flattering— 'Well,' I remarked to a sailor, 'they do seem to think we're valuable people!' 'Don't you kid yerself,' he said. 'Them ships ain't for *us*. 'Er astern's carrying *copper*.'

It was a pleasant voyage, warm and smooth: eight days to Glasgow, by way of Iceland. Once a Fokker-Wolf came eyeing us from far aloft; once our destroyers dropped depth charges; but we were undisturbed.

I, though, was much disturbed by an outcrop of boils which, spreading corruption through my limbs, made me hobble about in pain: the result, I suppose, of two months' starvation. I 'went sick' (the *Scythia* was run like a military camp), and was told by a supercilious medico of the R.A.F. that I had nothing wrong (does the opiate of the Officers' Mess still suborn young novices from the hospitals into the easy prescription of a 'M-and-D'?). By the time we made fast in the Clyde one fragrant Sunday morning of first summer, I could hardly walk.

Ashore, I had another interview with young men of 'Intelligence'; and then set off to find a doctor, limping painfully along the Sunday-somnolent by-ways of Glasgow, drab avenues of dormant aspidistras. I felt, I remember, a bit perplexed by my clothes: how, if I found a doctor, should I account for this odd appearance? I decided, to escape giving a tedious explanation, to speak in broken English and keep up the masquerade. I came upon a brass plate; and timidly rang the bell. The door was opened by a small man wiping porridge from his mouth—a man of such nobility and gentle kindness that I honour his memory still.

'Me ill,' I said, 'leg, him very bad'; picking up the skirt of my djellaba to show my festered knee. With tender skill he dressed my leg; he asked no question nor showed surprise at being visited during breakfast by such a curious patient. I thought for a moment of those furtive doctors one sees in gangster-films who, lips sealed, unquestioningly remove bullets from midnight malefactors. Fumbling for money in my great scarlet purse, I asked how much I owed him. He waved a kindly Christian hand: 'Och', he said in charmingly broad Scots, 'I never take money from a member of a releegious orrder.' There was nothing I could do but reverently raise my hand in silent blessing, and in humility withdraw. My leg, almost at once, felt better.

In London I telephoned to my brother in Sussex (my sister Nancy was in Ireland), who asked me to stay. At Charing Cross I was a little chary of going through the platform gates, flanked by policemen, civil and military—I had none of the statutory personalia of war: no identity card, ration card, nothing; not even a passport. But the policemen waved me on with a flourish, almost with a salute. I felt like the Sheikh of Kuwait. Eardley and his nice new wife welcomed me sweetly, found me some clothes, and prescribed vitamin pills.

## 14

THE LONDON YEARS that came, until the end of 1946, were duller, for me, than most (though none of my life, thank heaven, has been *dull*); and notable chiefly in memory for my 'second row', my embezzlement of Lady Margaret Orr-Ewing's brooch and my entry into a 'career'. About time: I was 44.

On my mother's death I received the remnants, having spent most of it in advance, of my patrimony: about £1,000. I started to spend this, went back to old haunts and found again some old friends. But many had gone: Phyl de Chroustchoff was dead; Boris and Ida King, his sweet new wife, were remote in Wales; the Plough was abandoned. Nina Hamnett was in her usual place at the Fitzroy Tavern—now nightly a bedlam of rampaging drunks and a mart of male prostitutes; Charles Ashleigh I found, of course; Edgell Rickword and his wife Jonny; William Empson now and then. Dylan Thomas I would find often in the Swiss pub, in Old Compton Street; I didn't like him: gross, dirty, sprawling aggressively across the bar. But I never knew him sober, and thus never *knew* him. Another drunken poet who came to the Swiss was poor Brian Howard, a haunted soul hungry for tragedy, racked by the tormenting ecstasies of seeking 'the divine friend much desired'. He too was tiresome when drunk; but a vivid, susceptive person beneath the obfuscations of escape. And Brian, like so many of that delirious generation, later took his own life, in Spain;*swallowing the deathly pill, I believe, before the eyes of his mother.

But circumstances, in 1941, had edged me into a fresh sphere of life: Fleet Street. I had met Charles Foley, a captivating man whose immensely tall severity and clipped abruptness of speech, though concealing like a cloak of shyness great depths of human understanding, dismayed a lot of people; he possessed a brilliant, and exactingly professional, journalistic mind (which is like no other sort of mind) and very young had leapt to the lofty post of

Foreign Editor of the *Daily Express*. In that office he was known as 'the colonel': a reflection, no doubt, of the uncompromising surface of his manner. For some reason, we got on well.

In those days the *Express* was running on the leader page serial 'features' in six instalments, Monday to Saturday. Generally, after a few days of preliminary blurb, these started off with a wham on the first day, and then dwindled to a few inches of print on the last. Foley set me to write one of these; the narrative of my Moorish 'adventure'; and himself, when I'd done it, re-dressed it in *Daily Express* language. I still had my beard; and on the roof of that glass building, one day, put on again my turban and *djellaba* for photographs, which, in various postures, appeared in the paper about nine days running. When it was all over, Foley gave me a chit for £100 to take to the 'Accounts'. 'Would you like a cheque', they asked, 'or will you take it out of the petty cash?' I took it in notes: marvelling that so grand a sum could be thought of anywhere as 'petty cash'.

One of the consequences of this *Daily Express* effusion was an invitation from Chatham House to 'address' its members on the situation in Morocco. I thought this odd—who was I to address so grand a body? I shrank from the presumptuousness of it. But I was told that to talk at Chatham House put a bright feather in one's cap; and, after all, I knew the country better probably than any Englishman, and had lived there in an intimacy denied to the diplomats. (Many years later I was having luncheon at Buck's Club with a friend, a Member of Parliament, who was going to Morocco and wanted to hear something about it; we'd had plenty to drink and I was holding forth with fluent authority, volubly destroying the policy of Marshal Juin and the French Government—this was after my second, journalistic, stay in the country. Suddenly we became aware, at the next table, of a man with a long face and drooping moustache who, agape and agog, was listening to my harangue. It was the Marquess of Salisbury, acting Foreign Secretary. I've often wondered whether, that day, I influenced British policy in North Africa.)

I'm a clammy-handed schoolboy, tongue-tied, before an audience: I wrote myself a script for Chatham House and read it, I suppose, like a bad preacher in a low church pulpit. But what I wrote was good: a few years later it helped me into a job on *The Observer*. It was vigorous and polemical; the Secretary, a sparkling woman of double-first competence, afterwards exclaimed: 'That was the *old* Chatham House back again!' I don't know what she meant. One of the 'questions' still makes me chuckle; I'd suggested that not Hitler but Lyautey, during his penetration of Morocco, had invented the Fifth Column as an advance-guard of conquest. When 'questions' came, a severe woman rose witheringly—the sort of woman, I expect, who asks questions at every Chatham House meeting—and said with an air of having the last word: 'Would the speaker agree that it was not Marshal Lyautey who first employed the Fifth Column—but the ancient Assyrians?' I could only apologise to the Assyrians.

Another consequence of the *Daily Express* serial was a job on the *Daily Express*. I was to work on the Foreign Desk at eleven pounds a week. Over a pint of beer I had jumped into Fleet Street. I felt a fraud: it's from apprenticeship in the provinces that Fleet Street should be reached, or at least from a mass-producing news-agency like Reuters; journalism is a technical trade which ought, in all its processes, to be absorbed from boyhood as cobbling or cabinet-making used to be absorbed: so that by the 'feel' of the familiar the craftsman recognizes what's journalistically *right* and rejects what's wrong. Nowhere better than a small-town newspaper office can this journalistic instinct be acquired; no 'course' in a red brick university can give it. The solecisms of style and vulgarities of taste natural to provincial journalism don't matter, because they're yet more insidiously natural to Fleet Street; only individual talent and personal sensibility can correct those, and it's journalists who have these qualities who find themselves one day working on the *Guardian*, *The Times* or the Sunday journals written with the mind and not with the organs of sex. Newspapers get the journalists they deserve.

One of the pleasures—there weren't many, for I detested the paper—of working on the *Daily Express* was the presence in the office of Tom Driberg, whom I knew already and liked and was to know and like better during the Korean war. His William Hickey was, I suppose, the only 'column' of sustained wit and intelligence that newspaper has ever carried; and when Tom left, Arthur Christiansen hastened to cleanse it of all intelligence and wit. But I didn't stay long with the *Express*; my 'second row' brought that episode to an end.

But before I reach the week's visit I paid to Brixton Prison, I must tell briefly of a series of negotiations with various war-faring bodies like the Army and Navy—none invited by me, and each snapped off short on the verge of fruition by some hidden hand, called, perhaps, 'security'. Shortly after my *Daily Express* stories and Chatham House paper—sequel, too, perhaps of the sundry 'intelligence' interviews during my journey home—both the Admiralty and War Office got on my tracks. The Army sent me to Oxford, where a secret staff was working on a North African landing; to them I told what I could, which wasn't much, about Morocco's Atlantic beaches. I was summoned to interviews in a War Office *palazzo* in Northumberland Avenue, and met bristling majors for drinks. At the same time the Royal Navy was summoning me to the Admiralty; I got quite high up there—I think I talked to an admiral; and almost reached the moment for getting myself measured for an R.N.V.R. uniform with a wavy green Intelligence ring. But abruptly, the door was slammed; I was told I wouldn't be wanted.

Then I got a letter from a David (or was it Michael?) Balfour—a brother perhaps of Patrick Kinross?—asking whether I'd be interested in working for 'Political Warfare'. But this offer, too, was suddenly withdrawn.

A little later somebody in the B.B.C. asked me to enlist there, for broadcasts to the Near East. I filled up several forms; and sat with sweating hands before an 'interviews board'; I passed all the tests, and was informed the contract was being prepared. Then the curtain bumped down again—some irremediable technical hitch. . . .

I sought none of these jobs; they came to me: in diverse spheres of effort I was thought competent enough to be of use. But when I was looked up in 'their' little black book, the door banged to. I was disqualified obviously either by my Previous Conviction or my Communist past or both; Britain's alliance with the Soviet was plainly a betrothal of expediency and no doubt a spell of anti-Hitler communism was still a ground for outlawry. But I don't know how my sojourn in Wormwood Scrubs could have enfeebled England's war effort.

Then I blotted my copy-book again; or rather it was blotted by the police, making tactical use of that whimsical concatenation of circumstances called luck. I had a small flat in Doughty Street, handy to my Fleet Street office and to the precincts of my private life—Bloomsbury, Camden Town and beyond, Soho and Charlotte Street. I'd had in these months a few impermanent liaisons, and was ever on the lookout for more: one summer Saturday, idling on the sward of Highgate fields, I fell into a languid conversazione, suitable to the sensuous torpor of the day, with a pleasant, darkly handsome Jewish boy from East London, aged 15. The green heath was covered with his gambolling companions; they were inmates of a school, enjoying a Hampstead outing. We chatted; and arranged to meet on the next Saturday afternoon to go swimming. Then we walked to Kentish Town tube station, where he and his schoolmates departed for Bethnal Green. That was all: plainly no 'offence' could have been committed; and an intention, a hope, the voluptuous imaginings of the mind, commit no breach of the law. With the pleasant curiosity of boys he had asked me about myself—my name, work and so on; and because I always trust people whose faces I like I told him.

A week later I kept the appointment at Old Street underground station. But instead of the boy, two 'bogeys' met me, in their emblematic mackintoshes and soft hats. 'Can I see your identity card?' they said; and after glancing at it: 'Well, I'm not satisfied. I must ask you to accompany us to the police-station.' In that tiled mortuary, which police stations are, there was a pause of backroom confabulation; then out they trooped and a uniformed sergeant formally charged me: 'Insulting Behaviour'—I had, the charge shamelessly averred, while under observation accosted three separate boys each of whom displayed resentment. 'That's a lie,' I said, 'and if you had me under observation, you know jolly well it's a lie.' They didn't reply; then one of the bogeys said: 'We know all about you, you know.' I saw what had happened: the Jewish boys had reported the encounter of one of them with me; he had told my name and the place of our appointment; the police, being informed, had looked up my 'previous'; from there, it was easy.

I was bailed, of course, till Monday morning. Next day, Sunday, I failed to find a solicitor; and on Monday went down to Old Street police court. I meant to ask for a remand in order to be legally represented. I knew that magistrates will generally accept the sworn evidence of two detectives perjuring themselves in unison (as in the sad cases of those youths 'done' for 'suspect'); but I supposed that an agile cross-examination could have exposed contradictions between the two fictitious statements—in the descriptions, for instance, of the non-existent boys, what they were wearing, the colour of their hair. After I'd been locked in the communal cell with the other prisoners, the drunks, the prostitutes, the barrow-boys, I was greeted with friendliness by the senior of the two detectives who'd arrested me; he led me into a corner and spoke to me kindly. 'You'd like a bit of advice now, wouldn't you? You'd like to get this settled quietly, with no fuss, wouldn't you? If you was to plead guilty, the whole thing'd be over in a couple of minutes—'e can't do you for more than a guinea fine, not for Insulting 'e can't. Just plead guilty, pay your guinea, and you'll be outside in no time. I couldn't give you better advice than that, now could I?' Put like that, his advice sounded sensible; would fighting the case be worth the publicity, the worry, the expense, the prolonged humiliation? Wouldn't it be better to get it over quickly and quietly, at the expense of a small lie? His manner was so kind, so solicitous, that I didn't for a moment doubt his word. I agreed; went into the dock; and pleaded guilty. The magistrate listened to the formal fiction of the detective, looked at me severely for an instant, and snapped: 'Fined one guinea'—just as the bogey had said.

But the moment those words had been pronounced, up jumped that treacherous dick: 'May it please y'r honour . . .' he hurriedly began; and told the story of my 'previous'. (I think probably there was a legal flaw here; before fining me, and so closing the case, the magistrate should have asked, 'Anything known . . . ?'; instead he allowed the detective to reopen it.)

'Oh,' said the magistrate. 'Oh. I shall remand you in custody for eight days for a report.' And so I went to Brixton.

I bore no special grudge for my own sake against those perfidious, lying policemen—they're the victims of a police 'morality' which, fighting corruption, is itself corrupt; I was grateful to them: they gave me a close view of an interesting process I couldn't else have seen. But how often, I wonder, in British police courts is the same trick played on scared, vulnerable little men for the sake of adding another conviction to their 'previous'?

So it was the black maria again. Brixton was principally a 'remand prison': people were waiting for something to happen: waiting to come up at the Old Bailey, to be released on payment of a debt, to lose an appeal and be hanged. Because I was there for a 'report' I was put in the hospital: a spacious ward with real beds where we could talk and smoke and where fatherly old warders played cards with the 'patients'. We wore our own clothes and ate nursery food like rice-pudding. Among us were four murderers. I remember two: a half-witted cripple, arrested for killing a small girl—he was brought in, deformed and drooling, while I was there; and a youth of 20, sentenced to hang for battering the life out of an old man for the sake of a few pounds: a young man so harmlessly ordinary to look at, it was hard to envisage his doing anything more violent than kicking a football. I sat opposite him at breakfast on the day his appeal was heard; he ate a lot, and talked with a confidence that was harrowing. 'It's in the bag,' he said, 'it's in the bleeding bag.' Of course he didn't come back: for him, that evening, it was either freedom or the condemned cell. I didn't feel like asking which.

I had a restful week; reading a certain amount, watching and listening to my fellows. I was taken to some senior functionary for a lengthy interview: the basis, I suppose of the 'report'. With him I argued spiritedly about homosexuality, trying to lead him into an objective, academic discussion: dissimulating nothing but refusing to play the penitent. He, however, insisted on clinging to the attitude of the Inquisition: heresy was heresy, and spread heresy. I imagine that the 'report' marked me down as incorrigible; I never learned what it contained.

At the end of this curious week I was taken back to Old Street; still charged, of course, with that guinea's worth of 'insulting behaviour'; and the magistrate, who seemed no longer interested in the 'report', could merely reimpose the original fine. When I paid it, like buying a ticket to freedom, the policeman who wrote it down in a book said: 'You better 'ave done with them foreign 'abits.' He didn't know his own country well.

I should like to have heard that magistrate's juridical explanation of his sending me to Brixton; charged as I was, his powers were limited by the tiny law of 'insulting behaviour'. I suppose, though, his private purpose was to inflict, by the device of the 'report', what extra-legal punishment he could manage—not for something I had done but for what I *was*.

The personage in Brixton with whom I discussed, or tried to discuss, homosexuality, made a big point of the harm done by people like me by spreading the practice right and left as if it were an infectious disease. This of course is nonsense—I speak from experience. Homosexuality isn't catching: people biologically and psychologically 'normal' recoil from it as homosexuals recoil from 'normal' physical contacts. It's a truism, I think, that most adolescents are bi-sexual; as they near maturity their intrinsic inclination gains strength and gradually ousts the other: the naturally normal settles into a course of normality and the naturally 'queer' into that which his nature whispers is for him normal; no outside influence can for long deflect either. I have through the years continued friends with a number of men I had known, and 'corrupted', as boys; those destined to be 'normal' successfully married and happily bred families, and looked back at our own relationship as something normal at the time but since outgrown; those essentially homosexual remained so.

Sentencing, early in 1962, a bunch of men for homosexual crimes, Mr Justice Stable called homosexuality a 'moral leprosy' and declared that the prisoners' statements proved that it could be spread like a disease. With due respect to the Judge, I don't suppose the 'statements' of men desperately seeking to whitewash their conduct can be scientifically worth much—'I was led astray', and the like. What the Judge could have said with truth is that the company and influence of other homosexuals can provide an opportunity for gratification which might not otherwise exist: the *practice* of homosexuality obviously can be spread, but not the condition—which is as subjective and 'uncatchable' as a bronchial chest, a taste for onions or an unquenchable urge to compose music. The argument of the prejudiced that homosexuality is 'spread' like influenza must usefully seem to justify their prejudice.

This private disaster wasn't heard of outside the police court; but the mortification of the outcast, and a sense of fitness, made me resign from the *Express*.

While briefly earning £11 a week I'd been spending £25; but I had still two or three hundred left in the bank. This fund, as funds to me always do, seemed inexhaustible; and I felt, besides, too vulnerable to hawk myself round for a job: I felt again that secret eyes were watching me, and traps being laid. So I went on squandering money; until I woke one day to find it gone.

I was born, I suppose, money-blind, as others are born cross-eyed or colour-blind. Or money-blindness, perhaps, is a common delinquency of adolescence which, when prolonged into after-life, becomes a form of mental deficiency—for it's a default of one's nature, not a voluntary choice like saying 'stealing's less trouble than working.' It's a gap in the mind, an inability to see beyond the money that burns for the moment in one's pocket or to grasp the reality that 'money', or the liberty that money means, isn't, like the air one breathes, free. It must be a psychological condition, like the lust to burn down haystacks; yet one doesn't hear of people being psycho-analysed for money-blindness, though its sufferers flock daily to the police courts.

All my life, even when earning money, I haven't been able to avoid overdrawing at the bank, getting into debt, borrowing from friends, finding myself penniless. I've rarely, certainly, been able to earn a lot—I'm bad at earning at all; but have had a fatal aptitude for spending a lot when I've had anything to spend (and yet, paradoxically, my personal way of life is generally parsimoniously modest, even squalid—I've never wanted 'good living' and flinch from ostentation). This incurably *louche* improbity of mine over money, this blind spot in my nature, is, I think, the gravest of all my turpitudes—if only because, when one borrows from one's friends one loses them. I suppose it's a failing of arrested adolescence: uncles are expected to tip their nephews.

But I would rather be guilty of financial laxity than of that basest offence which some of my self-righteously solvent acquaintances blandly commit: the mortal sins of intellectual dishonesty and moral improbity: writers who write lies for money's sake; men who, seeking notoriety, falsify fact for the sake of self-aggrandisement; social aspirants who live a lie in order to hold a place in the firmament of glamour; men whose worldly repute is founded upon intellectual sham. These are the unpardonable offenders against integrity; and they, of course, pay their bills on the dot and owe no man a penny—yet even this punctiliousness is a functional part of the pose: they're concerned not with moral 'honesty' but with the maintenance of social and financial credit. Where money is, honesty for honesty's sake cannot thrive.

I've been tempted, by shame, to leave out of these memories the episode of Lady Margaret's brooch; but since this book, if it's to have value, must try to delineate in its entirety a character that may for its flaws and deviations be of interest, that episode must go in. I stole Lady Margaret's brooch.

In 1943 my penury was severe. I seemed unable to find work; and had by then acquired a kind of 'complex' about that hidden force which four times had stepped in and denied me a job of usefulness. Eardley, my brother, was kind during this period, and so was dear Aunt Edie who, for all her tiresome dogmatism, was the soul of goodness: I often had luncheon with her in the convent to which she had retired in Orme Court where, surrounded by little Spanish nuns to wait on her, she lived, so to speak, like a princess of the Church. Once, she lent me £50. To her I went again in a time of despair; she had no ready money, she said, but there was Margaret's brooch, bequeathed in memory of their long friendship. Though it wasn't of much value, perhaps I could raise a little money, using it as security? She meant me, of course, to deposit it with my bank and return it to her later; but I, naturally, couldn't go near my bank and took the brooch to Attenborough's. Months later, in a moment of madness and renewed despair, I sold it. I suppose I pretended to my conscience—as, often, more honourable people lie in their own minds to excuse actions equally shabby but less indictable—that Aunt Edie had *given* it to me. But she hadn't; I stole Lady Margaret's brooch.

An advertisement in *The Times* took me to Wigmore Street and a job. The Times Book Club, for the Red Cross and St John, was conducting a countrywide collection of unwanted books for people in the fighting services. I did this work for three weeks; until in those polite gardens of Bournemouth where people play clock-golf I became infatuated with a boy. He was spending a summer holiday with an aunt; but lived in a remote West Country town. I determined to live there too; and wrote to the editor of the local newspaper. The name of Fleet Street is potent; and so were my powers of persuasion when, by prompt invitation, I dashed westward for an interview, staying with the kindly parents of my new friend. The evening paper hired me as a sub-editor; within that whirlwind week I had gained a new love, a new job, a novel environment, and a new home: I was taken as a lodger into my boy's home.

The National Union of Journalists allowed me to rejoin; I was back on the journalistic road. I stayed there about six months; then, the infatuation on both sides wearing thin, as infatuations do, and the parochial affairs of a small town palling, I felt the call of larger events and got myself a sub's job with Reuters in London. I'd gained technical dexterity on that useful provincial paper; with the 'World's Greatest News-Agency' I learned a trade.

I came to believe, in the decade that I was a foreign correspondent, that it *was* the world's greatest news-agency; it had fewer shortcomings than most, and its name, with the confident modesty of brown bread, had become a symbol of soundness. Every young journalist wise enough to want to learn should seek a spell with Reuters. It's a factory; where news-stories are a mass product shaped to suit diverse markets all the globe over. One works to a formula: each story, structurally, follows the same pattern; a sensible pattern which, for the mediocre, ensures a minimum of competence, and for talent, a workmanlike foundation. Reuters teaches one to spot instantly the 'lead' to a piece of news, to 'check' facts, to document with the right amount of 'background', liven with the right amount of 'colour', and assess promptly the length it merits. These are the bones of a story, essential in any sort of newspaper writing. Reuters teaches one also to drain a news-story of that tendentiousness that news so easily absorbs from the instant of its happening, and to fasten 'opinion', if any is expressed, unambiguously to the source of its expression. On most newspapers one is taught the opposite: to 'slant' a story to accord with the proprietor's preferences, or simply for sensation's sake.

The American news-agencies, when I knew them, often allowed exuberance to get the better of judgement; and European agencies, like Agence France-Presse, were generally instruments of their governments. Reuters had integrity, so far as that's possible in an organization owned by a consortium of newspaper-proprietors; or a desire, at least, for integrity.

The man who kept the Reuter machine in tune was Sid Mason: a splendid, explosive little Cockney, one of the best journalists I've known, and one of the nicest men. News was Sid's diet: the world existed for the generation of news, and Reuters for its 'processing' into a marketable commodity; by his infectious enthusiasm for news, the brilliance of his precept, and the magic of his gor'blimey charm, he got the best out of a poorly paid and constantly changing staff (nobody stayed at Reuters—it was a junction where one changed trains). Up on the aloof Seventh Floor some superior 'executives' attended on Sir Christopher Chancellor, whom one never saw, and Walton Cole, whom one hoped not to see; but down on the Fifth Sid Mason did the work, and was burning himself out in Reuter's service.

It must have been 1944 that I got to London: I was in the Reuter building the night the first flying bombs came—designated, I think, in our earliest stories 'pilotless planes' (cf. 'horseless carriage'). At Reuters I was put to work on the 'Nor Desk', producing a news-service designed to tempt American editors into buying it. Later I and a delightful cynic called Ronnie Williams, languidly competent as a silver knife, ran 'Nor' between us. We had a staff of half a dozen, working in shifts round the clock: an agency, of course, never stops. With about 50 'tape'-machines, incoming and outgoing, and some 100 typewriters, all rattling and tapping together, the Fifth Floor at Reuters sounded what it was—a workshop, where minds too were mechanized. It was no place for ivory-tower writers.

After I'd been with Reuters for a year or so I impertinently wrote a paper about some shortcomings of office routine, and passed it to Leonard Curtis, the Night Editor. The ideas in it impressed him enough to send it higher; and suddenly I was appointed Chief Night Sub-editor—the first title I'd had (Reuter was a great place for titles).

This was quite a grand position. I sat at the head of the General Desk with a dozen or more rewrite subs to do my bidding. I assessed the worth of incoming news; 'gave out' the copy, with quick directives, for rewriting; corrected the 'processed' copy thrown into my tray by the subs (often flinging it back for redoing); passed copy I approved to the teletype operators ranged with their clicking machines behind me; and was on the lookout for news in the inflowing cables worth 'flashing'— urgent enough for the first 'take' to be read hotfoot on to the teleprinter.

I did this job well: I've often been amazed by my bursts of high proficiency. I was stiffly praised from above; while from below I had the odd experience of being treated with respect, and even sometimes with an embarrassing timidity—as if I were of some importance. But after six months of working at terrific pressure from 4 p.m. till midnight, I decided it was no job for me. Never having had ambition, and preferring quietude to prestige, I asked to return to the tranquillity and autonomous obscurity of 'Nor', where late at night I could, unseen, keep a quart of beer beneath my desk.

That was my office life at Reuters: eight hours a day, at a factory-bench. It was fun; and invaluable. Outside the office I'd not been friendless; and for two years or more an interest of prime importance had been an Irish boy named Paddy.*By the autumn of 1946, he was sixteen. Paddy's was one of my most interesting friendships; and different from most in that, although composed of mutual homosexual affection, it dispensed with homosexual acts. Paddy was shy of passion, and shrank from physical contact that went beyond affection; so I, aware of this disinclination, never in all that time of close intimacy 'touched' him. It seems comic that what might be called my 'third row', like my second, should

have arisen from an affair which, in the light of the criminal law
if not in my own mind, was innocent: poor Paddy, that winter of
1946, landed himself (unknown to me) in an approved school;
and my concern for his welfare caused (unknown to him) my
wretched 'previous' to raise its head again.

Paddy lived in a King's Cross slum; and was a natural delinquent.
Nothing—except engrossment in occupations that pleased him,
like painting and acting—could have kept him out of trouble: he
had an honest mind, but couldn't help stealing; he loved exercising his lively talent, but wouldn't keep an errand boy's job for
two days. (His character, in fact, was like mine.) He came to see
me most mornings: painted or read till lunch-time, or performed
imaginative adventure-dramas which he *ad libbed* as he went along;
after lunch, we would go swimming or to the cinema until it was
my time for Fleet Street. For a while I lived beside the Regents
Canal in Paddington, in 'Little Venice'; and had Lucien Freud
for a neighbour. Lucien and Paddy got on well together: between
them they covered the bare walls of my room with murals—I
remember Lucien's slapping on a life-size horse, and Paddy's
absorbed working at the baroque figures of knights and barbaric
potentates he devised. Paddy's wistful nature wasn't a serene one;
but in those days he was happy—as happy as ever I saw him;
and so was I. I liked Lucien Freud immensely: a solitary person
then; quiet and gentle, soft-footed as a cat; wiry and fragile to
look at, and very young; as delicate in his movements as in his
painting, wanting only to work and avoid bores. He was going to
do a small picture for me—I gave him, I recall, a cheque on account
for thirty shillings! But I left the terrace by the canal, and soon after
left England. I never knew Lucien in his social days.

He had agreed that Paddy possessed talent; whom I persuaded
to enroll at a school of art. But he didn't stay there long; he liked
the work but didn't like, I suppose, being told how it ought to be
done. Paddy couldn't stay anywhere long. But when he spent his
days with me in these unexciting, humdrum ways he was content,
and kept out of trouble; I suppose I could give him the things he
needed: affection, intelligence and sensitivity, an audience for his
imagination. I know that Paddy drew satisfaction, mental and
emotional, from our companionship; and that, because of this
satisfaction, he felt no need to go out committing little crimes.
That, to me, was worth knowing. I loved his companionship, with
his brightly coloured mind and charming looks—soft, curling

fair hair and the Irish oval of his pale face; the great greenish wistful eyes set strangely wide apart, like a leopard's—an individual face.

I blamed myself for losing Paddy, and for the corollary; though it was bound to happen. I took a flat in Brighton, sleeping Monday to Thursday in an office bedroom beneath Reuters' roof; and saw less of Paddy—there was nowhere for him to spend his days. And then for weeks I didn't see him at all, nor hear of him; until one day a letter came, addressed to me at Reuters—from an 'approved school' in Surrey. He was 'in' for stealing, he said: he'd explain when we met. He asked me to visit him—we could meet for tea in the village.

Had I been sensible, bound to my 'previous', I'd have ignored that letter; but the Old Bailey itself couldn't have stopped my answering that appeal. Besides, I argued, Paddy and I had broken no law. I typed a breezy reply; enclosed a half-crown postal order and (confident that letters in and out of such a place would be censored) said I would visit him if he was sure he could get leave to meet me for tea. Back and forth our letters went, tacitly approved, I presumed, by their unmolested passage through the institutional censorship. After two or three weeks, I felt confident enough to propose a day for meeting, and asked for an immediate reply. None came; a week later I wrote again, suggesting another day. Still no reply; and then, blinded by worry to the red light of danger which Paddy's silence of course was, I sent a telegram announcing the time of my train's arrival next day. This was an act of madness; but I was made mad by the unaccountable arrest of Paddy's smooth flow of letters. At Banstead station I was met by two detectives, fat and blustering. 'We know all about you,' they said. 'We got your record.' They could do nothing else; at first they pretended that Paddy had given them 'evidence' of offences, but dropped this bluff when they saw I knew they were lying. There was nothing more they could do; I caught the next train to London, sickened by thoughts of what Paddy may have gone through while he was being questioned about me. I never saw him again; nor heard of him.

I didn't blame the heads of this approved school for investigating me; it was their duty. It did look, though, as if, having done so, they wanted me to put my foot in a snare. The irony of the incident was that the man whom they snared was probably the one person whose influence on Paddy was good.

This 'third row', diminutive as it was, grew in significance the more I looked at it: plainly, unless I became a different person, I should be back in prison before long. But I couldn't change into a different character; therefore, I must change my domicile—get out of England. Yet, with eyes open to the dangers of England, I still couldn't learn caution: I did openly what it was reckless to do at all, because what I did seemed the natural, and therefore the innocent, thing to do. One of the crazy things I did—the risk run makes me shudder when I look back—was to whisk up in the Reuter lift, when I was living in one of the rooms on the Eighth Floor, a 14-year-old Negro half-caste, a friend of mine at the time. It was lunacy to take any boy up there—past the door-keepers, into the busy lifts; it was madness to sweep in with a companion so exotically conspicuous as this dusky 'Charlie Mouth'.

Somebody told me that David Astor, then *The Observer's* Foreign Editor, was looking for foreign correspondents. This sounded like a visionary's dream; yet, confident that so distinguished a paper wouldn't give me a second look, I wrote to Astor: I couldn't resist having a dab at perfection. I sent him copies of my Chatham House address and the *Daily Express* serial; and diffidently proposed returning to Morocco as an *Observer* 'stringer'. He sent for me—he told me it was the Chatham House paper that had attracted him. 'I didn't think much of the *other*,' he said with that shy, slightly quizzical smile. At that first meeting I formed an instant liking which didn't diminish through the years I worked under him: I felt the spell of a rare veracity of mind, an honesty of interest—there was nothing spurious about him. David Astor's wonderful charm wasn't a *social* charm, turned on like an illumination; it was the charm of sincerity, of a sensitive mind's disinterested curiosity.

So I went back to Morocco at the beginning of 1947: David Astor had given me my apprenticeship in foreign reporting.

One again I started a new life. In Paris I called on high functionaries at the Quai d'Orsay; in Algiers had luncheon with the Gouverneur-Générale; in Rabat went to banquets at the Résidence-Générale, where now reigned, in the place of feeble General Nogués, a charming Liberal civilian, full of excellent intentions but equally feeble in a delicate political situation. Rabat, outwardly the same, was spiritually and intellectually in course of revolution: since the war, the nationalist idea had become a banner, and the

French were politely but helplessly waging a cold war with *Istiqlal*, the Party of Independence.

My first concern was to find Mustapha. I scoured the places where he was likely to be but could find no trace; until one Sunday we came face to face by the main door of the cathedral, and caused surprise among the ladies of Résidence society who were going in for Mass by weeping for happiness upon each other's necks. He was now 23, married with a child, and working as chauffeur to a French government official. Dear Oumi Malika was dead; Fatima had married again. We picked up our friendship; and Mustapha was kind, in an avuncular way, to my new boy Sidi Salah.

Sidi Salah (whose exquisite face is immortalized, if the British Museum Library confers immortality, in Robin Maugham's *North African Notebook*, published about 1949) belonged to the great holy family of the Cherkaoui, the shrine of whose sanctity is in the town of Boujad. That's why he bore the title of Sidi, 'My Lord': every Cherkaoui boy is born a saint, and even his mother addressed him as 'My Lord Salah'. Morocco has a scale of courtesy titles founded on sanctity: so my 14-year-old saint was called Sidi Salah.

*The Observer* was able to maintain a web of correspondents abroad by selling to intelligent newspapers over the globe its admirable *Observer* Foreign News Service: a bi-weekly envelope of political or descriptive 'features'. Correspondents, besides filing a Saturday news story for the Sunday paper, were expected to write a couple of these during the week for O.F.N.S. It was mainly for this I was supposed to be working in Morocco—a country that wasn't then producing much news worth cabling to London. I wasn't good at first. A foreign correspondent learns half the tricks from other foreign correspondents and gets from them too half the material for his stories. It's a predatory trade: one tries to keep to oneself as much of one's own information as one can, and to filch from one's competing colleagues as much of theirs as possible. But in practice it's expedient to give as well as take; and to count for 'exclusiveness' on one's own interpretation of the news and shaping of the story. It's ability that matters: not 'getting a story'. In Morocco, however, a neophyte in the game, I was on my own and had to find my own way.

But before long I had my 'contacts' in the French administration and within the midriff of Istiqlal conspiracy. I was naturally, by disposition, on the side of independence—at least until independence was won; but logic too was telling against the French who, like Canute, were trying to turn back the inevitable nationalist tide.

The most interesting character in Rabat, because beautifully paradoxical, was the Sultan's: the exquisitely subtle father of the present king Moulay l-Hassan (then as I remember him, a dark-skinned playboy of about 18, fascinated by fast motor cars and European clothes). The Sultan Mohammed V was, for the French, turning out to be a boomerang: the man they had themselves fashioned was becoming their principal executioner. They forgot, when they put him on the throne, that it's difficult to make a puppet of a god whose shrine is in eight million hearts.

The French chose Sidi Mohammed while he was still a boy to succeed his father, Moulay Youssef. They set out to make a Frenchman of him and school him to a docile vassalage to France. Probably they dosed him so much with the sugary sedatives of 'la France amie', 'la France civilisatrice', that he became nauseated. They'd chosen a youth far too intelligent to be taken in by such charming duplicities; what in effect their careful education did was to add to his native Arab shrewdness a perfect understanding of the French mind and an ability to play the Arab game in the French way.

He had charm, dignity, beauty (hieratic or kingly, as circumstances required) an acuity of mind and a strong will—the sort of figure about whom useful legends arose. Mustapha said that the Sultan, like Haroun er-Rachid, often wandered through the town at night alone, sometimes in Moorish dress, sometimes in European; going into cafés, chatting unrecognized in the bazaars. Perhaps it was true. The French assured me, over confidential little dinners, that strange things went on in the inviolate penetralia of the great sugar-white palace with its lovely green-tiled cupolas; and that van-loads of money came there daily to be stored away by the Sultan—money extorted from the tribes by emissaries of Istiqlal. Perhaps that was true; but the French liked to whisper little scandalous stories about the Sultan, as later the British in Cyprus circulated insinuations of a lush life against Makarios.

I was in the palace when Juin paid his first ceremonial call as the newly arrived Resident-General. Juin's replacement of the nice Liberal at the head of the French administration was like Harding's appointment to Cyprus in the stead of nice, liberal Bob Armitage: both were strong-arm men, both sent their chief antagonists into exile, and both were precursors of what they came to prevent—independence. Juin was France's chief soldier and Algerian-born: not the man to stand any nonsense in North Africa from a misguided little sultan and a bunch of nationalist agitators. One could see allegory that day in the throne room in the contrast between the Sovereign and the envoy of the Protecting Power—David and Goliath, perhaps: Juin, burly, rubicond, martial, his right arm lost in battle, resplendent with ribands and medals; the Sultan slender, simple, almost ethereal in a robe of diaphanous white, his young face, pale like china, medievally framed in the cowl of his djellaba.

They stood facing each other while each in turn read his speech of formal courtesy; and then, pursuing protocol, adjourned to a couple of arm-chairs for a few minutes of drawing-room conversation. But Sidi Mohammed, for polite small-talk, substituted barbed banter. 'I hope, General, you have come to do justice to Moroccan aspirations?' he began; and the brief conversation became a series of acid exchanges like these: 'I would suggest to your Majesty that a wise man listens to those whose advice he has agreed to accept.'—'A wise monarch, General, listens to the voice of his people.' At that first State meeting Mohammed V deliberately showed Juin where he stood; but his position as the leader of the independence movement had already been made clear by his great journey to Tangier through the Spanish Zone—it was the prodigious assault which breached the walls for the first time of the Treaty of Algeciras. No Sultan since 1905 had dared venture into the dominions which were his only on paper; and when in the summer of 1947 Mohammed went northward like a triumphant conqueror it was France's turn, and Spain's, not to dare to stop him. On that day, really, the Sultan won his country's independence. He wasn't the architect of independence, but he was its animator and oriflamme.

A friend of mine in the political branch of the French administration told me the secret of the Sultan's plan. But no breath of it had yet leaked out; I had the story to myself. The enormous importance to North Africa's future of this Moorish challenge seemed to me obvious; I wrote the story with my assessment of its significance and cabled it to Tudor Street: I had, I knew, a 'world scoop'. It was a blow to be told in reply that I musn't waste money on cables. . . . But every correspondent has sometimes this experience: there's often a curious myopia in a London newspaper office—or a wild astigmatism when looking at a situation a few thousand miles away. In Tel Aviv, during the Arab-Jewish war of 1948, I got one day a cable asking if I would 'cover' the Transjordan side as well as the Israeli; it was like requiring a reporter during the Hitler war to commute between London and Berlin.

I went to Tangier in the royal train (the only European aboard it, I think), with the Shereefian flags draped about its engine's brow. A Triumph in imperial Rome must have looked like a village fête beside that imperial progress. The single-track railway was lined by delighted Moors. Beyond the Franco-Spanish border the train pulled up in open country, beside a huge imperial marquee where the Sultan was welcomed by the grandees who lived under Spain and where we reclined for hours over a Moorish banquet. Tangier, crammed with tribesmen from mountain and plain, was as turbulently joyful as London on Victory night. The fantastic success of this royal desecration of the 'colonialist' temple surprised even its Istiqlal instigators.

Good old George Greaves met me at Tangier station and put me up during the royal stay; and, more important, took me to Dean's Bar and Dean himself—it was like being presented to a Cardinal; and thereafter I wondered how the Tangier I'd known six years before could have existed without Dean and his Bar.

There are two other special memories of that period: the circumcision of Sidi Salah's younger brother, and Winston Churchill's illness in Marrakech.

Now and then Salah and I would go off for a week or two to his tribal pastures south of Casablanca (Cherkaoui fractions were dotted about the country). It was bare rolling *bled*, treeless and dry, but good sheep country; there were plenty of sheep, though they didn't belong to Sidi Salah; they were his uncle's. We were poor; we lived—Salah, his brother, his mother, one or two babies, and I—in a small straw hut like a beehive which stood, with the donkey, in a small quadrangle of loose stones. There was a patch of ground which Sidi Salah's mother tilled for the rich uncle, and somehow she and the babies lived.

The age of circumcision varies in Morroco, following tribal tradition. Sometimes it is put off because of poverty: it's an important rite, full of powerful magic (the severed foreskin is loaded with *baraka*—Oumi Malika kept Mustapha's in a little leather pouch which she wore round her neck); and requires festivity, with the sacrifice of a sheep, or at least a goat; and that is expensive.

Sidi Salah's brother was about eight years old; a barbarous age, I thought, for the operation. I got a sheep from the rich uncle (and didn't, I think, pay for it); and on the chosen day the barber from the nearest *douar* was brought. It's the barber who circumcises; and he knows nothing of sterilization or anatomy. I kept out of our straw hut while the operation was going on; I couldn't bring myself to watch.

The agony and pathos of what followed the departure of the barber remain with me still. The child was bleeding badly, soaking into the rush mat he was lying on. The mother, gently moaning, was censing the boy with the smoke of benzoin; and muttering the names of the family saints. I told her I was going to fetch medical help—there was a first-aid post two miles away. But she went for me furiously: no French medico would come near her son, she said. I told her the man was a Muslim. 'Maybe', she said, 'but he uses Nazarene medicine.' The bleeding would stop, she assured me; her son would be all right; she *knew*. . . . I went outside, and sat on the stone wall of the compound, asking myself what could be done. Without skilled help, the boy would die; and his mother would let him die while she fought off medical help as a she-tiger with cubs would fight off a vet. If God and the saints and the djinn, she would argue, wouldn't save her son (himself a saint) obviously they had their reasons: how, then, dare she invoke infidel aid?

However, infidel aid was invoked. A shriek came suddenly from the hut, and the mother, her hair falling over her face, flung herself out of the door into the dust of the yard: rolling on the ground, wailing, tearing at her cheeks till they bled. Salah· went to his mother. Expecting to find the child dead, I entered the hut. He wasn't; but the bronze of his cheeks had already that tinge of duck's-egg green one sees in the faces of orientals whose life is draining away. I set off for the clinic, hoping the mother's hysterics would last a long time; I think I ran all the two miles of the downland track. The man was asleep; I shook him awake. His duty, he maddeningly said, was to stay where he was. The boy was dying, I said; he shrugged his shoulders. I offered a bribe of 1,000 francs; he put some medicaments together. I don't suppose that Moor had ever walked so fast as he did with me behind him.

But he saved the child's life. The mother, in a state of moaning collapse, was unable to resist. The man was excellent once he was on the job: he stopped the bleeding, dressed the wound, and told me what should be done. Within a few days the boy had recovered. For me, that afternoon is still a recurrent nightmare, and a sharp challenge to my sneaking belief that the simple happiness of ignorance is preferable to the hideous complexities that knowledge brings.

That winter a cable to Tangier sent me scampering to Marrakech where Winston Churchill's illness had been grave enough to attract a large number of correspondents, their papers waiting like vultures for the death. He was up and about again by then: the paper wanted a 'Marrakech Notebook'—the Notebook was a weekly *Observer* feature of comment and 'colour' from some place abroad where 'news' was in the making. Churchill didn't look like dying, sitting each evening through a long dinner in the public dining-room of the Mamounia Hotel and providing the watchful journalists with all the 'copy' they wanted of the cigars-and-brandy kind. I got the impression that the old man and his companions—men like Lord Moran and Professor Lindemann—rather enjoyed these goldfish-bowl meals at the Mamounia, throughout which every eye in the room was fixed on their table and every ear cocked for a fragment of talk: they could easily have dined in private. The only member of the party who appeared among ordinary folk in the bar was Sarah Churchill.

The Haj Tami el-Glaoui, Governor of Marrakech and 'Lord of the Atlas', was a friend of Churchill's whom in some aspects of temperament he resembled. Both loved power, both had sardonic charm and humour, both were domineering and irascible, both enjoyed a rich life and despised the mediocre, both were masters of the political game and had something of the buccaneer—in my 'Notebook' I called them the Tweedledum and Tweedledee of Marrakech: the perfect opposite of each other in appearance, they were as beautifully matched as Laurel and Hardy.

Knowing the Glaoui seemed like knowing a contemporary of Louis XV. He belonged to the age of highwaymen and the Barbary pirates; and was one of the last lordly tyrants, I suppose, to rule in the tradition of the Sultan Moulay Ismael.

He was nearly 80 then: tall and lean, with narrow shoulders and a long leathery face which slightly recalled that hawk-headed deity, or demon, of antique Egypt. He wore the pilgrim's green of Mecca in his turban, and the gossamer-soft *burnous* of patrician dignity; he looked, I imagined, like Henry Irving playing some gaunt and inexorable part—Othello perhaps. His skin was very dark: a near progenitress had been an African slave. He drank tea with the noise of a horse at a trough: cupping the glass in both hands, he sucked upwards like the sea's sucking through the scuttles. In conversation he was adept in ambidexterity. This sly art he needed, being compelled by the circumstances of his vast wealth and power to run with hounds and hare.

It was fun talking to this fabled rogue. Power should always be contemptible; but it can seem impressive when clothed in the panoplies of a romantic past. The Glaoui—medieval, almost mythical—was impressive; and at the same time contemptible, as he proved himself in the end when, his vast power crushed like a puff-ball with the worsting of his treachery against Morocco's independence, he went crawling on his abject bony knees in submission to Mohammed V.

One day somebody will make a film about the Glaoui. It could be a good film; though I've never heard that he performed a noble or heroic deed. But that wouldn't matter—it would be written into the script.

So much for that stay at the Mamounia; the next came a few months later, on my way to Timbuctoo. It was, and I hope still is, one of the world's most gracious hotels. Through the commissionaire at its door, at that time, one gained the entrée to the house of the Shillah dancing boys. I don't mean, of course, those troupes of equivocal youths who, with women's belts round their slim hips, wambled ambiguously among the crowds in the J'maa l-F'na and at every public festival; but that secret house, reached furtively in a cab instructed by the Mamounia commissionaire, where another troupe, running down the ages of adolescence from 18 to 12, performed naked the same Shillah dance; adding, though, embellishments that weren't equivocal at all.

That autumn of 1947 in Tangier I met Robin Maugham. I'd never heard of him until Dean one evening told me that somebody of that name had been asking for me. I said I would come back later; and went out wondering who it could be. I knew no Maugham; I'd read some of Somerset Maugham and vaguely thought that Neville Chamberlain's Lord Chancellor had been a Lord Maugham. The newcomer turned out to be the nephew of one and the son of the other; just over 30, a writer of travel books and novels and something of a student of Arab affairs. Somebody in *The Observer* office had suggested he should look me up. In his *North African Notebook*, published about 1949, Robin describes that evening in Dean's Bar:

I was waiting for Michael Davidson, special *Observer* correspondent in Morocco. I imagined a squat man with a severe face and a stiff collar. Half an hour later a slender man with an open-necked shirt, a well-cut shabby tweed coat and sandals slipped into the bar. This certainly could not be Davidson. I examined him as he sat drinking. He had a lean knobbly face with a large nose and very light blue eyes beneath heavy eyelids. His lined neck was set at an odd angle on his stooping shoulders. He looked like a humorous camel. At that moment he saw me staring at him.

'I'm Davidson,' he said.

Twenty-four hours later it was all settled. We would buy a jeep and travel through Spanish and French Morocco. We had another drink to celebrate.

From there started 15 years of friendship: an association often difficult, sometimes impossible, but when neither of these quite enchanting.

Robin bought the jeep. We drove the length of the Riff, to Abd el-Krim's birthplace; to Fez, Meknes, Marrakech, and over the Atlas to the edge of the Sahara. Robin, I remember, told me as we drove the story of the novel he was then writing—'Line on Ginger', later turned into a film called 'The Intruder', with Jack Hawkins playing the lead. Since then I've discussed with Robin most of his books during their gestation and read them in manuscript; I'm a pretty good critic, I think: having an eye for verity and a mind that spots anomalies and solecisms as a mine-detector metal. He's had a lot of my advice in these 15 years.

After a month or more of Moroccan journeying, Robin went on to Algeria, Tunisia, Libya and Egypt; and I took the jeep to Tangier where I sold it on his behalf to the local golf-club, for towing the mower over the greens. This shocked me: it was like hitching a good hunter to a baker's cart; but I got the price that Robin had paid.

A recent settler in Tangier was Sir Cyril Hampson, a shy little man who looked what he once wanted to become: a jockey.

Instead, he became a *conoscitore* of primitive and oriental painting and a bit of a primitive painter himself, using the various hand-maidens of his household for models; and, on the surprise death of a remote cousin, a baronet with a lot of property. There always seemed an air of surprise about Cyril; as if he found not only other people's actions, but his own as well, extremely odd. Few things surprised him more than his own purchase of a second-hand 'Walrus' flying-machine, an amphibious biplane with a single 'pusher' engine mounted aft. Having bought it and had it shipped to Tangier, Cyril thought he'd better get somebody to drive it; and hired a young man called Vivian lately of the Fleet Air Arm.

In Dean's Bar, near Christmas 1947, four of us were spending a clamorous evening: Cyril, George Greaves, young Vivian and I: we were arguing about what, now that Cyril had got the Walrus, he ought to do with it. About midnight, when we were all pretty high, I suddenly shouted: 'Let's go to Timbuctoo!' This was greeted with a whoop of assent; more drinks were fetched from sardonically smiling Dean and toasts were drunk to Timbuctoo. Next morning, when we thought about the Walrus and its de-ficiencies, the idea didn't look so attractive; particularly to George and me, who both were terrified of any sort of flying. But none of us had the courage, after such an alcoholic display of bravado, to back out.

We must have been out of our minds. We were setting out to fly 3,000 miles into the middle of Africa (not counting the way back) in an obsolete aircraft that had no radio, no spare parts, no tools; a petrol capacity of 300 miles—the distance of most of our proposed hops between refuelling points; tyres already so worn that Vivian said they might burst with any landing; over country devoid for the most part of communications and in some parts of humanity; on a course we had to find ourselves. The R.A.F. at Gibraltar sent us charts, so we could do without the school atlas we'd first meant to use; we had one spanner and a tyre-pump, but no spare tyres. 'If anything goes, we've had it,' said Vivian. (Another peril made its appearance when we turned inland from the West African coast and headed for the Niger: in that sultry heat the engine temperature rose critically, and Vivian, to correct it, had to climb, cursing the drain on our petrol—once we landed with tanks dry: a margin of moments.)

Yet we reached Timbuctoo; the merit must have been Vivian's: that nice, offhand, dog-end, suburban-tennis-club manner concealed a navigational and engineering genius—or if it didn't, we got there by a miracle.

First stop was Marrakech; where, leaving next morning the Mamounia, we saw the last of comfortable living, and where we ran into Peter Rodd, husband of Nancy Mitford and brother of the 2nd Lord Rennell (whose book about the Tuareg, 'People of the Veil', is a rare classic; I found it, after a long search, in the excellent Westminster City Library). Rodd and ourselves were bound for the same place: he was travelling in a white van inscribed LONDON—TIMBUCTOO *PICTURE POST*; I don't know what happened to him on that journey, but he didn't reach Timbuctoo.

The Walrus lumbered over the 10,000-feet snow of the Atlas like a lobbed tennis-ball just clearing the net; and we flew down to Sidi Ifni, a Spanish enclave, north of the Rio d'Oro; and then southwards along the African coast, between limitless, lifeless sand and a stagnant ocean: water and sand met in two slabs of staring blue and yellow, like a child's painting. For hundreds of miles there seemed no life; though sometimes, flying at 50 feet, we put up a few gazelle, and once a leopard bounded over the dunes; and in the sluggish sea a huge shark hung in the oily green, as if preserved in spirits. Abruptly, we came on Black Africa: the Senegal river gleamed, and the earth turned green with the suddenness of a changed lantern-slide.

From Dakar, we had a brief English interlude in The Gambia, a ramshackle British colony which, clinging almost to the banks of the Gambia river, bores like a gimlet into the territory of Senegal. Our descent upon the river at Bathurst, because it was a violation of routine, upset most of the colony's officials. I wrote this at the time:

We were met in a launch by the Director of Public Utilities, who is also Director of Civil Aviation, Director of Stores and Supplies, and Director of Posts and Telegraphs. 'I'm the odd-job man,' he said. 'But I don't draw all the salaries.' Ashore we were received coldly by the Police Inspector, the Revenue Officer, the Harbour Master, the Health Officer, the angry Control Officer at the airfield ('You should have known the flying-boat base has been out of use for a couple of years'), and other officials.

There was then no hotel; we slept at a disused B.O.A.C. rest-house where, oddly, I found Peggy Ross, widow of that Amyas

Ross, who had been a friend in the Bloomsbury days of 20 years earlier. She was engaged in some sociological investigation and told me she had found an envoy of the British Council lecturing local African mothers on Child Psychology.

From Bamako, in the French Soudan, guided by the silver shape of the Niger, we flew 300 miles north-east to Goondam, a 'lost city' on the Saharan fringe and nearest airstrip to Timbuctoo, 60 miles to the east. It was here that we landed with empty tanks. We'd been slowed by a hostile wind, and it was dusk when we came over the town, unable to spot the landing-ground. Twice Vivian made to alight on what looked like a broad highway between houses; the first time a camel loped slowly across our bows and he had to pull the Walrus steeply into the air; the second time it was an ox. By then it was dark, and George and I were sick with fear. Even Vivian didn't know what to do; nothing upset Cyril. All at once a flare blazed in the dark distance, and then two beacons were burning steadily. It was the airstrip; and somehow Vivian landed—with tanks dry. The charming French administrator, seeing us inexplicably floundering about over his astounded realm, had rushed in his jeep to the landing field and certainly saved our lives.

Next morning he drove us to Timbuctoo. The road was a camel track through the thorn trees, arid as the sand they were rooted in. We drove through flocks of goats, belonging to nomad tribes, which stretched up to the spiked branches like giraffes to get what green there was. Our Frenchman was delighted when he ran down a goat: 'These brutes add each day a bit more to the Sahara,' he said. I'd seen the same relentless erosion proceeding north of Fez, where the voracious goat was steadily replacing woodland with wilderness; and in Cyprus it is a penal offence to graze goats within a quarter of a mile of forest—but in the confines of the Sahara such laws cannot be enforced. In the Sahara, no law can be enforced.

Those 60 miles took us four hours: then, beyond the grey mist of thorn, the low brown outline of the town appeared, like a distant landfall. 'Oh, go to Timbuctoo!' we used to say to each other as children. Well, here I was; it seemed very odd. I quote here some scraps of what I wrote at the time for the *Observer* 'Foreign News Service':

You come up through clusters of thorn trees dotting the bright sand; in the distance it might be a bit of England in hay time.

Suddenly you are in the town. . . . The seven French civilians here sometimes get no mail for two months. They're hoping to organize a camel relay service with their nearest neighbours. The Dakar newspaper I have just seen is three weeks old. There is no electricity. . . . Women . . . wear only a wrapped skirt of coloured cotton. Necks, ears and heads are hung with ornament and amulet; all have silver anklets. Children of both sexes up to near-puberty go quite naked in the bright sunshine, their dusty bodies like brick darkened in a flame. Hair-dressing is more elaborate than any known to Bond Street. . . . The market-place is a fusion of coloured movement and patient immobility. Women with skins shining like anthracite squat before red, green, amber piles of spice or fruit, silver fish from the river or horrid fly-blown meat. The air trembles with a symphony of smells. Tuareg men, carrying spears and great two-edged swords, stalk aloofly to the camel market. Nomad Moors from Mauretania, with long wild hair, slip through the crowd with hungry eyes. Red-skinned Peulh, nomad race with a language of their own who breed and ride the humped cattle called *zebu*, stand in proud groups apart. . . . What Timbuctoo really stands for is salt. Each year three caravans, numbering anything from 5,000 to 25,000 camels, travel 500 miles to Taoudeni, in the heart of the Sahara, to load the famous rock-salt mined there. There are no wells on the way . . . with a lump of rock-salt for currency you can do all your shopping. . . .

The Tuareg roam with their camels and herds over a million and a half square miles of Sahara. . . . The 'nobles' are warriors, and do no work—none would deign to pick up a bucket; their wrists are so slender that no ordinary man can get his hand through the ring attaching the warrior's dagger to his arm. Besides the dagger, he wears a sword like a crusader's and a long throwing spear. A 'noble' keeps a member of the religious caste to say his prayers for him (nominally the Tuareg are Muslim). The negro slaves are . . . the property of their 'noble' masters. (French law long ago freed them; but in the Sahara French law has no voice.) Tuareg men are veiled. They will ford a stream naked, but the veil must stay on; eating, they poke the food under the veil and into their mouths. Beneath it, the skin of their faces is stained blue with the indigo of the cloth used. Like gypsies, Tuareg will not sleep under a roof; their tents are of matting in the dry heat, oiled ox-hide in the rains. . . .

A facile explanation of the Tuareg veil is that it is a defence against the desert. But no other desert peoples wear it; and that it has ritual significance is shown by its solemn assumption by a youth on reaching manhood. 'A boy may wear the sword at 12 or 14 years,' a Tuareg told me, 'but the veil not until he is a man.' And F. R. Rodd (Lord Rennell) says in 'People of the Veil': 'The veil will be found wherever the Tuareg live, and only when the riddle of their origin is solved will an explanation probably be forthcoming.' Wherever they sprang from, whatever the causes of their strange dissimilarities from other races, it's obvious the Tuareg were in some remote time influenced by Christianity: the cross is a frequent theme in their ornamentation, and a number of Tamashek words are variants of Greek and Hebrew words used in the Gospels. But Boris de Chroustchoff, in a recent letter to me, throws perhaps a new light on Tuareg antiquity. Because he is a student of African anthropology and collector of African primitives of various kinds, I sent him a talismanic tobacco container given me in a Tuareg camp north of Timbuctoo in 1958: an elaborate affair of inlaid leather on a foundation of the lovely green which dominates all Tuareg leatherwork, from camel-saddles and scabbards to tiny amulets. 'A most interesting thing about the design struck me which I am sure is a new observation connected with the origin of the Tuareg,' Boris wrote. 'Incorporated in the cut-out design a symbol appears which is I am convinced a direct descendant of the sign of Astarte-Tanit, the sign of the Moon Goddess whose symbol it was among the early inhabitants of the Mediterranean coast between Carthage and the western part of North Africa.'

The Tuareg will continue to survive while the Sahara survives: there, the *grand nomad* is as free as the eagle, and as hungry, and beyond the reach of the restraints of law. The end of the Sahara— the industrial consequences of oil, perhaps—will mean the end of the Tuareg; nothing else will.

I saw Timbuctoo again almost exactly ten years later, in February 1958, and stayed this time about a month*. There was a cinema and electricity for the European residents, a government hotel and a one-way street; otherwise the town hadn't changed—unless it was shabbier, emptier, more tumbledown. There were still a

* Robin Maugham has written an account of that expedition: *The Slaves of Timbuktu* (Longmans, 1961).

few salt caravans to Taoudeni, but reduced now to a sorry handful of camels.

I flew one more lap in the Walrus, from Goondam to Gao; but was by now so frightened of that machine that I would have walked back to Tangier rather than climb again into its rattling belly. Instead of walking, I went up into Algeria by lorry: six days across the Sahara, over 1,200 miles of sand. Driving night and day, cooking when you're hungry and snatching odd spells of sleep, you average 200 miles in 24 hours. I went with a convoy of three trucks carrying ground-nuts to Colomb-Béchar. Here are some extracts from my O.F.N.S. articles:

... From Gao the course runs for a few hours with the Niger. Then it leaves the river; you plough north into the desert. The world is still alive; soon it will be dead. At night your headlights freeze gazelle in the postures of panic; hyena, snarling into the beam before they lurch to the shelter of darkness; surprised looking, wide-eared Saharan foxes, and little stoat-like creatures that vault and whirl in terror. In the morning, with the sudden sun, there may be glimpses of ostrich distant in the thorn.

Thorn gives place to parched whisps of camel-grass tufting in the sand; then stone succeeds sand—black, shale-like stone stretching endlessly as if life itself were blitzed. A tract of weird outcrop, even in sunshine the colour of threatening cloud, humps low over the desert like crouching reptiles. On some of these rocks I found rough carvings of giraffe and antelope— whose hand, I wonder, had carved them? But the dry hand of the Sahara is still steadily widening its grasp: once, when there was still life here, giraffe roamed in herds. In recent years less than a dozen have been counted in the southern Sahara.

Occasional dunes break the horizon. To the east the Hoggar mountains, stronghold of Tuareg, rise black against the sky. Once they are out of sight, you are in the empty sand.

Some forms of madness must be like this. Three days of yellow vacuum: not a bird, nor a lizard, nor an insect (the flies in the lorry's cab are stowaways); not a dune or escarpment relieves the narrow circumference of void. Here the desert hasn't the spacious distance which, north and south, makes it grand: for those three central days you are hedged in by a dead-flat circle of sand; your horizon is the rim of a glittering platter of brick-dust. You cannot describe nothingness; this utter void that continues for 600 waterless miles (the water you see is mirage). There—just over there—a strip of clear water gleams blue as the sky. The lorries following behind you ford—you can see them splash into it, see plainly their reflections in it and the ripples their wheels make. But there is no water.

Sand creeps into all your possessions. When you blow your nose, you blow sand. . . . There is no road through the sand. You follow the tracks of the wheels that passed last. Next autumn, after the summer break in trans-Sahara traffic, drivers will pick up our tracks. Wind (that wind which blows icy cold at night) may sand them over; but a later wind will bare them again. Once a driver left his watch in the sand. Six weeks later he picked it up. The sand has its mysteries. We found an umbrella, 200 miles from anywhere; who could have brought an umbrella to that spot? Wandering over the sand while a lorry was being dug out, I came on a fountain-pen. There was ink in it.

Third day through the void, and the desire to see something alive becomes a craving. A vulture in the air, a strayed gazelle across our bows, were like drops of water. Approaching Reggan, first oasis for 600 miles, we saw, far ahead, a man leading a saddled camel. It was like home-coming. . . .

Back in Tangier I wrote a 'Timbuctoo Notebook' for *The Observer* and the story of the whole trip which the *Observer* Foreign News Service sent out in a grand way: a six-day serial with map showing 'Davidson's Route', my own photograph and half a dozen of the better pictures I'd taken.

One evening of high summer when I went into Dean's he greeted me with languid urgency. The Eastern Telegraph Company, he said, were looking for me; an important cable had arrived. I swallowed my drink and rushed to the cable office: telegrams, when one's a journalist, are galvanizing. This one was electrifying: *The Observer* offered me a job as staff correspondent in Israel, covering the war with the Arabs which had just begun; flights had been booked for me Madrid-Rome, Rome-Haifa.

Sick with excitement I wired my acceptance; and walked back to Dean's to celebrate.

THE PLANE I caught in Madrid missed the K.L.M. connection in
Rome—the last commercial flight to Israel: fearful of the war, the
air lines had cancelled their services.

For nearly a week I hung round the travel agents' offices, waiting
for something to gather courage enough to fly to Israel. At last I
scrambled myself on to a charter aircraft whose 50-odd passengers
were Jews from over Europe; Rome was then an assembly point for
people heading for the Promised Land. Besides the crew, I was
the only gentile aboard; and the only passenger with a Greek
transit visa—a fact that made me feel ashamed when, at Athens,
where the plane stopped overnight, I alone was allowed out of the
airport and into the town; my fellow passengers had to camp
out as best they could—labelled 'Jews' until the very frontier of their
own land, where to be a Jew was to be a proud free citizen at last.

The flight next day over Cyprus and down to the coast of
Palestine provided a spiritual experience of a kind which moved
my heart and imagination as few others have. As the aircraft got
within sniffing distance of Israel, the passengers seemed to become
reborn, to feel a resurgence of life as birds do when the sun comes
out after a storm. Rousing from the wretched somnolence of
chivvied travellers, their eyes became bright and their cheeks
warm; and they began to sing or pray; and shout quick Hebrew
hosannas of triumph or love or joy. Soon they were all singing or
chanting together; while the plane droned on through the high
blue haze and the pencilled line of Israel's shore drew nearer. It
was extraordinarily beautiful: like the poetry of the Psalms, of
Isaiah; and I thought that those ancient Jews whom Moses led
must have sung and prayed and cried out in just the same chorus
of praise. These people had left all that was familiar to them, except
their Judaism; they were approaching a strange land at that moment
being attacked by armies ten times their number—yet, if ever
anybody in history was, they were coming *home*.

At the Haifa hotel I found a letter left by Patrick O'Donovan who, because of my delay, couldn't be there: an amusing and highly individual guide to the politics and personalities of Israel. Next morning I went to Tel Aviv, then the seat of government. Because this war was the biggest world 'story' of the moment, the bars of the two chief hotels were crowded with correspondents; here I was going to get some real schooling.

Journalism, more than any other, is the trade in which one can be sure of a high level of companionship—I can't imagine a more excellent miscellany of minds than that of an average crowd of correspondents round a table-load of drinks. Nobody goes, or drifts, into journalism who isn't slightly mad, and it's the touch of madness in a man that's interesting; who isn't something of an insurgent against the tenets of the 'establishment' and therefore *individual*; and who hasn't that depth of intelligence without which he wouldn't last in the trade—who hasn't in fact a sufficiency of wit and personality to save him from being a bore. And most journalists—certainly correspondents abroad—are mentally honest and strive to satisfy their consciences as well as their proprietors; and there are a few, like James Cameron, who will send their proprietors and their jobs to blazes rather than betray their consciences.

One day in the bar of the Kaethe Dan hotel, I was introduced to a man with a long, dark, thin, somewhat vulpine face; a face of such powerful and sensitive vitality that within the space of moments it could express tender affection, the fury and scorn of hatred, twinkling amusement, the austere nobility of a thinker, the sneer of ineffable contempt; a face that seemed the incarnation of intellect and emotion. This was Arthur Koestler; I had met him briefly in London at the time of the Reichstag Trial, but hadn't really known him; now I was fortunate enough to become friends with him and his incomparable wife, Mamaine. We drank together almost every day, in their flat or at the Kaethe Dan; and dined in one of the oriental Jewish restaurants where we had food of the Greek and Levantine school, drinking lots of *arak*. Often to dinner would come Walter Lucas, then working for the *Daily Express*: a gentle, languorous person who looked more like St James's than Fleet Street. I can't think of two more disparate men than Arthur and Walter: one, intellectually and emotionally, as scintillant and unpredictable as fire-crackers in China; the other slow, indolent, stuttering slightly, his mordant wit emerging with the fruity leisure of a club steward bringing the vintage port. But each relished the other's mind; and to me both were adorable.

Mamaine who, cruelly for all who loved her, died in 1954, had been one of the famous Paget twins; slight and fair, her small and delicate face possessed, besides a shining intelligence and the Paget beauty, a faintly fay other-worldliness: something as imponderable as the flight of the birds she loved. After her death Arthur wrote to me in Rome: 'It was a mistake of creation: she ought to have been born a bird; bird-watching was her great passion. Nobody who hasn't seen her face transfixed when watching a rare bird, has known the real Mamaine.'

The last time I saw her was one spring evening in 1953 when Arthur and I dined at her little Chelsea house (he, I suppose, was living in Montpelier Square). That evening was memorable too for the unexpected appearance after dinner of Nicholas Monserrat, then riding on the crest of 'The Cruel Sea' success; and yet more for Arthur's splendid malediction of him. Arthur could be wonderfully offensive to people who merited his scorn; I've never seen him ruder than he was then. To his heavy shot I added my grape; we had had far more to drink than Monserrat, and this put a zest into the attack which his riposte lacked. The attack was not on his writing; but on his 'fascism' and his advocacy, as South African government propagandist, of Pretoria's policy.

I wasn't much interested in the war (I find few things duller than military manoeuvres); but I reported its progress and attended the daily 'briefings' given at the P.I.O. by Moshe Pearlman, a young English Jew who was Israel's Public Information Officer. I went once or twice with the splendid Israeli troops on an operation—in one, I remember, a detachment of General Glubb's Arab Legion took part; it was said that its British officers politely took the day off rather than do battle with a State Britain had helped to found.

But I was interested in the Israeli Army—in the soldiers of which it was made: brave, ardent boys and girls who drilled in the streets with poetry in their eyes; and yet more in the exciting processes of building this eager and resolute young State: it was like watching creation going on before one's very eyes. In *The Observer* of 23rd April 1961, Patrick O'Donovan wrote (in a piece from Jerusalem about the Eichmann trial): 'People seem to live in a continual conscious state of elation over being a State. I have seen

nothing to compare with it in any other new State.' Yes: *elation*—
that too was the appropriate word 13 years earlier; it's good to
know that this thrilling joy of accomplishment may still be felt
there: that those creative people still rejoice in their creation. I
think it was Moshe Shertok (or Sharratt), then Foreign Minister,
who said to me: 'We don't need capital; we have our own Jewish
capital—Jewish muscle, Jewish brains, Jewish soil.' That perversely
seems to smack of the Nazi mind; yet it perfectly defines the
uniform spirit of these multiplex people; who, coming from a
dozen different worlds, with a dozen different languages and
cultures, bound together only by blood, faith and history, came
ready to raise up their State and nationhood if necessary with their
bare hands. I stayed in 'Kibbutz Buchenwald', the creation of
about twenty boys and girls scarcely out of adolescence; all with
memories almost from yesterday of the concentration camp, each
bearing the tattooed brand of Buchenwald; one or two still mentally
or emotionally ill. But these waifs, who'd been so close to tragedy,
seemed filled with a kind of divine fire; they worked and lived
together in a mood of communal exaltation that wasn't neurotic
or hysterical but that put into my mind the followers of Moses
reaching the Promised Land. Spade or pick in hand, rifle slung
over shoulder, girl or boy, they seemed to me the emblem of a
reborn Jewish chivalry.

In his book 'Promise and Fulfilment' Arthur Koestler quotes a
remark I made just as I was leaving Israel: 'I came to Israel pro-
Jew and anti-Zionist; I leave it pro-Zionist and anti-Jew.'

That was true; though, like most such glib sayings, it exaggerated. Before I saw Israel, I'd thought Zionism a romantic, 'literary'
aspiration, impracticable and visionary; and I believed, too, that
its fulfilment meant a double-crossing of the Arabs. But when I
saw this miracle of creation going on; when I was told that the
Emir Abdullah, Jordan's first king, being shown the verdant
fecundity of the Jewish settlements in Palestine, had exclaimed as
if in prayer: 'This green! This wonderful *green*! Ah, if only I had
people like these Jews to make my country *green*!'; when I felt the
ardour and gallantry of those young knights of Kibbutz
Buchenwald—when I knew these things I became a zealous
Zionist.

As for my departing 'anti-Jew': after three months of total
circumscription by hortative, proselytizing, didactic, boastful,
effusive Jews, I felt shut up in a hothouse full of over-scented

plants; I longed to breathe. I didn't leave Israel feeling anti-Jewish; I only wanted to have a rest from Jews.

I think I was the first journalist to write about the physical change occurring in Jews of the second and third generations born in Palestine. Many schoolboys in Tel Aviv in 1948—boys born, that is, in the '30s—had snub faces, fair hair and eyes blue enough to be 'nordic'; with perhaps a shadowy hint of orientalism in the mouth and nose. This must, I suppose, have been the consequence of climate and of an out-of-door life; if this is so, it seems extraordinary that the effect should so dramatically become manifest within two or three generations. But I hope that the ancient racial characteristics are not really tending to disappear; it will be a pity if the people of Israel become in time as nondescript in appearance as most Europeans. Shlomo—whom I met bathing on the wide shore where the leisured water is so shallow that you wade out for a furlong with it no higher than your shins—looked more like a pretty cockney than a child of the eastern Danube; he was a 14-year-old *sabra* ('cactus'—slang for Jews Palestine-bred) who knew almost no English and hadn't been to school; he couldn't tell me, as his educated contemporaries constantly did, that 'modern' Hebrew was going to be a language far superior in every way to English. There was nothing brash and boastful about Shlomo; he was a confiding friend, like a faithful dog.

Arthur was a natural conspirator; he romantically enjoyed I think, the idealist dangers of 'illegality', and the heroically malevolent atmosphere of the classic anarchist plotting in attic secrecy; and he knew most of the important Stern Gang terrorists who weren't in Jaffa jail. He introduced me to one or two; and when, on that remarkable day of the prison mutiny, I went with Louis Heren of *The Times* to Jaffa, we were pleasantly received by the Stern Gang who had taken command of the jail. They'd locked up the Governor and official warders and appointed their own; they went out into the town to bathe, go to the cinema or do some shopping, returning later conscientiously to their cells; they ran the prison and themselves with an exemplary discipline. It was an uproariously funny situation in the eyes of everybody but the Israeli government.

I became great friends with Louis Heren and his sweet wife Pat: a friendship, happily for me, which extended for some years up and down the Far East. He and I worked often together: we had the same notions about integrity and truth, injustice and hypocrisy. If any young journalist asked me for advice, I'd say: 'Be like Louis Heren.' Besides the obvious needs like a controlled brain, alert judgement and perspicuous prose-style, he has an uncorruptible conscience and the courage of his honesty. Content in the anonymity of *The Times*, he's never had the temperament of the prima donna—that occupational mania to which correspondents are prone. (How many readers of *The Times* realize that its strength lies largely in its ostracism of the pronoun 'I'?)

I learned a lot from Louis as a correspondent; as a friend he gave me a lot. He was about the first of my Irish-English Catholic friends; and better friends than they I've never had. The Irish-English Catholics (one has to bracket them, they're so interwoven) cling endearingly, if a shade comically, to the mantle of martyrdom worn by their forerunners of penal times; they're cliquy, often, as are other groups conscious of persecution present or past; and their suave certainty of being personally on sure ground can sometimes seem a little smug. I, an infidel, loving them can gently laugh at them; knowing, though, that of all the Christians they are the most *Christian*; they may drink like fishes, swear like troopers, and practise, some may think, the most charming idolatries; but nobody practises so ungrudgingly the charity of Christ towards their fellow beings, Catholic, heretic or infidel; no other group of people is so free of malice, so understanding of human weakness, so unfailingly *kind*, so impulsively unselfish. The difference in this respect between such a number of the Catholics in England and the non-Catholics there seems to me to prove that the Catholic Faith contains some powerful incentive to *goodness* not possessed, say, by the Church of England. Does it lie, perhaps, in the ideal of the *imitation* of Christ instead of merely praying to Him—an imitation which entails a love of people in fact as well as in church on Sunday mornings? And the tremendous belief that Christ reappears in the flesh at every Mass must be a mighty inducement to strive after the imitation.

If I *had* belief I should want to become a Catholic—not too exact a Catholic; one must reserve some rights: a little like Don Camillo, perhaps—*monsignore ma non troppo*; and I should pray for grace enough to attain to one-tenth of the charity and human *goodness* which my Irish-English Catholic friends breathe out in their everyday lives as unselfconsciously as sweet peas their scent.

In October a cable called me home; and suggested I move to Vienna whence I should 'cover' the neighbouring Iron Curtain lands. Arthur Koestler flew with me as far as Paris; what a splendid companion he is! Never less than amusing or interesting; his glittering mind pouring forth thought or fantasy or exegesis or vivid illustration, the vigorous stride of voice and language gaining a charming levity from the right amount of un-Englishness in the accent.

One trend, on leaving Israel, seemed disquieting. Jews black as Arabs from the Yemen and from North Africa, illiterate and primitive, were pouring into the country; and already, but a few months after Israel's birth, there were signs that they were becoming a 'depressed class'—that between them and their sophisticated brothers from Europe a colour-bar was arising.

In London, my mind on Vienna, I spent ten days or so getting the military permits required then for Austria and Germany still occupied by the Allies; and then, one Wednesday 'office lunch' at the Waldorf Hotel, David Astor said suddenly: 'Michael, I think you'd better go to India.' So to India I went: the prelude to nearly five joyous years in the Far East.

A Sikh in London had kindly arranged that his father in New Delhi should put me up for a day or two while I was finding my feet. At the airport, therefore, I found a grand motor car awaiting me and was driven to the huge mansion of Sir Somebody Singh in Queensway. Almost as soon as I'd said how-d'you-do to my host, Sir Whatnot Singh arrived; and then Sir Thingummy Singh and Sir Something Singh. They were all enormously rich contractors (as Sikhs are apt to be), all holders of British knighthoods and all formerly members of the Viceroy's Council. When we had settled round the tea and gin, they started on me. 'Now, Mr Davidson,' they said, 'we want you to help us. It's vital to India's prosperity that British rule be restored. All this socialism—' I said: 'I'm sorry: I'm afraid my paper hasn't sent me out here to preside over the reassembly of the British Empire.' After that, the knights went away one by one, and I became aware of a certain coolness. I told this story to Nehru—I thought it so funny. So did he.

I moved to Maiden's Hotel in Old Delhi; not far from the Red Fort and the great dusty maidan where lay, eyes craving for alms, the living skeletons of the starving, taking an awful long time to die; and where the massage-boys looked for clients, ready to pound and knead their muscles on the spot.

Like most Indian hotels, Maiden's had in the compound detached annexes where one lived behind one's own front door. A few minutes after my luggage had been carried into mine, a sweet-faced Hindu youth came lithely in and said: 'Me Peter, me your private bearer.' 'Oh?' I said. 'D'you belong to the hotel?' 'No, no,' he replied decidedly, 'me your private bearer'; and turned on the hot water in the bathroom, opened my bags and started unpacking, rated the hotel bearer for not bringing me towels, and took charge of me and my belongings. 'You want *chumpi*?' he said. 'Me very good massage-boy.' And so, having hired me, so to speak, to be his 'master' without my having much say in the matter, Peter remained my faithful and beloved private bearer for the next six months; and when I had to fly to Burma we both wept in the street where I caught the airport bus. It wasn't till long after that I learned he had a wife and two babies; he was about 17.

My first meeting with Nehru was a formal 'interview'; in his room within the great circular parliament building like a Colosseum in the Lutyens manner. As always, reaching his door, I felt sick with a guilty shyness; the instant inside, it was like meeting an old friend. Some journalist said that Nehru 'exudes charm'. That is exactly the wrong word: 'exude' suggests ooze, trickle, drip—something sticky and sickly; but Nehru's charm is as natural and unsugared as the beauty of his face is intellectual. I found him just as I expected after reading a lot of what he'd written: wonderfully simple in manner and unpompous, wonderfully humble as only the spiritually great can be.

The relation of politics to truth is easily stated: there's none; no man can wholly serve both. It's always seemed to me one of those historical tragedies that a man of Nehru's nobility, by being destiny's only possible choice for the political leadership of India, should be compelled to yield up a portion of his moral and mental integrity. I can't believe his conscience has been easy over his Kashmir policy, no matter how 'right' it may be strategically; it began with a trick, when the Hindu Maharajah signed away his Muslim subjects to India, thus making the Indian occupation of the State 'legal'. When I was in Kashmir at the time of the truce, I had a long talk in Srinagar with Sheikh Abdullah, the Prime Minister. In the presence of his 'minister of information' I asked him if he couldn't subscribe to a design giving to Pakistan the Muslim territories which ethnically and geographically belonged to the northern Punjab, to India the Hindu territory of Jammu, and leaving the central 'Vale', where the people thought of themselves neither as Pakistanis nor Indians but as Kashmiri, an enclave of independence—a Himalayan Switzerland—guaranteed by its two great neighbours and by Great Britain and any other powers needed. The Sheikh answered unequivocally that he could agree to that and would. This interview, through the *Observer*, was published naturally far and wide; I felt I'd contributed something positive to a solution of the conflict. I was appalled when I read one day that, from New Delhi whither plainly he'd been summoned, Sheikh Abdullah had denied that he had said anything of the sort. And soon after, in spite of this obedient denial, he was imprisoned.

The last time I saw Nehru was at a garden-party at his house in honour of Lady Mountbatten and her daughter Pamela; a huge slow queue of guests crept through the hot afternoon to shake hands with the Prime Minister, his daughter, and the Mountbattens. It was a remarkable crowd: though I felt that princes in semi-finery are more suitable to a garden-party than elderly Congress politicians showing lengths of shadowy thigh through the lewd transparencies of the *dhoti*—the most indecent of all the world's garments, I think; perhaps because its wearers professionally assume a look of puritanical propriety.

But the most lovable person I met in India was Rajagopolachari, last Governor-General before India became a republic. He was such a fund of reasonable humanity. He always wore the *dhoti*, even when driving in the State landau with outriders and escort of lancers. He looked like a little old humorous monk. In Government House, where a long line of English grandees had dwelt in greater splendour than their sovereigns at home, he lived as simply as an anchorite. On his desk, with the sacred Hindu texts, lay a bible; he told me he read some every day. I asked him whether the portraits of his vice-regal predecessors that hung in Government House would be removed. 'Certainly not,' he said. 'They're as much a part of Indian history as the Moguls.' But I wonder if those portraits are still there; when I think of the onslaught upon me, because of Government House, by the daughter of the formidable Sardar Patel, I wonder if the broad and reasonable humanity of Rajagopolachari has survived against the rancour of the Miss Patels.

His aides-de-camp discovered that reasonableness. Government House was as 'dry' as the Band of Hope; and the four A.D.C.s who lived there couldn't get a drink. But because the Armed Forces were the special and honoured offspring of the British Raj,

THE WORLD, THE FLESH AND MYSELF

alcohol, following tradition, still flowed legally in the messes and
wardrooms. The four A.D.C.s took it in turns to go to the Governor-General and beg leave to return to their units—they felt
ashamed, they pleaded, to be enjoying the comforts and security
of Government House while their brother officers were roughing it
in Kashmir and elsewhere. One day His Excellency summoned the
four of them. 'Very well,' he said slyly. 'One bottle each a week.'

I was in the parliamentary press gallery one Question Time
when a puritanical and anti-British member asked the Prime
Minister if he would take steps to stop the supply of 'foreign liquor'
(meaning Scotch whisky) to Indian officers' messes. 'No sir,'
Nehru bluntly answered, in the best House of Commons manner.
I imagine that India's Services are still getting their whisky.

I was in Karachi when Patrick Gordon Walker, Commonwealth
Relations Minister, arrived on his way to Delhi; and *The Observer*
wanted to know why he was going. Gordon Walker was very kind,
and talked to me for a long time sitting under a tree in the High
Commissioner's garden. He explained in detail matters he was
going to discuss in New Delhi—economic matters. No doubt all
he told me was perfectly true; what he didn't tell me was that he
and Nehru were to turn India into a republic. How silly my feeble
economic interview looked when later the republic story 'broke'!
I've been kicking myself ever since for missing that story, and for
forgetting that one must never be satisfied with what the most
honourable of Cabinet Ministers tells one.

When I got to Peshawar I remembered a letter my cousin Hugh,
Secretary of State for War, had written from the North-West
Frontier in 1890: ' . . . we were received by the colonel of the
Khyber Rifles . . . after which we started in dogcarts, with very
good little horses and boy drivers.' I got one of these dogcarts
with its boy driver; and he stayed with me while I was there,
parking his pony and trap outside my bungalow 'quarter'; or
waiting outside Government House while I dined with the Governor of the North-West Frontier (the last Englishman to hold a
provincial governorship in Pakistan). The charming young driver
was a Pathan, dark skinned and handsome; with bones as slender
and limbs as wiry as his pony's. But he couldn't drive me all the
way to Waziristan; I went there in a jeep, and stayed with the
famous Frontier Scouts who by then were officered entirely by
Pakistani. They were all as charming as they were splendidly
efficient; they were like the Aden Protectorate Levies—those

excellent Arab soldiers in southern Arabia led by 'dedicated' British officers. These Scouts were Pathans; the officers were selected volunteers from the Pakistani Army. This was the kind of soldiering the most rabid anti-militarist could love: Rudyard Kipling stuff, Bengal Lancer romance; chivalrous boy-scout warfare with a six-pounder mountain pom-pom the deadliest weapon and honest men on both sides. We would drive over the wild mountain roads in a patrol jeep and often there'd be the crack of rifle or the whine of a spending bullet: some Pathan shooting at us for fun or out of spite; or perhaps a prowling member of the Fakir of Ipi's invincible army.

For this was his country; or rather the stony heights at the other side of the valley were. For fifteen years this old man had fought the British Empire from his mountain stronghold with an army of never more than 500 men and one gun, which now and then he dragged by camel into range of the Scouts' post. Now he was continuing his war against Pakistan. The Pakistani believed he was in the pay of Nehru; as they believed also that it was Nehru who was behind the 'cold war' which Kabul was waging all along the Frontier. Nehru, to the Pakistani at that time, was the devil; I did my best to persuade them that he was a nice man who wouldn't stir up the Afghans against his neighbour.

When a precarious truce stopped fighting in Kashmir I thought it would be interesting to move from one side to the other across no-man's-land. From Lahore I went to Rawalpindi to see the soldiers about this plan. There were still plenty of senior British officers in both Armies—a nice little general called Sir Douglas Gracey was Pakistan's last English C.-in-C.; but they, in this fratricidal conflict, were not showing themselves: Sandhurst was already well represented on both sides, and there was no need for British brigadiers to plan publicly each other's destruction. I think Abbottabad (who, I wondered, was Abbott?) was the H.Q. of the Pakistani major-general directing operations in Kashmir; I've an idea he was Ayub Khan, a decade later President of his country. Like all the generals on both sides, he was quite charming and a perfect product of the British Army. 'Want to cross over, do you? Jolly good show,' he said. 'I'll put you in the picture. This is the form—' The Indian generals spoke the same language. 'By the way,' he added, 'you'll be seeing old So-and-so; he's in command on the Indian side. Do give him my warmest regards. Great pal of mine—we were at Sandhurst together.'

It was a curious war, and a sad: like the wars of antique Sicily, where sister cities, Greek or Phoenician, were allies one month and fighting each other the next.

The Pakistani, always delightful, were efficient as well; they made signals to their enemies, the Indians, warning them that I was coming; and drove me north to the long lovely gorge that turns eastward and debouches into the Kashmiri Vale. As the valley widened between lofty hills I noticed how the steep slopes were terraced like giant staircases for cultivation, just as I'd seen in parts of Morocco; and as I was to see again on the island of Bali and other parts of the Orient, and on the island of Ischia and elsewhere in southern Italy. Mountain people, wherever they be, find the same ways of taming their mountains.

Near the edge of the Vale, the opposing lines lay. We left the jeep, and I was escorted to a forward Pakistani post. From there, carrying a hold-all containing my bare needs (including, of course, a dinner-jacket; one couldn't travel in the Sub-Continent without a dinner-jacket), I set out for the Indian post. I don't suppose it was more than 200 yards; it seemed a mile, wondering as I walked whether I'd be shot first in the back or the belly by the two machine-guns aiming at each other with me in between. There wasn't, obviously, any danger really (no more than there is a dozen years later when the world, crouching between the Kremlin and the Pentagon, wonders which, by mistake, will press the trigger first); but it was an eerie saunter.

The Indians were as charming as the Pakistani; and when I reached Srinagar I gave the Indian general his opponent's message. 'Great pal of mine, old So-and-so,' he said, 'he was at Sandhurst with me. Jolly good show. Well, I'll put you in the picture—'

If it's true that the prospect from the Roman theatre at Taormina is the loveliest in the world, the Vale of Kashmir isn't far behind. Both have a breath-taking beauty that seems almost unbearable; both the perfect propinquity of towering, snow-topped mountain and gentle champaign; both a satin expanse of oyster-still water and the sweet haunting haze of luminous distance. Neither, one feels, can be quite real; one yearns after a while for a solider landscape, less entranced.

After seeing Sheikh Abdullah I hurried back to India; hopping in a Dakota over the terrifying range that walls in Kashmir from the south, and gliding steeply down to Jammu, Amritsar and on to Delhi; where dear Peter was waiting. But soon I had to say goodbye to him; in April 1949 I moved to Burma, where there was grim and chaotic civil war, and never saw India again.

In Calcutta, on the way, I was slightly surprised to see in broad afternoon a burly bearded man striding down the centre of the main street with lordly step and as naked as he was born. I wasn't of course shocked; but I thought it odd. No police, however, came running up to arrest him; no outraged citizens, female or male, screamed in horror; nobody thrust a newspaper at him for the concealment of his privates. Nobody minded. I was told he was a *sadhu*, a holy man entitled to do what he wanted. I thought it was a more sensible kind of holiness than its extreme opposite, which wants to cover up the body entirely and pretend it doesn't exist.

That evening I found sitting on the pavement against the wall of the Great Eastern Hotel a row of shabby Bengali holding out dirty postcards to likely customers. I always enjoy pornography and bought a few, putting them into a trousers pocket. Next morning I boarded the flying-boat for the Rangoon river, bubbling with happiness over the thought of being 'on the road to Mandalay'.

I didn't know that I was the first British journalist to arrive in Burma since the deportation of a *Daily Mail* correspondent and a certain Colonel Tulloch accused of rousing the pro-British Karens to revolt against the Burman government. There'd been a big rumpus about this; and I, unknowingly, came in in its wake. So I was taken aback when, the other flying-boat passengers passing swiftly through customs, I was held under guard while for three hours my luggage was searched and every scrap of writing in it read. Meanwhile, I was feeling awkward about those dirty postcards; being watched all the time, I couldn't get rid of them; nor could I hope that my pockets wouldn't be searched. And of course, when I was taken into a 'search cubicle', they were discovered and impounded; but nothing was said: a little indecency was of no account compared with a possibility of my plotting with the Karens. After three hours or more I was set free; thankful for the proximity of the Strand Hotel bar. No further official word of all this was heard; though there was an unofficial sequel which, since it brought no humiliation, was quietly comic. A few days later a Burmese acquaintance pointed out to me a headline in a newspaper published in that language; he translated: 'English Journalist Caught Importing Immorality'; below came the details. I can't believe that this juicy piece of news wasn't noted in the British

Embassy—yet I was cordially received by the Ambassador and became close friends with one or two of his staff. Perhaps this paragraph, if it was seen, was assumed to be a characteristic fiction of the 'vernacular' press; the Burmese papers could be delightfully inventive. Those in the English language often committed attractive and touching solecisms; I remember one headline which, speaking of some politician, ran: So-and-So MEETS HIS WATERLOO A SECOND TIME.

The Karen war was taking place about eight miles north of Rangoon, at a place called Insein. I went to see the brigadier commanding the Government troops—a delightful man named Douglas Blake with whom I at once became friends. His mother had been Burmese; he was therefore 'Eurasian': a condition, he told me, which probably would prevent his rising beyond his present army rank of brigadier.

Blake told me he was going to have a battle next day: would I like to come? Hating battles, I said I'd be delighted; and next morning took a taxi to the battle-field. When a small mortar-shell burst 50 yards from the taxi, the driver pulled up. 'Double-fare, or I go back,' he said. I agreed to double fare; wishing that I had the courage of my cowardice and could say 'let's go back.' The battle proceeded through some fields thickly dotted with trees. We advanced: little men ran from tree to tree, crouching and firing rifles; not far away other little men were doing the same thing, firing in our direction. Sometimes there was the ping of a bullet; yet I felt I was sitting in a cinema watching this battle on a screen. But unlike a film battle, nobody fell down in the dramatic postures of death; I saw nobody hit at all. We put the Karens, I think, to flight; and went to Douglas's headquarters to drink beer.

Earlier in this story I've mentioned Maung Té-hung: my small, brown, loving companion for all my Burmese stay. We used to go out to the broad silvered lagoons north of Rangoon; chartering a small sampan, bathing and basking on the long slim banks of sand; we spent long contemplative hours among the gilded Buddhas of the great and wonderful Shwé Dagon pagoda, where the yellow-robed boy monks ate their rice among the golden gods and Maung Té-hung offered flowers to his favourite idol. When I moved into a room at the Pegu Club he came with me; none of the members—English civil servants working for the new State, senior employees of Burmah Oil, a bank manager perhaps—seemed to consider it odd. Thinking now, as I often do, of that enchanting and *good* boy, I feel a fraud: how could a man as selfish as I, one so generally unworthy, have been granted the sweet devotion that Maung Té-hung so unstintingly gave?

I saw a lot in Rangoon, and always enjoyed it, of Leslie Glass, political secretary in the Embassy. His competence was impressive and his company charming and entertaining; I was to enjoy both again in Cyprus seven years later.

After a week's trip in a tiny oil tanker to the Arakan coast, a cable ordered me to Singapore to 'take over' the Far East from Patrick O'Donovan. I discovered, when taking my ticket, that I couldn't fly to Singapore without a valid vaccination against yellow fever—which became valid only ten days after the actual stab. This was awkward; I had but twenty-four hours. That evening I went to an embassy party; and found myself talking to a Pakistani doctor. I told him my problem. 'Oh,' he said suavely, 'd'you want the vaccination itself, or merely the certificate?' Next morning he gave me a stab and certificate—dating it ten days earlier.

I was happy in Burma. To give one happiness a country must provide not only physical and emotional needs like an appropriate climate and sexual contentment, but also a temperament, an *esprit* in tune with one's own. A colonel in the Salvation Army wouldn't be happy in Macao, nor a native of Bali in Glasgow. I wasn't happy in India; it's not a light-hearted land, not a country of the joy of the moment. India takes life seriously; there, I felt, people fond of statistics could be happy, or Fulbright scholars composing theses. But moving from Delhi to Rangoon was like exchanging a London suburb for the pink and yellow and blue of a Mediterranean fishing town; there's a joyousness and warmth of spirit that can be felt through the most obstinate misery. I wrote once in *The Observer* that South-East Asia was 'the last repository of simple human happiness'; there were still parts of those lush and lovely wilds where the horrible hand of politics hadn't yet reached, where violence and cruelty weren't thought of, where the earth was quietly generous without demanding too much human effort; blissful places like the island of Bali and parts of north-eastern Malaya where people could exercise their natural talent for happiness unperturbed by commercial 'progress' and political 'advance'. But today, I suppose, in the scramble between centres of power for the allegiance of the inoffensive, those conditions of contented backwardness and underdevelopment have come to an end.

I think 1949 was the last year of the flying-boat service that linked the Rangoon and Bangkok rivers with Singapore harbour. Waiting at the customs barrier I found a tall, sprawling young man in white shorts and shirt; with a charmingly clumsy face, untidy dark hair and an impish grin. He could have been nicely cast for Synge's 'Playboy'. This was Patrick O'Donovan; one of the best writers who ever worked on a newspaper and one of the most delightful companions, witty as well as wise, at once earnest and boisterous; alas, I knew him only in memorable snatches, too few and too short; and then, after getting married, he went to Washington for a decade. I haven't seen a book of his since 'For Fear of Weeping', his swift and touching travel-notes in China and thereabouts; last time I saw him, nearly ten years ago, he was going to Ampleforth, his old school, to finish a book about Africa. I've never seen that book. In those days he was a broadcasting 'star'; I fear that perhaps he's now become a 'TV personality'. That's bad for him; and, if it means that he's rarely writing, bad for us.

Patrick early took me to see Malcolm MacDonald at Bukit Serene, across the causeway in Johore, a spare palace of the Sultan's, where he lived in shirt-sleeved, workaday grandeur with his great collection of jade and chinoiserie; snatching moments from his work to watch the birds in his garden; and breaking down, by the magnetisms of his charm and simplicity and by the delicacy of his intelligence, the prejudices, fears and jealousies which were poisoning relations between the races of Malaya. His title was Commissioner-General for South-East Asia—a kind of Minister-Resident or Super Ambassador—and his parish reached to the frontiers of China. But the work which, I think, was nearest his heart and for which his memory will live as long as the Federation of Malaya lives, was his precious help in preparing the psychological and spiritual foundations for the multi-racial State of Malaya. If this enthralling experiment succeeds; if the Malays, Chinese and Tamil Indians of Malaya manage to rule themselves by being *reasonable* instead of destroying themselves with racial antipathy and communal rivalry, they will have to thank for their success firstly themselves but secondly Malcolm MacDonald. A lot of the British old stagers, drinking their *chota pegs* in the Tanglin Club, and especially their wives, those frightful matriarchs of Singapore, looked down their noses at Malcolm; he played to the gallery, they said, seeking cheap popularity with the 'locals'—appearing at an evening party in black tie and shirt-sleeves. Of course his simplicity wasn't a pose at all; it was the simplicity of an honest man who detests pose. To visit him one put on, naturally, a tie and coat; and was instantly invited, once there, to take them off; it seemed to him absurd to sweat for formality's sake. This simple frankness, this almost humble ordinariness, was half the battle in his egalitarian familiarity with the Malayans; the other half was the integrity that shone through his charm and governed his mind.

I was in and out of Singapore for the next three years. I suppose the centre of my affection for Singapore remains the Padang: round its periphery flutter, in my mind, like flags my many happinesses there. The Padang is a vast sheet of green turf between the Cathedral and the sea; with at one end the pavilion of the Singapore Cricket Club and at the other that of the Eurasian Cricket Club. In the late afternoon, when the day's heat was subsiding and the breeze from the harbour could be gently felt, when the governing caste had finished its cricket and tennis—then the Padang came into its own: hundreds of workaday Chinese streamed on to the wide sward to watch their children playing in the cool: the whole expanse became an enchanting kaleidoscope of coloured movement and happy faces; children, hundreds of children, with their solemn, bony, contented elders in black polished pyjamas: children playing ball, boys flying kites, leathery granddads happily watching tiny Chinese toddlers romping. It was a beautiful and moving sight which I tried to enjoy each evening—either drinking beer on the *loggia* of the Cricket Club or wandering over the Padang making friends with the children.

As dusk came with tropical suddenness, the Padang assumed a furtive cloak: the children had gone home to their tenement warrens; and 'vice' took over. Shadowy youths lurked under the surrounding dark trees; and a few women and boys hung hopefully about the cathedral wall. ('What?' exclaimed the Anglican bishop when asked by the aviation director for leave to put a warning beacon on the tip of his spire. 'Quite enough goes on in my churchyard at night without my putting up a Red Lamp!')

I'd heard in my youth that Singapore was 'the wickedest city in the world'; and was disappointed when I found it wasn't. There was, though, an amusingly squalid bar called the Criterion, where epicene youths, Malay, Chinese, Indian, warbled the latest lyrics in shrill falsetto. I remember an entertaining evening when after giving dinner and a great deal of drink to a Foreign Office dignitary, I took him for devilment to the 'Cri'. He was a man who valued respectability above riches; who would resign from his clubs rather than be seen carrying a brown-paper parcel in Bond Street; in whose eyes the slightest departure from the canon of English normality merited excommunication. But that night the allurements, aided by alcohol, of an ephebe of Indian extraction led him steeply down from grace. Next day he sent a brief note by hand excusing himself from a later engagement; poor fellow, it must have been some time before he felt socially shriven.

At the beginning of July 1949, when Patrick left for England, I flew to Hong Kong. On arrival, after the aircraft's terrifying slither down the cliff-side on to the old Kai-Tak airfield, I went straight to the Reuter Office. In all my journalistic time abroad Reuter was unfailingly kind; but nowhere more than here, where the great Bill O'Neill ruled with rollicking competence—'great', I say, because such he was in bulk and in heart; and he had been for years one of the great figures of the Far East. Bill was an Old China Hand, and had been a prisoner of the Japanese in Changi jail in Singapore. Behind his roistering Irish jollity and that wonderfully handsome Irish face were an acute and sensitive mind and one of the sweetest, most humanly generous natures I've ever been lucky enough to know. Fortunately for me he moved a little later to Singapore, whence he governed Reuter's Far Eastern realm, and where I spent a lot of my time.

The Hong Kong office of the 'Commissioner for Kwangtung and Kwangsi' wanted thirteen photographs with an application for a visa to enter China; I see from an old passport that I had three such visas, so I must have supplied thirty-nine photographs: no wonder that the Kuomintang Government, engaged in filing all these photographs, couldn't spare a finger to lift against the army of Mao Tse-tung. No wonder, on that last October day in Canton, I found George Yeh, the Foreign Minister, sitting on a packing-case in his Foreign Office, praying for a British aircraft to fly him to safety in Hong Kong. But that was later; my first visit was in July, when the train still ran through from Kowloon in British territory to Canton, tranquilly bustling between the emerald padi and gentle yellow downland. Demure girls sold you cups of bitter tea, handing out hot towels, steaming wet, for the mopping of First-Class faces. It was called, naturally, the Smugglers' Train: from roof or windows passengers by the dozen dropped bundles on the appropriate side of the frontier to be picked up by waiting friends.

Since there were a few British in Canton, there was The Canton Club; to which I fleetingly belonged. In the last days no more than half-a-dozen members kept it going by drinking there: two or three from the Consulate, a few journalists, and the Bishop. 'Compared with colonial bishops generally, he is a very liberal man,' wrote Hugh Childers nearly 100 years ago concerning some disputed prelate. So was the Bishop of Canton; a humble and *human* person, simple and brave; the night before Mao's troops marched in he told me that nothing would induce him to abandon his flock; and stay he did. Perhaps he is still there: I hope the Communists allow him whisky.

By October, when the Communists were on the threshold of Kwangtung, the Government's panic found whimsical expression in the prohibition of fire-crackers, on the 'Wolf, wolf' theory, I suppose, that the squibs might turn out to be a machine-gun fire; a measure that must have made the otherwise indifferent populace hope for the early arrival of the Communists, fire-crackers being a necessary household prophylactic against demons. Coffers like offertory-boxes were set up at street corners, and patriotic citizens were invited to drop in the names of Communist agents known to them; this, obviously, was an opportunity to get rid of business competitors, creditors, rivals in love and so on; persons denounced were arrested, taken to a main street, made to kneel down hands bound behind them, and shot in the back of the head. I didn't watch these executions.

It was on the last day that we saw George Yeh sitting in his empty office. Chiang Kai-shek had already taken wing for Formosa. Couldn't we get him a British plane? pleaded the poor Foreign Minister. Wouldn't the Hong Kong Government send one over to fetch him? I don't know what was in his mind: whether, in those hopeless hours, he was thinking of the comfort of private life in a British colony; in the event he joined his master in Taipeh, and when later on there I saw him again, he had regained his breezy English University assurance.

That night the Communists marched in; and I boarded the last ship to sail down the Canton River. As the vessel slid past the dark quays where a century earlier the British merchants had precariously had their 'factories', there was a sudden volley of musketry and bullets spattered on her plates; I remember dropping

in a flash to the saloon's deck. The joke was that the shots couldn't
have come from the Communists; they were fired by the Kuomintang—in anger, we presumed, because our ship had slipped
away leaving certain fees, or perhaps bribes, unpaid.

Most of the journalistic drinking in Hong Kong was done on
the eighth floor of the Gloucester Hotel. We ate, when we wanted
to be expensive, at the Parisian Grill (the 'P.G.'); or, cheaper and
nicer, in one of the many Chinese eating shops along the waterfront whose cooks, between them, could provide food in the varying
idioms of almost any province of China. One of the last meals I
had at the P.G. was luncheon with Ian Morrison and Hugh Astor
—a few months before Korea, where Ian was killed.

Ian, correspondent of *The Times* in the Far East, was, through
the year before his death, my greatest friend. We both wrote for
'serious' newspapers; we looked at life more or less through the
same eyes. But there the resemblance ends. When I first met him
in Singapore, where he lived with his brilliantly original Austrian
wife Maria and their children Nicky and Petra, I felt I was meeting
a knight in shining armour, a character out of Malory. Of all
people I've known, Ian struck me as *sans peur et sans reproche*.
In face and figure he was beautiful: soft, slighty tousled hair,
vivid blue eyes, and almost perfection, I always felt, in his boyish
face; yet transcending his physical features was the loveliness of
his expression: that sweet, slightly mocking smile, and those
laughing eyes. Ian was one of those elect few, like Rupert Brooke
or Raymond Asquith, to be endowed with supremely Greek
beauties of body and mind; and like them, he died in battle.

No one who knew him can forget that debonair walk, the
easy gait of a dancer; the languid clear voice that turned the accents
of Winchester and Oxford into music; the chuckling verbal wit
and kindly teasing of his conversation; the loftiness of his devotion
to things that were beautiful. And who can forget the Shan satchel,
embroidered and tasselled, that inseparably swung jauntily from
one slim shoulder?

He was a son of 'China Morrison', a renowned Victorian missionary—the first person, I believe, to translate the Bible, or parts
of it, into Chinese. China, his father's love, remained to the end
Ian's: he told me just before Korea that it was his ambition to
settle in Pekin as *Times* correspondent—he was no communist
but, China having 'gone' Communist, he wanted to watch her

progress from there: to watch it in the company of Elizabeth Tan, who (after his death) published under the name of Han Suyin a novel called 'A Many-Splendoured Thing' and made, no doubt, a fortune out of it.

I was the first person in whom he confided his infatuation for Elizabeth Tan. It was while we were in Hong Kong together; early in 1950 perhaps. I remember his arranging for me to be invited to the house where she was staying, so that I should first meet her in a 'social' atmosphere; and his touching anxiety that I should like her as he wanted me to. I found myself being introduced to one of the most exquisite creatures I'd seen: tall and slender, her face almost perfectly Chinese with only a hint of half-Belgian parentage; a ready charm and, instantly apparent, a rare intelligence. She was the widow of a Chinese general, with a daughter of eight or nine.

After that meeting, I became the confidant of both; and because I loved Ian I naturally took his side and Elizabeth's although I knew that dear Maria in Singapore was in for untold pain. Ian's passion for Elizabeth seemed inspired like scripture; he was like a prophet, transfigured by a divine revelation. We would walk over the Peak together or sit drinking over a Chinese meal, or bathe in the warm silken sea; while in his beautiful flowing voice he talked about his love and assured me that he could not, would not, live without her. The intensity of his love was awesome; that Elizabeth's for him should be enduring seemed to me all-important. She was a doctor in a government hospital—an excellent doctor; she assured me that she and Ian should go together to China. 'China is my country—she needs doctors,' she would say. 'My place is with my people.' Vehemently denunciatory of colonialism, she repeatedly told me: 'My place is in China, with my people.' I remembered that insistence afterwards.

She gave me to read a fragment of a novel she was writing, wanting my opinion. I told her it was wonderful stuff, which it was; but pleaded that, since it was an unreserved and intimate narration of an adultery, since the adulterous husband was unmistakably a semi-public figure well-known throughout the Far East and the injured wife a woman of distinction in Singapore, she should make her portraiture less recognizably exact. When, much later, we were in Korea together, Ian showed me her letters; they were epithalamia of passion; to him the arrival of each was the moment of consecration. Then he was killed. I cabled Elizabeth, that dreadful midnight in the Reuter office in Tokyo, hoping feebly to break the news less harshly than next morning's headlines. I knew that Maria would be told officially.

Six months later I returned to Hong Kong; and in the Press Club found her festively dancing with nice Joe Fromm, of the *U.S. News and World Telegram*; I can see them now, as I walked in: she lithely tall, radiantly lovely; little Joe's trim head about level with her small, Chinese breasts. This unreasonably shocked me; I hadn't expected that my first sight of her would be festooned in gaiety. But I told myself it signified nothing: Ian wouldn't have wanted her to mope in the weeds of misery. A little later she married a British colonial policeman; and moved to Malaya, where I didn't go to see her. So much for her dedication to her people in China. Then, in 1952 I think, Louis Heren, who had replaced Ian for *The Times* in Singapore, told me he had read an advance copy of 'A Many-Splendoured Thing' and had been appalled by the pain it must cause Maria; and dismayed by the enthusiastic preface given it by Malcolm MacDonald. Louis and I drove straight out to Bukit Serene and begged Malcolm to withdraw his preface. But it was too late; the thing was printed. He explained that he had introduced the book purely as a work of art, which it was, and hadn't seen it in the light of Ian's memory and Maria's unhappiness. It was a beautiful book; and I would have loved it if it hadn't photographically portrayed Ian in acts of betrayal and cruelly piled humiliation on to Maria's suffering. Truth, to remain inviolate, needn't be merciless.

The book became a best-seller, and was followed by a popular film. Elizabeth must have made a lot of money out of Ian's love.

Yet in one personal way I was beholden to the book: it gives the one picture of myself at war that I can value. I am a minor character towards the end of the book, a newspaper correspondent transparently named David. A letter of Ian's from Korea is quoted:

Charles, a young Frenchman with beautiful manners, gently cynical. . . . He told me that he travelled down from Taejon to Taegu with David on a train. Poor David was so moved with pity for the refugees that he flung open the door of the coach (reserved for American personnel and correspondents) and bade them all come in, spent all the local money he had on buying them apples and melons and rice, distributed all his cigarettes, and nursed a small child on his knee all the way.

I remember perfectly that journey; and that small wide-eyed Korean child. That is how, if I'm thought of at all, I'd like to be remembered in the setting of that ghastly war. 'Charles' was Henri de Turennes, a small and very young correspondent of Agence France-Presse, shy and fastidiously intelligent. He wrote, I think, the only book in French about the Korean war.

Looking through the book again recently, I found a remark I well recall making, and would make again today. The Korean war, just started, is being excitedly discussed; and 'David' exclaims: 'It's the biggest story in the world, and how I loathe the prospect!' So I did: I knew I was going to the vilest, most pitiful of wars, and in advance I was appalled. A good correspondent, of course, is expected to go forward to his new assignment with eager eyes aglow. I didn't, to that one.

I spent most of two months before Christmas 1949 up-country in Malaya; reporting political and military happenings in the face of the Communist rebels in the jungle—known officially as 'the bandits'. I think it was then that I got my 'scoop' concerning various deficiencies from which the British troops were suffering. Almost by chance in Kuala Lumpur I found that the Army in the whole of Malaya had only one surgeon for the on-the-spot operations which alone could save many a wounded man's life, whereas the establishment laid down there should be three; and, working on from that point, that helicopters promised by Whitehall a year earlier hadn't yet arrived. This meant that wounded men sometimes were carried through the jungle for twelve hours instead of being picked out of it and whirled to hospital in an hour or so. This cable caused a big stir; and Sir Linton Andrews, editor of the *Yorkshire Post*, a subscriber to the *Observer* service, caused questions to be asked in the House after 'leading' his paper with my story.

After filing this story, I went up through Kedah State to the Siamese border, and from there down to Penang; where I found a cable saying my facts had been officially denied—what had I to say to that? I wrote a cable beginning: 'I stand by every word I wrote . . .'; and set out to unearth further administrative delinquencies—such as the absence of armour-plating on troop-carrying lorries which could have avoided many casualties when convoys were ambushed. Another absurd anomaly I reported was official insistence on 'peace-time accounting' because of the

:echnical quibble that the Army wasn't at war but 'aiding the :ivil power'. This meant that soldiers deep in the jungle had to account for every sock, tin mug, jungle hat or round of ammunition lost in battle or on patrol. My stories were triumphantly vindicated; surgeons, helicopters and armour for trucks were rushed out. Generals and régimental officers thanked me; and the headline to a column of editorial comment in the *Yorkshire Post* was FORTH-RIGHT MICHAEL DAVIDSON. That headline, and the paragraphs under it, gave me enormous satisfaction; if I have to be qualified by an adjective I can't think of a nicer one than 'forth-right'.

From Hong Kong I went to Macao, the oldest European settlement in the Far East. The place cosily lolls over a tiny peninsula from which, through a medieval archway, one looks into Red China: architecturally a strange matrimony of raucous Chinese concrete with the sleepy languor of Portuguese colonial building. Half the colony is given over, in terms of Hollywood, to gold, gambling and girls; the other half to Eurasian holiness: through the riotous colour and ear-splitting clamour of the streets, fraught with vice, move grave crocodiles of sweet-faced half-caste nuns, monks, sacerdotes, seminarists, choristers; while church-bells tinnily sound through the rattle of fire-crackers and the shouts and explosive expectorations of the populace. One goes over in the 'gamblers' ' ferry that for three hours or so chugs past the fairy islands and the misty secrets of the debouching Pearl River; settled into a brash water-side hotel at breakfast-time a polite valet appeared at my door: 'Manager's compliments, and did I require a woman?'

I had drinks with the ornate Portuguese governor, a superior naval officer out of an earlier century; but the real rulers of Macao were Mr Lobo and Mr Fu. Gold-smuggling was the foundation of Mr Lobo's fortune; prostitution, gambling, real-estate and the rest were subsidiaries of his empire. A shy man, born of mixed parentage in Portuguese Timor, he refused to be interviewed; he disliked inquiries into his affairs. Mr Fu had only one ear; the other had been lopped off by Pearl River pirates and sent to his family by way of inviting quick payment of a ransom. He ran the Central Hotel: a huge building of many floors on each of which some variant of gaming or carnality was provided.

But most, in Macao, I enjoyed wandering through the little leafy Protestant graveyard within its lichened walls. Here were the mossy tombstones of English sailors who had died in the

Opium Wars; I wish I hadn't lost the touching old epitaphs I carefully wrote down: contemplating them, evoking pictures of the young pigtailed mariners they commemorated, was like those charming, repining churchyard reflections of Walter de la Mare.

Ian and I were in Hong Kong when the frigate *Amethyst* came dashingly down the Yangtse River with Commander Kerans conning her from a packing-case lashed above the bridge. It was of course a 'terrific' story: as good a tale of high adventure and gallant impudence as any; with Kerans' historic signal from under the Chinese guns: 'Am rejoining the fleet, God save the King.'

The escape, of course, gave a huge fillip to Britain's prestige; Hong Kong celebrated it by keeping *Amethyst*'s crew drunk for a week. Party after party was given; drink was poured down their throats; and ambulances waited at the door to carry the heroic guests away. When they sailed, they were pallid wrecks; with more parties awaiting them all the way home.

I watched her sail. It was the aftermath of a ferocious typhoon; in which *Amethyst*, with all the wise ships, had put to sea and anchored, head into the wind, with her propellers turning against it (the ships that unwisely didn't were blown ashore). That morning the rain poured steadily from a low-lying sky of heavy slate; the wet, glistening quay was almost deserted. When she arrived, she'd been given a Triumph: bands, admirals and generals and guards of honour; she left in nothing but the rain. As she pulled into the fairway I stood beside a solitary rating huddled into his blue naval raincoat; we watched little *Amethyst*, still with the wounds in her flanks, sail out of sight with her paying-off pennant streaming damply aft, twice her own length. With water dripping from his nose, the seaman suddenly said: 'There goes the 'eroes—lucky fuckin' 'eroes.' That seemed to sum up the whole nostalgic sadness of the moment.

An enchanting companion here and there in the Far East, but especially in Hong Kong, was Christopher Rand, of the New York *Herald Tribune*: a regular writer for the *New Yorker* and the best American magazines; a person with a meticulously truthful and deliciously original mind, a bubbling sense of fun, and a writing style sharp as diamonds. Chris had a family of daughters in Connecticut; but was happiest when disappearing for months at a time into the wildest regions of north-west China and Central Asia, with no companions but the natives he lived amongst. Then he would suddenly turn up; and write a series of incomparable articles, unique in their charm, humour, perception and integrity. He was a little plump, with shorn sandy hair, a bank manager's moustache and pink face; he walked springily and fast, rising on his toes like a cockerel. Chris was an emotional vegetarian; and refused to have any leather about him: his shoes were of canvas or rubber, his belt of fabric. He surprised head waiters by ordering half a dozen fried eggs. Yet Chris was no ascetic: he loved strong drink and was fond of his opium pipe. He took me to see his friend Mr Wu, who kindly helped me to make my first, and last, attempt to enjoy opium. Mr Wu was an author; engaged at that time on a novel which was to be several thousand pages in length and to consist mainly of philosophical discussion—a kind of Chinese 'Back to Methuselah'. But he was able to compose only after several pipes; he would smoke during the later hours of the day, and devote the night to writing. Mr Wu was a little wizened man with tiny bones and a face like a beautiful skull; he seemed to have no flesh. One of the defects of opium-smoking, considered as a *divertimento*, apart from the nausea it arouses in the novice, was, I thought, the bother of it all: that preparatory fiddling with needle and sticky mess; and then, with a thick tube of bamboo in one's mouth, sucking noisily in and out like a winded hound. I tried, under Mr Wu's directions and with Chris's encouragement, a couple of pipes; but the only sensation I obtained was that of feeling a bit sick.

With Chris I went to the lofty island called Lan Tao, and climbed for two hours up the hillside to the Buddhist monastery on the summit. On the upward march, we came every so often to a convent gate whence issued gnomeish women bringing cups of bitter tea. We made a few days' Retreat with the Buddhist monks, eating the sparsest vegetarian dishes, drinking no alcohol, and saying our private prayers in the temple. The monks were jolly, casual people; who, busying themselves in the pagoda would lay their lighted cigarette on the edge of the deity's pedestal while their hands were required elsewhere; their pretty devotions seemed to have a lot in common with the Catholic: incense, chants and responses, and tiny tinkling bells. Dear Chris, what fun we had together! I wonder where he is now?

In Hong Kong I made friends with a sweet slender Chinese boy, like a porcelain figure, named Chou. His little pinched underfed face was made beautiful by a perfect nose; it's the nose, as well as the hooded eyes and the alabaster skin, that makes the Chinese the loveliest people in the world; just as, inversely, it's the nose—that sorry lapse of creation—that makes hideous so sadly many northern Europeans. Chou was a studious boy, and I sent him to school; tenderly faithful, he needed a mother's affection. I saw him last in the huge grandiose Peninsula Hotel on Kowloon-side, like Euston Station, when I came back from Korea; he used to write to me after I had gone for good.

Like G. K. Chesterton, like most of the English Catholics I've known, General Francis Festing had a lively fondness for beer; and in his delightful company, when he was G.O.C. Hong Kong, I drank a number of pint-pots of it at Flagstaff House (charming, evocative name from England's Kiplingesque past; now disappearing, I suppose, with the colonies it adorned).

I've known a lot of generals: none so engaging, so intellectually interesting, as Frankie Festing (though Templer was a fascinating complexity); I felt that, like Wavell, he had a *mind* as well as a training—that he might even read poetry. His was one of those personalities that attract affection: all ranks, behind his back, called him 'Frankie', and when he was struck gravely ill there was a wide sadness. Again like many Catholics, he was essentially simple: he would be as happy, I felt, in a Northumberland cottage (as long as he had beer and a horse) as in gold-laced grandeur. These were his loves: his native Northumbria; hunting (riding 17 stone, he told me); the Church; and plainly the Army. His huge handsome bulk was a fine sight when he strode across the pier to his launch, for the crossing to the New Territories, carrying a great staff like an episcopal crozier.

I suppose he was a lieut.-general then—but everybody said his brilliant capabilities would take him to the top. 'Frankie will make a splendid C.I.G.S.', somebody said. Then startlingly he collapsed; and a little later was carried on a stretcher to a homebound aircraft. 'Frankie's finished,' it was sadly said. His brain was affected; he'd never recover enough, the doctors feared, to return to the active list. It seemed unbelievable: like some impossible disaster: yesterday so healthy and alert, so absolutely master of himself, today struck helpless. Yet he did recover; and did become Chief of the Imperial General Staff; and as his appointment roughly coincided with the change in military thinking concerning Cyprus I've wondered whether his liberal intelligence, sweeping away the shibboleths of the hide-bound generals, didn't directly allow the solution to that island's problem.

At Christmas 1949 I was among the lovely Annamites, in French Indo-China: exquisite people with Chinese faces that were yet not quite Chinese; as one advances from Malaya through the lush beauty of those coloured countries one moves too along a subtly modulated scale of facial fashioning: Siamese, Burmans, Cambodians, Annamites, the Thais of Tonkin—all are moulded in a conforming 'style' but each is the work of an individual artist; they are like a school of painting, of which every member marks with his originality the canon of the whole. I suppose the stripling ricksha puller who in Saigon became my friend was, stripped of his rags, as perfect a confection of human beauty as can be devised; poor child: doomed to wear his heart out between the shafts.

Soon after I arrived, those parts of Indo-China where French writ still ran became nominally independent under Bao Dai, and England's charming consul-general in Saigon, Frank Gibb, found himself a Minister. Gibb, going up to Dalat to present his credentials kindly took me with him—I received beforehand a wonderful imperial command to luncheon. We flew up in the Emperor Bao Dai's personal Dakota, bearing on its bows the imperial dragon—Frank in white uniform and sword. We were received on board by an imperial 'hostess': an extremely personable young Eurasian: Bao Dai chose his feminine entourage with care. He was a nice young man, handsome and with fine French manners. After luncheon he and I withdrew for a political talk; he spoke with intelligence and knowledge but, though his country was in chaos and his throne precarious, without interest; he seemed bored by the tormenting problems his government faced. The one thing that interested him was this: How could he obtain some English turf for the laying out of his putting green?

One of my most enduring memories of southern Vietnam is my sojourn with *le colonnel* Leroy among the swamps and deltas of his Catholic realm in what used to be called Cochin-China in the extreme south. Vietnam was a great country for political religion including the Caodai-ists, a powerful and splendiferous Church of local creation whose pantheon of saints included Winston Churchill and Maurice Chevalier. The Catholic Church reigned in vast areas of Tonkin and northern Annam, where the bishops ruled absolutely; my friend Col. Leroy was the Catholic ruler of his own kingdom—his private property—the size of an English county. The French told me that his colonelcy was acquired by simply sewing the badges on to his shoulder-straps; but Graham Greene, who also knew him well and who wrote a preface to a book the colonel later published in France, has assured me that he indeed held colonel's rank in the French army.

Leroy—the name seemed to predestine him for his monarchy—was a Eurasian: son of a French adventurer and an Annamite mother. He had acquired, some by inheritance and some by private conquest, a vast domain of padi land, which he ran excellently by tyrannical government; maintaining his own army and compulsorily converting his subjects to Catholicism. He built schools, churches, dwellings for his people; made roads and introduced modern methods of rice cultivation; and at the same time carried on his private guerilla war with the insurgents, Communist and other, who infested the waterways of Cochin-China. He was an enchanting little man, bubbling with humour and gusto; keen as mustard on everything he did, and possessed of an insatiable thirst for whisky. I don't think I've ever drunk as much whisky in so short a time as I did while staying with him. He took me all over his realm, by jeep and by motor-boat; we went to obscure fishing hamlets where piratical outlaws lived, and to villages on the fringe of the zones of insurgence; everywhere he was welcomed as a king, as a father, as a god almost. It was in a sense a replica of the medieval Norman baronies in Calabria and Apulia of 1,000 years ago, except that he was a 'good' baron.

Poor little Col. Leroy: he was, under the Annamite domination after the defeat of the French, ousted from his kingdom; and retired to private life in France. I hope he was able to take with him some of his riches.

Indonesia wasn't a country I enjoyed much. It seemed to me a country of political chaos, governmental corruption and social squalor. It was an exasperating story to 'cover': I would interview, say, the Foreign Minister and carefully read over my notes of what he said to make certain of his concordance. As soon as my report was published, he would publicly deny his own words. Besides, it was a dangerous land to travel in, and I've never liked danger (but not nearly as dangerous as Malaya which, paradoxically, I loved). In Djakarta, too, there was the smell of putrefaction; the effluence, doubtless, of the slimy, stagnant canals: in which communal defecation, teeth-brushing, bathing by both sexes, and the washing of dirty clothes, all took place together.

From Hong Kong, early in 1950, I flew to Taiwan (which Vasco de Gama, sailing by, called Formosa, the Beautiful): interesting chiefly for exhibiting a Japanese culture imposed superficially upon a Chinese population settled around a remnant spine of Aboriginals: kinsfolk of the natives of Borneo. I remember the dreary food at the American 'club'; the delicate hands of the 'room-boy' at the Japanese-style hotel where I stayed; the jauntiness of George Yeh (the obverse of Canton); the harsh inelegance of Taipeh; and a genial English employee of the great buccaneering firm of Jardine, Matheson who, with his island sweetheart, lived in a pretty Japanese cottage on the volcanic slopes above Chiang Kai-shek's house and amused himself in moods of evening exuberance by cutting off the Generalissimo's hot-water supply: which, drawn from the mountain's natural hot springs, was conducted to privileged houses by a cunning system of easily interrupted bamboo pipes.

I've said that if Malaya achieves stable political good health, she will have to thank Malcolm MacDonald for much of it. She will also have to thank a perky little English engine-driver called Jack Brazier, Trade Union Adviser to the administration during the worst years of the Communist insurrection.

In an admirable pamphlet published by the Fabian Society in 1960, 'John Lowe' writes: 'Whether seen in relation to the racial problem or to the question of working conditions . . . the trade union movement of Malaya is one of the major assets of the nation. It is a genuinely non-communal movement in which the unions have a racially mixed membership. . . . It proves the possibility of breaking down inter-racial barriers in Malaya through working co-operation. . . .' Those are wise words; and the success they record was chiefly due to little gor'blimey Jack Brazier's lovable truculence to the authorities (he was one of the very few who stood up to Sir Gerald Templer), warm and endearing humanity among his multi-coloured workers, and brilliant organizational competence.

Before I knew where I was Jack was whisking me off, bag and baggage, to stay with him and his gentle, motherly wife in their house perched on a knoll beyond the fabulously rococo railway station. (Before it's too late, somebody like Sacheverell Sitwell should write a book about British colonial architecture, starting with the grandiose lunacies of Rangoon and Kuala Lumpur.)

Jack was the best of company: a bubbling kettle of cockney pugnacity and vituperative criticism; always at war—with governmental ineptitude, with the rubber and tin-mining magnates, with all the obstacles of cant and lassitude and self-interest that were blocking his splendid enthusiasm and political wisdom. 'You're telling *me*,' was his way of clinching an argument; in his mouth the empty phrase seemed to annihilate his opponents and establish unchallengeably his own position. 'You're telling *me*,' he would snap, swallowing a big gulp of whisky; and that was that. Yet interwoven with his aggressiveness was a wonderful humour, and he loved his unions and the union leaders he was moulding as a father loves his children; and they loved him. One of his greatest prides was the Taxi-Girls Union—he had organized the Chinese 'hostesses' in the dance-halls who were hired as dancing partners at so much a minute; they elected him their honorary president.

A patrol in the high jungle was an uncanny promenade; I imagine that even the soldiers, whose job it was for days and weeks on end, didn't lose that sense of being wound up like a spring that the slightest touch could release; for, once enclosed by that infinite entanglement, one knew that every oncoming instant could bring a bullet from an unseen enemy. The jungle had an eerie, satanic beauty; I thought that the country beyond Styx must have been like that: a dark-green haunted world without a sky; hushed as eternity, and teeming with the soundless unseen. In the daytime not a creature nor insect stirred; yet the stillness was fraught with latent life; and the forest rose to such a huge opaque height (like the roof of Hades, perhaps) that one felt one was walking in a rank garden deep in the earth's belly. I was dressed in jungle clothes and taken in by the Green Howards who were 'jungle-bashing' in Pahang, the biggest and wildest of the States where the tiger and the small Malayan elephant still live. We were a subaltern and half a dozen men: their precise and unperturbed comprehension of the jungle was superb, advancing with breathless eyes and finger on the trigger; and when suddenly a 'basha' came into view (a tiny 'bandit's' hut of branches and leaves) the party instantly froze like a pointing gun-dog: *was it occupied?*—that was the intoxicating question: was there to be a kill? That brief patrol lasted five hours; yet I don't think we covered in distance more than two miles, so difficult was the slithery and tangled terrain, so extreme the caution. Five hours, for those young soldiers, of

unremitting tension: I don't think, in England, the silent gallantry
of the Army in Malaya was ever properly understood.

All travel in Malaya was to me, a born coward, a nightmare of
apprehension. The *orang ulu*, the 'people of the jungle' (that is,
the Communist rebels) had perfected the art of the ambush—not
difficult in perfect ambush country; driving along those serpentine
roads, past the treacherous ranks of the ghostly rubber trees, beside
the threatening wall of jungle, my heart was in my mouth; and
when, ahead, one saw a small brown figure fleet from the under-
growth from one side to the other one breathed: 'This is it.'
Probably it was only a harmless rubber-tapper; but one *never
knew*. I was fortunate, for I did a lot of travelling. Only once did
I come under some sort of fire; and then, luckily, I was in an
armoured car of the 4th Hussars.

Among those moments of great beauty which remain undying
in my mind is the awakening in the brief dusk of a tropical dawn
at the embattled homestead of a rubber estate: those few twilight
minutes when, alone in an equatorial day, the air is as fresh and
sweet as spring water; going out on to the balcony wearing only a
sarong and breathing the immense paling silence of the morning.
The arc-lamps flooding the defensive palisade of barbed wire
had been switched off; and among the darkling trees beyond, the
scarlet blooms of Flame of the Forest were glowing like coals in
the awakening light, while below in the garden the red and orange
canna shone like burning candles. In a few moments the sun
would be beating down and the earth sweating again; but in that
tiny interlude of rebirth the world seemed as clean and its people
as gentle as an English spring. Then, looking down, I was watching
the Chinese 'home guards' being raggedly fallen in by their little
Malay police corporal; and the horror of this sweet land's slaughter
became real again. Dear Malaya: *ti voglio bene*.

Although I knew Sir Henry Gurney only 'officially' I saw
enough of him to admire him and even become fond of him for his
gentle courtesy and delicately perceptive mind; and when, in
Malta late in 1951, I heard on the wireless that he'd been ambushed
and killed, I felt personally bereaved. He was criticized; I've
heard him called 'too feeble', whatever that meant; but the plan
which finally defeated the rebels, and for which Templer later
got a large part of the credit, was his: the 'Briggs Plan', by which
the men in the jungle were deprived of their chief provisioners—
the 'squatters' who, outside the embrace of administration, lived

on the verges of the jungle—was conceived under Gurney, worked out by Gen. Briggs, and put into operation by Templer. In London a few years later I was standing at the counter of the Chartered Bank off the Haymarket when I heard a bank clerk say to a woman I'd hardly noticed: 'Good morning, Lady Gurney. . . .' For a second I wanted to tell her how much I'd thought of the husband who'd been killed shielding her with his body; but I was too shy.

King's House, the official home of the High Commissioners, stood charmingly on the highest summit of the undulating and attractive Lake Gardens, which also contained the Lake Club, a stronghold of the *pukka sahib* over which, on top of my quick-firing row with Sir Gerald Templer in 1952, I was to have yet another public row.

In one plebeian corner of the Lake Gardens, far from those illustrious mansions, the broad brown waters of the lake disgorged their surplus through a weir of high masonry. Here, at most times of the day, a multi-coloured galaxy of naked boys splashed and dived and swam; and most unbusy afternoons I idly watched them from the shade of a banyan tree. One day, in this enchanted spot, I made the acquaintance of a lissom Chinese of about 16 named Wong. Neither could speak a word of the other's language but each had a small vocabulary of pidgin-Malay; and we became friends. I was then staying in a Chinese hotel too 'low-class' for any other European; here in my room, which had a shower-bath and was divided from neighbouring rooms by matchboard partitions through which the sounds of quarrelling and expectoration noisily came, Wong joined me. I'd long wanted to visit the north-eastern States of Trengganu and Kelantan; I'd met in Singapore a brother of the Sultan of Kelantan who'd urged me to visit him on the 'Beach of Passionate Love', a kind of *le camping* which he owned on the foamy, palm-girt shore of the China Sea. I now felt, romantically allied with Wong, that the Beach of Passionate Love was just the thing.

There are few pleasures keener than that of introducing the young to a new experience, giving them an unaccustomed thrill: watching the spellbound eyes of a child at the circus, sharing the eagerness of a boy's first ride on a pony. This blissful pleasure I had when Wong climbed aboard the Malayan Airways Dakota and we flew to Kuantan, on the east coast of Pahang: the pleasure of *feeling* the wonderment registered in his glowing narrow eyes.

From Kuantan we took a wobbling Chinese bus to Trengganu; and next day, another bus up to Kota Bahru, in Kelantan.

The Sultan's brother let us for a tiny rent a nice little bungalow on the sands, 30 yards or so from the breakers. We did our eating, and I my drinking, at the Sultan's brother's restaurant. Very few other people were indulging in passionate love, and we practically had the place to ourselves.

After a week's idyllic sojourn, we embarked for Singapore in a small Straits Steamships vessel; there were about six other passengers, all English; nobody seemed to think it strange that Wong should share my cabin and sit beside me in the saloon. He understood nothing said to him, except by me; but had beautiful manners, though was little at his ease with knives and forks. We loved, he and I, as the ship ploughed through the gilded China Sea, to stand right in the bows and look down at the prancing porpoises which for the whole voyage *led* the ship on her course; they didn't follow alongside her slicing stem but unerringly swam a few feet ahead, as if consciously piloting her along her way. At one point off the coast of Pahang or northern Johore, we passed over the sepulchre of *Prince of Wales* and *Repulse*.

At Singapore Wong stayed one night with me in the Cockpit Hotel, smuggled into a bungalow annexe; and next morning, having to depart on some assignment, I tearfully put him on the train for K.L. When next I was there, after Korea, I looked for him; but he had gone. I suspected that he, like great numbers of Chinese youths at that time, had heard the glamorous call of Red China and taken ship for the fatherland. I hope he wasn't disappointed. Dear Wong: he was a good companion on the Beach of Passionate Love.

THE EMPEROR FREDERICK II of Hohenstaufen remarked in the thirteenth century: 'God wouldn't have chosen Palestine for his own, if he could have seen my own kingdom of Sicily.' I'd be inclined to say the same of the island of Bali. It must have been as close a copy of the Garden of Eden before the Fall as anywhere; and up to 1950 there'd been no Fall yet on Bali: its lovely, innocent people were as free of the civilized sins of violence, vulgarity, cant, ostentation, humbug, deceit and sticking their noses into other people's business as, I suppose, it's possible to be.

When the paper gave me a month's local leave, I rushed there; and for that month lived a god's life—without the tiresome quarrels and jealousies of Olympus.

In the first place, Bali's beautiful in its own right as well as its people's: a green and flowering mountain rising rampant from the sea, with skirts of feathery palm and a violet volcanic crown; a fragment of verdant paradise between the eastern tip of Java and the isle of Lombok. In the second place, it's an island of happiness, the happiness of the specially blessed. In the third, it's the sort of island where, when you're thirsty, a boy swarms like a monkey up a palm trunk and knocks you down a coconut.

I think a Greek island in the bloom of Pericles' time may have been a little like it: an island of aristocrats whose life of pleasure and flourishing art was supported by slavery—the slavery, on Bali, being provided by the generous earth. One did enough work in the padi fields to harvest rice enough to satisfy one's belly and the Rice Goddess, the Rice Mother; for the rest of the time one was happy: one danced (so many dances, theatrical or ritual, perfectly performed by exquisite little girls or handsome, epicene youths); or one painted delicate pictures of monkey-like people stooping over the padi and human-like monkeys playing among the palms; or listened to tremendous Brandenburgian *concerti* played by an orchestra of gongs thirty musicians strong; or carved strange goblin figures in wood; or chiselled the easy soft stone into temples worthy of the gods; or fashioned head-dresses like mitres, like Cleopatra's tiara, out of the blooms of jasmine; or one squatted under a banyan tree making much of one's fighting-cocks or playing with one's crickets captive on a thread. One drank, stronger than coconut milk, the delicious 'beer' called *tuak*, brewed from the sugar-palm; and ate with one's rice, off palm-leaf plates, pork or chicken, dragon-flies, flying ants and the larvae of bees; and one went down to the golden sands, palm-fringed, where the cata-marans were beached, and bathed in the gay breakers, not swim-ming out because of the killer *barracuda* and vaguely covering one's genitals with a fluttering hand for convention's sake (as the mouth is covered when yawning). One wore the soft flowing sim-plicity of the sarong; and one chatted cosily with one's village Prince, careful only to sit on a lower level than his, and to address him in his superior upper-class language while he spoke to oneself in one's baser, lower-class language (five tongues, I think, were spoken, including Brahmini 'sanscrit' and excluding Dutch) and one gazed, if one were a barbarian from industrial civilization, in humble wonder at this sweet and gentle human happiness, set against the torrential greens of padi and palm: a happiness that sprang from beauty and the spontaneous creation of beauty. Everyone was an artist from infancy; they were people of the *mind*, as well as of the body.

When one arrived at Denpasar airstrip, the first thing one saw was a notice admonishing, in English (I can't remember the exact phrasing): 'It is forbidden to photograph ladies with un-covered breasts, this practice being degrading both to photo-graphers and photographed.' The ladies of Bali had no notion that their breasts, covered or uncovered, were degrading until officially told so; and even then, presumably not believing it, they continued to clothe themselves in the waist-high sarong. This was one of the first assaults launched on Bali's unconformist singularity by the Muslim Mrs Grundys of Java's new busybody rulers; today 12 years later, there's probably little left of the old Bali; and the Fall is writing off that Eden's happiness.

By some caprice of history this tiny remnant of the earlier Hindu empire had survived in almost unsullied purity: an impudent bird of paradise in a garden of Muslim sparrows. Even physically the Balinese had retained their ancestral type: unlike their Malaysian neighbours, they had large luminous Indian eyes, though in their

gentle faces there was a sufficiency of Mongol merriment to soften
the stern air of suffering which Hindus often wear. The caste-
structure of the island's tiny society was elaborate and ornamental;
with a hierarchy of nobles, appropriately entitled, feudally ruling
under five Rajahs; yet manners were charmingly free-and-easy and,
observing the small formalities, one was, so to speak, one's prince's
pal.

While the sun circled about the earth, the world, of course, re-
volved round Bali; the Gunung Agung, the great central mountain,
was the 'navel of the earth'; wherever one might be, one could
always find the North by looking toward to the mountain, making
navigation simple.

High on the mountain, Theo Meier lived with his Balinese
family: a delightful and talented Swiss painter and a kind of
father-figure to his villagers: to him, possessed of useful medical
knowledge, they brought their maladies as well as their domestic
problems. His people were great brewers of *tuak*; and visiting him,
one could be sure of a splendid roistering time and a performance
of the dance special to his village: by which small dainty girls,
crowned with flowers, exorcized the devils of anybody who chanced
to be possessed of some.

On the way up to Theo's, there was a hamlet called Selatt,
surrounded by terraced padi-fields. Here one stayed in a rest-
house where, for a few *rupiya* one could get a dish of rice, a flagon
of *tuak* and a small room; and where, after gently making known
to the Mayor one's amorous preference, one's desires were
mysteriously fulfilled. Nothing was said; nobody appeared during
the evening's supping and drinking; but when one went to bed
one would find, wistfully smiling from the gloaming of the room,
a tender brown creature who took it for granted he was staying the
night. There would be no question of payment: the Balinese
weren't interested in money; but if one made a present of a new
sarong, there would be abounding and touching gratitude. That's
how I came to know Ktut—alas, I have treacherously forgotten his
name, for Ktut was merely his 'title', meaning 'second son': one
of the sweetest and most affectionate companions I've had, who
stayed with me for all the rest of that blissful month and travelled
with me all over the island.

But then, like all one's loves made fleeting by the compulsions
of time, bliss came to an end; I had to go back to work: I had to
leave Ktut, pathetically forlorn, but enriched by several new

sarongs and, I hope, some sweetness of memory. After sadly putting him on the bus for his home in Selatt I found that my aircraft was delayed and I had to stay in Denpasar for an extra bereaved day. In Powys Mathers' translation from the Arabian Nights: 'Were I to stay, I'd see the places where her absence is, And hear her silences: Let me away.'

Oh, in those remotenesses of the Far East, how I loved the kindly, gentle innocence of the ignorant: knowing nothing of the horrible scramble for power and position, of the absurd race for flashy prestige, which the deforming discords of civilization have made the human aim!

At the beginning of July 1950 I was about to set out again for Indo-China when that pleasant prospect was dashed: the moment I heard the broadcast news of the march into South Korea I knew that THIS MEANS ME, in the idiom of those hortatory placards which the Army used to put up in its far-flung cantonments. Sure enough, the cable ordering me thither came; and Ian Morrison got his. We flew together to Hong Kong; and he had a short time with Elizabeth Tan. By ill luck his plane on to Tokyo was sold out when I tried to book; and I had to follow on a day behind. As always when flying, because I'm so frightened, I drank a lot on that trip; but I remember the tingling pleasure of dropping over Tokyo bay, with the tiny toy islands below and the fair cone of Fuji like a huge pile of gravel tipped on to the land, and saying to myself: 'I'm actually *arriving in Japan*!' I was met by George Fraser, latest of a long line of English poets to hold the Chair of English Literature in Tokyo University and, until then, spare-time correspondent of *The Observer*. Next day, July 5th, I set about the complicated business of getting to the Korean front. The Press Club was full of American correspondents; there weren't yet many British besides Ian and myself—soon came a pair from *Picture Post*, among the earliest killed. At last, after the expenditure of a couple of days, I had what was needed—'movement order' from MacArthur's headquarters in the Dai-Ichi building, Korean visa from the Korean Diplomatic Mission, the various injections which the American Army insisted upon; I was equipped to thumb a ride from Haneda airport.

I dreaded it—dreaded the flight, in a slapdash U.S. Army plane; but especially dreaded the war which I *knew* was going to be the nastiest of wars. I'm not going to write here much about the

Korean war; it's all been written—and most, by now, forgotten; I shall retrieve merely a few personal memories that may be amusing or interesting.

On that first flight into Korea my enchanting British companion was 'Wardie' Price—G. Ward Price of the *Daily Mail*, one of the most famous foreign correspondents there have ever been; he had been 'covering' wars and international sensations ever since the Balkan War of 1911. Wardie, a man of infinite gentleness and unselfish patience, must then have been getting on for 70; he went to this war wearing a neat felt hat, a nicely pressed suit, gloves and tie and carrying a walking-stick (I, in high summer, was in my usual white shirt and shorts and Waziristan sandals). The war for us didn't begin well; the aircraft had no seats and we sat on loose drums of petrol (not inspiring furniture for a dangerous flight); and our pilot, in heavy mist, lost his bearings and took us far over enemy Korea at almost ground level, searching for a river he had mislaid. I was sick with fear; but dear old Wardie remained unperturbed: observing the serpentine valleys we were perilously pursuing as calmly as if he were driving in a carriage-and-pair through the Park. Somehow we safely reached Taejon—then, briefly, American advanced headquarters. I can see Wardie now, that night in the deserted school where we slept. He took off his tie and carefully folded it; fastitidiously arranged his hat and stick on the floor and lay down beside them, with the air of getting into bed at the Bath Club. Some time afterwards, in Tokyo, Tom Driberg and I went up to the ninth floor of the Maronouchi Hotel for a midday drink with Wardie who had a flat there. The ninth floor was high up and when, on the stroke of twelve, the earthquake happened, that building swayed like a rolling ship, at the same time oscillating up and down like a dancing bear. Tom and I clutched each other, white with terror; but gallant old Wardie was perfectly calm. 'The thing to do in this situation,' he said in his precise way, 'is to place oneself beneath the lintel of the door.'

Most correspondents in Korea would agree that flying in and out of it was more frightening even than the war. I was on an airstrip south of Seoul one day, at the end of 1950, waiting for the Australian Air Force 'courier' which was to take me to Tokyo, watching a U.S. Dakota loaded with G.I.s going on leave. The pilot climbed out of the cockpit and came aft to the door of the aircraft. 'This kite's overloaded,' I heard him say. 'Three of you guys has got to get out. Come on—you an' you an' you.' The three addressed made no move. 'Come on,' said the lieutenant, 'get out or we don't take off.' 'Aw, shit,' said the three, and made no move. The argument continued briefly, until the pilot shrugged his shoulders in disgust. '*Aw, shit,*' he said savagely—climbed into his cockpit, revved up his engines and took off. I don't know whether that aircraft reached Tokyo.

That first day in Taejon I went to the 'briefing' by a nice major-general, shortly after captured. I remember a feeling of dismay when somebody asked how many North Korean tanks had been sighted. 'Oh, I guess about a dozen,' answered the general; upon which a staff officer said: 'Weren't there about 100 reported, sir?' 'Oh yes,' said the general vaguely, 'yes, yes—about 100.' Such vagueness didn't make for confidence. I remember, too, an American youth, badly wounded in the stomach. He lay on his stretcher shouting: 'I didn't join the army for this—I joined for *eddi-cation.*' That was the truth: the soldiers in Japan hadn't thought of doing any soldiering; they were in the most spoiled army, probably, since the Praetorian Guard. It was an odd army: in which the colonel commanding a battalion and his privates squatted together over the after-breakfast trench head-to-tail, like a file of circus elephants—not a dignifying spectacle. One officer explained to me that it was a *democratic* army; and this democracy was illustrated during a stay with an Air Force colonel about Christmas 1950. For some reason, on my way up to Seoul, I had to stay the night on an airfield; the hospitable colonel in command did everything to make me comfortable. During supper with him in the 'mess hall' (where the officers' table was distinguished from the enlisted men's by a table-cloth), a plainly drunken sergeant lurched up to us, plumped himself down on the bench next the colonel and said: 'Say colonel, you're just the man I'm looking for. I want you to loan me a jeep, colonel.' The colonel asked why he wanted a jeep. 'I'll tell you, colonel,' said the sergeant. 'I'm up here from Pusan getting provisions for my outfit. I want a vehicle to take 'em down to my outfit. You see, colonel, I'm up here *trading weapons for whisky.* Now, you'll loan me a jeep, won't you colonel?' The colonel shook his head sadly. 'Sorry sergeant,' he said, 'I just don't have no vee-hicles.' Grumbling, the sergeant shuffled off; and the colonel said to me with a puzzled look: 'I guess that man's been drinking.' That dialogue, exactly photographed in my memory, would seem, I'd suppose, inconceivable even in a Congolese army; yet that nice colonel didn't so much as blink over the notion of 'trading weapons for whisky'.

In those very early days of July at Taejon there weren't yet many correspondents, though they were flowing in with every plane and before long numbered three or four hundred. One, then, was Christopher Buckley of the *Daily Telegraph*, killed with Ian Morrison; who looked and talked like a schoolmaster because he had been a schoolmaster. Ian, Buckley and I lived together as a rule, and went out together on stories; if I hadn't at the time been in Tokyo I should probably have died with them when their jeep hit a land-mine.

With Ian, shortly before he was killed, I came upon a spectacle so terrible and evil that it's haunted my mind ever since: the cold, deliberate torture of men about to die by men momentarily possessed of power. I'd sooner see a thousand mangled bodies than this frightful reality of human cruelty to humans.

Driving through a peaceful green countryside that even, for Korea, seemed kindly, we came suddenly on two open lorries standing just off the road. Clinging to the side-boards of each lorry were three or four Korean soldiers who every so often poked with their rifles at something inside. When we came abreast, we could see what was inside.

Each lorry was packed tight with Koreans. They were kneeling, hands tied behind their backs: kneeling in files one behind the other, packed tight like pigs being taken to slaughter. They were being taken to slaughter: shortly, after a few more hours of waiting under the burning sun, they would dig their own mass grave and be shot. Every time one moaned or moved, a soldier from above clubbed him on the head with his rifle. Some probably, mercifully, were dead already: for hours they'd been so penned, with the sun beating down on their bare heads. They knew they were going to be killed.

They were 'communists', 'spies', or merely personal enemies of their captors. There was nothing we could do; except report it, too late, to the Americans and cable angry, anguished stories about it to our newspapers.

That was why I loathed Korea and the Koreans, and the whole beastly war: that spectacle seemed to sum up all the grim, cynical cruelty of it; with the terrible atmosphere of defeat and flight which we then were breathing, and the disgust felt at the lamentable clique of corrupt politicians the United Nations was trying to succour. Most of us correspondents deplored the cynical aggression from the Communist North; but there was no warmth in our support of Syngman Rhee's South.

I saw that Taejon was about to fall; and took the train down to Taegu (the journey described in 'A Many-Splendoured Thing). Besides wanting to avoid being killed, I wanted to avoid a boring and perhaps painful captivity: the North Koreans had a knack of coming round a position and cutting it off like a tuft of grass with a sickle. One correspondent of a London newspaper was in the habit, Ian told me, of getting up in the morning, thumping his bare chest like Tarzan in the film, and exclaiming: 'Today I get me another Gook.' He then set out with a rifle, on the butt of which his kills to date were notched, in search of North Koreans. ('Gook' was the American term for a North Korean; c.f., wog, dago etc.) That didn't seem to be a correspondent's job: I didn't want to write heroical stories about myself, beginning in the first person. I wanted to report the progress of the war, which was what my paper wanted me to do (quite exceptionally, the syndicated *Observer* Foreign News Service was requiring a daily news cable, so dominating was the Korea story all over the world).

After a while, I decided that the best place to cover the war from was Tokyo. In Korea itself one saw the segment of the war immediately before one's eyes, and that was all; for the rest one had the Army's official daily hand-out, useless by itself. But in Tokyo, in the Press Club, I had the brains to pick of 100 or more correspondents; at four o'clock I had the Army 'briefing', operational and 'intelligence'; and through the evening, thanks to the unfailing generosity of Reuter's, I had a sight of the cables from half-a-dozen Reuter correspondents in Korea. I found that this formula worked splendidly: that it did, was shown by the flattering messages I got from my London office and from a number of editors subscribing to O.F.N.S. My stories were quoted in different parts of the world; and Sid Mason, in the Reuter head office, did me the honour (I learned long after) of distributing copies of one of my reports to all his correspondents as a model to emulate! From the moment I started working from Tokyo, my most successful period as a correspondent began; I found that by collating and checking as much information from varied sources as I could collect, and examining it with my untidy but not over-blunt intelligence, I could often 'throw the story forward', as the jargon has it, pretty accurately. Every so often, reluctantly and cold with fear, I braved the flight to Korea and went there to do some on-the-spot stories.

The least helpful of these sources of information was the official 'briefing' by American staff officers, one 'G' and the other 'I'. As the war situation became worse, the information they gave us became more unrealistic and evasive; we correspondents became angry. Breaking point in my own exasperation came one afternoon late in the war, after the Chinese had joined in (I'd spent a month in north Vietnam in the autumn of 1950, and was whipped back when China took an active hand at the end of November): the Intelligence colonel was pointing to a wall-map with his wand, and saying: 'A horde of Chinese is pouring down *here*, more hordes are on the move *there*, and another is massing on the 39th parallel *there*.' This, I felt, was too much. 'Can the colonel tell us,' I asked, 'how many hordes go to a platoon?' This facile and unmannerly intervention brought down the house, sent the colonel into retirement, and injected a bit of common-sense into future 'briefings': Tommy Thompson, of the *Daily Telegraph*, put it into the first book published in England on the Korean war.

One day I met at the Press Club bar, for my enduring pleasure, a nervy, restless man with a lean, questing, satirical face: recalling, I liked to imagine, Pope's or Swift's: a face moulded in bitter humour and cast in intelligence. This was James Cameron, come out for *Picture Post* after the death in a crashed aeroplane of his predecessor: he was already one of my journalistic heroes. He had recently resigned from the *Daily Express*, whose 'star' writer he was, because his 'copy' had been altered on the subs' desk to suit, not truth, but Lord Beaverbrook's policy. Jimmie will always live as one of the great journalists because, writing superbly with his own intellect and not with his proprietor's bias, his integrity has been inviolate: he will send all Fleet Street to hell rather than write what he thinks is a lie. He left *Picture Post* on a point of moral probity; and since has stubbornly followed his conscience, in a kind of pilgrim's progress, through the avenues of princely salaries he's been offered. But unlike some, this pilgrim is no prig; and for a dozen years I've been honoured with a warm and tolerant friendship.

After Ian's loss, *The Times* sent Louis Heren: the next best thing from the paper's point of view and from mine. Another welcome arrival was Tom Driberg, whom I'd known for several years: come to do stories for *Reynold's News*. I found his quiet, comforting intellect consoling, like the presence of a doctor with a good bedside manner; and his great force of mind was accompanied by a gentle charm and wit. It was while Tom was there that I wrote my *Tokyo Notebook*—we were writing our pieces in the same room. It was a great success, and began: 'We, the Occupationaires, are the new patricians. . . .' The Americans had invented this frightful word, 'occupationaires', to denote all who 'belonged', so to speak, to the Occupation—the Army, diplomats, newspapermen, businessmen even: all, in other words, who weren't Japanese. And Patricians we were: we were at the top down to the humblest G.I.; after that came the Japanese, starting with the Prime Minister (the Emperor was pigeon-holed by himself; nobody quite knew where he came in the order of precedence). We, the Occupationaires, had hotels set apart for us, houses were emptied of their Japanese occupants for our sake, we were above the Japanese law, we paid no purchase tax, we had special petrol at special rates, we had special trains and special coaches, special bars, we alone had the right to take taxis, we had the run of the PX (and, if we were British, of the Australian N.A.A.F.I., when the Commonwealth contingent came, for cheap whisky). In fact, we never had it so good. Douglas Macarthur, having deposed the Emperor from godship, seemed to have raised himself to it in the imperial stead; when, daily, he drove from the U.S. Embassy which had become his 'residence' to the Dai-Ichi building, the streets were cleared, all traffic along the route was stopped; he didn't drive, he royally progressed. The Japanese we consorted with were pathetically—to me painfully—obsequious; five years after the war's end the intention still seemed to be to humiliate the Japanese. I remember having to luncheon at the Press Club a group of former generals and admirals, including the Ambassador in Washington who first heard, to his embarrassment, of Pearl Harbour from the Americans. They were sad, crushed little men, with barely enough money to live on: barons and marquesses deprived of their coronets, hobbling about in frayed suits on their walking sticks, looking wistfully at the empty, forbidden Peers' Club. I dare say they deserved it; but I never think of deserts when I see sorrow.

Once, of a close friend, I said that he was the 'nicest shit I'd ever known'. Of Randolph Churchill, I think I'd say he's the most agreeably boorish man I've ever met. Arrogant, ungracious, blustering, boastful, brutally tart—he can be all these things;

yet I've found him an endearing person, with great charm behind his ill-manners, and kindness under his egotism. And he's such huge fun: that brilliantly flashing mind, fraught with epigram and repartee, loaded with the perfect barbed phrase, used to keep me—over a well-wined luncheon, or through an evening of flowing drink—in agog delight. I suppose he could easily, if he troubled, be the ablest political journalist of both sides of the Atlantic; and if he chose, with that polemically sparkling brain, make any falsehood plausible. I dare say, were he inclined, he could argue Communism better than Marx could.

Randolph came for the *Daily Telegraph* after Christopher Buckley's death with Ian; and was soon gently wounded in a brave, probably foolhardy, exploit. Then in Tokyo, after getting himself barred, by some outrageous rudeness from the Press Club, he made the Maronouchi Hotel his headquarters. This hotel, excellent for eating and drinking in, had been taken over by the Australians —the Commonwealth division was commanded by an Australian general. Only one thing spoiled the Maronouchi for me: in Tokyo's flaming midsummer, when even breathing was a problem, this notice appeared in the hotel foyer: 'Visitors to the Hotel are required to wear jacket and tie after 6 p.m.—(Signed) X.Y.Z., *Lieut.*, O.C. Hotel.' This enraged me: 'O.C. Hotel', indeed! One knows in any war about R.T.O.s and Town Majors—but O.C. Hotel: surely the basest way, of any, to fight a war. And even the Royal Navy, in the tropics, wear 'Red Sea Rig' in the wardroom at night: evening trousers with cummerbund; open shirt and no coat. I was constantly breaking this 'order', and being told that I should be 'reported to O.C. Hotel'; but, on principle, I continued to break it.

Among Randolph's gifts is a wonderful memory; he can quote faultlessly things like Shakespeare or the speeches of his father; and he's an entrancing raconteur and mimic. I think it was he who told me the story of Winston Churchill's contemptuous dismissal of a proposal—made, I think (in the story), by Admiral Cunningham—for some changes in the structure or principles of the Royal Navy. 'The Royal Navy', Churchill devastatingly replied, 'has for long been founded upon Nelson, rum, buggery and the lash; and so founded it shall continue.' I know it was Randoph who told that his father, after being introduced to the middle-aged bride of a well-known public figure*well known for his private unorthodoxies, grunted: 'Oh well—buggers can't be choosers.'

During one evening's conversational drinking—there were Randolph, Frank Owen, Louis Heren, myself—Frank had been recounting the mutations of his journalistic life—how he'd parted company with the *Evening Standard* with 'separation money' of so many thousand pounds, with the *Daily Express* receiving so many more thousands and, quarrelling with the *Daily Mail*, of which he'd been for a time editor, departing the richer by so many thousands more.

'My dear Frank,' observed Randolph softly, 'you were born with a silver knife in your back.'

I was overjoyed when, six or seven years later, I ran into Randolph again in Cyprus; where together we had a luncheon lasting from noon until nightfall.

I find it's impossible to write about Keibo:*because, I suppose, he's too close to me—though it's eleven years ago now, I feel he's in the room with me. Of all the loves I've had, his has lasted longest; of all the boys I've loved, he, more than any, was the 'divine friend, much desired'—the perfect one. He was 15 when I met him in the Hibiya gardens in Tokyo; today, at 26, his affection is as perfect as ever; and mine for him, though changed in structure, is unalterable in strength. After I had had to leave him behind (his adoring mother, sweet little Mama-San, had said to me: 'Do you want him for your own? I will give him to you'; and thereafter he had begun his letters: 'My fatherly Michael'), he wrote to me for ten years, and sent me presents from Tokyo; and when, at the age of 23, he became converted to the Catholic Church, he had himself baptized after me—'Now I'm Christian so my name is Michael of course after yours,' he wrote to me.

I have many of his letters written down the years, and when I re-read them I am humbled to the point of shame by the fierceness of their naively expressed devotion: ' . . . we were always together. You came every day for lunch and dinner to my house and I was stay with you every day and night, first we were hotel then you found our house in Satagaya. . . . My dear Papa, since you left Japan I felt very lonely and sorrow then I became very norty boy but I have grown now. Mon père, I was hard to live alone, I thought I'm going to mad, you can't imagine how I was missed you so. Oh I wish I can look after you. It will be very nice isn't it? . . . ' Love, which should be always kind, can be as cruel as torture when arbitrarily wrenched apart; I've often felt, during the many harrowing partings of my life, that one has no right to love when one knows that circumstances must brutally cut it short; by loving and being loved, one is storing up pain.

Yes: our house in Satagaya . . . the perfect simplicity of life on the yielding kindliness of the *tatami* floor, the softly sliding doors; the gliding grace of a Japanese house and the steaming luxury of a Japanese bath. And how we laughed afterwards, that night in the European-style hotel (our window looked full out to the blue-white immaculacy of Fuji-San) when an impudent earthquake rolled us out of bed with a bump. The shopping expeditions to the PX and the Australian canteen to buy luxuries like sugar for Keibo's family (it was a grave offence even to *give* 'occupationaire' provisions to any Japanese). I suppose, in all my life (since the perfection of my childhood), those six months with Keibo were the happiest; and his incomparable *goodness* made even the grim inhumanity of the Korean war seem worth while.

We said good-bye twice: in October 1950, the war in Korea seeming to be near dubious conclusion, I was sent to Hanoi, in northern Vietnam; not knowing that in six weeks' time I should be back with Keibo, after the Chinese 'hordes' moved south. Before leaving Tokyo, I was asked to 'string' in Vietnam for the *Christian Science Monitor*: a delightful offer that brought me the pride of getting during the next few weeks four or five column-length stories on the front page of that excellent American newspaper and the pleasure of a large number of dollars (two years later, while living on the island of Corfu, I received out of the blue a cheque for 70 dollars from the *Monitor*, which they 'had found on their books': a nice example of newspaper integrity).

I loved Hanoi, and the great green hills and plain of the Red River valley. I drove northwards, towards the Chinese border, through Catholic country (where, the faithful said, no church was hit by the godless shells of Ho Chi-minh) and along roads sentinelled by the high wooden watch-towers described in 'The Quiet American', to a French outpost, where I drank wine with the officers and listened to their courageous fatalism. In Hanoi the French were bluntly defeatist, from the general staff down: 'another three weeks and we'll surrender', colonels would say, or: 'we're evacuating our families immediately'. The galvanizing presence of de Lattre de Tassigny, who arrived just after I had to leave, turned fading French morale upside-down—I was glad that I did, later in Malaya, meet that great and curious man ('he is a romantic figure', writes Lady Diana Cooper in her autobiography. 'One pictures him with Flemish lace laid on his armour. Such intrepid gallantry, such bold effeminacy.').

I remember, in Hanoi, being charmingly enticed into the little island temple on the edge of the lake (Buddhist, would it have been? Or Confucian? I think I saw, in the twinkling dimness of the interior, a gilded image among the black and crimson lacquer) by an acolyte and shown delights which can't, I'm sure, have been liturgical.

In the first week of December I was back in Tokyo; and a week or so later in Seoul, the capital of South Korea already being threatened again. I recall chiefly the agonizing cold, and Christmas at the front with the Middlesex Regiment, who were cheerfully entombed beneath ice and snow in the wild hills some dozen miles north of Seoul.

I left the Korean war for good on 17th January 1951. I can't remember, I'm glad to say, the actual parting from Keibo; I know that I sobbed for half an hour after take-off: saying my prayers for his sake to Fuji-San's white pile on the starboard beam. I've howled so often and so much in aeroplanes during the last twenty years and more, that I no longer care about appearing an ass in the other passengers' eyes.

In 1961 I saw Keibo in Europe: the same incomparable person; but a decade older than boyhood.

Then came a happy, though roistering, time in Singapore and Malaya. My principal companions, besides Louis Heren and Bill O'Neill, were S. Rajaratnam, brilliant Indian leader-writer on Aw Boon-haw's brashly intelligent *Singapore Standard*—'Raja', married to a charming Hungarian, was later, I think, Minister of Information in the first Governments of free Singapore; Arthur Jansen, the Dutch Consul, and his entrancing Siamese wife Pakh; Jack Brazier, the splendid railwayman; Alex Josey, a bearded, rollicking free-lance journalist whose Left-Wing pen, virulent as a blow-pipe dart, was a thorn in administrative sides and whose Anglo-Sino-Malaysian consort seemed as fragilely exquisite as a humming-bird; Frank Sullivan, a sensitive Australian with a fine, sad mind: today, I believe, private secretary to Malaya's Prime Minister, Tungku Abderrhaman; and often dear Dato Onn, a sweet man with a gentle, civilized intelligence: at that time still the leading Malay politician in the Federation. It's sad that those elder statesmen of Malayan independence, the architects, really, of Malay-Chinese co-operation, Dato Onn and Sir Tan Cheng-lock, had to be passed over by history when independence came.

Most of these men had their wives with them, and most of the wives were my friends—yet by now my private life was well known: I didn't try to hide it; and when Somo became my friend I took him nearly everywhere. A few, perhaps, privately commented: 'Michael really is rather the limit'; but these people were too humane, too *intelligent*, to look down their noses at me or treat my business as theirs; they were among the best friends I've had. I confess I went a bit far with Somo; I even took him, almost flauntingly, into the suburban-minded Singapore Cricket Club (which, unlike the Tanglin Club, allowed members to entertain 'local' guests).

I don't, as a rule, go much for 'beauty' in a face, but for its *interest*, for some touching quality, for the person it reflects: Keibo's face, spellbinding, wasn't pretty. Somo's beauty, though, was breath-taking—like a hothouse flower. Languid and sinuous, delicately sensual as a slim orange rose; he was a southern Indian to whom some infusion of paler blood had given a skin of old gold. He was, too, meltingly, lazily affectionate and made a charming pretence of performing the duties of 'bearer' in my Cathay Building flat. He couldn't be a substitute for Keibo; but he was somebody to mother, to be fond of, and to show off.

I paid another visit to Indonesia; and then, in the summer of 1951, Robin Maugham invited me to join him for a yachting cruise in the Mediterranean. One ought, I felt, at least once in one's life play at millionaires; and I asked *The Observer* for three or four months' leave-without-pay. I was in England long enough to go down to Sutton Courtenay for luncheon with David Astor, where I found the Rev. Michael Scott: physically fragile, but morally heroic: òne of those rare parsons who see Christianity as a practical crusade against political injustice and the very opposite of Butler's 'a clergyman is supposed to be a kind of human Sunday'; and to meet in London, with Patrick O'Donovan, Seretse Khama and his loyal English wife.

In August 1951 Robin and I flew to Nice: his yacht was lying in Villefranche harbour. Robin's Uncle Willie, Somerset Maugham, came to the quay but refused to come on board, being averse to small craft; we dined at the Villa Mauresque, his home on Cap

Ferrat: a gay evening, he in unusually good humour, in his dry way. I talked about Malaya to his son-in-law, Lord John Hope: chiefly, I expect, in protest against the obstructionism, at that time, of the big rubber interests to the policies of men like Malcolm MacDonald; and the direly envenoming effects on racial harmony of Singapore's diehard British matriarchy. I can't remember whether Hope, a nice, bony, youngish man, was yet a Minister.

This yachting life, to me, was a wonderful extravaganza: escapism perfected, lifting one illusorily above the ordinary restrictions of life and lightly lacquering one's little unreal world with a semblance of riches. Aubrey Beardsley, in a letter from his death-bed, said: 'Boats are sucn blessed things, one loses all sense of responsibility upon them.' That's the secret of yachting; one's responsible to no one but oneself and is free of the tyranny of time-tables and the dictations of bureaucratic authority; one goes where one will and leaves when one wants; and one looks with pitying disdain upon the feeble, ordinary folk who can't go yachting. It's absurd and unreal, but delightful.

On Capri we found Norman Douglas, drank *negroni* with him at a cliff-top café behind the *piazzetta*, and took him to dinner in the small *trattoria* that he loved and where he was loved. He was brimming with fun and wit: very old on his legs but youthful in mind: the deep-set blue eyes still lively and laughing, the splendid Augustan face still relishing 'copious conversation, copious wine'. He talked of Boris de Chroustchoff and Irving Davis, Pino Orioli's partner, and others of the old Bloomsbury days; and gave us each a signed copy of the Maurice Magnus pamphlet, that venomous castigation of D. H. Lawrence. With him came always a 12-year-old boy, whose duty was to guide Norman's tottering footsteps back to Anacapri. 'I've always liked,' Norman said (I paraphrase slightly), 'a very small possessor attached to a very large possession.' Two months later he was dead. I've sometimes wondered whether those gay and festive days with us didn't hasten his death—he was, after all, over 80; but if they did, he certainly enjoyed them. I suppose his Attic and witty writing, with its exquisite workmanship, infinite sensibility, and exact, scholarly observation, will always be read by people who love the perfect—in spite of the captious and envious denigration of Richard Aldington. Surely 'Old Calabria' must remain in the first rank of England's literature.

Crossing the Malta Channel from Augusta, in Sicily, we nearly foundered: it was a night, in fearful reality, when strong men's lips were moving in prayer. One engine went dead, and some cylinders of the other; the bilge pumps failed, the engine-room was flooded, the ship in darkness; without navigating lights, we limped—oh, how we limped!—through huge seas. Yet somehow Malta was found; and as the night began to pale, we made fast to H.M.S. *Manxman*'s stern buoy. Next morning Captain Trevor Lean, D.S.O., looked over the rail of his quarter-deck and exclaimed: 'Good God, I've laid an egg!'; and by midday we were having drinks with him in his cabin.

About the beginning of November the 'troubles' in the Canal Zone of Egypt flared into near-war. I cabled *The Observer* offering to go to the Canal; and before they could answer a chance came to sail with the first Naval reinforcement; at an hour's notice I went on board *Chequers*, of which Prince Philip had once been Number One ('bit on the strict side, 'e was,' a rating who'd served under him told me). Meanwhile Trevor Lean, by now a great friend, had dashed with *Manxman*, fastest ship in the Navy, to Tripoli in Libya to bring a contingent of the Guards Brigade to the Canal; *Chequers* and *Manxman* met somewhere near Ismailia, and Trevor made a signal asking me to join him at Suez. A day or two later, I went down the Canal from Ismailia in a tug called the *Empire Dolly*, manned by the Royal Navy: an absurd little craft in the long, slow convoy of huge oil-tankers and merchant vessels. Then *Manxman* became my home for the next few weeks.

In one respect, a ship of the Royal Navy is a journalist's dream: you're living and travelling with your cable-head (his 'communications' are a correspondent's first concern): the ship radios your stories to the Admiralty, whence they're passed to your paper. But a ship lying in Suez harbour doesn't produce much 'copy'; my aim was to join the Army (the 'brown jobs', the Navy called the soldiers) ashore where the news was. This however, ridiculous though it sounds, wasn't possible: though I went into Suez every day with Trevor or his officers, I did so illegally even from the British point of view. We weren't at war with the Egyptians (again, the armed forces were acting 'in aid of the civil power'); and the British, intent on correctitude towards Egypt as well as on downing the Egyptians, insisted that even accredited correspondents should have an Egyptian visa before entering the Canal Zone. But there was no Egyptian authority to give me a visa; nor, had there been, would I have been given one. I felt like a man penniless but for a fifty-pound note which nobody will change. Then I was told that in Khartoum, the Sudan being yet an Anglo-Egyptian condominium, visas were still being marketed; from there I could fly legally to Cairo, and thence go into the Canal Zone. So, *Manxman* having a mission in Port Sudan, I sailed down with her and took the train to Khartoum—one of those charming, sleepy long journeys of gazing out of the window at a strange land; and seeing, waving from the railside bush, Kipling's Fuzzy-Wuzzys in the flesh. In Khartoum an English official gave me a visa; but news came that people with Sudan visas were being arrested on arrival in Cairo. With a man from the *Daily Express*, who was in the same quandary, I chartered a tiny Dove aircraft and flew back to *Manxman* in Port Sudan. But before leaving Khartoum I interviewed Abderrhaman El-Mahdi, a stately and beautiful old man like a Moorish Pasha: it was awe-inspiring to be talking to the son of that fabled Mahdi whose soldiers had slain General Gordon and against whom Kitchener had marched.

At Port Sudan we were joined by a new Ambassador to Saudi Arabia whom, with his wife, we were ceremonially to land at Jeddah. The approach to Jeddah is one of the world's trickiest: a maze of shoals and sandbanks through which a narrow channel treacherously winds. The pilot came on board: a little withered Arab wearing a dirty old tarboosh and ragged European clothes. It was a diverting sight, standing on the bridge—this confident little scarecrow virtually taking command of one of the King's mightier ships and chatting gaily with her Captain as if Trevor had been the master of a felucca. Unerringly he took *Manxman* to her anchorage where, after sending off our Ambassador in his gold lace, our guard of honour was kept jumping to attention for a succession of Saudi Arabian dignitaries. That afternoon the Ambassador lent us his motor car, and Trevor and I said: 'Let's go to Mecca'; of course we couldn't get there—the way's barricaded against infidels some miles from the city; but it was a fine feeling driving down the Mecca Road.

All my time in *Manxman* I slept below in an empty officer's cabin but grandly lived and ate with Trevor in the roomy day-cabin forrard of the quarter-deck where he ruled in 'the loneliness of command'; on his writing-table were photographs, signed in childish hands, of the two princesses he had known while serving in the old *Victoria and Albert*; and along the bulkheads hung pictures of his earlier ships—notably *Roebuck*, in which he had performed a dashing exploit at Narvik. Trevor had everything one wants to find in a sailor: great good looks (with that nautical fringe of whisker carefully left along the line of the cheek-bone) charm and humour and a sort of kindly strength: adored by his officers, gentle and patient with the problems of his men; I never heard him use a sharp word, and the ship ran like happy clockwork.

But, sadly, I had to leave. At Port Said, from the deck of the cruiser *Liverpool*, I watched dear *Manxman* sail for Greek waters; and then managed to smuggle myself ashore and in a convoy of Army lorries down to that horrible camp of barbed wire and corrugated iron at Fayid. I will skip that grim December in Fayid and Ismailia; I loathed each moment of it. It was a month of hideous vengeful violence, squalid discomfort, bitter desert cold, and unvarying ugliness, physical and spiritual. I knew, what anybody could know except apparently Whitehall, that Britain would have to leave the Canal Zone shortly, which indeed she did very soon after hundreds of men on both sides had been uselessly killed; I knew that terrorism can never be defeated by counter-terror: only by understanding and removing the reasons for that terror (a lesson which, after Ireland, Palestine, Egypt and Cyprus, the politicians may by now have learned). My heart wasn't in my job of reporting this cycle of treacherous ambush and squalid reprisal—like that awful day when a huge British force drove the frightened poor from their slums in a Suez suburb. It wasn't the soldiers' fault; they were brave and restrained in circumstances of agonizing perplexity. It was the crass, blind, brutal policy that I hated. The Christmas cable calling me home was the most welcome I ever had; I didn't know it meant the sack.

I sailed in a Tank Landing Craft to Cyprus; and two days later was in London.

At the office in Tudor Street I felt at once an oracular chill; I didn't see David Astor but was received by the Chief Sub, Ken Obank, whom I'd always liked as a man and admired as a journalist; and Tristan Jones, an administrative personage whom I'd never liked and who had never admired me. They told me I wasn't wanted any longer; they didn't say why, and I didn't ask: to this day I don't know. But instantly I thought of my 'previous', of my indiscretions in Singapore and elsewhere; heaven knew what scandals had been brought to London.

The paper was generous: I was to go back to Malaya until July at £200 a month, and receive a cash payment of £500 at the end. To me, with my adolescent blindness to the meaning of money, this seemed a boundless fortune that would last for ever; I was delighted, and saw myself settling in some Elysian place to write a book about Malaya. I was indeed grateful, and have remained so, to *The Observer*; its gift to me at the end was very generous; but much more precious than that were the five years of happiness while I was with the paper and the honour of working for it. I was yet to work for it again, as a 'stringer': in Cyrpus and in Aden.

Before leaving London I was commissioned to write my Malaya book—another that I spinelessly failed to finish; and by mid-January was back in Singapore.

Soon after I got back, the appointment as High Commissioner was announced of Gen. Sir Gerald Templer: responsible directly to the Prime Minister, Winston Churchill, and armed with absolute powers. We didn't know much about Templer, but it was plain we were to have a military dictatorship; and those of us shuddered who believed that communism's power over the people's minds must be opposed (while the communists in the jungle were fought militarily) not by oppression but by the gift of something more attractive than communism, like the much-desired advance towards independent self-government. The arrival at King's House of a uniformed satrap, we felt, wouldn't encourage the scared little people, black, brown and yellow, to suppose that that 'freedom' lay round the corner; especially as it it was made known by hints subtly dropped, that a proper tartar was coming among us. I remember the mood of drama at K.L. airfield when he arrived: the nervous colonial servants, the soldiers on their toes, the journalists agog for a 'story'. A sparse, frail, jumpy figure, light on its feet as a child, almost feminine in its gait, stepped off the Dakota; with a gaunt, pinched face like a suspicious mandrill's, gnomish and sly—a face, though, that could break abruptly into a sweetly impish grin; a fascinating face, quite unmilitary in spite of the small moustache; and a restless trick of taking off and putting on his spectacles and looking pedagogically at one over their top.

I quickly found in him a character of rare interest; and developed for him a sort of love-hate: an irreconcilable mingling of admiration and contempt. He was a bundle of nerves: chain-smoking, gin-nipping; impatient, petulant, tactless—yet had an endearing charm and an admirable brain (even after our big quarrel he threw at me, at some official function, a wryly roguish grin). He would have gone to the top, I was sure, in any profession—the law, scholarship, philosophy perhaps; but I felt he'd chosen the wrong one: his huge ability and surging personality were constricted by the sam-browne belt and stifling corselet of an army lifetime. 'But having put the cassock on, it poisoned him; he was strangled in its bands,' said Thackeray of Swift; that's just what I felt about Templer—that his great spirit would have soared if it could have breathed.

He seemed to delight in playing the *enfant terrible*; and stories of his rancorous asperity piled up. Here are three which I know to be authentic.

Lady Templer was to make her first public appearance at some ceremony; and a young European was sent up to King's House by the government information office to find out the programme so that photographers could be present and publicity made out of the function; Templer came upon the young man in an ante-room. 'What do *you* want?' he said. Stammeringly, the mission was explained. 'Can't my wife go out without *you* being on her tail?' the High Commissioner snapped—not the way to win the confidence of a junior official.

At Seremban a leader of the Indian community was presented to him. 'Oh—you're an Indian, are you?' said Templer. 'Well, I *don't like Indians*.' I suppose the remark referred to the supposition that Indians were inclined to sit on the political fence; it can't have increased Indian regard for him.

During the time of the notorious curfew at a village called Tanjong Malim, I went to a cocktail party in K.L. at which Templer was introduced to a revered Chinese professor, an old man of high standing in the Federation and Singapore. 'And what part do *you* come from?' asked the High Commissioner. From Tanjong Malim, replied the sage. 'Oh, you do, do you?' Templer barked. 'Well, who let *you* out?'

This sort of mischievousness could be amusing to the spectator and, probably, to himself; but it didn't endear him to people. I don't think tactlessness is a British failing; but it was embarrassingly often exhibited in colonies by the ruling to the ruled. At that time, near Kuala Lumpur, the wife of a senior official 'opened' a welfare centre in one of the New Villages—the wired-in encampments where Chinese squatters gathered in from the jungle verge were 'resettled'. 'I've always,' said the good woman addressing the villagers, 'been so interested in women, and children, and welfare, and *all that*.' Probably none among her listeners but the hand-clapping English comprehended what she was saying.

Templer at once began to put into operation the Gurney-Briggs plan to cut off the men in the jungle from their supplies; apart from the few patches of tapioca they could grow inside the forest, the terrorists depended on the settled population for food, and upon the humble Chinese 'squatting' wherever they could scratch a living. 'Resettlement' and the New Villages became the talk of the day: plainly, depriving the 'bandits' of food was a quicker approach to their defeat than hunting them interminably through the jungle and killing or capturing about one a month. (When King's House was being fenced with barbed wire, an Indian gardener pottering near by remarked: 'Everybody's being re-settled these days: I see they're resettling the High Commissioner.')

Resettlement, barbed wire and all, was a sensible and humane thing; savage vengeance upon innocent people another. Tanjong Malim brought the question of 'collective punishment' to the front pages of London's newspapers, certainly of *The Observer* and *The Times*—Louis Heren felt as strongly about it as I did. Recalling the medieval savageries of Charles of Anjou in Sicily, 'collective punishment' became one of the instruments of oppression under Templer in Malaya and under Harding, later, in Cyprus: it seems horribly inherent in a revolutionary situation where military dictatorship meets resistance and resistance is followed by reprisal. Tanjong Malim was a biggish village known to have been a source of supply to the terrorists; it was curfewed and wired—and even then some villager threw bags of rice over the wire for the rebels to pick up. Templer retorted by halving the entire village's rice ration; which meant that the unculpable many, with their children, would—by British decree—go short of food. This seemed to me not only unforgivably brutal but also an easy way of making Communists.

I drove out to Tanjong Malim with Leslie Hoffmann, a delightful Anglo-Chinese journalist, later Editor of the *Straits Times*. We found only soldiers in sight; shops were shut; the people imprisoned in their homes. The soldiers, going from house to house, were distributing and then collecting Templer's famous 'information forms': sheets of paper on which the Chinese citizens of Tanjong Malim, mostly illiterate, were asked, under guarantee of secrecy, to 'inform' against their acquaintances. To make this a personal matter strictly between the High Commissioner himself and the citizen, each 'form' was accompanied by a printed envelope addressed: 'To His Excellency General Sir Gerald Templer, K.C.M.G., K.C.B., D.S.O., M.C., etc. etc., High Commissioner in Malaya'—I couldn't think what the Chinese would make of that; and I liked to think of what *may* have been written in some of this private correspondence with the High Commissioner.

Information about the terrorists, side by side with supplies to them, was a crux of the Emergency situation; and was almost impossible to come by. Wherever there is rule by fear—fear of Government, fear of an unseen, vengeful power—in western Sicily, in Cyprus or Ireland during the 'troubles', wherever terrorism and oppression are locked in their terrible embrace—there's bred a conspiracy of silence which is most perfectly described in the Sicilian word *omertà*: it's a schoolboys' code of honour which forbids their giving away each other, and if they do, brings them swift vengeance. A murder is committed before twenty people's eyes; but not one of them has seen it: that is *omertà*. It is impenetrable and inscrutable; and, as was found in Cyprus, a lot of torture is needed to breach it, if it can be breached at all, and very rarely will a bribe of £5,000 cause it to crack. *Omertà* can beat armies and outwit field-marshals, and, if one's a policeman concerned with 'intelligence', must be exasperating to the point of dottiness. In Malaya it was universal, and I don't suppose those letters to His Excellency let much light through it.

Dictatorships, obviously, can't tolerate criticism: 'who isn't with me is against me'; and Templer, being a dictator, was understandably enraged by it. It was after the storm raised by Tanjong Malim that he summoned the entire Press to King's House to listen to one of his lectures. Alternately glowering at us over his spectacles and giving us his enchantingly mischievous grin, he solemnly proposed that we should choose one of our number to receive from him, on behalf of the rest of us, his versions of what was happening and from them do our reporting; we were to put away our own eyes and minds and use his. Of course we turned that down. 'Very well,' he snapped. 'Let's have a drink'; and with his light-footed, gangling tread, led us into another room.

A burning question then was elections: the Malayan politicians were clamouring for them; and those of us British who were 'liberal' believed that if promises of future independence were to mean anything in the public mind, a visible move towards an elected parliament was vitally important; that the manifest emblem of good faith which elections would be must wrest from the Communists a lot of hovering sympathy. (I can't now remember chapter and verse; but I imagine this must too have been Malcolm MacDonald's view; but he and Templer were poles apart. I knew what Malcolm thought of the High Commissioner; I could guess what he thought of the Commissioner-General.)

Over a whisky I said to Templer: 'Are you going to hold elections, sir?' 'No!' he said shortly. 'Nothing above village pump' (one or two municipal councils were being elected). 'No elections till terrorism stops.' That was what I wanted to know; I knew I couldn't file this important bit of news at once—anything he said was 'off the record'; but, according to the rules, I could work it in later without 'attributing' it to anybody.

I sat on this extremely important knowledge for a couple of weeks, and then decided it was my duty to publish it: both politically my duty and journalistically. Using one of those formulas like 'I understand from a reliable source,' the worth of which hangs upon the confidence his Editor and readers have in a correspondent, I cabled the story and gave a copy, as I was empowered to do, to the *Singapore Standard*, that paper 'taking' the *Observer* service. I was in Singapore when it was published and, going blandly into the government information office, found that Kuala Lumpur had been furiously telephoning for me. On the line I was told: 'H.E. wants to know immediately what the source of your story was.' Normally that's a question one doesn't answer—to do so would be a violation of the confessional; but this time I was safe. 'His Excellency was my source,' I said cheerfully. There was some spluttering on the line; then I was told Templer wanted me at King's House at noon next day. I flew up in the Dakota; a leisurely hour over the great green lake of jungle: one looked down and thought of those little implacable killers somewhere in its infinite dark depths.

One of his staff was in the room: there's always a witness on these occasions. He didn't shake hands; nor, when he took a cigarette, offer me one. 'You don't mind if I smoke, sir?' I said at once, taking one of my own. He said I had betrayed his confidence, given 'in my bloody drawing-room, drinking my bloody whisky'. I told him that I'd respected the 'off-the-record' nature of the information; that I was bound in duty to use it, and that the way I had used it was morally proper and journalistically correct. We argued like iron against iron about the propriety of my behaviour and the wisdom of his policy; and then he said: 'Well, I think you're a shit.' 'Well, sir,' I said, 'I don't think too much of you.' A ghost of that goblin grin flickered; and we went at each other some more. Then he stood up: 'Well, we agree to differ,' he said; and added with sly menace: 'Who's got the *Observer* now—Astor isn't it?' It would have spoiled the fun to have told him that I was leaving the paper anyhow. He did shake hands when I bid him good morning.

I was already engaged for luncheon a few days later with Sir Donald MacGillivray, the Deputy High Commissioner; but within a few hours of my interview at King's House a telephone message came from his secretary to cancel the engagement. I was being sent to Coventry.

Another newspaper story, before I left Malaya, was to enhance my unpopularity. The annual dinner of the St George's Society, to which all the bigwigs were traditionally invited, was that year to be held at the Lake Club, a stronghold of the British *tuan*. I was told by a senior Government official in whose word I had absolute faith, that the committee of the Lake Club, learning that the Sultan of Selanger (a later King of Malaya) was one of the invited, was insisting that his name be taken off the list—'natives' were not admitted to the Club. This juicy piece of colour-bar, coming at a time when Malcolm MacDonald and every man of good will of every sort of skin was striving for harmony between the races and the creation of a Malayan Nation, was of the utmost importance: here was an influential section of the British 'aristocracy' sabotaging a principal intention of British policy. It was also, of course, the kind of 'unfortunate' happening that the authorities would have liked hushed up while it was quietly smoothed out being the scenes. But I thought, and still do, that the only way to destroy such criminal snobbishness was to shame it out of existence. My story in the *Singapore Standard* raised a hullaballo: denials from the St George's Society and the Club appeared that day in the afternoon paper; the Secretariat was in a ferment and Templer ordered an inquiry. In the end, the Sultan went to the dinner; I can't remember whether it was held at the Lake Club.

A friend of mine from England, a member of parliament,* who, visiting Malaya, dined at King's House, told me that (over the brandy, I suppose), talk coming round to my critical insubordination, Templer said: 'Well, I don't like buggers anyway.' This was so much in character, it made me laugh; it also disturbed me:

had that cursed 'previous' cropped up again? Perhaps he'd heard a rumour of my heresy: though that seemed unlikely—I'd never come near scandal; more sinister was the doubt whether a colonial vice-regent, seeking to silence a political recalcitrant, had the right to ask Scotland Yard for any secret weapon that might exist. Twice afterwards, in Cyprus and in Aden, the same doubt brought me to a wrong decision.

I think, on balance, I adored Templer more than I hated him. I hated his policy, his methods, the military corset that deformed his spirit; but I adored his modesty, his uniqueness, the charming twinkle of mischief that hovered behind his outrageous brusqueries. He was without pretension or sham, without a hankering for small grandeur; I knew he wouldn't seek a peerage as firmly as I knew, in Cyprus later, that Harding would want one. Templer had in him the glow of greatness, too confined to come to flame; Harding had none.

In July I came to the end of my great Malayan happiness; and of my happy alliance with *The Observer*. Sadly I said goodbye to Louis Heren and his wife Pat, whose companionship had for so long been an almost daily pleasure; and went to Naples, and on to Greece.

I WAS 55 years old; yet still insensible of reality: I felt that with £500 and my Malaya book to write I needn't worry again— a new life of ease and gentle pleasure stretched delightfully ahead, and no notion of old age yet clouded the shining horizon. I didn't know old age existed—except in the already old: a race apart, I thought, whom one pitied with respectful contempt. I ought, of course, at once to have sought another job; instead, I lay back on my pillows of fantasy.

I found a tiny cottage on Corfu, in a steep grove of old olive trees, looking out across the sea to the mountains of Albania; and for three months, with a sweet yellow-haired youth named Yorgo to cook and clean, I daily worked sitting under a spreading fig-tree. I wrote some 50,000 words of my Malaya book. It wouldn't have been a good book, in the sense of being authoritative and balanced in political judgement: for that is needed an exact and 'brainy' mind, disciplined and logical; but it was lively, and fraught with unorthodox and impudent ideas. Alas, I never finished it. Because of currency fears I moved to London: a disastrously foolish move; better finish the book, cut off from money for a while, than waywardly spend the money and find the book gone stale. But that is what happened in London. I became powerless to write; anybody who has sat in front of a typewriter unable to put a sentence together, feeling his mind resistant like a clogged coffee-mill which one holds between the knees and hopelessly tries to turn, will know the despair that day after day I felt. It was mental paralysis almost physically felt: Malaya, so lively and blooming on Corfu, had gone dead in me.

Throughout those London months I saw a lot of Robin Maugham and when, in the summer of 1953 he took a house for a month in Dorset, he asked me to come with him. We stayed at Brockenhurst on the way: Trevor Lean had asked us on board H.M.S. *Adamant* for the Coronation Review; his last ship before

etirement from the Royal Navy. The night before the Review
ve went over to Beaulieu to dine with Edward Montagu; and next
lay drove into Portsmouth. *Adamant* was lying next to the aircraft
carrier allotted to members of both houses of parliament, so
Montagu, being a peer, boarded her. Trevor, in *Adamant*, was
lost to a crowd of retired admirals, generals, air-marshals, and the
ike with their wives: the party began at about eleven in the
morning and lasted until the evening—a day of uninterrupted
patriotic drinking. That evening we met Edward in a Portsmouth
bar; luckily we had a driver to take us back.

It wasn't long after returning from Dorset to my Bayswater
home, that the telephone woke me up one midnight. The call
came from Beaulieu, from a friend staying there: Edward Montagu,
he said, was being charged with 'a certain offence' and so was
another man; would I instantly go round to that other man's flat
and tell him what was happening? I went round to his mews flat,
banged the poor fellow up, and gave him the confounding news;
nobody could know better than I how he then felt: I suppose
there's no knowledge so *shocking*, in the same physical way, as the
knowledge (whether one's innocent or guilty) that the whole
ghastly trail of police-court, trial, and perhaps prison, lies ahead;
it affects one's *bodily* health as well as one's mind's. One's transported in a flash from a real world of ordinary things like bus-stops,
tobacconist's shops and sitting in cinemas beside ordinary people
to whom policemen are men who will tell them the time—to a
nightmare world, a city of dreadful night, where the *knowledge*
gnaws at one's mind like a rat. Punishment begins long before
judicial punishment can be imposed. For a little time after this I
was running errands in connection with the defence, seeing
Edward and the other while they were on bail and so on; and then,
in August, Robin proposed that we should go to Ischia for a holiday,
offering in his generous way to stand me the fare. So it was on that
island weeks later, that I read one morning in a Naples paper the
dumbfounding news that a brand new charge had been brought
against Edward; and that this time Michael Pitt-Rivers was
implicated. The police had been out to 'get' poor hunted Edward;
and in doing so had triumphantly scooped up two other men as
well.

There's a frightening social paradox in the truth that often in
these squalid sexual cases (squalid because anything initiated by the
police and swilled from the newspapers by the salacious public

instantly becomes squalid) the person condemned is essentially a *moral* one, a nature *finer* than those of the little men condemning him. I didn't know Michael Pitt-Rivers very well; but he had seemed to me a man whose interests were principally of the *mind*, who sought philosophical goodness in such systems of thought and experience as Buddhism, whose occupations were spiritual and intellectual in a world where minds were chiefly dirty with commerce. It seemed to me laughably silly that so moral a person should be imprisoned for physical contacts of no minimal importance in any context whatever.

Ischia, in 1953, and still less in 1951 when we first knew it, hadn't yet become the touristic goal for every tripper and asylum of international layabouts that it is today; the Porto was the tranquil haven of a few yachts and there was a sprinkling of foreign painters and writers, including Wystan Auden, around the fishing village of Forio. One memory remaining from those few weeks in the villa Robin took—suitable for *Punch*, or perhaps Thurber— was the night Leli Colucci upset the soup down the princess's frock. Signora Colucci, wife of Vincenzo, a painter of some local renown and owner of Robin's villa, asked us to dinner, her other guests being Prince Henry of Hesse (Enrico d'Assia, as he's known in Italy, whose King Victor Emmanuel III was his grandfather) and an enchanting little German princess aged about 19, whose name I've forgotten: a cousin of Enrico's and of the Duke of Edinburgh. Unhappily Leli, flustered perhaps by the presence of so much royalty, began the meal by emptying a plate of soup over the princess's skirt: it was a delicate garment, if I remember rightly, of primrose satin.

Robin was flying home from Naples; I moved to Forio: into a little house with domed Phoenician ceilings, washed in Forian blue; and a brass door-knocker in the mould of a hand like those which in Morocco ward off the Evil Eye. I drank a lot of wine at Maria's, and in her visitors' book, between verses by Auden and by his collaborator in operatic libretti, Chester Kallman, wrote some doggerel which even Auden wasn't unkind about. I ate on the beach at Filippo's—a sweet-tempered, gentle-hearted American married to the daughter of a Forio wine-grower; a gifted cook, he was also painter, actor, philosopher, and quietly humorous and endearing companion. Thousands of American and European visitors by now know his restaurant, the nicest on the island; I hope he's made a fortune out of them.

I had a boy who idly cared for my house and me: a winning honey-skinned lad named Mario, of fisher-descent; with yellow tumbling hair and indolent Hellenic face. He was, so to speak, a renegade fisherman; for the fishing people there, as everywhere in the Italian south from Naples to Taranto, are an aloof, exclusive sect who, like the Zingari, live in an enclosed, xenophobe privacy with a mystique of its own: suspicious and contemptuous of all outside it. They are as a rule arrogant and craftily rude; yet there's no rhythm of movement on earth so perfect, no visual euphony so pure, as the unison of four standing rowers leaning united to their oars and recoiling with an assured flick of the wrist for the next stroke, bodies and limbs synchronized as one flexing muscle: a stripling boy and his double-bent grandfather working as one with the generations between. To watch the boats coming in thus between the sea-walls of the harbour was like standing beside Homer. The only other absolute concord of movement I can think of is the splendid unison of the fiddlers' bows perfectly propelling a Bach concerto.

During those months in Forio I wrote—and finished—a little novel which I called 'Love on a Greek Island'; founded upon an erotic drama I'd watched enacted next door to my Corfu cottage and containing in a central female character an infusion of all my Childers aunts and some of myself. It was barely 40,000 words long, but people who read the typescript were amused. Mamaine Paget, Koestler's wife, then working for Derek Verschoyle, a publisher later out of business, wanted to do it if I could tie up some loose ends; and tantalizingly suggested persuading Osbert Lancaster to do some drawings (but then dear Mamaine died; and her successor turned it down). Sonia Orwell, widow of George Orwell and later Michael Pitt-Rivers' wife, 'reading' for Weidenfeld, wrote a long interested report on it: adding 'I should like to see more of this young writer's work' (!); and some other publisher said it was like 'desiccated Firbank and Douglas', hardly the compliment I hoped it was. For four years I forgot all about it; and then a kind friend who had it sent it to Hutchinson's; whence I was told they would almost certainly accept it if I could stretch it to full length and buttress some of its debilities. After a couple of years, I did both; and ruined it; since when it's been resolutely rejected by half the publishers in London. I don't quarrel with their judgement.

On Christmas Day I reached Rome. I secured one or two newspaper 'strings': the *Evening Standard* and *Daily Herald*, and now and then a story for *Illustrated*; but Rome produced little news wanted by those two condensed dailies.

For *Illustrated*, Odham's picture magazine, I saw a lot of Mike Hawthorn after he'd nearly been burned alive in a motor race. I'd expected, when I first went to the international hospital, to find a brash, boastful 'hearty'—that's what I supposed racing drivers were like. I was wrong; he was a quiet, thoughtful young man, modest and diffident and, I thought, a little unhappy: some inner unhappiness which, perhaps, sought escape in the inebrieties of speed and danger and the contest: the nicer charioteers in the Greek games must have been like him, I thought. He was, that first time, sadly bandaged and still in pain; but his eyes smiled bravely through the swathings, and as he got better he seemed to think of nothing but a quick return to the race track. He was a knightly person, full of gentle and courageous charm; yet feverish, he seemed, with an obsessive lunatic ambition—the ambition I suppose, to drive faster than anybody else.

With Tom Clarke, sports writer of the *Daily Herald*, I sat in a ringside seat and saw Randolph Turpin knocked out within the first half-minute by a fair-haired young Italian who looked like an athlete by Phidias. I hated the violence and blood of it; yet the turbulent, roaring scene, like a Roman Games (and Jack Solomons, beside us, like the emperor), was perversely exhilarating. The afternoon before the fight we spent in Jack Solomons' royal suite in the Grand Hotel drinking his whisky and smoking his Churchillian cigars. He was walking splendidly up and down his spacious parquet floor, looking every inch a boxing promoter; but a rebuff was rankling: the Pope had declined to receive him. 'What d'you say,' he was complaining over his cigar. 'I asked 'Is 'Oliness for an *audition* an' 'e wouldn't give me one!'

For the glorious pomp of Pius the Tenth's canonization I had a perfect stall—the press box—above the portico of St Peter's: where God's Vicar enthroned heard the merits of his forerunner argued and the make-believe protest of the Devil's Advocate. Watching this gorgeously medieval scene was like sitting in the middle of one of those huge historical cartoons of Raphael: the coloured phalanx of prelates, their damask mitres serried like the shields of crusading soldiers; the Noble and Swiss Guards, the Knights of the Sovereign Order and of the Holy Sepulchre; diplomats in their liveries, visiting royalties in their ribands, chamberlains and princes looking like packs of cards; and, of course, the pure divinity of the ethereal white Pontiff, carried like God on his palanquin and surrounded by the symbols of spiritual and temporal royalty. Like most people whose functions gave them some scant insight into the penetralia of the Vatican, I had no lofty opinion of Pope Pacelli; yet seeing him that day was like coming face to face with an Archangel. 'He is no longer flesh and blood; he has no taint of mortality; he is like a white soul robed in white', wrote Oscar Wilde in a letter from Rome in 1900. 'I'm not a Catholic; I'm simply a violent Papist. No one could be more "Black" than I am.'

But through those months in Rome I couldn't make ends meet. I lived in horrid cheap rooms or horrider, less cheap hotels; and ate, when I ate, on a precarious scaffolding of credit. Often I had no money at all. Through the summer heat I lolled on the Tiber's edge of sand and scrub, deep and secret like a moat below the city's level; and bathed in the tepid swirl of its fast yellow stream with gusts of boys bred in that dark symmetry of beauty special to Rome. In the winter, or through those drenching fits of un-relenting Roman rain, I divided my empty hours between the churches and, when I could afford the sixpence they cost, the *louche* cinemas of which I knew three or four, where the audience kept changing seats as if playing a lascivious musical chairs.

My favourite church was Sta Maria Maggiore: superb on her cobbled height and containing within the contentment that comes from a sense of perfect proportion, perfect balance: the sort of contentment that the 'Ode to the Nativity' brings. I loved the long, chaste rectangle of her painted ceiling and simple usefulness of the splendid columns. I liked to think of St Luke painting that portrait of the Virgin. 'Move your head a little this way, please—that's it; and that fold in your mantle, could you—'.

Though often hungry, I was mainly happy—there's so much in Rome to make the most miserable happy; and every so often I emerged from my beachcomber's underworld for sallies into worldly grandeur: an English peer's wonderful luncheon parties; an Embassy reception at the Villa Wolkonsky; a drive to a ducal *castello* outside; or an encounter with an exquisite legend like Lady Diana Cooper or an inspired self-advertiser with a talent for painting like Salvador Dali.

And then, towards autumn, Byron Pavlides came: a member of one of the richest Greek families in Cyprus. In Italy on business for the Pavlides firm, he had been sent to me by a friend: I was to pilot him about Rome, which he was seeing for the first time.

Byron's was a lavish, Byzantine personality: endearing and exasperating: rich with charm and bubbling gaiety when things went as he wanted them, when 'crossed' as sulky or passionate as a spoiled child. He looked like an Emperor of the East: tall and broad, with regal stance and imperious nose; and a voice to chop off heads; always elegantly dressed and, for his huge bulk, walking with buoyant grace on small, delicate feet. For me, his arrival in Rome that summer was one of those odd fortuities of fate that change men's lives: it led to the founding of the *Times of Cyprus*, a newspaper whose small Levantine voice was soon to make itself heard loudly in Whitehall, and to my conflict with Field-Marshal Sir John Harding.

I BELIEVE THAT the *Times of Cyprus* truly made a contribution
to the Cyprus peace: to the sensible, and only possible, solution
which we who wrote the paper had foreseen and which Sir Hugh
Foot and the Archbishop brilliantly transformed into fact. What we
did, during those insane years of EOKA's terror and the hangings
of Harding, was to insist upon keeping, in the English language,
some intellectual sanity athwart a political situation that in 1956-57
was galloping into dementia; to insist on maintaining an oasis of
*honesty* in a wilderness of lies by exposing the dishonesty of the
Harding administration (there weren't so many lies on the EOKA
side: they didn't need them). We were writing less for the Greeks,
than for English minds—in civilian and even governmental
Cyprus, in the Army, in the United Kingdom; and I think we
were able, in measurable degree, to perforate some of the un-
thinking English blindness to the awful stupidity of the Macmillan-
Harding policy. I think we helped to accustom the English mind to
the notion of common sense.

For some ten years there'd existed on the island an English
daily called the *Cyprus Mail*: a camp-follower of British policy
read by people who liked seeing their names in the cocktail
column and their chauvinist opinions comfortably confirmed in
print; this paper, before being bought by a jolly Greek-Cypriot
named Jakovides, had been a Government sheet; and amiable
'Jacko', regarding his paper as a tobacconist regards his shop, had
done nothing to change its nature. But some rich Greeks (commercial and industrial barons who, before EOKA, were the leaders
of 'English-educated' opinion) wanted an independent English
paper which would be bluntly critical and become, if it could be
done, the war-head of an *English* opposition. All this was discussed
between me and Byron; between him, by post, and his friends on
the island; and by me, one morning at Ciampino airport, and an
emissary, flying through to London, of C. P. Manglis, the

island's greatest tycoon and biggest single economic power. The upshot was that about November 1954 Byron took me to Cyprus.

He was flying from London: I was to join him at Ciampino. When I reached the airport bar, he was there: I saw his great looming back and the imperial tilt of his head; and, childishly (because the pair of us were like that), I began an excited game of hide-and-seek, dodging about like a buffoon behind his knees. I could see that a man standing near him thought my behaviour odd; and Byron, when he saw me, displayed confusion. 'I present you, Michael,' he announced like a chamberlain at the court of Constantine, 'to His Excellency Sir Robert Armitage, Governor of Cyprus'; and I found myself sheepishly shaking hands with an attractive smiling man whose young face looked delightful and intelligent. This was my first meeting with 'Bob' Armitage: whose integrity and understanding of Cypriot aspirations I learned to admire, and whom I dreadfully pitied when, at the end of 1955, I watched him cruelly booed off the island.

Why, since 1879 (when Cyprus was 'leased' from the Turks), have British governments, loathed from the start by the population, hung on stubbornly to the island although politicians like Gladstone towards the end of last century and Churchill at the beginning of this, have proclaimed its 'Greekness' and the legitimacy of its Greek aspirations? A multitude of justifications have been proffered in these eighty years for the maintenance of British sovereignty over the island: it was 'vital' to security, to commerce, to communications. In 1956-57, Harding, nearly every time I saw him, was vehemently arguing how strategically 'vital' its retention was. 'Look at the map!' was one of his pet exclamations; and, like the American in Korea with his Chinese 'hordes', the Field-Marshal would indicate with his finger the courses of invading armies from the north-east, all converging on the eastern Mediterranean.

In 1880 Admiral Sir Beauchamp Seymour, who had been at the Admiralty while my cousin Hugh was First Lord, wrote to him: 'I went to Cyprus and everything I saw there confirmed me in my opinion that we are in an entirely false position there. You knew my ideas on the subject when, at Strawberry hill (Lady Waldegrave's), we were just informed of its having been ceded.... There isn't a harbour on the island ... if we wanted Cyprus as a sort of *tête-de-pont* to the Suez Canal we should have bought it out and out. Far better it would have been never to have gone near the

island. . . .' The island still has no harbours; the 1956 Suez fiasco
showed that it was no use as a *tête-de-pont*.

I believe 'prestige', a sad clinging to a vestige of imperial grandeur, was at the back of these justifications; and of the frightful
months of the Cyprus 'troubles'. One has only to go back in
history to see that the prestige of Empire was a principal force
which brought the island to England and sealed its subjection all
this while. Bertrand Russell, who was born while Disraeli was still
Prime Minister and whose grandfather had been an even earlier
Premier, writing of Disraeli's return from the Congress of Berlin
with the words 'I bring you Peace with Honour,' says acidly:
'The "Peace" was a decision not to go to war with Russia; the
"honour" was Cyprus.' And Algernon Cecil, nephew of the Lord
Salisbury who went to Berlin as Disraeli's Foreign Secretary,
says in 'Victoria and her Prime Ministers' that the acquisition of
Cyprus bore witness to the splendour of the blossoming Imperial-
ism which Disraeli had by 1880 achieved. The Cecils are a family
of tradition: it was no surprise when in 1957 the present Marquess
of Salisbury resigned from the Cabinet because Makarios was
released from the Seychelles: what was a prize in the hands of
Beaconsfield and an earlier Salisbury couldn't easily be given up
by their successors and heirs.

It was this element of 'prestige' that rankled principally in the
fiercely independent hearts of the Greek Cypriots—that intransigent
Hellenic independence which made Athenians fight Athens and
Spartans Sparta in defence of the sovereign Statelets of Magna
Graecia. I don't know how Archbishop Makarios adroitly managed
to slip out of the complexities of *enosis*, 'union with Greece', into the
straightforward common-sense of republican independence (the
solution which I'd predicted and wanted)—I'd left the island by
then; but I believe it was this which the Greeks there wanted at
heart, beneath the romantic hero-worship that was the content of
*enosis*: to get rid of the foreign ruler who called them 'Cyps' and
begrudged every penny spent on the country's good. I expect that
Makarios, with his subtly brilliant political intuition, knew this all
along; and cunningly used the heroical banner of *enosis* for its own
expedient extinction.

When I arrived in Cyprus, the island was physically placid,
but emotionally turbulent. It was ruled by British colonial servants;
the Greeks were boycotting tactical efforts to bring them nominally
into a legislative façade; the last two Greeks still members of the

Executive Council, the late John Clerides and Byron', brother, Sir Paul Pavlides, were soon to resign. The island was simmering with hatred; but 'trouble' seemed still remote.

It was in this political atmosphere that I met Costas Manglis. I liked him, though his wasn't the type of man I ordinarily like: small and wiry, brisk and curt; with a mind like a knife and a small alert face that seemed to be on its guard against displaying emotion; he was, I felt, carefully remembering that he was a tycoon. But there were charm and gleams of humour beneath the mask; and he had a *mind*: he liked books, and had a fine library at his house; he liked colour photography, and diving deep into the subaqueous world of the rocky Kyrenia coast. Manglis, a mainland Greek and a financial associate of Bodassakis—one of Greece's most resilient makers of millions—ruled an industrial empire: wine-making, distilling, brewing, textiles, electrical equipment, plaster-board, engineering, agencies, retail selling; but his greatest province was the Hellenic Mining Company which operated the pyrites mines in the south-west and thus controlled the island's most valuable export. He owned the only Rolls Royce on Cyprus and (the mark, surely, of the true tycoon) had his hair cut while working at his directorial desk. Naturally, he was hated by some of the lesser magnates; while the British were guardedly suspicious of a man who wielded greater economic power than themselves.

He explained to me that a daily newspaper with guaranteed advertising—and through his numerous companies he would see to that—could pay its way from the beginning, after laying out about £5,000. Could I find a capable editor who could find that amount of capital? I said I knew the very man if he could be persuaded to come: Charles Foley, Foreign Editor of the *Daily Express*.

Receiving my zestful proposal backed by facts and figures, Foley came to see: secret conferences with Manglis, with a master-printer, and—perhaps most valuable of all, so wise was 'Gubby's' counsel, so absolute his intimacy with the island—with Shahe Gubbenlian, Reuter's man in Cyprus, known as Gubby to hundreds of the world's journalists who've drunk his beer and valued his invaluable help.

Gubby's spirit was unique, I think, in that the various gifts that composed it weren't kept in separate compartments and displayed in different moods: his shrewd, assured competence and quiet sagacity, his gusto and inexhaustible store of human kindness, all functioned together and simultaneously like the components of a cocktail: small, nimble and darkly handsome, he was a magnetic coil of ebullient intelligence and charm. Still in his 30s, he was an incomparably good 'agency man' whose English, Greek and Turkish were as perfect as his own Armenian; who worked 24 hours a day yet never was too busy to be hospitable or helpful; who understood better than anybody on the island its perplexities and paradoxes, yet was never too professionally avaricious to share the wisdom of his judgement or the riches of his knowledge; who had a multitude of friends yet whose expanse of generous friendship was boundless; who, bred in a social morality where polite improbity was genteel, possessed a natural integrity that was incorruptible; who, through crises of journalistic stress or physical peril, maintained an unruffled air of gay and debonair calm.

We let Gubby into our secret, and with him his partner and future wife, Jill Russell, herself an able London journalist, because we couldn't do without his advice and co-operation. Foley, during that fleeting visit, had his first sight, as I think we all had, of one of those great surging schoolboy riots which later became a Cypriot habit; it was no fun running the gauntlet of 1,000 stone-throwing zealots aged from ten to twenty-five.

In the first quarter of 1955 we started our paper. There was a discussion about what we should call it; then I said: 'Well, there's *The Times* of London, the New York *Times*, and Mabel Strickland's *Times of Malta*: why not the *Times of Cyprus*?'; and so it became.

On an island of Byzantine Levantines the curtain of secrecy we'd tried to hang round our project couldn't long stay light-proof; and one evening in the Dolphin, Nicosia's only 'night-club', breezy Victor Bodker, editor of the *Cyprus Mail*, said to me: 'What's this I hear about you and Manglis starting another paper? Well, I'm not frightened—healthy competition, eh? Jolly good thing, what?' And, of course, after we'd started, it was widely thought that Manglis was the paper's real owner. In fact, the paper was Foley's, and only Foley's: his money paid for it and Manglis had no share in its ownership. Manglis assured its basic advertising revenue; and, I don't doubt, allowed Foley his credit facilities for the buying of costly primaries like type and newsprint. But Foley, with his wife Dorothy a director, was the sole owner and the sole controller of policy.

When, later that year, Foley moved the paper from its first home to a print-shop belonging to the Archbishopric and within almost

the precincts of Makarios' tumbled-down palace, our enemies
seized the chance of saying that not only were we the puppets of
Manglis but also of the seditious Church. But the Archbishop
never had, nor tried to have, a say in the conduct of the paper: we
paid a commercial rent for printing plant and offices which, happening to stand idle and empty, fitted our needs.

It was useful to me, doing most of the political writing, to have
the Archbishop living at the bottom of the garden. I could see him
any day I wanted to; or, if he were away, his brilliant and delightful
principal secretary, Nicos Kranidiotis (the island's first Ambassador, I think, to Greece).

I adored Makarios; but I could never have *liked* him: that foxy
charm was too insidious for the confidence implicit in *liking*. But
I adored his splendid medieval presence, the perfection of his
*dressage*; his lordly, and justified, confidence in his own brilliance;
that superb mastery of the art of charmingly hoodwinking, or at
least baffling, his adversaries in polemic. There was oriental
grandeur in the ruthlessness of his sweet smile, in the craftiness of
his Byzantine beauty. His courage, too, had the quality of a martyr's: right through Harding's autocracy he knew that his liberty,
and even his life, were daily weighed in the scales at Government
House; he smiled. Yet I felt, always, nothing 'spiritual' about him:
not even his cowl and crosier reminded me he was a priest, and his
title of 'Beatitude' seemed to me purely a worldly one. He was like
a crusading prelate in some medieval chronicle. 'No tonsured clerk
ever sang mass who did such strong things with his body,' runs a
description in René Hague's lovely translation of *The Song of
Roland*. 'The Archbishop . . . cuts through his body from one side
to the other and throws him dead in an empty place. The French
say, "This is a good soldier, the Cross is safe with the Archbishop.
. . ." ' That is how Makarios appeared to me; and, doubtless, to
EOKA. I stood beside him once on the balcony of the Archbishopric while a pitiless schoolboys' battle with soldiers was raging
before the Greek Gymnasium below, through the compound of the
palace and even over its roofs; stones clattered everywhere; sweating
British tommies warding them off with wire shields and clubbing
the advancing ranks of boys with truncheons. Impassive, implacable, Makarios leaned over the balcony looking down: he was
like a headmaster watching his boys playing an important football
match.

For public utterances, like an 'official' interview, he used Greek.

But sometimes in private he spoke English: not very well, though his subtle mind was well abreast of its subtleties. To the world, of course, Makarios appeared as a divine of austere habit, made immune by sanctity from such small fleshly temptations as smoking. When, though, after his abduction to the Seychelles, I explored his private rooms at the bereft Archbishopric (I was first there after the military had turned it inside out) I found boxes of cigars and cigarettes in his bedroom and ashtrays full of dog-ends; and stole, for sentiment's sake, a couple of the apostolic cigars. Humble parish priests of the Orthodox Church, with no pretensions to promotion, were allowed (as a reward perhaps of their humility) to take a wife; Archbishops weren't; and the Army and police, after their search of Makarios' palace, allowed it to be whispered around that they'd made some 'interesting' discoveries, including a cache of pornography. But since these rumours, unsupported by visible evidence, quickly died, I took them to be merely the weapons of tactical malice.

I nearly went to the Seychelles to try to see Makarios. The Church, or rather the Ethnarchy (the secular side of that ingenious political edifice)—and perhaps, for all I know, EOKA too—wanted to send me there some months after he'd been exiled. Kranidiotis quietly made the suggestion (he was, in effect, 'acting Ethnarch', though the Bishop of Limassol was the nominal caliph). I was enchanted by the idea: I saw the tremendous political 'scoop' I might get (though Foley could have nothing to do with an expedition thus financially sponsored); and the romance of a modestly historical mission; I saw myself basking in the warm soft Indian Ocean, among a warm, exotic island people. But, after tantalizing reflection, I had in honesty to tell Kranidiotis that I hadn't a hope of getting near the Archbishop: by that time my name stank politically at Government House—it seemed unlikely I'd even be allowed to land. (It would have been interesting to see two such discordant characters as Makarios and the Bishop of Kyrenia locked up together: like making Churchill and de Gaulle share a bedroom.)

Shortly after we'd started publishing, the first of those EOKA raids on police stations, with weapons for booty, happened with brilliant surprise in the island's wild south-east, below Famagusta. Clearly, when such an occurrence was still a dramatic novelty a good story was to be found: I drove to Famagusta and picked up our local correspondent. This was a charming, but plainly unstable,

Greek youth of 22: bursting with keenness and brash conceit; a government clerk who, aware of his vocation, was playing journalism in his spare time. Nicos Sampson: a name that eighteen months later was the most 'wanted' in Cyprus: as loudly execrated by one half of the island as Harding's was by the other. We hired a car and spent the day in the bleak, dried-up villages of this savage zone where nobody ever went and which drove like a roughened tongue into the sea (the heart of EOKA-land, I called it in my story): villages with gleaming Hellenic names like Xylophagou, Paralimni, Lipetri, Sotira. We sat in the coffee-shops among swarthy, reticent men with peasants' moustaches, instantly hostile in the presence of an Englishman; all the houses were daubed with EOKA slogans, all those men, I suppose, were EOKA: they wouldn't have thought twice about shooting me, yet their stern Cypriot hospitality couldn't allow me once to pay for our coffee. On this trip Nicos' companionship was delightful; a perfect interpreter, asking the questions as I wanted them put, enticing with his charm the frankest answers possible in the circumstances; he was the impersonal reporter, never the partisan. Indeed, in all my early acquaintance with him, he seemed to me detached from politics. It wasn't until he'd spent three months in prison later that summer that he became fanatically 'converted' to EOKA terrorism. But that day he was interested only in himself: he talked naively of his own abilities and ambitions, volubly vain in a boyish way. 'I was the best reporter in Cyprus,' he boasted to the police when on trial for his life.

Two years later he'd been sentenced to death twice, on charges connected with a sten-gun; he'd been acquitted of murdering two policemen—in the face of an almost delirious desire in Government House and the armed forces to see him convicted; and was being popularly accused, though no charges could be brought, of a dozen or twenty other shootings in the streets of Nicosia. In the public mind this charming and intelligent, though certainly vainglorious, youth had turned into a mass murderer without parallel; before his arrest, the Government issued a 'special notice to all security forces': a photograph of Sampson headed: 'WANTED: This is the man believed to be responsible for shooting your comrades and innocent civilians. LOOK FOR HIM—EVERYWHERE'; and after his arrest, he said in a 'confession' rejected later by the Trial Judge: 'People say I did twenty murders. No, no, no! It's not true! Every time there's a killing they say "Nick Sampson!

Nick Sampson!"' He was never convicted of a shooting; but he never denied that he became an EOKA terrorist.

What turns an ordinary, 'good', boy into a terrorist? What incredible emotional force can persuade a studious, well-behaved youth to shoot cold-bloodedly in the back somebody he doesn't know from Adam—can turn his whole nature upside down and transform, in his eyes, what yesterday would have seemed a ghastly crime into, today, an act of shining chivalry? It seems impossible, beyond one's comprehension; yet it happened every day in Cyprus in those demented years, as it had happened in Ireland and Palestine and will happen wherever the nationalist fever rises beyond the temperature of tolerance. One might have supposed that, by 1955, the political diagnosticians in the Colonial Office would have learned to foretell the exact point in the development of any given nationalism when it would boil over into terrorism; it should be as predictable as the course of physical fever.

Larry Durrell, in 'Bitter Lemons', tells of finding in a detention camp two boys he had formerly taught in the Pancyprian Gymnasium. ' . . . I realized for the first time that the appeal of EOKA was not to wrongdoers, congenital felons, but precisely to the most spirited and idealistic element among the youth,' he writes. One of the boys, he says, he upbraided 'with severity' for his folly. 'Ach, Mr Durrell,' the boy replies, 'it was just a *little* bomb.' Primly Durrell adds: 'I passed him by in silence.' To the other boy schoolmaster Durrell said: ' "What a twisted brain, what a twisted stick you must be as well as a fool!" He winced and his eyes flashed. "War is war," he said. I left him without another word.' (Durrell must have forgotten, I suppose, that the same sort of 'twisted stick', when stabbing a Nazi sentry in the back anywhere in occupied Europe, was a hero of the Resistance.)

When Michael Karaolis, the first of the terrorists to be hanged, was executed early in 1956 for shooting a policeman, I explored his character and past life, interviewing his family, friends, schoolmasters, employers—every compartment of his career that I could enter; and published the result in the *Times of Cyprus*. I found that this serious young student, just started in the government service, was indeed 'most spirited and idealistic'; and more: he was a young man of the highest principles and moral character—until, with cold deliberation, he killed an unsuspecting Greek Cypriot policeman. There is the terrifying paradox.

'Idealism' is the explanation: a romantic, heroical idealism that's like an uncontrollable infatuation. The British can't understand this: they're not idealists. The British don't go to war for an ideal, but for some material or even moral purpose that seems to them necessary though dull—never for a Holy Grail. The British were bewildered by the un-Englishness of the Greek Cypriots: Sir John Harding couldn't understand why an Archbishop of Cyprus didn't behave like an Archbishop of Canterbury. In July 1957 the Field-Marshal was reported in the *Yorkshire Post* to have said: 'What I personally find most irksome is the knowledge that so far I and my administration have been unable to bring home to the ordinary, decent, law-abiding Greek Cypriots the magnitude of the disaster which a rash and inept political leadership seems determined to bring upon them.' Almost the very day I read that I went to a moonlight picnic with a party of 'ordinary, decent, law-abiding' Greek Cypriots: a doctor, a leading business man, a couple of government servants, a newspaper editor, a chauffeur—a very ordinary, decent lot. We were high in the northern hills, by the crusading castle of St Hilarion: below were the fairy lights of Kyrenia and the smooth oyster sea, and level with the Anatolian haze a glowing rim of sky left by the buried sun. We were miles from the nearest military; and when a fair deal of white wine or whisky had been drunk my friends, as Greeks do, broke into song —EOKA song.

'Of *course* we're with EOKA in our hearts,' said one. 'Every one of us Greeks in Cyprus is with EOKA. We don't want violence, we hate it. But don't you see that EOKA came because they *had* to come? The British Government left no other course open to the Greek Cypriots—except to lick its boots.'

'We're *all* EOKA!' somebody shouted, taking a good swig— and echoing the famous dictum of Dr Themistocles Dervis, Nicosia's pugnacious mayor.

These were ordinary, decent, law-abiding men having, probably, no organizational tie with EOKA. Their emotional identification with EOKA was the force which a man so one-eyed as the Field-Marshal couldn't comprehend: it was the force which defeated him.

The Greek Cypriot's temperament is one of extremes. His joy becomes ecstasy, a lost temper turns to dementia; a small rebuff or affront is an intolerable pain. Romantic emotionalism easily flares into hysteria: we who saw, in the great schoolboy riots, the demoniacal faces of youngsters who but a few minutes earlier were quiet, studious, gentle creatures interested chiefly in passing examinations, know how terrifyingly sudden this change can be. Bertrand Russell relates somewhere that George Santayana remarked to him at Cambridge: 'I'm going to Seville tomorrow. I wish to be in a place where people do not restrain their passions.' In Cyprus too passions aren't restrained, whether they spring from hate or enthusiasm, political anger or sexual jealousy, they're given full throttle. In EOKA's time, the most vehement passions were political—yet they weren't really 'political': they were romantic, heroical, almost mystical. Then, the 'ideal' was *enosis*, union with Greece; today it's probably *eleftheria*, liberty. Then, the yearning for 'Greekness', to be Greek in name as well as in heart, was a form of hero-worship; and hero-worship seemed as necessary to the young Greek Cypriot's emotional satisfaction as love. Often, indeed, it took love's place; or the two merged into one exaltation. The overall 'hero', the heroic abstraction was the romantic Hellenism they felt to be their heritage, a mystical sense of being one with the glory that was Greece. But boys and girls prefer heroes made of flesh and blood: what handier and more splendid heroes could be found than the martyrs and martyrs-to-be of EOKA? There were heroes in plenty: products of a strange partnership: EOKA and the British Government: every fresh 'martyr' brought to EOKA a flow of starry-eyed recruits to martyrdom. In this atmosphere and with this temperament, it wasn't difficult; for many of these ardent young people it was but a short step from hero-worship to seeing themselves the hero; from adoring the martyrs already made to aspiring themselves to martyrdom. It was the short step between emotional participation in EOKA and a sacrificial gamble: the terrible step of ecstasy that made a boy accept tasks from which in ordinary rational life he would have shrunk in horror.

In Sampson's case it was those three months in prison among a crowd of EOKA boys that put him on the frightful terrorist road: three months of gnawing resentment at the injustice of his imprisonment. I believe it was unjust: I have photographs of that riot in Famagusta which show Sampson sitting on a wall taking journalistic notes. I knew enough of his character to be convinced that this was just what he would be doing— the role of reporter was for him sacramental: 'I was the best reporter in Cyprus'; and when he told me he was innocent of the rioting charge, I knew that wasn't the sort of lie he would tell me.

I saw a lot of Larry Durrell: not only because he was the Government's information officer and hence an almost daily object of my duty as a journalist, but also because I enjoyed him: his wit and intelligence and slightly derisory friendliness, his jolly laughing cynicism and his air of an endearing chimpanzee. The Alexandrine novels hadn't yet been published; he was known only to a few for his poetry and his delightful Grecian *reportage*. I don't think he was a good government propagandist—I don't think his heart was in the job, especially after Harding came. He was too 'cultured' for the vulgarisms of political publicity: when I arrived he was bent on launching a literary magazine with contributors like Lord Kinross and Patrick Leigh-Fermor—but the Cypriots weren't readers of literary magazines. Larry was an adept of culture, and a bit schoolmasterish: even when wandering abstractedly about his house with no clothes on, opening bottles of beer. His was a multitudinous character—as multitudinous as the characters in the Alexandrine novels, each of whom almost is a facet of Larry. But any one of us who is interesting to others is constantly a contradiction of himself: it's only the dull, I suppose who has a simple character.

Larry gave lovely parties: one I remember specially for the gay presence of his brother Gerald Durrell, author of 'My Family and Other Animals' and a succession of delightful animal books, with his tiny elfish wife; and another party, with Freya Stark, like a frail headmistress: telling of her passion for Alexander the Great, whose footsteps she was about to pursue; and saying with a vague sigh: 'how would *you* like to be married to a cocktail party?'—I can't remember in what context.

One day a pale young man walked into the office and asked for a job; he'd been sent to us by Larry, with whom he was staying. Foley and I talked to him: an unobtrusive young man with a quiet intelligence, a wry smile and the sad face of an undergraduate who's been up all night. 'What can you do?' we asked. 'Nothing,' he said. I said: 'Well, we need an intelligent proof-reader; it's quite easy.' As he went off, hired as our new proof-reader, Foley asked his name. 'Lumley,' he said briefly. Next day, after he'd started work, a bulky man with a wing-commander's moustache called Walker-Brash, who for a spell was compiling our gossip column, came into our room flushed with high news: the new proof-reader was no less than a viscount: heir to the earldom of Scarbrough, son of the Lord Chamberlain. Gracious! we said.

Richard Lumley was a good proof-reader and a delightful companion: languidly amusing and charmingly intelligent; many jolly meals we had together at the Gourmets and drinks at the Ledra Palace; but the suave quietude of his discerning mind seemed to be founded on an ingrained unhappiness, as lichen charmingly colours the hardness of stone. He left us for the 'news desk' of the Public Information Office, where he studied the subtle art of official double-talk; and in 1956, after Harding's arrival, became— alas for the niceness of his nature—an extra A.D.C. to the Field-Marshal, living in Government House and animating the sessions of vice-regal rock-an'-roll. The Field-Marshal liked titles, and roped in any that appeared on the island. But Richard, though bred into court life, had too much *mind* to remain a courtier; before long he returned to England.

At the time Richard came to us he was staying in Larry's little house; where the Greek Cypriot maid used to call him in the morning, saying: 'And how is Our Lord this morning?'

It was the mighty riot in Metaxas Square towards the end of 1955—on a night when nearly all the senior officers of Government were out at cocktail parties—that caused poor Bob Armitage's recall from the governorship. It was the night the idiot vandals of EOKA burned down the British Council library, destroying 15,000 books; I remember going home under a sky scarlet with flame. Murder and explosion had become commonplace; that wasn't, of course, Sir Robert Armitage's fault—both became worse under Harding. Armitage was the scapegoat for the policy of Downing Street.

I went down to Larnaca, where the Governor and his wife were boarding a steamer for home. There were the guards of honour and a row of senior officials drawn up for the silent good-bye hand-shakes—and beyond the barriers and police cordons a howling crowd of jeering, catcalling Greeks adding their insults to the British Government's humiliation of a good man. I loathed the Greek Cypriots that day; and wept with anger at their cruelty to a man who had wished them well and done his best for them within the hopeless confinement of his power. The formal farewells over, he walked along the jetty to the launch that took him to the ship lying off-shore; and as he walked, like a man going into exile, the hoots and taunts and whistles of the crowd hounded him away in a dreadful gale of derision. My impulsive impertinence made me run after him to the launch. 'Good luck, sir,' was all I could say: there were tears of pain in his answering smile. That agonizing catcalling wasn't, of course, directed at Armitage personally: once again, this time by the EOKA boys, he was being made the scapegoat for the British Government; but that evening I wrote an angry story—though it's wasted breath trying to teach manners to the politically intoxicated.

When we heard that the Field-Marshal was to be Governor, I realized that we were in for a military dictatorship; but, I said to myself, under Harding we'll have the least noxious, the gentlest possible, sort of military rule: a man with *that* smile, with *that* ineffable charm, can't be coming merely to repress and exterminate; a man of that intelligence, I thought, must, before accepting the job, have equipped himself with an understanding of the Greek Cypriot mind and obtained from Downing Street a tacit cancellation of that nefarious dictum 'never'. Templer had gone to Malaya knowing that independence was to follow his defeat of the terrorists; I assumed that Harding wouldn't have agreed to come to Cyprus without something of the same sort in his contract. (What an ironical comment on the ineptitude or humbug of politics is the historical fact that barely three years after repeated pronouncements in Whitehall that 'never' would Cyprus be relieved of British rule, Cyprus became indeed independent.)

But certainly the Field-Marshal made some terms. His pay, according to the island's official estimates, was nearly double what Armitage's had been; I forget now whether it was seven or eight thousand a year—Sir Robert had had £4,000: a tidy sum, since he lived practically free. He got some 25,000 troops; and the Life Guards and the Blues came to the island turn and turn about to act almost as his personal 'household' cavalry. I'd guess, on 'internal evidence', that it was understood that a peerage when he'd completed his task would be enjoyed.

Sir John got the peerage; but he had failed. I'd been deceived by my hopes: events quickly showed that he'd come only to 'restore order', with nothing but weapons in his bag; a task which, with all his battalions and all his passionate reprisal, he failed to perform—as people who comprehended the Greek Cypriot mind and who had learned the lessons of history knew he must fail. Nobody could blame the Field-Marshal for his failure: that was the doing of a political insensibility larger than his own; I blamed him for accepting the falseness of a position in which—after two years of murder, hanging, punition and unbearable tragedy—he was bound to leave things, from the British point of view, worse than he found them. Surely, by the end of 1955 the British Government's Intelligence, and thence the Field-Marshal, must have known that the Archbishop and EOKA weren't to be bought off with the short-weight of a 'liberal constitution', with the sudden offer of funds for economic development which had been denied the island for eighty years; that EOKA, embattled in their mountains and in the hearts of the people, would answer mere violence with yet greater violence. Harding came, I believe, with a mistaken notion of the situation: he thought his job was the extermination of a 'gang' of criminal 'thugs', after which the 'ordinary, decent, law-abiding' citizens would hail him as their deliverer; he couldn't understand that the temper of the people was such that each hanging, each vengeful curfew, each fresh imposition of 'collective punishment', only enhanced their will to resist and added strength to EOKA's arm. 'I am incensed!' he exclaimed on the wireless one night after an Army officer had been killed in Famagusta—as if his personal anger were a good reason for not shooting British officers. He couldn't understand that nobody cared whether the Governor was incensed—that what the people cared about was the continued presence of British officers. He couldn't understand the refusal by prominent Greeks to 'denounce violence' publicly— a formula which he appeared to suppose would have the force of exorcism. Of course Archbishop Makarios, Dr Dervis and the other mayors, and even 'moderates' like John Clerides and Sir Paul Pavlides, couldn't 'denounce violence'. Had they done so, they would quickly have been removed and with them what influence for reasonableness they possessed—or if they remained alive they would have been written off by the people as 'sold' to the enemy; and secondly, they *couldn't* denounce violence with sincerity: 'violence' was no longer a thing that one condemned or condoned: it had become, as my friend at that moonlight picnic had said, a political inevitability: to 'denounce' it would be like denouncing the nuclear bomb after it had gone off. We on the *Times of Cyprus* couldn't 'denounce violence', appalled by it as we were; had we publicly condemned it our usefulness, coming from Greek confidence in us, would have evaporated overnight.

I suppose Greek Cypriot terrorism was as horrible, as mean and

treacherous, as terrifyingly barbarous as any in history—shooting
innocent young soldiers and policemen in the back, murdering an
office-boy working at his desk, killing a man helplessly sitting in
the barber's chair, shooting to death a sacristan during a church
service; but it was no longer a matter of ethics or morality or
decency or humanity: it was a hideous product of politics, like the
Bomb: an inevitable chemical reaction to the British Government's fatal 'never'. It wasn't something that could be stopped by
a repressive tangle of Emergency Regulations, by the 'deterrent'
of the scaffold, by reprisal and vengeance, by empty pieties like
denouncing violence. It could be stopped only by correcting the
errors which inexorably engendered it.

On the strength of my acquaintance with the Field-Marshal in
the Far East, I got an 'exclusive' interview with him the day after
his arrival. I remember telling him that recently soldiers had
opened fire on 'demonstrating' villagers, killing one or two; and
begging him to give strict orders about that; and then I said (with
the patronizing air of an old hand giving kindly advice to the newcomer): 'If I were you, sir, I'd wear uniform as little as possible:
military display can only exacerbate political feeling.' This didn't
go down at all: I saw a glint of temper behind the charm; and the
Field-Marshal didn't reply. Of course it was cheek, but I still
was nursing the illusion of a man moved by goodwill, anxious to
understand and tranquillize.

I think Harding's salient endowments were these: that smile and
that charm—a charm that made one feel he *liked* talking to one,
when certainly he didn't; his debonair good looks and the confident
military grace that enlivened his slight form; a wonderful fluency
in conversation—an agreeable unhesitant diction and certainty of
phrase which gave an impression of acute intelligence; and a disarming candour that sometimes, perhaps, was more disarming than
candid. Once, when the scaffold in Nicosia prison was working
almost in time with the new moon, I asked him if he didn't think
that the exercise of his prerogative of mercy might pacify the island's
atmosphere for any possible negotiations. He answered, with
splendid forthrightness: 'I will not sacrifice principle to political
expediency!' I was momentarily impressed: here, I felt, is a man
whose candour is like an open window, whose integrity is manifest.
Yet this was the same man who was offering a safe conduct off the
island and free passage to any destination he chose—terms far
more generous than those granted Napoleon by Wellington—to

Grivas, to the arch-terrorist, the architect of continuous murder, the designator of the victims of the little infatuated killers who were being hanged. Where here was principle, and where political expediency? It was a fine-sounding utterance; but it was nonsense. He was contradicting it every day of his governmental life—right down to the day in 1957 when, reluctantly obeying Whitehall, he reprieved even Nicos Sampson. It's the nature of government to subordinate principle to political advantage.

King George III, in the throes of the American rebellion, said: 'I have no wish but the prosperity of my own dominions, therefore I must look upon all who would not heartily assist me as bad men, as well as bad subjects.' That was the Field-Marshal's view: he assumed the divine right and believed himself infallible. But not only would he not suffer opposition, he couldn't *understand* how anybody could oppose him. 'I *can't* understand the attitude of your paper', he said one day to Foley and me (while we were still on speaking terms)—there was genuine puzzlement in his candid blue eyes. He could tolerate no criticism of his acts or of the consequences of his acts: when, under his administration ('Harding's contemptible administration,' Mr Stelios Pavlides, C.M.G., Q.C., a former Attorney-General, called it in a letter to me late in 1957), every principle of British Justice was torn up by the Special Courts (always excepting Sir Bernard Vidal Shaw), which became, in effect, a branch of the police bent on getting convictions, he became enraged by public protest against some of the decisions and published an Emergency Decree making criticism of court judgements an offence—the same law that was in force under Roger II of Sicily in the 12th century: 'A man who questioned the sentence of one of the King's judges could be tried for sacrilege' (Georgina Masson's biography of Frederick II of Hohenstaufen). That same Norman king's laws laid down that 'the king's right came from God alone, and it was sacrilegious to oppose him'. Criticism of Harding certainly took on the odium of sacrilege: if in the Ledra Palace bar one referred to him aloud without proper reverence, one was treated by the soldierly drinkers as if one hadn't stood up for 'The Queen'.

The cult of personality was vigorous in Cyprus in Harding's day. I don't know how much, if any, of this was his doing; or whether it spread like the warmth of morning from the devoted adulation of his entourage (who of course agreed with him); or from a need communally felt among the island's British for an

Olympian figure of their own to offset the Mars and Jupiter of Grivas and Makarios. The Security Forces adored him; he had a genius for making any man he spoke to believe it was *him* the Field-Marshal was personally interested in. Whatever the cause, the Governor became the island's British deity—or British Stalin: in the second year of his regnancy especially, as his temper became publicly more testy and he withdrew further into the embattled isolation of Government House, he seemed to have conferred on him by his courtiers and the senior officers of Government and Army the qualities of godhead. To all those Britons who accepted absolutely his absolutism, Sir John's utterances and edicts had the infallibility of revelation and his sorties in a caravan of armoured cars seemed sacramental:

> He was the Word that spake it,
> He took the bread and brake it;
> And what that word did make it,
> That I believe and take it.

—this was the unquestioning loyalty of all who agreed with him: 'That I believe and take it.'

The Field-Marshal enjoyed the grandeur of himself being the grandee (I don't think Templer cared tuppence for it); and he adored titles and the attributes of aristocracy: he surrounded himself in Government House with A.D.C.s who were heirs to earldoms and with officers of the Household Cavalry. It must have been a big day for him when he was appointed Colonel of the Life Guards and became Gold Stick-in-Waiting: the Somerset Light Infantry must have seemed a long way off.

As soon as he arrived he began cutting out what he thought was the dead wood of the administration: poor old John Fletcher-Cooke, the Cyprus colonial secretary, was pigeon-holed into an 'advisory' sinecure: one day when I went in to see the Field-Marshal I found Fletcher-Cooke sitting in the ante-room: 'I've been waiting for an hour', he said plaintively, 'but I can't get in.' He appointed a brainy bureaucrat named Reddaway to head the civil service. But apart from Reddaway, his only civilian 'advisers' were the new Attorney-General, Sir James Henry, imported from East Africa (who drafted the accumulating Emergency Regulations and instituted prosecutions under them), and the new Police Commissioner, Col. White, who had worked with Harding in Trieste. He had no political advice, beyond what came from Whitehall.

From this situation arose an example of governmental dishonesty. Harding's immunity by default to political advice and understanding had for long been a worry of the *Times of Cyprus* and of people in England who weren't happy about the Field-Marshal's governorship. A question about it was put in the House of Lords by Lord Listowel; the bland answer was that two senior members of the Foreign Office were constantly at the Field-Marshal's elbow, proffering their advice. This was a lie. The only two senior Foreign Office men on the island were the head of the Middle East Political Office and Leslie Glass, newly appointed Director-General of Information under Harding. The first of these had nothing to do with the Emergency or Harding or Cyprus; he was on the island because the Commander-in-Chief Middle East Land Forces was there—his field was the Middle East, not the internal affairs of the island. The second, Leslie Glass, was neither asked for nor allowed to give political advice, though he'd been appointed to Cyprus for that purpose; his first-class political acumen and experience were ignored and his excellent brain confined to the department of 'information' (Reddaway had secured control of 'propaganda'). The truth was, I think, that the Field-Marshal didn't want to take anybody's advice; and this parliamentary reply was a mendacious evasion of the truth.

Looking back on those dreadful years I wonder how anyone who went through them emerged sane from that repetitive nightmare of terrorism and counter-terrorism, murder and curfew, ambush and execution—the weapons of repression seemed, to me, as hideous as the cold cruelty of the EOKA terror. It can be properly argued, I suppose, that if it's true that EOKA terror was the ineluctable consequence of 80 years of political perversity, then the government's counter-terror was equally inevitable. That must be true up to a point; but the point where it ceases to be true is marked, surely, by the independent Republic of Cyprus—the clear, common-sense demonstration that what was accepted as wise in 1957–58 would have been infinitely wiser in 1955–56: *before* a ghastly number of lives had been violently lost.

I was frightened nearly all the time: walking through the streets of 'Murder Mile' in Nicosia, where any youth one saw might in the next 30 seconds be one's killer; riding my scooter on the lonely country roads with, as in Malaya, my heart in my mouth at sight of a sudden figure looming from the verge. I drank a great deal, like most British in that tense time. I remember one early morning, still in bed, being woken from a doze by the short staccato burst of a sten-gun in the street below, sickeningly recognizable; and knew at once that someone had been killed; knew that within a few hours, long after the killer had returned to anonymity, the punitive curfew would descend on the town, cooping up 30 or 40 thousand inhabitants indoors for a week or so; knew that dozens of youths would go to detention camps and others to Ormophita cells for 'interrogation'; knew that when this curfew was over, there'd be another murder, starting the whole hideous cycle again. By that time it had become a war of tit-for-tat: each act of violence on either side brought reprisal from the other; one knew that a hanging would be followed by a fresh killing. Sure enough, that morning when I ran out, I found that two policemen had been shot down just round my corner: an Englishman and a Turk, two ordinary coppers on the beat.

In the centre of Nicosia we on the *Times of Cyprus* were safer than most British: we were known by sight, I suppose, to the local 'killer squad' and probably excused death because we were anti-Government. But there were too the terrible bonds of the EOKA oath: if a boy were ordered from above to go out and shoot the first Englishman he saw he would do so, knowing he'd die himself if he didn't. Stelios Pavlides, Q.C., while defending a self-confessed terrorist, asked him during a visit in prison: 'Would you have shot Michael Davidson?' 'Oh no', the youth answered, 'he was my friend.' Pavlides said: 'But supposing Dighenis (Grivas) had *ordered* you to kill him?' The boy hesitated, and then said awkwardly: 'Oh—I don't think Dighenis would have done that.' Under EOKA friends killed friends, if ordered to.

A lot of nice people came through Cyprus. Dear Jimmie Cameron, fortunately for me, often looked in for the *News Chronicle*—an hour in his company is always like a great draught of clean fresh air after a stuffy room. We were together at the Ledra Palace bar when we learned that the Suez operation of 1956 was 'on': in the same breath we exclaimed: 'I feel ashamed to be English!' When Randolph Churchill came, Nicos Sampson, working as a reporter on a paper called *Phileleftheros* (ironically, the Greeks' affectionate nickname for England in Lord Byron's day: 'Friend of Liberty'), begged me to get him an interview: of course kindhearted Randolph agreed, and the three of us were photographed together at the Ledra Palace.

I was writing most of our leading articles and political stories,

generally critical of Government policy; and being equally out-
spoken, when justified, in *The Observer* and the *News Chronicle*,
whose 'stringer' I was; and it wasn't long under Harding before I
was one of those 'bad men'. But we were still fairly amicable when,
in the spring of 1956, I interviewed him for television. We did it
on the lawn of Government House, walking out together gaily
chatting (for the camera) and then, sitting side by side, saying our
set pieces. TV interviewing hadn't then become the medium of
malicious exposure for the public pleasure it seems to be today: it
was a vehicle for the expression of the 'interviewee's' point of view
and the interviewer gave the 'lead'. I did various other men too,
such as Makarios and Dr Kutchuk, the Turkish leader, now Vice-
President of Cyprus; and then Christopher Chattaway, an expert
on the job, came out from the B.B.C. and took over.

I can't think what Kutchuk's interview looked like on the screen;
his English was almost unintelligible and he talked in a jerky
fashion like a dog barking, as if he wanted to bite your head off.
He was a medical man (said to be a good one); in his consulting
room stood a large jar containing a pickled human foetus—to show,
I supposed, how good he was. Perhaps it wouldn't be fair to the
Turkish community to say that if it's true a people gets the leader
it deserves, then Kutchuk was their man. I found him an uncouth
fellow, shaped like a squat brandy bottle, with small manifest
intelligence and much personal ambition. He possessed a ranting
demagogic talent which could rouse a crowd of Turkish youths to
frenzies of excitement and incendiary zest when he harangued them
from his upper window near Ataturk Square. His was the sort of
leadership they wanted. Dr Kutchuk's meeting with Queen
Elizabeth at Nicosia airport must have been funny.

Yet I knew three or four Turks of immense charm: cultivated
men like M. N. Munir, Q.C., the Solicitor-General; Raouf
Denktash, former Senior Crown Counsel who resigned to lend his
intellect to Turkish politics; and the bookish owner of Nicosia's
only bookshop, where a lot of Turkish political plotting took
place.

I dare say that among Harding's political follies, the 'divide-and-
rule' pitting of the Turks against the Greeks came second only to
the abduction of the Archbishop. When I came to Cyprus at the
end of 1954, Turks and Greeks were living in comfortable harmony; by early 1957 they were burning each others' houses down,
a barrier like the Wall of Berlin was run across Nicosia to keep

them apart, and the Government had recruited a new force of 'special police' composed of undisciplined Turkish hirelings.

It's difficult to think of a sillier measure than the exile of the Archbishop. If it was hoped that his removal would also remove from the island the source of EOKA inspiration, or the centre of EOKA direction, or the fount of Greek intransigence, it was ineptly hoped: these things were simply strengthened by the deportation. If any one act of the Harding administration angered the Greek population into a mood of immolation it was the kidnapping of Makarios. I'd have thought that, from the British point of view, it'd have been far more sensible to have kept him going as the visible leader of the people—confined perhaps to his Archbishopric; whence, surely, a skilful intelligence service could have valuably explored any intercourse with EOKA. But, with the Ethnarch raped from their midst, the Greeks stuck in their toes deeper and terrorism, instead of diminishing, waxed fiercer.

In November, just after Suez, Robin Maugham wired an invitation to stay with him: I asked Foley for a month's holiday without pay, handed my London 'strings' temporarily to him, and went. In England, until then, I'd always found Robin living in an attic flat in his father's house in Cadogan Square (where, meeting old Lord Maugham for the last time in 1953, he told me he'd been that morning to the Royal Academy exhibition—'I searched and searched through all the rooms, and couldn't find a single nude'; an interest in the flesh that I thought praiseworthy in a man getting on for 90). But this time Robin was living in Brighton; and there I had one of my happiest times with him; and met, for the first time, Gilbert Harding.

A lot has been published about Gilbert since his death; I can only add one more testimony to his essential *goodness*; not only his kindness and generosity—those are fairly easy virtues—but a goodness of *mind* so sensitive to modern badness that, appalled by the vulgarity and cheapness of the entertainment world into which his brilliance had landed him, it sought illusion in whisky. It was a very shy, easily hurt goodness; and the life in which he found himself hurt too much.

He had a tremendous intellect; but circumstances had made of him a 'comic': to get and keep the security he wanted, he had to be comic all the time—even when he wasn't being paid for it. When he went into the Star and Garter or some other Brighton pub, he was instantly required by his professional fame to be irascible, iconoclast, devastating—to be the Harding of the television. One face of him enjoyed it; the obverse hated it. An audience, though, had become his necessity. When he came to a party he came to a stage, an audience. Where did he get his stories —did he invent them himself? They went on for a long time: the 'build-up' was everything—brilliantly done, full of decorative detail and swift lines of character, perfectly phrased in a tone of deadly earnest; and leading up to a hilariously unexpected curtain. Nobody could tell a story like Gilbert; and he was furious if he was interrupted.

There was a party in Hove: Gilbert, of course, started telling a story—a long story. Somebody let out of its cage a budgerigar which, fluttering about the room, kept alighting on Gilbert's shoulder and croaking into his ear what, to us in the audience, sounded like *silly old fool, silly old fool*; Gilbert, going steadily on with his story, irritably kept brushing the bird away as if it were a fly. The last straw came when, as the story was approaching its climax, a certain member of parliament brightly said: 'Oh, I know, Gilbert——' and finished the story off for him. Poor Gilbert was so angry that he didn't, I think, say another word before he left.

There was another party some time later, after a charity 'brains trust' (in, no doubt, the Corn Exchange: with Gilbert, Nancy Spain, Alan Melville and Godfrey Winn on the platform—what a rum punch of mixed natures!), when Gilbert, late at night and very drunk, said to me—saying it, though, more to himself, more to the glass he was gazing into: 'I hate this world, I *hate* it. . . .'

My last sight of him, in 1958, was when leaving him at his house in the small hours after a long and happy evening; he was beyond speech. We'd begun at his house at six in the evening; there was no audience, and he talked charmingly and with wisdom about his pictures and about music—and with bitterness because he was required to 'introduce' or comment on a wireless programme of records he despised. Gilbert was genuinely sensitive, as to everything, to music; he could, of course, have declined to do this programme which offended that sensitivity. Yet he agreed: lamenting, that evening, his degradation. The fact was, I suppose, he couldn't bring himself to reject the money; there was no streak of avarice in his nature—his quiet generosity proved that; he was haunted by fear of poverty—fear that his 'box-office' value would fall, that he'd

lose the livelihood which hung upon popular taste and be doomed
to a hard-up old age.

After many whiskies we went, with his devoted housekeeper
Miss Smith, to the Star and Garter where he ordered wine for
dinner, and then to Howard's Grill. I can't remember what we
talked about; but I know he was in fine form, amusing and
caustically gay—still less can I remember much of the hours' more
talk back again in Montpellier Villas. In the early hours he became
incoherent, slumped and mumbling in his chair, yet still drinking.
I was drunk, of course, but I could speak. 'Oughtn't we to stop his
having any more?' I asked Miss Smith (he'd been very ill in
hospital not long before). Silently she shook her head; and then I
realized: he must have given instructions that if he wanted a drink
he was to have it: I realized that he *wanted* to drink dangerously.
I never saw him again. He was a 'great' person, unique, and he
possessed in his wonderful mind and spirit all the constituents of
happiness. Yet he was stubbornly unhappy, while making millions
laugh—perhaps that was why he was unhappy: he wanted to make
them *think*. Harlequin, stricken with melancholia, consulted a
doctor. 'Melancholia?' said the doctor. 'That's easy—go and see
Harlequin.' Alas, it didn't work with Gilbert Harding.

One of the people I wanted to see in England was Lord Radcliffe.
In Cyprus, where I'd met him when he came to explore the
political ground before writing, at the Government's desire, a
constitution for the island, I'd been bewitched by his intellectual
elegance and the *depth* of his courtesy—it was much more than
'charm', which is a quality pretty near the surface, shielding often
many a deficiency. His graceful mind seemed to work with the
power, the precision, and the quiet ease of a Rolls-Royce engine.
He asked me to the lovely Hampstead house he then had; and on
another day I had tea with him at Brooks's. He couldn't, obviously,
disclose much about the constitution he was working on, nor about
the Government's mood; but we discussed Cyprus busily and I got
the impression, reading between the lines, that Cyril Radcliffe
didn't feel great sympathy for the Government's policy there or
for the Field-Marshal's handling of it. I don't think he can have
been much surprised when the Greek Cypriots rejected his constitution; it was bound, at that time, to stop short of what they
wanted and finally got. What I above all admired Lord Radcliffe
for was his *objectivity*, his purely intellectual position, his superi-

ority to *power*. He could, I dare say, have had any job he wanted: the Great Seal had he gone into politics, the wig of the Lord Chief Justice if he'd had punitive tendencies, or, retiring from the Bench, a post of vast power in the City. But he preferred the power of his superb mind: applying it to such objective tasks as fitting a constitution to a country's needs, conducting inquiries—the study of human affairs and the pursuit of truth, which is more than justice. That's why he seems to me to tower above his employers who've achieved eminence through politics. He's the sort of Judge it would be a pleasure to be sentenced by.

I rang up St James's Palace and arranged to meet Richard Lumley in Jules' Bar in Jermyn Street. That encounter was the greatest fun; unfortunately it led to Richard's quarrelling with me when next I saw him two years later. I used that meeting, when I got back to Cyprus, in a 'snob' column I wrote for the paper. It was a good column: amusingly recording my doings in England, urbanely anecdotic about the people socially and politically distinguished I'd met, and loaded with titles—I wrote it mainly in order to annoy the Field-Marshal. I was sorry to discover, two years later, that it had annoyed Richard too. He was a very nice young man; whom the falsities of a courtier's livery didn't really become at all.

One day I read in *The Times* that my editor, Charles Foley, had been charged under the Emergency Regulations with publishing matter 'tending to cause alarm and despondency' and to 'prejudice the maintenance of public order'—there were two alternative charges, on the swings and roundabouts principle: he had printed in the *Times of Cyprus* a despatch sent to the *News Chronicle* by a visiting correspondent, and published by it in London. That same day I got a cable from Foley telling me to brief the best counsel that could be found.

At the House of Commons, I saw Francis Noel-Baker, Labour M.P. for Swindon, in one of those dungeon-cells below ground in which members do much of their work. He sent me to a splendid solicitor named Derek Clogg, who took up the case with zest; in his hands the choice quickly lay between John Simons Q.C., a Tory M.P. (later, I think, one of Macmillan's junior ministers), and Sir Frank Soskice, former Labour Attorney-General and member of the Shadow Cabinet. For tactical reasons I rather favoured Simons—his being an important Conservative, I thought, could carry weight. But the choice depended on availability; and it was Sir Frank who luckily was free for the date of Foley's trial. With Derek Clogg, I had a consultation with him one early morning at the House of Commons; and he accepted the brief. Nobody could have more brilliantly pleaded Foley's case than did Soskice: the Cyprus Attorney-General, Sir James Henry, was like plasticine in his hands; but he could do nothing about the judge: who found Foley guilty of the charge Sir Frank knew he was technically innocent of, and acquitted him on the second which Sir Frank thought had probably been proved.

I was back in Cyprus by the middle of December; and almost at once went on an 'anti-terrorist operation' in the Troodos mountains. Talking with a nice brigadier called George Baker—Harding's Director of Military Operations—I asked if, while I'd been away, he'd caught any of EOKA's 'big boys'. 'There's one man we've *got* to get', he said. 'Who's that—Grivas?' I asked. 'No', he answered. 'Sampson'.

That's how I discovered that Nicos Sampson, my young colleague of more than 18 months before, had become the Security Forces' most hunted, most execrated, most feared quarry—the man accused of being the killer of 'Murder Mile', of being the gunman in 20 or more Nicosia shootings, including the September murder in Ledra Street of two off-duty British policemen out shopping and the wounding of a third. It was flabbergasting: until I'd left for England six weeks before I'd been seeing Nicos fairly frequently, generally when he called at our office; I'd no inkling that he'd any connection with EOKA.

The rest of my time in Cyprus, until August 1957, was occupied by three things: the decay into medievalism under the Harding administration of British 'justice'; the five trials—six if one includes a reference to the Supreme Court on the admissibility of a 'confession'—of Nicos Sampson; and the use of 'ill-treatment'—the official euphemism for what most people called torture—in the working of that medievalism.

Sir Sydney Abrahams, until his death in 1957 legal adviser to the Colonial Office, had been brought out to design a special judicial structure for handling trials under the Emergency Regulations: a sweet old man who liked talking about athletics better than about the organs of punishment—he was one of the three renowned Abrahams brothers, of whom in my memory, Harold, a mighty runner, was the most famous. It seemed unfair that the last memorial to Sir Sydney's professional name should be the Special Courts of Cyprus: he merely devised their shape; others turned them into the tumbrils of the Emergency.

Glafkos Clerides, a brilliant young barrister called from Gray's Inn who fought over Germany with the R.A.F., and a son of the late John Clerides, Q.C. (I think today he's Speaker of the Cyprus Parliament, or perhaps a Minister) said to me: 'The most terrible consequence of the Emergency is the collapse of British justice, the one department of British rule in which the people had real confidence. It would take a hundred years of good administration now to restore that confidence.' I hope Glafkos there exaggerated: the Cypriot Bar and Judiciary, schooled in the Inns of Court, have the ability, the principles and the tradition to regain the people's confidence. The danger perhaps is that the people, remembering only the bad side of British judicial methods, experienced during the Emergency, will now reject the good as well and demand a new, perhaps Greek, system.

It soon became plain that what the Cyprus administration wanted was as many convictions as possible and as many 'deterrent' sentences as the courts could inflict—if innocent men were sometimes convicted that was all to the good: in the eyes of authority no Greek Cypriot was innocent. To achieve this all Emergency cases had to be taken out of Cypriot hands. Soon two Special Court Assize judges were brought from England and four—and later more—magistrates (called Special Justices); five Special Crown Counsel were recruited from the English Bar; cases were prepared by imported British C.I.D. officers; and the Cypriot Attorney-General was replaced by a British, a native of Northern Ireland employed in the colonial service. I expect, had it not appeared too barefaced, the Government would have liked to remove the two Cypriot Puisne Judges—a Greek and a Turk—from the Supreme Court and left the British Chief Justice to decide appeals by himself: one could almost hear the anger in the Attorney-General's office when a dissenting voice in the Supreme Court secured the quashing of one of the two death sentences passed on Nicos Sampson.

One of the Special Justices once said privately: 'I administer the Law—but I administer it in the light of the Emergency'—which sounds rather like a Returning Officer saying: 'I run the polling booth but I run it in the light of the Conservative Party.' Another, who sometimes acted as an Assize Judge, with the power of the death sentence, almost monotonously included in his judgements this clause: 'I believe the evidence of the British police officers; I do not believe the evidence called for the defence. Therefore I find the accused guilty.' Of a third, one of the Crown Counsel said to me: 'So-and-so knows so little law that almost any decision of his stands a good chance of being reversed in the Supreme Court.'

At least one Special Justice was excluded by his fairness from this generalization; but the great and historic exception was the principal Assize Judge, Sir Bernard Vidal Shaw. Mr Justice Shaw, the most upright Briton on the island, found himself in the egregiously paradoxical position of winning the hatred of the British community by steadfastly upholding British principle. Because he remained unwaveringly loyal to his professional standards, to the rules and practices and traditions of British justice; because he refused to stretch the laws one way or the other to suit any interest but the Law's; because, therefore, when by British standards the evidence or lack of it required an acquittal he *acquitted*—because of this undauntable legal integrity, most British would have liked to see him sacked. Thus had the Emergency brought low the British heart.

Resisting this perversion of British justice, I was accused of being on EOKA's side. Of course I wasn't: I loathed the beastliness of terrorism no less than I loathed the beastliness of hanging. But I was on the side of British decency and fairness, of those British legal standards which Cyprus still had respected: and was appalled by the shame of their being dragged down to terrorism's beastly level. That's why I gave evidence in Sampson's defence at his murder trial; and why I exposed in the *Times of Cyprus* the Government's mendacity about 'ill-treatment' in the interrogation cells.

Almost alone among England's representatives Shaw showed the Greek Cypriots that there were still men from the United Kingdom who could be just, still Britons who put their conscience and their duty before the demands of politics. His departure from the island in June 1957 was England's loss more than the Cypriots': there was almost no one else to uphold Britain's name in the one sphere in which she'd won honour: the law.

In the summer of 1956 Shaw was shot twice in the head by terrorists as he was driving home from the Law Courts; it was a miracle that he lost no more than the use of one ear. But just as he didn't allow the Government to sway him from his principles while on the Bench, nor did he permit this murderous attack to tinge his conduct of a trial with vindictiveness. He was too big a man for that. He was too big a man for the British community's taste.

When he was shot, no word of concern, I was told by one of his closest friends, came immediately from Government House. When, in 1957, he acquitted Sampson of murder, a British colonel near me in court exclaimed: 'Shaw ought to be flung off the island!'

It would be unjust here not to say that the little group of Crown Counsel working on contract in the Special Courts—Ronnie Grey, Hilary Gosling, David Griffiths-Jones and one or two others— stuck rigidly to English Bar standards: they were hired to prosecute, and they prosecuted; but with absolute fairness and no taint of the vengefulness which the Government's Legal Department was bent on injecting into the courts. These men didn't hide their contempt for the processes of the Special Courts and for one or two of the justices, or their distaste for some of the methods of the Attorney-General's office.

Sampson was six times tried—if one counts two preliminary hearings, two assize trials, a reference to the Supreme Court during the murder trial of a 'confession' which the Attorney-General sought to introduce and which Mr Justice Shaw had rejected, and an appeal to the Supreme Court against two death sentences. For four months he was on trial for his life.

Well, what's wrong with that, one may ask—if what was said of him was true: if indeed (which was never proved) he was a murderer many times over? What's wrong with trying to put a rope round his neck, if one believes in the justice of capital punishment? There's the point: the motive wasn't *justice*, it was vengeance. There was no 'justice', in the English legal sense, in any of the prosecutions conducted against Sampson; they were makeshift attempts to satisfy a phrenetic craving to hang him for vengeance' sake, cost what it might to British principles and British law: an attempt at legalized lynching in which nearly the whole British community joined, from Government House down.

When the murder charge failed, Nicos was at once back in the dock on lesser charges—but ones which under the Emergency Regulations carried the death sentence. First he'd been charged with 'possession' of a sten-gun—but that wouldn't do, because punishable only with life imprisonment; it was changed to 'carrying'—he was holding the gun when four policemen burst into his bedroom in the middle of the night. A second charge was 'pointing' a gun; this was arrived at after 'discharging', 'attempting to discharge', 'aiming' had been tried and rejected at various stages: the police object was to hit on a couple of charges both punishable by death, one of which at least would fit what evidence they could produce.

Under the Emergency Regulations, the crime of 'murder' didn't exist: the offences were 'shooting' or 'killing'. So the Attorney-General, Sir James Henry, had Sampson charged under the ordinary criminal code with 'murder'—because, I suppose, it sounded worse. The Prosecution in this trial depended almost wholly on a 'confession' obtained immediately after Sampson's arrest when he was badly hurt, sopping wet, shaking with cold and kept without medical attention. The Defence said this 'confession' was extracted by 'ill-treatment'.

Sir James Henry had chosen himself to conduct the prosecution; the only other case he had appeared in personally was that against Foley and the *Times of Cyprus*. He took the extraordinary line, which astonished barristers in court, of trying to influence Mr Justice Shaw's decision by demanding his sympathy for the Special Branch policemen who had been accused by the Defence of brutality and unnecessary ill-treatment; he said, in effect, 'if you reject this confession on the grounds that it was improperly obtained, if you acquit Sampson because you find he made this confession as a result of force or fear or threats, you will be ruining the careers of these splendid officers'. It was a recurrent theme of his throughout the trial—indeed Sir James's only attempts at oratory were devoted to convincing his lordship of his duty towards the policemen. Legal rectitude seemed to have been ousted by the official anxiety, insistent at the time, to save the good name of the Security Forces and at the same time hang Sampson.

The Judge threw out the 'confession'. He acquitted the Special Branch men of Sampson's charges of torture during and after his arrest; but described their treatment of him as 'unconscionable'. He said in his ruling: 'In my experience, and it goes back over some 47 years, I can recall no case in which the Crown has set out to prove a confession and at the same time to admit that the accused received the sort of treatment this man received. . . . I find it difficult to understand how these brave officers came to act as they did. But if they do act in this way I do not think they can reasonably complain if the Court entertains a doubt as to their bona fides. . . .' The ruling exonerated the Security Forces of charges of 'torture' while in the same breath giving them the first trouncing they'd officially had. It took their breath away—and Government House's too. It was a triumphant end to Mr Justice Shaw's career in Cyprus—triumphant because he showed the island that true British judges were immune from political pressures.

Government House's interest in the trial was keen. On the morning of Shaw's delivery of his ruling on the vital 'confession' issue, the place was thronged with distinguished visitiors: the Chief Constable, the Solicitor-General, who during the reading of it went out once or twice to telephone; members of the Field-Marshal's personal staff; officials from the Secretariat (the island's 'Whitehall'). Before long a message came from Government House asking that a copy of the ruling be sent up there the moment a typescript was ready. There was plainly consternation in high places: this was at the height of the virulent controversy over allegations of 'ill-treatment' against 'interrogators' of the police and army; and here the Special Branch were getting a thrashing.

'Do you want to go on, Mr Attorney?' asked Mr Justice Shaw when the trial resumed after the Supreme Court had rejected the 'confession' and Stelios Pavlides, C.M.G., Q.C., had submitted that Sampson had no further case to answer. Sir James Henry said he did; and urged the worth of the only piece of evidence he had left: the identification of Sampson by the survivor of the three police sergeants shot in Ledra Street. This sergeant was a perfectly honest witness; but he had admitted in cross-examination that his memory of what took place after the shooting might have become blurred. But he had insisted that about the shooting he was in no doubt. 'I see the shooting in my dreams', he said. 'I know it, I know he is the man.' Mr Pavlides, cross-examining, had also undermined the value of his evidence about his first 'recognition' of Sampson as the gunman who'd shot him—when he 'happened' to be in the police-station yard at the very moment that Sampson was being taken to court. The sergeant agreed that Sampson was the only prisoner in the yard at the time; he agreed that he was handcuffed and that his ankles were shackled, and that he was surrounded by police; he agreed that he knew Sampson had been arrested and was suspected of being the man who did the Ledra Street shooting, and that he knew that Sampson was being taken to court that morning. Yet it was during the 'chance' glimpse that recognition flashed in his mind: there was the man who'd shot him five times.

Mr Pavlides reminded the court that this witness had said in the box the sole difference between Sampson in the dock and Sampson as he saw him during the shooting was that then he had a much thicker moustache. Then Pavlides called me.

I said I couldn't remember when exactly I'd last seen Nicos before he was arrested; but that he'd been in and out of my office fairly constantly through 1956 until I left for England on November 8th.

'Had Sampson a moustache when you knew him?' asked Mr Pavlides. 'Never,' I answered.

Mr Justice Shaw then acquitted Sampson; saying it was a most unfortunate thing if a guilty man should go free, but no British Court could consider convicting if there was an element of doubt.

My giving evidence in Nicos' defence when the entire Government and all the Security Forces wanted to see him swing was a serious act of sacrilege. People in high authority smouldered with anger; lesser men cold-shouldered me in the bar of the Ledra Palace. Yet I would have done the same had I been *convinced* of Nicos' guilt: firstly, I suppose, it's one's duty to state any relevant fact when a man's on trial for his life; and secondly, I was so angered by the official conduct of the case and the frenzy of vengeance that animated it that I felt compelled to show that British decency and fairness still were to be found on the island. It was less for Nicos' sake that I went into the box, than, so to speak, for England's.

Stout British anger with me even caused a correspondent of the *Daily Telegraph* to cast doubt on my little bit of evidence by altering it—an extraordinary thing for any newspaperman to do: instead of my categorical 'never', he cabled that I'd said 'I couldn't remember' seeing Sampson with a moustache. When I complained to the *Telegraph* about this inaccurate report, the paper wrote that the two versions were 'substantially the same'; I couldn't be bothered to argue back that they were substantially very different.

Another judge tried the next pair of charges against Sampson, both hanging jobs; and quickly sentenced him to death twice over. One of the death sentences, that for 'pointing' a gun, was quashed on appeal (the British Chief Justice, Sir Paget Bourke, dissenting); the other, for 'carrying', stood—and Nicos went to the condemned cell; where he wrote letters containing phrases like, 'we take courage carrying the cross of martyrdom, and our tears forgive those that massacre justice', and small, aching poems—'I long for the past, The happy years. . . .'

The long and complicated series of hearings during which Nicos sat in the dock on and off for four months formed really one single process which the Crown and police were determined should end in one way: the rope. When the murder charge failed, they weren't satisfied with the obvious charge of 'possession'—an offence which he never denied and would have brought him 'life'; they didn't want to give this immature, unbalanced, hysterical fanatic of 22 (who, in a kind of sacrificial rapture, saw himself as a martyr) a chance to grow to mental and emotional sanity: that course lacked the ingredient Government and Security Forces were clamouring for—revenge. That's why the Attorney-General and the police started on a course of action which before it was over had stripped them of dignity and brought the repute of British legal procedure lower surely than it can anywhere have fallen before.

Sampson's case was the most notorious; but daily other cases were going on that equally illustrated the betrayal in one way or another of British legal principle. There was a boy of 18, Pallika-rides, sentenced to death for 'carrying' a weapon on donkey-back along a mountain path. Nobody thought that he would hang; the death sentence was mandatory under the Emergency Regulations for that offence, but reprieve seemed certain. Yet this boy was executed; on the very eve of an EOKA cease fire. He was hanged, it was learned later, because the police 'knew'—it was said they had a 'confession'—that Pallikarides had committed more serious crimes than 'carrying', crimes with which he was never charged—crimes to prove which, presumably, there wasn't evidence enough even in a Special Court. But, for the medieval morality of the 1957 administration in Cyprus, there was enough evidence to hang him.

All through the winter of 1956 and the first half of 1957 the burning question on the island was 'ill-treatment'. The Government frenziedly denied that it existed; while at the same time obstinately refusing to allow an objective inquiry. The Government, being the accused, itself investigated the charges brought against itself, and over and over again announced that it had found itself innocent. The island became like a private school in which hundreds of boys complain of belly-ache because they've been given bad food while the headmaster angrily tells them they haven't got belly-ache at all. 'Every complaint of belly-ache has been fully investigated and I am satisfied it doesn't exist', the headmaster went on repeating, adding that complainants of belly-ache which they hadn't got would in future be caned.

Of course 'ill-treatment' existed: it was a regular practice in the interrogation cells. Everybody knew it was; including, obviously, the Government. But nobody accused the ordinary soldiers of brutality—their restraint and good humour during duties like imposing a curfew were admirable; nor were the ordinary uniformed police accused of ill-treating people they arrested. The men charged with using violence to obtain information or confessions were certain members of the Special Branch, a very small number of Army 'intelligence' officers doing interrogating work, and 14 special 'interrogators' recruited in the United Kingdom at salaries of about £1,600 a year. Some irreverent Englishman christened this body of specialists H.M.T.—Her Majesty's Torturers.

Nobody knew better than the Greek members of the Bar what went on in the interrogation cells: the evidence was on the bodies and limbs and faces of their clients; and there could be few more reliable witnesses than most of these lawyers, trained in the disciplines and traditions of the Inns of Court.

On 5th February 1957, Stelios Pavlides, who throughout defended Sampson with brilliance and wisdom, sent this telegram to the Governor:

Your Excellency at interview 3rd Jan. intimated that complaints illtreatment prisoner would receive attention. Have just returned from Omorphita prison where I saw Nicos Sampson arrested last Tuesday. He complained of brutal treatment including insertion broken glass into fingernail to extract confession. I testify to appalling condition in which I found him. . . . Respectfully pray immediate directions examination by independent doctor accompanied by own doctor and full investigation at which a Law Officer and myself should be present. I never saw a prisoner in such condition I felt sick looking at his pitiful and appalling state and this on seventh day after arrest—Stelios Pavlides Chairman Bar Council.

Mr Pavlides, a level-headed man of absolute integrity, wouldn't have lightly sent that telegram. Seven days later, Mr Reddaway, the Administrative Secretary, replied: 'The complaint of illtreatment has been fully investigated . . . I am to inform you, therefore, that His Excellency the Governor is satisfied that Sampson's complaint . . . is wholly unfounded.' Those sentences were repeated whenever a lawyer complained to the Government of ill-treatment of a client: such formally lodged complaints numbered more than 300.

The 'full investigation' was made by one British C.I.D. sergeant accompanied by a Greek interpreter. As has been seen, during the trial later, Mr Justice Shaw cleared the police of inflicting deliberate 'torture', but his remarks showed that Sampson's complaints weren't 'wholly unfounded'.

The interview with the Field-Marshal to which Pavlides refers was the result of an invitation from the Governor to discuss allegations of ill-treatment: with Mr Pavlides, C.M.G., Q.C., chairman of the Cyprus Bar Council and a former Attorney-General, went the late Mr John Clerides, C.B.E., Q.C., chairman of the Human Rights Committee and formerly a member of Sir Robert Armitage's Executive Council, and Mr Chrysafinis, president of the Nicosia Bar Association. These were serious men, as devoted to their professional honour as any High Court Judge in London—and them, at this meeting, the Field-Marshal accused of 'encouraging EOKA propaganda'.

Of course EOKA made the most of the propaganda value of ill-treatment—it was propaganda handed on a plate by the 'interrogators'; and the Government, by publicly accusing honest lawyers of falsifying facts at the behest of EOKA, were equally making propaganda.

The whole island knew these things went on; and sometimes the men who performed them would provide confirmation: I was told by a man working at the Troodos interrogation centre that a colleague of his (he gave me the name) was in the habit of tying a string to a prisoner's genitals and giving a tweak when his questions weren't satisfactorily answered. In May 1957 an English Special Branch sergeant said: 'I shan't ask to renew my contract when it's. up. You know what goes on—we all know. I've had enough.'

In June 1957 the Cyprus Government rushed into print a White Paper on 'Allegations of Brutality in Cyprus' with a foreword by Field-Marshal Sir John Harding. This followed Sir Bernard Vidal Shaw's castigation of Special Branch police in the Sampson trial and a cluster of Special Court cases in which similarly procured 'confessions' came to light. Introducing the White Paper, the Field-Marshal wrote: 'Wherever terrorism has been employed in the pursuit of political ends, part of the technique has been to try to discredit the forces of law and order by accusing them of scandalously abusing their powers and of indulging in terrorism on their own account. . . . Time and again I have made it clear that I will not tolerate misconduct by members of the Security Forces, that complaints supported by evidence will be fully and fairly investigated and that offenders will be punished. The forces of law and order must not allow themselves to be contaminated by the brutal and unprincipled men with whom they have to contend.'

Unfortunately for the White Paper, 'unprincipled' was the word which described it—a craftily mendacious document designed primarily to be read in the United Kingdom and abroad where the publicity given to allegations of brutality was doing the Conservative Government no good. An example of this lack of principle is this statement: 'A very large number of the Police Officers who are accused of such monstrous conduct are in fact members of United Kingdom Police Forces whose traditions of restraint and humanity have long been the admiration of the world. . . .' This was a falsehood aimed at the sympathy of Britons who held properly in high esteem those nice men in blue—a falsehood because no accusations had ever been made against 'a very large number of police officers': over and over again it had been made clear that only a very small group of 'interrogators' and Special Branch men were believed guilty of brutality. This sort of deceitfulness ran right through the White Paper. I analysed it, sentence by sentence, with Glafkos Clerides; and then wrote a detailed reply, taking each paragraph in turn and surgically exposing the fallacies. Foley was away, and I was acting editor: I printed it across the top of the front page of the *Times of Cyprus*; the morning it appeared it was a sensation. It was, I think, a clever piece of analysis; and it destroyed the White Paper. Government House was in a rage; it was reported to me that either the Field-Marshal himself or one of his closest collaborators—I was unable to find out exactly—exclaimed: 'We're going to get that man!'

Neither I nor Foley and his wife were that year asked to Government House, to drink the Queen's health on her Birthday!

Towards the end of July I met one evening Victor Bodker, until recently editor of the *Cyprus Mail*, in John Odgers' bar—nice, rotund, sardonic John Odgers: the perfect publican—even his name was right. 'In the Nicosia Club just now,' said Victor, 'they were saying the C.I.D. were looking for charges to bring against you—of course, I know nothing about it; but that's what they were saying.' He finished his drink and stumped out. Kind old

Victor: professionally we'd been at daggers drawn; but personally always on good drinking terms. This was news that set me thinking: if they could have found charges under the Emergency Regulations they'd have jumped at the chance long ago. But what other charges? My private life had for long been immaculate; there was no evidence there. And then once more the spectre of the 'previous' appeared: what if the Field-Marshal and the Attorney-General's office had secured from Scotland Yard my 'record'? In Cyprus the police could easily have hired a couple of young Turks and framed an accusation against me, comfortably supported by my 'previous'—that's the way my thinking went. Probably I was wrong; I'm sure the Field-Marshal wouldn't have countenanced such a thing; though the police, once they knew I'd been convicted, might certainly have so acted on their own. I dare say I was cowardly: I felt I was too vulnerable to face the possibility of such a case; I decided it was time I left Cyprus. Foley was generous; so too were Byron Pavlides and above all dear Gubby. In the first week of August I secured an 'exit permit' and slipped away; I didn't feel secure until I was aboard the Italian ship at Larnaca.

I went to the tiny island of Procida in Naples Bay and wrote my Cyprus book, the heart of which was the study of a terrorist, Nicos Sampson. It wasn't a good book: it was too hot with recent anger, and the British reading public, exasperated by the wickedness of Greek Cypriot terrorism, weren't in the mood for a condemnation of that terrorism's attempted repression. Gollancz were probably right to reject it; André Deutsch later wanted to do it if I would put more 'balance' into it and bring it up to date: but by then I found it impossible to bring Cyprus up to date.

When I learned that Sir John Harding was leaving Cyprus and being succeeded by Sir Hugh Foot, I felt I'd won that contest: the Field-Marshal's policy of repression had been reversed in London and on the other side had come up my own. But the Field-Marshal won in the end; Field-Marshals, I suppose, always do. He finished me off, unknown doubtless to him, in the colony of Aden in south Arabia.

Back in London from Naples in April 1958 I went naturally, wondering what to do with myself, to my friends on the *News Chronicle*—Jimmie Cameron and Norman Clark, the paper's Foreign Editor at the time of the Cadbury surrender. Norman said one evening: 'I'd go to Aden if I were you: there's going to be a story there for a long time. We'd want you as our "stringer" for a start.' So I went to Aden in the middle of May: as 'string' correspondent of the *News Chronicle*, *Observer*, *New York Times*, the United Press news agency, *Financial Times* and later *Daily Herald*—a nice bagful. It meant writing each story five or six times—and getting paid five or six times. I seemed to have started, at the age of 61, a new and agreeable career. I went even with the encouragement of the Colonial Office, where I was blessed by a number of functionaries. I suppose (in the light of later happenings) they hadn't then looked me up in their black book.

No landscape that I've anywhere seen so much suggested the mouth of Hell as did Aden. Yet I loved the place: the livid south Arabian climate; the 'John Company' type colonial architecture; the mighty romance of the world's ships lying in the roads for bunkers; the thronging multicoloured populace. I even loved its explosive and rather comic politics; but especially my young Somali bearer, with the face of an Assyrian god and a skin like Guinness' beer.

After I'd happily been there for some ten weeks, when I was beginning to earn a tolerable income and had about recovered the cost of the fare out, the blow fell: I was told by the Immigration Police that my residence permit wouldn't be renewed and I must leave the colony within a few days.

This was dumbfounding. Aden was the one British territory where I had actually *supported* Government policy: my despatches had been praised by Horace Phillips, the political secretary; I was friends with a number of senior members of the Government. My private life, even, had been immaculate—or almost: my Somali bearer was my *bearer*—a perfectly respectable office; nobody could guess that he was to me far more important than His Excellency the Governor and that when he poisoned his knee I put him into my bed and waited on him like a nursemaid, sleeping myself on his mat. I had no qualms about my private life, and none about my political; I was baffled by the meaning of this personal disaster.

Horace Phillips and other dignitaries said blankly they knew of no reason but that anyhow nothing could be done. I asked to see the Governor; and was refused.

(I hope, by the way, that this Governor, Sir William Luce, is more courteous in his new office of Adviser to the Sheikh of Bahrein than was his predecessor. When the Irak revolt broke,

my various papers wanted me at least in Bahrein, whither rein-
forcements were being rushed. Needing a Bahrein visa, I consulted
the senior immigration policeman—the same who announced my
expulsion; he counselled me to send a *reply-paid* cable to the
Adviser asking for one. I did so; it cost £13 in cash. *No reply ever
came.* That's why I hope Sir William Luce is more polite than his
predecessor: I feel that reply-paid telegrams costing £13, even by
British officials in the Persian Gulf, ought to be answered in the
ordinary course of manners.)

I cabled the *News Chronicle* asking them to take action, which
they immediately did; so did Frank Fisher ('Fish' to all Fleet
Street), the downright, delightful and able head of British United
Press. There came a series of cables from Sylvain Mangeot, then
Foreign Editor of the *News Chronicle* (son of that André Mangeot,
the violinist, in whose quartet my brother-in-law, Chris Southward,
had played forty years earlier). The first ran:

> Have cabled Governor Aden direct demanding explanation
> withdrawal your permit. Question to Colonial Secretary being
> put down House of Commons this afternoon.

Two days later two urgent telegrams followed each other hotfoot:

> Governor has replied negatively to Editor also to Frank
> Fisher. Colonial Secretary unwilling interfere his decision. . . .
> Assuming you still wish press parliamentary question regards
> Mangeot.

And the second:

> Colonial Office hint real reason personal nonjournalistic.
> Parliamentary questioner wishes be certain you don't object
> possibly unfavourable publicity if Colonial Secretary's answer
> based personal allegations. Reply all speed as House rises
> tomorrow regards Mangeot.

This last was blackmail by the Colonial Office: 'Drop your
question or we'll show you up in Parliament.' But *what* could
they show up? *What* was the personal shame or ridicule they were
prepared to expose me to if I insisted on embarrassing them with
the question? I couldn't believe that a brief career as an anti-
Hitler Communist thirty years ago could be accepted by the
House of Commons as a valid reason for expelling from Aden
a competent and judicious journalist. So, once again, I jumped to

the conclusion that my blasted 'previous' must be to blame. I had, before replying, only a few minutes to think in; I foolishly wired back that if there were anything *personal* they could bring against me it was twenty-five years old and asked Mangeot to use his judgement about going on with the Question (I had to consider too the matter of embarrassing the *News Chronicle*). This I've regretted ever since: the Question was dropped, and I was later persuaded that the Colonial Office blackmail was founded not on my conviction but on my effective opposition to the Harding administration in Cyprus. Had that been thrown at me in the House and Press, there were critics enough in both of the Field-Marshal's disastrous rule to take my part: I would gladly have fought on that issue. But having no time in those few minutes to reflect, I was jolted by that blackmail into surrender.

In London, I discussed the business with a close friend who was a Tory Member of Parliament: not a lawyer, but a man who knew intimately the mind of the Government and particularly of the Colonial Office. He convinced me that no Government—especially not *that* one—could have the face to produce in the House a little sexual conviction of a quarter of a century ago in justification of a journalist's expulsion. Obviously, my political 'naughtiness' in Cyprus was the reason. 'They couldn't rely on you,' he said. 'They were afraid, with your Cyprus record, that if the Governor of Aden ordered troops to fire on women and children, you'd criticize him for it in the Press!'

I wish that Question had been put: I'd like to know what Mr Alan Lennox-Boyd's 'unfavourable publicity based on personal allegations' could have been.

I suppose, had I reflected after Cyprus, I might have guessed that Sir John Harding's reports to the Colonial Office would probably bar me from working again in any British colony where there was some sort of 'emergency'. I would, I expect, have remembered: 'We're going to get that man.'

\*     \*     \*

One friendship I haven't put in its context and do not identify here: it could be embarrassing to the friend.\*He was with me for nearly three years: from his schooldays until he was nearly 18, when I helped him into a career in England in which he immediately did brilliantly. Each morning, while we were together, I sent him to school on his bicycle; I did the shopping, and had a hot lunch ready cooked by the time he came back. On Sundays, while he was at Mass, I'd have a chicken in the oven. I think I was a good mother. He wrote regularly after he left; in a letter written after he was grown up he said: 'You will always be the best friend I had. . . . When you are old and I am married, you shall make your home with me and my wife.'

And so I come to the end of a dissolute life. I've hardly any regrets; my unhappinesses were inherent in my nature. I wouldn't have been different, not for ten City directorships; because without my unnumbered faults, I suppose, I wouldn't have had my few qualities. Looking back, I've enjoyed it all; sometimes it's been disagreeable, but never uninteresting. I don't think I've done much harm; I don't believe anybody's been unhappier for knowing me, and perhaps some have been even a little happier. If that be true, I couldn't wish for a better epitaph.

I've done nothing to be proud of: much less than most people, who have lots to be proud of—their families, the good work they do, their neat lawns, their bank balances, the world's esteem. I've never cared a damn for the world's esteem; though I've been privately proud of some of my journalistic endeavours, such as my work for racial harmony in Malaya which brought me, after I'd left, a charmingly warm letter of appreciation from Malcolm MacDonald; and my work in Cyprus, which brought nobody's thanks. And I haven't done *very* much that I'm ashamed of— though the world, of course, must say that I ought to be. I'm ashamed certainly of having selfishly done less than I could have to repay those who selflessly loved me—people like my mother and my sister Nancy. I'm ashamed of my incurably adolescent money-delinquency—of my unpaid debts to friends and of that sorry episode of Lady Margaret's brooch. But I'm not very much ashamed.

Now there's little left but the horrible business of getting old: *è brutta la vecchiaia*, a hobbling old Italian five years my junior grumbled the other day. Yes, old age is ugly, nasty, brutish—all the things that *brutto* can imply. I'm already old enough to have discovered the nonsense of those charming opiates about 'the mellow evening of one's life' and 'the quiet contentment of a serene old age'. Brother Ass, one's beastly body, becomes mis-shapen and incapable; one's ears elongate into huge dried bisquits of gristle; one's Victorian nose, too long already from birth, gropes pendulously down towards one's sagging mouth; the skin of one's neck becomes reptilian and the backs of one's hands mottled with senility. Yet, cruelly, one's mind stays young; one's yearnings and interests are still a boy's; one wants still to climb rocks and dive from above into the sea, but one's tottering old skinny legs have lost their notion of balance and one's afraid of losing one's teeth. And yet, if one makes wily use of these last years or months there's still some fun to be got out of life's ending: until the moment comes when 'We cease to grieve, cease to be fortune's slaves, Nay, cease to die, by dying.'

# INDEX

# NOTES TO THE TEXT

*These additional notes derive from the author's own personally annotated copy of the original edition.*

page 52: Ernest Claude Millard, son of a stockbroker (no connection with C. S. Millard, q.v.)

page 73: Ismael bin Ibrahim

page 111: Theron Hughes, whose Welsh parents had settled in Durban.

page 116: Mrs Violet Lazard

page 151: Braun, Secretary of the International Red Cross.

page 152: Walfried Reile-Reiljon: father Latvian, mother Berlinerin.

page 208: Actually in the South of France, not Spain.

page 219: Terry

page 282: Tom Driberg, M.P.

page 283: Eikivhi Suzuki, nicknamed Eibo

page 287: . . . a very small boy, attached to a very large cock.

page 296: Billy Maclean, the Tory M.P. for Inverness.

page 344: Joseph Anthony, a Maronite Cypriot.

*also in* **Gay Modern Classics:**

| | |
|---|---|
| **Francis King**<br>**THE FIREWALKERS** | ISBN 0 907040 71 3 (pbk)<br>72 1 (cased) |
| **Francis King**<br>**A DOMESTIC ANIMAL** | ISBN 0 907040 32 2 (pbk)<br>34 9 (cased) |
| **James Purdy**<br>**NARROW ROOMS** | ISBN 0 907040 57 8 (pbk)<br>58 6 (cased) |
| **James Purdy**<br>**EUSTACE CHISHOLM**<br>**AND THE WORKS** | ISBN 0 907040 33 0 (pbk)<br>35 7 (cased) |
| **Andre Gide**<br>**CORYDON** | ISBN 0 907040 53 5 (pbk)<br>54 3 (cased) |
| **John Lehmann**<br>**IN THE PURELY**<br>**PAGAN SENSE** | ISBN 0 907040 55 1 (pbk)<br>56 X (cased) |
| **T. C. Worsley**<br>**FELLOW TRAVELLERS** | ISBN 0 907040 45 4 (pbk)<br>51 9 (cased) |
| **Edward Carpenter**<br>**TOWARDS DEMOCRACY** | ISBN 0 907040 73 X (pbk)<br>74 8 (cased) |
| **Edward Carpenter**<br>**SELECTED WRITINGS**<br>**VOL. 1: SEX** | ISBN 0 907040 43 8 (pbk)<br>44 6 (cased) |
| **Gillian Freeman**<br>**THE LEATHER BOYS** | ISBN 0 907040 61 6 (pbk)<br>62 4 (cased) |

GMP also publish a wide variety of books in other areas, incuding art and photography, biography, current affairs, fiction, health, history, humour and politics. Our full catalogue is available on request from GMP Publishers Ltd, P.O. Box 247, London N15 6RW, England.